D1336749

DESIGNING
SUSTAINABLE CITIES

Edited by
Rachel Cooper
Graeme Evans
Christopher Boyko

WILEY-BLACKWELL

A John Wiley and Sons Ltd., Publication

This edition first published 2009
© 2009 by Blackwell Publishing Ltd
Blackwell Publishing was acquired by John Wiley & Sons in February 2007. Blackwell's publishing programme has been merged with Wiley's global Scientific, Technical, and Medical business to form Wiley-Blackwell.
Book design © Scott Abbott 2008. All rights reserved. Moral rights asserted. All photographs that do not appear within figures © Simon R Leach. Used under licence to Lancaster University. All rights reserved. Moral rights asserted. All photographs that appear within figures © the authors unless otherwise stated.

Registered office
John Wiley & Sons Ltd, The Atrium, Southern Gate, Chichester, West Sussex PO19 8SQ, United Kingdom

Editorial offices
9600 Garsington Road, Oxford OX4 2DQ, United Kingdom
2121 State Avenue, Ames, Iowa 50014-8300, USA

For details of our global editorial offices, for customer services and for information about how to apply for permission to reuse the copyright material in this book please see our website at www.wiley.com/wiley-blackwell.

The rights of the authors to be identified as the authors of this work have been asserted in accordance with the Copyright, Designs and Patents Act 1988.
All rights reserved. No part of this publication may be reproduced, stored in a retrieval system, or transmitted, in any form or by any means, electronic, mechanical, photocopying, recording or otherwise, except as permitted by the UK Copyright, Designs and Patents Act 1988, without the prior permission of the publisher.

Wiley also publishes its books in a variety of electronic formats. Some content that appears in print may not be available in electronic books.

Designations used by companies to distinguish their products are often claimed as trademarks. All brand names and product names used in this book are trade names, service marks, trademarks or registered trademarks of their respective owners. The publisher is not associated with any product or vendor mentioned in this book. This publication is designed to provide accurate and authoritative information in regard to the subject matter covered. It is sold on the understanding that the publisher is not engaged in rendering professional services. If professional advice or other expert assistance is required, the services of a competent professional should be sought.

Library of Congress Cataloging-in-Publication Data
Designing sustainable cities / edited by Rachel Cooper, Graeme Evans, Christopher Boyko. – 1st ed. p. cm.
Includes bibliographical references and index.
ISBN 978-1-4051-7915-7

1. Urban ecology. 2. City planning. I. Cooper, Rachel. II. Evans, Graeme. III. Boyko, Christopher.

HT241.D47 2009
307.76–dc22
2008034866

A catalogue record for this book is available from the British Library.
Set in 10pt Gill Sans Light by Dave Barratt Creative Ltd
Printed in Singapore
1 2009

CONTENTS

THE VIVACITY2020 TEAM
(in alphabetical order)

The urban design process

Naomi Pemberton-Billing – Lancaster University
Dr Christopher Boyko – Lancaster University
Daniel Cadman – Lancaster University
Professor Rachel Cooper – Lancaster University

Environmental sustainability and city-centre living

Dr Mags Adams – University of Salford
Jo-Anne Bichard – University College London
Professor Trevor Cox – University of Salford
Dr Ben Croxford – University College London
Professor Clara Greed – University of the West of England
Professor Julienne Hanson – University College London
Victoria Henshaw – University of Salford
Gemma Moore – University College London
Dr Mohamed Refaee – University of Sheffield
Professor Steve Sharples – University of Sheffield

Urban form and social sustainability for city-centre living

Dr Caroline Davey – University of Salford
Professor Julienne Hanson – University College London
Professor Bill Hillier – University College London
Dr Lesley Mackay – University of Salford
Ozlem Sahbaz – University College London
Judith Torrington – University of Sheffield
Professor Edja Trigueiro – University College London
Dr Laura Vaughan – University College London
Andrew Wootton – University of Salford
Reem Zako – University College London

Diversity and mixed-use: concepts, policy, design and experience

Rosita Aiesha – London Metropolitan University
Professor Graeme Evans – London Metropolitan University
Dr Jo Foord – London Metropolitan University
Frances Hollis – London Metropolitan University
Chiron Mottram – University College London
Professor Alan Penn – University College London
Irini Perdikogianni – University College London

Supporting urban design decision-making: ICT

Professor Ghassan Aouad – University of Salford
Professor Terrence Fernando – University of Salford
Charlie Fu – University of Salford
Professor Joe Tah – University of Salford
Jialiang Yao – University of Salford

VivaCity2020. Reinterpreting the research: artists-in-residence

Helen Bendon
Jessica Thom

ACKNOWLEDGEMENTS

The authors would like to acknowledge the support of the UK Engineering and Physical Sciences Research Council (EPSRC), without which this team would never have been brought together, nor been able to undertake the research that has informed this book. In addition we value all the support from our industrial collaborators and our steering committee. This project has required an enormous amount of access to information, people and places, and although we cannot list them all here we would especially like to thank Sheffield City Council, Islington Borough Council, Manchester City Council and Salford City Council for their continued accessibility and interest in our work. We also owe a significant debt to Professor Ian Cooper and Jeremy Grammer for their guidance, advice, support and time, which they gave willingly and in abundance, and which helped keep this complex project on track. In order to present our findings in an interesting and imaginative way in this book we have called upon the skills of an excellent creative team led by Scott Abbott, and we are grateful for the guidance and help of Madeleine Metcalfe and Beth Bishop at our publishers, Wiley-Blackwell.

Every team is, hopefully, more than the sum of its parts. In VivaCity's case those parts – the individual professors, doctors, research fellows and PhD students – were of the highest standard in the first place, and when brought together created an extraordinary team. It is to their credit that VivaCity has been such a successful and flagship project, and they have set the bar very high for future projects.

This type of large and complex research project requires an enormous amount of skill in bringing together the resources and the people to work effectively. This project has relied on the talent, diplomacy, persistence and organisation of one dedicated person, Joanne Leach, who has contributed not only project management but also intelligence and wisdom, for which we are sincerely grateful.

Finally, none of this would have been possible without the vision, imagination, dedication and patience of the project leader, Professor Rachel Cooper. She has diligently and delicately led the team through both smooth and turbulent waters, and has demonstrated that effective leadership is crucial to success. Rachel's dedication to this project knew few boundaries, and she has led by example, frequently working 16-hour days, six days a week, to get the job done. From the beginning VivaCity2020 has been an exemplary project, and there is no doubt this is down to Rachel.

Thank you.

PREFACE

By the time this book is published, we shall have passed a significant point in our evolution as a species. More than half of us will live in some kind of 'urban' settlement. Across the planet we have left behind our rural origins, and now find ourselves grouped together en masse into towns and cities. And it is predominantly here, in these urban environments, that we shall have to confront the twin challenges thrown at us by sustainable development and climate change.

How should we now live in cities? And what new or altered forms should our cities take? Is there a clear, emergent UK or European model that can be held up as exemplary, especially for those countries that are still rapidly industrialising and urbanising, and with whose actions so much of our joint destiny rests?

When the late Jane Jacobs (1961) tried to identify, from a North American perspective four decades ago, what was problematic about cities, she commented:

> 'Merely to think about cities and get somewhere, one of the main things is to know what kind of problem cities pose, for all problems cannot be thought about in the same way. Which avenues of thinking are apt to be useful and to help yield the truth depends not on how we might prefer to think about a subject, but rather on the inherent nature of the subject itself.' (p. 442, emphasis original)

She offered her own answer to this:

> 'Cities happen to be problems in organized complexity .... They present "situations in which half a dozen or even several dozen quantities are all varying simultaneously and in subtly interconnected ways". Cities ... do not exhibit one problem in organized complexity, which if understood explains all. They can be analyzed into many such problems or segments which ... are also related with one another. The variables are many, but they are not helter-skelter; they are "interrelated into an organic whole".' (p. 446, emphasis original)

Since then we have become more familiar with notions such as complexity theory and holistic thinking, just as we are with the requirement for so-called joined-up government. But, despite their increased familiarity, all three of these are proving very difficult to put into effective practice, especially where the design, operation and management of cities are concerned.

This book is one attempt to confront such difficulties. It takes as its focus of attention how to make the '24-hour city' more sustainable. It is the product of a research programme, supported by a UK research council, that has itself displayed extraordinary longevity, under one title or another. The Engineering and Physical Sciences Research Council (EPSRC) launched its first managed research programme of research into the sustainability of cities in 1993. Since then, it has funded further rounds on the Sustainable Urban Environment. Whatever their title, these programmes have been based on a shared belief — that through interdisciplinary research, conducted in collaboration with relevant stakeholders and end users, the UK's research community can construct an improved evidence base on which decision-makers can ground more effective actions.

Despite the longevity of the research programmes, it is not easy to track down, let alone collate and synthesise, the results of the research they have supported. So we should be grateful for this book, which emerges from the first round of EPSRC's Sustainable Urban Environment programme (called SUE1 for short). It brings together, in one place, the results of the VivaCity project and puts them between one set of covers so that we can begin to explore how, and to what extent, the UK's research community is fulfilling the expectations that have been placed upon it.

We should commend the EPSRC for its sustained commitment to research in this area. And we should be grateful to the VivaCity2020 project team for the exercise in collation and concision that they have undertaken on our behalf. With the publication of this volume, we can begin to assess another brick in the evidence base that the UK's research community has been diligently constructing over the past 15 years. Towards the start of this process, the late Michael Breheny (1996) warned that policy-making on sustainable cities was an instance of:

> *'Politicians racing ahead of academics, pressing for specific policies before the research community is able to say with any confidence which policies will have what effects.'* (p. 13)

A decade and a half later, the time for more mature and critical reflection on what is being achieved has now arrived.

Ian Cooper, Eclipse Research Consultants, Cambridge.

April 2008

References

Breheny, M. (1996) Centrist, decentrists and compromisers: views on the future of urban form. In M. Jenks, E. Burton & K. Williams (eds), *The compact city: A sustainable urban form?*, pp. 13–35. London: E & FN Spon.

Jacobs, J. (1961) *The death and life of great American cities.* London: Penguin Books.

INTRODUCTION

The Brundtland Commission defines sustainability as 'development that meets the needs of the present without compromising the ability of future generations to meet their own needs' (WCED, 1987). Sustainability requires that three main quality-of-life objectives are met (DETR, 2000):

- social progress that addresses the needs of everyone
- the effective protection of the environment and prudent use of natural resources
- the maintenance of stable levels of high economic growth and development.

The drive to promote sustainable urban regeneration through design excellence, environmental and social responsibility, economic investment and legislative change was outlined in the report *Towards an Urban Renaissance* (Urban Task Force, 1999). This presents a vision of thriving and sustainable urban centres that are high-density, compact, well connected and vibrant around the clock. The creation of this 'urban buzz' involves combining a mixture of urban uses with a balanced social mix of incomes and tenures. This introduction of the notion of mixed-use, day- and night-time economies has resulted in what is termed '24-hour cities'. Cities such as Manchester have restructured to realise this vision, and with this have arisen conflicts of interest between stakeholders with different objectives: for example, security versus free access; the needs of older people versus conditions that support other interests such as youth culture; and commercial activity versus environmental quality.

Ultimately, the users of urban environments and their lifestyles create or erode sustainability, with the physical, social and economic infrastructures forming the 'places' that locate such lifestyles. Therefore, for sustainability interventions to succeed, a human-centred approach must be adopted. Such an approach is central to this book. We shall address the complex relationships between the perceptions, evaluations and emotional responses of users to urban environments (Jones, 2000; Davey et al., 2002), and the short-term habits and longer-term lifestyles to which they aspire.

Design, sustainability and quality of life

Design has long played a role in promoting sustainability and quality of life, with designers addressing a range of quality-of-life issues through socially responsible design. In the 1960s designers began to actively consider the wider implications of design for society. Several approaches emerged, including green design and consumerism, responsible design and ethical consuming, ecodesign and sustainability (Dewberry 2000; GCCP, 2000) and feminist design (Whiteley, 1993). In particular, concern about pollution and health prompted designers to evaluate the social implications of high-density, high-rise buildings or 'concrete jungles' characteristic of cities, and to consider the impact of the built environment on quality of life. In the construction sector, a greater emphasis was placed on achieving low capital costs, using local labour and materials, creating jobs and, most importantly, enabling control by local people considered best placed to articulate their needs (DETR, 2000; GCCP, 2000).

Sustainable design decision-making

Cooper *et al.* (2002) have shown that designers are able to address quality-of-life issues while providing competitive advantage for the client, reducing costs arising from social or environmental issues, creating better environments and regenerating deprived areas. Clients, planners and developers, however, are sometimes unable to determine the costs and benefits of different design solutions, and fail to consider the longer-term consequences of their decisions (Hardjono & van Marrewijk, 2001). Under such circumstances, design professionals often find it difficult to pursue quality-of-life issues, and require support guiding the clients that employ them.

According to the DETR (2000), sustainable decision-making requires:
- costs and benefits to be considered over the long and short term, including those that cannot easily be valued in money terms
- disproportionate costs to be avoided and trade-offs to be made when pursuing a single objective, to prevent problems simply being transferred elsewhere.

To achieve sustainability, design professionals must develop innovative and creative solutions that are able to address social, environmental and economic issues at the same time. To this end, designers need to consult with key stakeholders and be supported in the process of innovation. Greater awareness by planners, policy-makers and clients of the value of design in tackling quality-of-life issues is needed to ensure that the solutions of today do not become the problems of tomorrow. This requires:
- research data on the urban environment and the interaction between social, economic and environmental issues
- methods of understanding the context in which urban design takes place
- guidance materials relevant to practitioners – i.e., codes of practice, case studies and guidelines
- process maps to help practitioners understand the context, make trade-offs, and develop design solutions that allow for change
- methods of testing and predicting the consequences of design proposals (e.g., virtual reality and space syntax)
- methods of monitoring design outcomes, identifying trends and envisaging future scenarios.

The VivaCity2020 story

This book is based on the results of a five-year research programme, VivaCity2020, which addresses the dimensions of sustainability in the urban environment. The book takes a multidisciplinary perspective (physical science, social science, engineering, architecture and design) to considering the problems and issues of city-centre living. VivaCity2020 recognised that the approach must include a breadth of disciplines, because individual perspectives simply cannot address the complex relationships that exist in a city and which need to be addressed by the various professional

stakeholders – both the professional designers (architects, planners, engineers) and those people who make intangible or tacit design decisions everyday, but who may not be aware that they do (e.g., policy-makers, developers, local government, and investment community). In addition, the research and the resulting findings are important for the more marginalised voices, such as non-professionals and locl communities. They are important contributors to the design process, and VivaCity2020 looked for a multiplicity of ways to engage and understand their role in the 24-hour city.

The VivaCity2020 method

VivaCity2020 was funded by the UK Engineering and Physical Sciences Research Council (EPSRC) as part of a research programme entitled Sustainable Urban Environments (SUE). It brought together researchers from five universities: Lancaster University, the University of Salford, The Bartlett School of Graduate Studies at University College London (UCL), the University of Sheffield and the Cities Institute at London Metropolitan University. The team included experts in architecture and design, acoustics, air quality and pollution, thermal quality, sociology, crime, housing, planning and IT.

Rochdale Canal, Manchester

It was clear from the outset of the research that a new method of working was necessary in order to reap the benefits of a multidisciplinary perspective. This was achieved by having common case study sites, determining the aspects of sustainability to be researched, and applying methods appropriate to the line of enquiry. The methods ranged from questionnaires, surveys and ethnographic studies to physical monitors collecting atmospheric and acoustic data. At the beginning of the project, the whole team undertook a period of intense discussion to consider the relationships between the different dimensions to be addressed. Throughout the period of study, everyone interacted and shared knowledge of case study locations, places and people. VivaCity was not concerned with merging datasets but with collecting the right types of data that would inform evidence-based design decision-making. The team developed a programme devoted to collecting data in eight key areas of sustainability:

- the urban design decision-making process
- the impact of design upon, and the relationship between, perceptions of actual environmental quality
- how people's knowledge affects the development of the built environment
- the relationship between the design and accessibility of public toilets and how people use the city centre
- the relationship between housing needs and types of housing provided in city centres
- city-centre crime and fear of crime
- mixed-use and economic diversity in cities
- how ICT can help decision-makers make more sustainable decisions.

The temporality and the scale varied from one aspect of the study to another, and consequently the results are at different levels of detail and perspectives. Thus the book flows at varying paces and depths of study. Indeed, it is clear that creating a 'sustainable' city is neither a macro-scale nor a micro-scale issue, but both. The following chapters will illustrate that often the devil is in the detail in all sustainability issues, and proxy indicators can be found on very small, detailed projects.

The VivaCity2020 project worked within three case study areas: Greater Manchester, Sheffield, and part of London (Clerkenwell), and this book is illustrated with photographs from these three cities. These areas were chosen for their large populations (over 500 000 inhabitants), high densities (over 1000 inhabitants per km^2) and the plethora of 24-hour urban issues relating to sustainability (such as crime, noise, environmental pollution, adequate housing and access to public conveniences). Studying cities with these qualities – versus smaller towns with lower populations, densities and fewer urban sustainability issues – provided opportunities for the researchers to explore the complex relationship between urban design and sustainability. It is becoming increasingly important to acknowledge the fundamental role of designing and developing sustainability for 24-hour cities, given that over 47% of the world's population currently lives in urban areas, and about 60% of us will be considered urban by 2030 (Population Reference Bureau, 2004).

VivaCity2020 was one of 13 research projects funded by the EPSRC as part of its Sustainable Urban Environments (SUE) research programme. The SUE projects covered four themes: the urban and built environment (VivaCity2020 was part of this theme); waste water and land management; transport; and metrics and knowledge management. Throughout the research programme links were made with the other SUE projects looking at other aspects of the sustainability agenda.

Structure of the book

Addressing sustainability issues in relation to the design and planning of the urban environment is a complex, multidisciplinary task, and solutions never arrive from a single perspective. This book uses design in a facilitating capacity to consider how, when and by whom decisions are made that contribute to the dimensions of sustainability (environmental, social and economic) in the urban environment, specifically in relation to the concept of the city centre over 24 hours.

The book is based on a series of case studies. This use of particular cities and particular localities raises questions about the degree to which conclusions are generalisable and transferable, and the degree to which we can make commonly applied conclusions. One attraction of this approach is that it reflects the heterogeneity of UK cities, and emphasises the importance of place-specific issues. By recognising what works or doesn't work in other cities and at different scales, local authorities, planners and decision-makers can adapt their own processes.

The book begins by providing a new conceptualisation of the urban design decision-making process, identifying the key stages and lead decision-makers. The following chapters take the reader through a process of understanding the dimensions of sustainability, and presenting case studies and tools by which these dimensions can be analysed. The later chapters illustrate the trade-offs and the relationships between the dimensions of sustainability and the use that can be made of IT in making design decisions. Finally, the book makes recommendations for future approaches to the design, development and the ongoing management of urban environments.

Section 1 The urban design process
Chapter 1 The urban design decision-making process: definitions and issues
This chapter reviews our conceptions of the urban design process, illustrating the types of guidance and processes that are in use. It discusses the notion of process in relation to urban design, introducing the concept of the urban design lifecycle and the notion that all urban development projects go through four stages: pre-design; design and development; use, management and maintenance; and decline, demolition and/or regeneration.

Weston Rise, London

Chapter 2 The urban design decision-making process: case studies

This chapter provides three in-depth case study examples of the decision-making process, in Sheffield, Salford and Clerkenwell. These cases are used to illustrate different levels of design decision-making and the complexities involved, highlighting the implications for sustainability.

Chapter 3 The urban design decision-making process: a new approach

This chapter discusses how the urban design decision-making process needs to be re-conceptualised, and where and by whom sustainable urban design decisions should and could be made. It illustrates this through a detailed model of the process, and explains the concepts presented in that model. This model forms the framework for the remainder of the book, illustrating how and where sustainability issues should be considered by those making urban design decisions.

Section 2 Environmental sustainability and city-centre living

Chapter 4 Urban environmental quality

This chapter reviews the positioning of the environment broadly, and environmental sustainability more specifically, in the urban design process. It examines the various approaches to how the environment is measured and perceived, and how they are used in urban design.

Chapter 5 The sensory city

This chapter delves into the relationship between our senses and the city, describing the research undertaken in the case study cities. In each city environmental quality was assessed in both the indoor residential environment (the home) and the outdoor urban environment (the street). The case studies have a strong focus on the resident users of the city and their perceptions of local environmental quality, enabling the evaluation of the trade-offs being made, both implicitly and explicitly, by people living in city-centre environments.

Chapter 6 Inclusive design of 'away from home' toilets

This chapter continues to investigate the user experience of the city, but in a specific manner. It looks at the provision of 'away from home' toilets in city centres, and is concerned both with the availability of toilets in a city environment and with the accessibility of both public and commercially based provision. This small issue is shown to have a much wider impact on our experience of the city than one might expect.

Section 3 Urban form and social sustainability for city-centre living

Chapter 7 Housing in the twentieth-century city

This chapter considers housing in the city: it illustrates this through case studies of 30 urban blocks in the three cities, which have been analysed from the perspective of form, morphology and user perspectives. The analysis illustrates the differences chronologically over blocks built from 1890 to date, and leads to recommendations on residential housing, open spaces, primary and secondary boundaries, axiality and liveability.

Chapter 8 Designing safe residential areas
This chapter discusses the tools used by planners, developers and architects to reduce crime, and critiques the theories upon which they are built. Through the use of case studies, it explains the application of such theories and the resulting outcomes. The chapter then makes recommendations on how to address crime prevention during the process, and signposts appropriate tools.

Chapter 9 Crime and urban design: an evidence-based approach
With access to a very large and detailed dataset, this chapter discusses the notion of form and space and its relationship to crime. It applies space syntax to understand crime in relation to residential and mixed-use areas, and provides advice to enable better spatial design and planning.

Section 4 Diversity and mixed-use for city-centre living

Chapter 10 Urban sustainability: mixed-use or mixed messages?
This chapter provides a conceptual analysis of the policy and development processes concerning mixed-use buildings and neighbourhoods. Diversity is represented in terms of the temporal, social and economic, and interrogates these dynamics at varying spatial scales, and in the design and usage of mixed-use buildings. Case studies of mixed-use areas in the urban village of Clerkenwell and in the city centres of Sheffield and Manchester assess quality of life from the perspectives of residents, businesses and the planning system. A detailed synthesis

illustrates how mixed-use operates at varying scales and intensities, the interactions between policy, planning and design, and sustainability challenges to the Compact City.

Chapter 11 The generation of diversity
The concept of social, economic and land use diversity is further developed in this chapter. Taking a biological–ecological analogy to sustainability, theories of how physical and spatial patterns relate to urban systems are used to present a model of land use patterns, agglomeration and clusters. These are tested in Clerkenwell, based on detailed land-use and pedestrian surveys. Agent-based modelling is then applied more widely to simulate urban growth and patterns of retail premises distribution and usage.

Section 5 Supporting urban design decision-making: ICT

Chapter 12 IT infrastructure for supporting multidisciplinary urban planning
This chapter discusses the use of ICT tools to support sustainable design decision-making. It looks at the nature of the stakeholders, their propensity to use ICT-based decision-making tools, and the skill levels required. The chapter goes on to describe the tools developed using the data and case studies from the research.

Printworks, Manchester

Section 6 VivaCity2020: artists-in-residence

Chapter 13 The role of art practice within VivaCity2020
Chapter 14 Present in public space
This section presents the reflections and illustrates the work of two artists-in-residence who worked with the VivaCity2020 project to provide an alternative insight into the issues of sustainability and the experience of city users and residents. Their images are presented alongside the chapter narratives, providing a cultural and creative perspective to our understanding of being in a city.

Conclusion

Chapter 15 The ongoing sustainable city endeavour
The book's conclusion discusses sustainable urban environments. It considers how achievable the objective of sustainability is, where and how trade-offs are to be made, and how knowledge must be codified into domains – such as policy and regulation, space and form, user perspectives and levels of accessibility. It goes on to apply this to the design decision-making process, and makes recommendations on how the process and the decision-making tools can be applied in practice.

References

Cooper, R., Davey, C.L. & Press, M. (2002) Design against crime: methods and issues that link product innovation to social policy. *International Journal of New Product Development & Innovation*, December/January, 329–343.

Davey, C.L., Cooper, R., Press, M., Wootton, A.B. & Olson, E. (2002) Design against crime: design leadership in the development of emotional values. Paper presented at the 11th International Conference, Design Management Institute, Boston, USA.

DETR (2000). *Building a better quality of life: A strategy for more sustainable construction.* London: Department of the Environment, Transport and the Regions.

Dewberry, E. (2000) Lesson from ecodesign. In S. Learmount, M. Press & R. Cooper (eds), *Design against crime*, pp. 127–146. London: Report for the Design Council, Home Office and Department of Trade and Industry.

GCCP (2000) *Construction the best government client: Achieving sustainability in construction procurement.* London: Sustainability Action Group of the Government Construction Client's Panel.

Hardjono, T.W. & van Marrewijk, M. (2001). The social dimensions of business excellence. *Corporate Environmental Strategy*, **8** (3), 223-233.

Jones, R. (2000) *The big idea.* London: HarperCollins Business.

Population Reference Bureau (2004) *2004 World population data sheet.* Washington, DC: Population Reference Bureau.

Urban Task Force (1999) *Towards an urban renaissance: Final report of the Urban Task Force.* London: Spon.

Whitelely, N. (1993). *Design for society.* London: Reaktion Books.

WCED (1987). *Our common future.* Oxford: Oxford University Press.

SECTION I
THE URBAN DESIGN PROCESS

THE URBAN DESIGN PROCESS

This section addresses the urban design process. It identifies a generic process resulting from a review and analysis of the literature and documented practice in a number of fields and disciplines, including business and planning. This model is then tested against three case studies involving urban design and development projects of varying temporal and physical scales. We explore a regeneration project in Greater Manchester over two years, a 'repair and enhance' neighbourhood in Sheffield over 15 years, and an urban block in London over 20 years. At the same time, the cases are analysed to identify the degree to which sustainability is considered by the decision-makers and where appropriate tools and guidance are employed. This section concludes with a reconceptualisation of the urban design process based upon a revisit of the generic process and an analysis of the case study findings. This new process outlines stages for more sustainable decision-making as well as incorporating new concepts to be used in the process, e.g., sustainability tasks and sustainability reviews.

CHAPTER 1

THE URBAN DESIGN DECISION-MAKING PROCESS: DEFINITIONS AND ISSUES

Rachel Cooper, Christopher Boyko, Naomi Pemberton-Billing and Daniel Cadman

Exmouth Market, London

This chapter opens with a discussion of urban design, offering a definition and describing its relatively recent proliferation, both in planning and as a discipline in its own right. The notion of process in relation to urban design will also be examined, illustrating the different stages and activities involved in the urban design decision-making process. Issues not addressed in the process will be investigated currently, particularly decision-makers, tools used in decision-making and sustainability. Finally, the urban design decision-making process will be shown as part of a larger life cycle for urban design, driven by a number of factors crucial to the development of 24-hour cities.

Urban design

Urban design can be viewed as a relatively new discipline: it was first mentioned in North America in the 1950s at Harvard University (Rowley, 1994). However, the practice of urban design is anything but new. Throughout civilisation, urban design has played an instrumental role in the creation of cityscapes, from Greek and Roman times until the present day (Greed & Roberts, 1998).

Historically in the UK urban design has been viewed separately from town planning and architecture. One outcome of this disciplinary division has been the development of schemes with no overall strategy to connect design with support services, shops, transport links and housing (Hall, 1998). Recent EU legislation and non-legislative guidance regarding urban sustainability (European Commission, 1993; Tewdwr-Jones & Williams, 2001), and the Planning and Compulsory Purchase Act 2004 (HMSO, 2004) aim to rectify these and other issues, resulting in a government drive towards a more holistic and interdisciplinary approach to design, planning and sustainability. Consideration of urban design throughout the lifetime of urban development projects is now perceived to be a vital ingredient in the creation of successful cities, and is central to improving urban design decision-making within the planning system (Office of the Deputy Prime Minister (ODPM), 2002).

Although urban design has been breaking new ground on the policy front, defining the term has been a more difficult endeavour. Urban design is multifaceted and complex, open to interpretation and extensive explanation (Moughtin et al., 1995). Different groups, such as government, the private sector, researchers, academics and the community, have an interest in urban design and will consider it in their own terms and contexts (Rowley, 1994). Even the words 'urban' and 'design' are difficult to define, as context plays a large role in their interpretation. Nonetheless, there is some consensus about the basic elements of urban design.

Urban design is a multidimensional concept that reinforces physical transformation within the urban environment (Barnett, 1982; Rowley, 1994; Gosling, 2002). Physical transformation may be guided by a variety of principles. These principles include, but are not limited to, the following:

- Character: a sense of place and history, responding to and strengthening locally distinctive patterns in the built environment
- Continuity and enclosure: clarity of built and natural form, clearly distinguishing between public and private space
- Quality of the public realm: sense of well-being and amenity in public spaces and routes that are both lively and pleasant to use
- Ease of movement: ability to get to and through a space; permeability
- Legibility: ease of understanding in a space; a clear image of a space
- Adaptability: ability for a space to change easily
- Diversity: spaces with variety, allowing people to choose from different options (Commission for Architecture and the Built Environment (CABE), 2003).

In addition to physical transformation, urban design also considers the role that people play in cities throughout a 24-hour period. People shape urban design through their changing social, psychological, aesthetic, functional and emotional needs. People are also shaped by the design of cities, providing a myriad social, political and environmental reactions and responses to what they see, hear, smell, touch, feel, and experience there (Reekie, 1972; Greed & Roberts, 1998; CABE & DETR, 2000). Thus urban design is a holistic concept (Buchanan, 1988), as much about a transformation as it is about a reaction to, and an ongoing conversation with, the urban environment.

This perspective enables us to form a working definition of urban design: *the dynamic art and process of designing, creating, making and managing spaces and places for people and with people in mind* (adapted from Rowley, 1994; CABE & DETR, 2000). The idea of urban design as a dynamic art and as a process is worth exploring further.

Urban design as a *dynamic art* refers to creativity and context, the latter being unique to each urban area. While urban design is seen as part of a wider national policy, and is reflected in guidance by national advisers to government (e.g., CABE), local authorities must be able to reinterpret these ideas to suit their local context (see Rogers & Power, 2000, for a description of context). The private sector and other local stakeholders (e.g., community residents) should also be able to bring their particular insights and experiences to each situation, helping to shape the specific urban design of an area (CABE & DETR, 2000). Community consultation within the planning system and local engagement with urban design are priorities that need to be addressed to facilitate the creation of lively and inspirational places that are safe, accessible, pleasant to use, human in scale and distinctive – in essence, a sustainable community (CABE & DETR, 2001; Carley et al., 2001; ODPM, 2002, 2003, 2005a, 2005b, 2006; HMSO, 2004; CLG, 2006). The basis on which decisions from the community are made is indeed an art, however, as it combines local priorities, a 'gut feel' or tacit knowledge from the community and, in some cases, scientific evidence.

Urban design as a process refers to following a method, procedure or series of actions that lead to the accomplishment of a result (Atkin et al., 2003; Concise Oxford English Dictionary, 2006). In general, processes are complex, non-linear and iterative (Rowley, 1994), involving a host of people, activities, feedback, issues, and trade-offs over time. Illustrating a generic procedure for urban design may help to bring a clearer understanding to the complexity. Through the development of a process map, important information can be gleaned about who should be involved in urban design projects, when they should be involved, what their roles should be, and what they need in order to make more informed decisions throughout the process. Process maps have been utilised in a number of industries (e.g., manufacturing and construction) to usefully illustrate the completion of an activity and the roles played by the people involved (Cooper et al., 2005).

The urban design decision-making process

A well-mapped and understood urban design decision-making process has been recognised as providing an appropriate balance between creativity and procedure (Boyko et al., 2005). Such a process gives structure to the design of cities, yet does not impose a strict set of criteria on decision-makers and stakeholders, which might remove originality, imagination and innovation from these environments. Moreover, the creation of a balance between creativity and procedure requires the collaboration of all individuals involved in the

St Marks Church, Finsbury, London

Clerkenwell Green, London

process, each with their own specialist knowledge and contribution. Considering people's needs and requirements throughout the process serves to enhance the quality of urban design in terms of the places that are built, and the social, environmental and economic realities of those places (Pemberton-Billing, 2007).

In the past – and arguably, the present – decision-making processes existed primarily within planning and stemmed from a rationalist perspective, relying on the so-called precision of 'hard' or objective data, such as mathematical models and economic formulae (for examples of rational processes see Lindblom, 1959; Etzioni, 1968; Faludi, 1973, 1987). From this perspective, information given by different groups, such as local residents, was often seen as too subjective or 'soft' (e.g., anecdotal accounts), and therefore was considered less appropriate for the planning process. As a result, qualitative information often risked being discarded outright in favour of quantitative data (Green, 1996). Thus planning was viewed as a dominant – yet still passive – decision-making process, with issues of urban design being largely ignored because of its emphasis on design as 'art'. However, planning 'mistakes', for example Pruitt Igoe in St Louis, Missouri, served as a wake-up call for planners to consider alternative ways of approaching the planning process.[1]

An alternative to the dominant decision-making process for planning is an urban design decision-making process (Rowland, 1995) that gives greater credence to the 'softer' qualities and contexts of cities – as well as to the relationships between such qualities and contexts – while also incorporating 'hard' data into decision-making. The value of this less traditional approach is that stakeholders have more opportunities to become involved in the process (Boyko et al., 2005). To date, however, little work has taken place that investigates the urban design decision-making process holistically. The remainder of this chapter outlines this process in the context of creating urban sustainability for the 24-hour city.

The urban design decision-making process in greater detail

To understand why urban design is a fundamental part of 24-hour cities, it is necessary to recognise the underlying framework and process (Cook, 1980). It is not enough to examine the outcomes of urban design and ponder why things have happened. The process through which decision-makers and stakeholders arrive at their decisions also must be comprehended so that 'mistakes' such as Pruitt Igoe can be minimised (Rowley, 1994; Kagioglou et al., 1998).

A comprehensive review of processes from a variety of disciplines and professions, including architecture (RIBA, 1999), business (Smith and Jackson, 2000), manufacturing, construction and engineering (Woodhead, 2000; Austin et al., 2001; Cooper et al., 2005), non-governmental organisations (English Partnerships, 2000; Heritage Lottery Fund, 2000), planning (Nelessen, 1994; Bressi, 1995; Wates, 1996, 1998; Okubo, 2000; Roberts, 2003) and urban design (Rowland, 1995; Biddulph, 1997; Canadian Institute of Planners, 2000) (see also Macmillan et

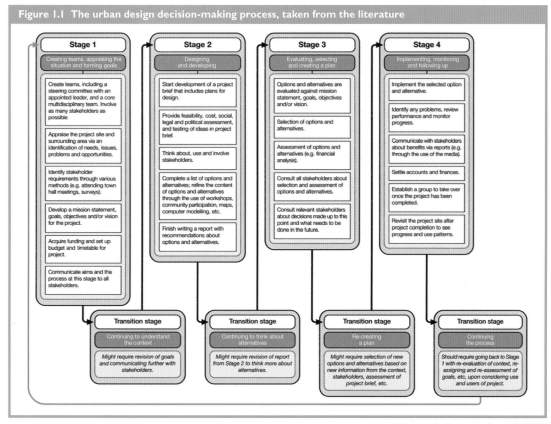

Figure 1.1 The urban design decision-making process, taken from the literature

Source: Boyko et al. (2005)

al., 2002) was undertaken to ascertain the types of stages and activities found within processes. These processes consist of a range of stages, from as few as three (see Woodhead, 2000; Roberts, 2003; Cooper *et al.*, 2005) to as many as 12 (see RIBA, 1999). The average number of process stages was between four and five. The review found that a precise process for urban design decision-making does not exist. However, there were substantial overlaps between the different disciplines' and professions' conceptualisations of their processes, allowing a hybrid or generic decision-making process to be created that focused on urban design. Figure 1.1 illustrates the stages and activities within this urban design decision-making process, which can be structured into four discrete stages, with four linking or transition stages.

The process and stages can be explained as follows:

A generic urban design decision-making process model

Stage 1: Creating teams, appraising the situation and forming goals.

The objective for this stage is to prepare for an urban design project. Here a number of activities occur, including the formation and establishment of teams, the appraisal of the project site and its surrounding context, the determination of goals, objectives, mission statements and/or visions for the project, the identification of stakeholders, the securing of funding, and the creation of timetables. These activities do not need to be followed in any specific order; they may take place concurrently; and they may change over the lifetime of the urban development project if and when this stage is revisited.

Wardour Street, Soho, London

Stage 2: Designing and developing.
The main activity here is the creation of design options and alternatives for the urban development project. This activity is based on a project design brief, an assessment and testing of ideas in the project brief, and feedback from stakeholders. Design options and alternatives are also informed by the context appraisal undertaken in Stage 1.

Stage 3: Evaluating, selecting and creating a plan.
This stage responds to the outputs from Stage 2 by evaluating the design options and alternatives. The goals from Stage 1 and the brief in Stage 2 are utilised to evaluate the designs. Once chosen, the selected option will be assessed again; stakeholders will be consulted on this decision, giving feedback where necessary; and the urban development project will be reviewed and detailed, in preparation for construction.

Stage 4: Implementing, monitoring and following up.
The urban development project will be built via the construction process. Once built, the urban development project will be monitored for problems by a group who will be established to manage the project in the future. Accounts will also be settled between the various stakeholders in the project (e.g., architects, engineers).

At the end of each stage are transition stages: 'Continuing to understand the context', 'Continuing to think about alternatives', 'Re-creating a plan' and 'Continuing the process'. The transition stages represent 'soft gates' for decision-makers to review their actions and plan their next steps (Kagioglou et al., 1998). By placing them at the end of each stage, the transition stages also underpin the iterative nature of processes. That is, decision-makers may need to revise actions from a previous stage before moving to the next stage. Keeping the process iterative illustrates that decision-making also involves reflection before proceeding. It ensures the urban development project does not finish when it is built, but continues to be monitored and assessed throughout the project's lifetime.

The above urban design decision-making process identifies a number of key stages and activities within those stages that decision-makers and stakeholders could follow when undertaking an urban development project. However, this process has been developed from existing literature and guidelines, and therefore fails to cover the details required to implement the ideas in practice (e.g., the lack of information about decision-makers, the identification of tools used in decision-making, and

Homes for Change, Hulme, Manchester

how sustainability is brought into the process). If such a process is to be applied, these details must be clarified. Indeed, if we look at defining decision-making in urban design, we find that little or no information is provided about the specific roles of the different people involved at each stage in the urban design decision-making process (Boyko *et al.*, 2005). It is crucial to understand these roles, as they may distinguish people's influences on the process and how those influences can lead to decisions being made. Thus it is very important to try to capture this information, both within each stage and throughout the process.

In addition to the lack of information about decision-makers, there is little knowledge about the kinds of tools used to undertake the various activities within each of the stages. Some of the activities, for example identifying stakeholder requirements via town hall meetings or surveys in Stage 1, are described in both the urban design literature and more generic literature on surveys and market research, providing suggestions on how to carry out the activities. Coinciding with the recent emphasis on stakeholder involvement in planning and sustainable communities (ODPM, 2002, 2003, 2004a, 2004b, 2005a, 2005b), numerous tools for engagement and consultation are being used by decision-makers to ensure participation in the urban design decision-making process. Many community-based and participatory planning exercises use hand-drawn maps, tracing paper, felt-tip pens and flip charts as a way of involving stakeholders without the confusion of complex, technological jargon (Wates, 1996, 1998). Holding locally based workshops and focus groups, performing outreach, and having well-trained facilitators at consultation events helps to promote stakeholder involvement across a wide selection of people (ODPM, 2004a).

While the use of non-technical tools is a viable option for consultation exercises, some tools to aid decision-making are more computer-based, and help users to visualise or identify areas on spatial maps. Figures, graphs, three-dimensional representations and contextual information can be created and layered using geographical information systems and other visual graphics packages found on computers (e.g., photo-editing software and computer-aided design). Other tools are Internet-based, allowing decision-makers to understand the planning process in which they will be working. For example, in 2004 ODPM created Planning and Regulatory Services Online (PARSOL), which gives local authorities access to e-planning and e-regulation services (ODPM, 2004a). Many local authorities also have an electronic public access system for planning applications, which allows anyone with an Internet connection to see what applications for development have been submitted. Many of these tools and their uses are illustrated in subsequent chapters.

Additionally, policy documents produced by national, regional and local governments concerning planning, urban design and sustainability issues are tools used by local authority planning departments to inform and substantiate planning and design decisions (e.g., HMSO, 2004). Non-governmental

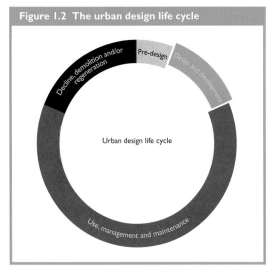

Figure 1.2 The urban design life cycle

Urban design life cycle

Source: Andrew B. Wootton

organisations, such as CABE and English Partnerships, also produce guidance to support government policy (e.g., CABE and DETR, 2001). These documents include planning briefs, histories of an area, photographic essays, written reports from commissioned surveys, questionnaires and studies (e.g., a feasibility study of a proposed urban development project). Decision-makers can use this latter set of documents to help understand the context of an urban development project.

A final set of 'tools' reflects the human-centred nature of decision-making, and includes understanding personality traits, interpersonal skills and the types of feelings that are desired in order to foster a good working team and a smooth-running process. These 'tools' are valuable in the decision-making process, yet are often overlooked because they are not as tangible as, for example, a computer program to visualise a new building, or a survey. Nonetheless, as with all tools, it is important to have the appropriate skills to use them, as well as to understand when to use tools in the process, and with whom.

Aside from tools, the process of urban design decision-making in the twenty-first century needs to include aspects of the myriad issues facing 24-hour cities, including sustainability (Thomas, 2003). However, the generic urban design decision-making process presented above is based on earlier processes, none of which mentions or considers sustainability at any of its stages. The process necessitates a holistic and interdisciplinary scope, and a temporal, long-term focus to ensure that decision-makers incorporate social, economic and environmental sustainability issues into their decisions. As sustainability is a significant part of well-designed places (CABE & DETR, 2000, 2001; ODPM, 2002, 2003, 2005a, 2005b, 2006; HMSO, 2004; CLG, 2006), greater efforts need to be made to illustrate how and where in the process sustainability should be considered, and who should consider it (Boyko *et al.*, 2005).

The urban design decision-making process within the urban design life cycle

The urban design decision-making process described above does not exist in a vacuum. It is part of a larger life cycle for urban development projects, consisting of four stages (see Figure 1.2):

- pre-design
- design and development
- use, management and maintenance
- decline, demolition and/or regeneration.

Urban design decisions are often focused on the second stage of the urban design life cycle, 'Design and development'. However, this stage is influenced by the activities that occur in the pre-design stage, 'Creating teams, appraising the situation and forming goals', and impacts on the activities that take place in the latter two stages, 'Evaluating, selecting and

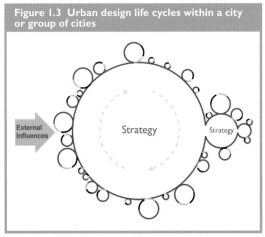

Figure 1.3 Urban design life cycles within a city or group of cities

External Influences

Strategy

Strategy

Source: Andrew B. Wootton

creating a plan' and 'Implementing, monitoring and following up' (see Figure 1.1). Furthermore, within 24-hour cities, several urban design life cycles will be occurring simultaneously. However, each life cycle may be at a different stage. Indeed, the life cycles do not progress in isolation. They are influencing, and are influenced by, the other life cycles, thus affecting the overall shape, look and feel of an area.

An example from one of our case study areas, the Devonshire Quarter in Sheffield (see Chapter 2), illustrates the dynamics of the urban design life cycle. A neighbourhood park called Devonshire Green has been experiencing decline as of late, as maintenance has not been kept up, there are not many people in the park during the day, and the area is perceived as unsafe at night (decline, demolition and/or regeneration). Next to the park is the Forum, a thriving café and restaurant complex with outdoor seating. It is used in the afternoons and evenings, and is managed by a competent team of professionals (use, management and maintenance). On the other side of the park is a relatively new, mixed-use development scheme called West One (design and development). The development, which is only now fully tenanted on the ground floor, includes public space, retail and roof gardens for its tenants to use.

The owners of the Forum have been speaking with the local authority to improve the park. In response, the local authority has been strategising with local residents and businesses about how to bring new amenities to the park, and link the new public spaces in West One with the park.[2]

Within a city or group of cities, many urban design life cycles are progressing at any one time (see Figure 1.3). There are many external influences on these life cycles, and one of the most important is government strategy, from the national, to the regional and local levels. Local government not only interprets national and regional policy about planning, urban design, sustainability and so forth; it also creates its own policy to suit local contexts. Thus both top-down and bottom-up approaches are utilised in driving the urban design life cycles.

Additional externalities play a role in influencing urban design life cycles. These external influences include the state of the economy, political will and pressure, funding, private-sector control over development, and popular sentiment about design. Depending on the city, one or more of the external influences will play a large role in the development of 24-hour cities. In a city that is struggling to become more economically independent from its neighbours, for example, local government may encourage *laissez-faire* development through its planning policies. Thus a combination of political will and a private sector with a lot of power over what it would like to develop may heavily influence the urban design of that city, and the progression of the urban design life cycles.

Royce Court, Hulme, Manchester

A significant internal influence on urban design life cycles is scale. Scale, in this sense, refers both to the spatial size and magnitude of urban development projects and to the temporality associated with how long the urban design life cycle lasts. Although not always the case, larger-scale projects may take a long time to complete – evolving from 'Pre-design' to 'Use, management and maintenance' quite slowly – because of the multitude of decision-makers, stakeholders and issues to consider. If a project has the capacity to impact on a large group of people, such as the regeneration of Central Salford in Greater Manchester, then it is likely there will be much debate about its appropriateness by a range of stakeholders. In contrast, smaller-scale projects, such as the addition of an outdoor terrace on the Forum building in the Devonshire Quarter in Sheffield, may take less time to progress through the first three stages of the urban design life cycle, and require less discussion amongst stakeholders. Thus it is important for decision-makers to understand the issues surrounding scale, as these issues will influence how smoothly the urban design life cycle progresses, and the time it takes to move from one stage of the life cycle to the next.

Scale is a crucial concept, not only for the urban design life cycle but also for the VivaCity2020 project in general. Through a discussion of the research undertaken on this project, many of the chapters within the rest of this book focus on different spatial scales, from the micro (e.g., Brewhouse Yard, Clerkenwell, London) to the macro (e.g., Central Salford, Greater Manchester). Temporal dimensions also are explored in the research. For example, the three urban design decision-making processes that were mapped in the case studies cover different periods of time, from two years – Central Salford in Greater Manchester – to 20 years – the Devonshire Quarter in Sheffield (see Chapter 2). This differential focus on spatial scales and temporal dimensions helps us to identify the connections and impacts between coexisting urban developments in an area regarding urban design and sustainability and the decision-making processes that are occurring simultaneously. Scale and dimension also help us to understand that decision-makers and stakeholders may be part of many different urban development projects in the same area, and therefore provide important input into urban design decision-making.

Summary

We have shown, then, that urban design is both a dynamic art and a process. We have developed a generic urban design decision-making process based on that which exists in the literature and in practice guidelines. We have found that this process tends to be prescriptive yet vague on a number of issues, including the details and definitions of decision-makers and their roles, the vast and diverse array of tools available to aid decision-making, and the inclusion of sustainability. Finally, we have discussed the urban design decision-making process as it sits within the urban design life cycle and in the context of influences such as the economy, government policy and scale.

The next chapter will compare the generic urban design decision-making process and knowledge against three in-depth case studies undertaken as part of the VivaCity2020 project. These case studies highlight decision-making processes from urban development projects in three UK urban areas: Greater Manchester, Sheffield and the Clerkenwell area of London. Each case study is used to address and focus upon the context, the methods, the tools and the process that occurred. The urban design decision-making processes are mapped and the decision-makers identified alongside the tools used and the degree to which sustainability is both implicitly and explicitly discussed and incorporated into decision-making. The process for each case study is compared with the generic urban design decision-making process described in this chapter, which will then be used to inform the development of a new process, described in Chapter 3.

References

Atkin, B., Borgbrant, J. & Josephson, P.-E. (eds) (2003) Conclusions. In *Construction process improvement*, pp. 292–298. Oxford: Blackwell Science.

Austin, S., Steele, J., Macmillan, S., Kirby, P. & Spence, R. (2001) Mapping the conceptual design activity of interdisciplinary teams. *Design Studies*, **22** (3), 211–232.

Barnett, J. (1982) *An introduction to urban design*. New York: Harper & Row.

Biddulph, M. (1997) An urban design process for large development sites. *Town and Country Planning*, **66**, 202–204.

Boyko, C.T., Cooper, R. & Davey, C. (2005) Sustainability and the urban design process. *Engineering Sustainability*, **158** (ES3), 119–125.

Bressi, T. (1995) The real thing? We're getting there. *Planning*, **61** (7), 16–21.

Buchanan, P. (1988) What city? A plea for place in the public realm. *Architectural Review*, **184** (1101), 31–41.

CABE (2003) *The Councillor's guide to urban design*. London: CABE.

CABE & DETR (2000) *By design. Urban design in the planning system: Towards better practice*. London: Thomas Telford.

CABE & DETR (2001) *The value of urban design*. London: Thomas Telford.

Canadian Institute of Planners (2000) The urban design process. Retrieved 24 June 2004 from http://www.cip-icu.ca/English/aboutplan/ud_proce.htm.

Carley, M., Jenkins, P. & Smith, H. (2001) *Urban development and civil society: The role of communities in sustainable cities*. London: Earthscan.

CLG (2006) *Strong and prosperous communities: The local government White Paper*. London: TSO.

Concise Oxford English Dictionary (2005) Definition of the word 'process'. *Concise Oxford English Dictionary*, p. 1144. Oxford: Oxford University Press.

Cook, R.S. (1980) *Zoning for downtown urban design: How cities control development*. Lexington, MA: Lexington Books.

Cooper, R., Aouad, G., Lee, A., Wu, S., Fleming, A. & Kagioglou, M. (2005) *Process management in design and construction*. Oxford: Blackwell.

English Partnerships (2000) *Urban design compendium*. London: English Partnerships.

Etzioni, A. (1968) *The active society*. London: Collier-Macmillan.

European Commission (1993) *White Paper on growth, competitiveness, and employment: The challenges and ways forward into the 21st century*. Brussels: European Commission.

Faludi, A (1973) *Planning theory*. Oxford: Pergamon Press.

Faludi, A. (1987) *A decision-centered view of environmental planning*. Oxford: Pergamon Press.

Garvin, A. (1996) *The American city: What works, what doesn't*. New York: McGraw-Hill.

Gosling, D. (2002) *The evolution of American urban design*. New York: Wiley & Sons.

Greed, C. & Roberts, M. (1998) *Introducing urban design: Interventions and responses*. Harlow: Longman.

Green, S. D. (1996) A metaphorical analysis of client organizations and the briefing process. *Construction Management and Economics*, **14**, 155–164.

Hall, P. (1998) *Cities in civilization*. New York: Pantheon.

Heritage Lottery Fund (2000) *Building projects: Your role in achieving quality and value*. London: Heritage Lottery Fund.

HMSO (2004) *Planning and Compulsory Purchase Act 2004*. London: TSO.

Kagioglou, M., Cooper, R., Aouad, G., Hinks, J., Sexton, M. & Sheath, D.M. (1998) *A generic guide to the design and construction process protocol*. Salford: University of Salford.

Lindblom, C.E. (1959) The science of muddling through. *Public Administration Review*, **19**, 79–88.

Macmillan, S., Steele, J., Kirby, P., Spence, R. & Austin, S. (2002) Mapping the design process during the conceptual phase of building projects. *Engineering, Construction and Architectural Management*, **9** (3), 174–180.

Moughtin, C., Oc, T. & Tiesdell, S. (1995) *Urban design: Ornament and decoration*. Oxford: Butterworth.

Nelessen, A.C. (1994) *Visions for a new American dream: Process, principles, and an ordinance to plan and design small communities* (2nd edn). Chicago: Planners Press.

ODPM (2002) *Sustainable communities: Delivering through planning*. London: ODPM.

ODPM (2003) *Sustainable communities: Building for the future*. London: ODPM.

ODPM (2004a) PARSOL: Planning and Regulatory Services Online. Available (15 April 2005) http://www.parsol.gov.uk/planning_services.html.

ODPM (2004b) *Diversity and planning: Research report on planning policies and practice*. London: ODPM.

ODPM (2005a) *Planning policy statement 1: Delivering sustainable development*. London: ODPM.

ODPM (2005b) *Sustainable communities: People, places and prosperity*. London: ODPM.

ODPM (2006) *The Office of the Deputy Prime Minister's Sustainable Development Action Plan. Securing the future: Delivering UK sustainable development strategy*. London: TSO.

Okubo, D. (2000) *The community visioning and strategic planning handbook*. Denver, CO: National Civic League Press. Retrieved 20 July 2005 from http://www.ncl.org/publications/online/VSPHandbook.pdf.

Pemberton-Billing, I. (2007) *How do regional towns and cities make sustainable urban design?* Unpublished doctoral thesis proposal, Lancaster University, Lancaster, England.

Reekie, R.F. (1972) *Design in the built environment*. London: Edward Arnold.

RIBA (1999) *RIBA plan of work*. London: RIBA.

Roberts, M.B. (2003) *Making the vision concrete: Implementation of downtown redevelopment plans created through a visioning process*. Unpublished doctoral dissertation proposal, University of California, Irvine, California.

Rogers, R. & Power, A. (2000) *Cities for a small country*. London: Faber & Faber.

Rowland, J. (1995) The urban design process. *Urban Design Quarterly*, **56**. Retrieved 14 July 2004 from http://www.rudi.net/bookshelf/ej/udq/56/udp.cfm.

Skateboard area, Queens Walk, London

Rowley, A. (1994) Definitions of urban design: the nature and concerns of urban design. *Planning Practice and Research*, **9** (3), 179–198.

Smith, J. & Jackson, N. (2000) Strategic needs analysis: its role in brief development. *Facilities*, **18** (13/14), 502–512.

Tewdwr-Jones, M. & Williams, R.H. (2001). *The European dimension of planning*. London: Spon Press.

Thomas, R. (2003) *Sustainable urban design: An environmental approach*. London: Spon Press.

Wates, N. (1996) A community process. *Urban Design Quarterly*, **58** (Supplement). Retrieved 14 July 2004 from http://www.rudi.net/bookshelf/ej/udq/58conf/cp.cfm.

Wates, N. (1998) Process planning session. *Urban Design Quarterly*, **67** (Special report: Involving Local Communities in Urban Design). Retrieved 14 July 2004 from http://www.rudi.net/bookshelf/ej/udq/67_report/method_10.cfm.

Woodhead, R.M. (2000) Investigation of the early stages of project formulation. *Facilities*, **18** (13/14), 524–534.

Footnote

1   Pruitt Igoe was a 2762-unit public housing development consisting of 33 eleven-storey tower blocks. Completed in 1954, the development was demolished by the local authority in 1972 owing to poor design and construction, variable tenant selection procedures, erroneous fiscal policies, and improper management and maintenance practices (Garvin, 1996).

2   Each of the urban design decision-making case study areas presented in Chapter 2 characterises different stages of the urban design life cycle. For the Devonshire Quarter in Sheffield, the area straddles the 'Design and development' and 'Use, management and maintenance' stages because of the new development occurring in the area and the use and management of existing city spaces. The Brewhouse Yard in Clerkenwell, London, is an example of a completely developed urban area that is in the 'Use, management and maintenance' stage. Finally, Central Salford in Greater Manchester is an example of an urban area that is being regenerated; as such, it spans both the 'Decline, demolition and/or regeneration' stage and the 'Pre-design' stage of its urban design life cycle.

CHAPTER 2
THE URBAN DESIGN DECISION-MAKING PROCESS: CASE STUDIES

Christopher Boyko and Rachel Cooper

Table 2.1 Spatial scales and temporal dimensions of the three case studies			
	Size of urban development project	Type of urban development project	Process timescale
Greater Manchester	Area	Regeneration vision	2 years
Sheffield	City-centre quarter	Repair and enhance	20 years
London	Urban block	New build with listed buildings	10 years

This chapter investigates the urban design decision-making process in detail by presenting three in-depth process case studies of urban developments in 24-hour cities – Greater Manchester, Sheffield and London – undertaken as part of the VivaCity2020 project. These case studies illustrate different levels of urban design decision-making, and the complexity involved, focusing on the implications for sustainability. Furthermore, the case studies represent three distinct spatial scales at which urban design decision-making takes place: a local authority regeneration plan for a 2200 ha area in Greater Manchester, repairing and enhancing a city-centre quarter in Sheffield, and a new-build project with listed buildings in an urban block in London. Different temporal scales also are represented in the case studies, emphasising the varied timescales and histories of the urban development projects (see Table 2.1).

To understand the urban design decision-making process for each urban development site, researchers gathered information using a number of sources. These sources included archival materials, observations, questionnaires, and interviews with a range of decision-makers and stakeholders (e.g., academics, architects, developers, governmental and non-governmental employees, members of voluntary organisations, property surveyors, regeneration specialists, registered social landlords, resident and community groups, retailers) (see Table

2.2). Once sufficient information had been collected, it was content-analysed, and process maps were created. With each map, a story unfolded in chronological order. In particular, the stories outlined particular urban design decisions, who made those decisions, what tools were used in decision-making, and whether or not – and how – sustainability was considered throughout the process.

For each case study, background information about the area and the urban development site is given. The urban design decision-making processes for each urban development site are then described, indicating the various stages and tasks within the processes, and the similarities to and differences from the urban design decision-making process outlined in Chapter 1. Finally, comparisons are made across the three case studies.

Case Study 1: Central Salford, Greater Manchester

At the beginning of 2002, the Chief Executive of Salford City Council, John Willis, decided that something needed to be done to improve the area of Central Salford. High unemployment, low education, fear of crime and inadequate and changing family structures are key demographics of the area. Willis desired a change to make Central Salford a good place to live, and a place where people wanted to live.

Willis's initial ideas, along with the participation of other important decision-makers, have been taken forward and expanded. As a result, Central Salford has been the focus of a major regeneration initiative. This case study highlights the early stages of the urban design decision-making process for Central Salford.

Table 2.2	Data collection period and methods used in the three case studies				
	Data collection period	Interviews (number of interviews)	Archival material	Observations	Questionnaire
Greater Manchester	10 months Oct 2004 – Jul 2005	× (12)	×	×	×
Sheffield	6 months Apr – Sep 2005	× (12)	×		
London	7 months Mar – Sep 2005	× (8)	×		

Figure 2.1 Boundary map of Central Salford, Salford

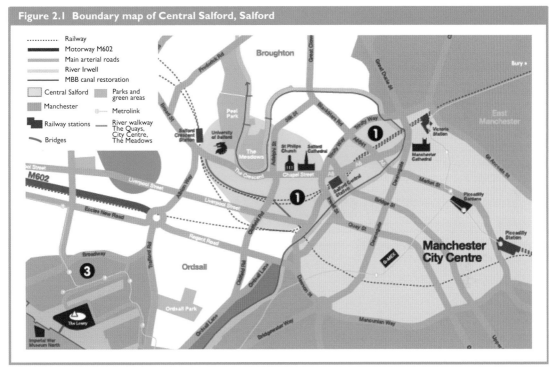

Source: Central Salford Urban Regeneration Company

• **Central Salford**

Central Salford is an area in the city of Salford, located in Greater Manchester. It is approximately 2200 ha in size and home to about 72 000 people. It is represented by seven wards: Broughton, Claremont, Irwell Riverside, Langworthy, Kersal, Ordsall, Weaste and Seedley (Salford City Council, 2004) (see Figure 2.1).

Taken as a whole, Central Salford is a locally deprived area on a significant scale and intensity. The 2004 Index of Multiple Deprivation indicates that the boroughs within Central Salford fall within the top 4% of the most deprived areas in the UK. The population has also decreased consistently, keeping pace throughout the 1990s and into the twenty-first century. Those choosing to stay in Central Salford are characterised by a higher-than-average

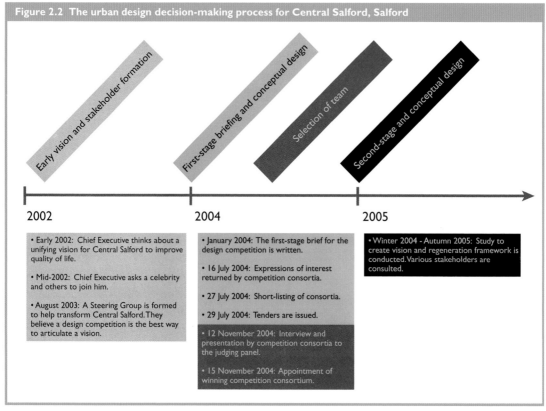

Figure 2.2 The urban design decision-making process for Central Salford, Salford

Early vision and stakeholder formation

First-stage briefing and conceptual design

Selection of team

Second-stage and conceptual design

2002   2004   2005

• Early 2002: Chief Executive thinks about a unifying vision for Central Salford to improve quality of life.

• Mid-2002: Chief Executive asks a celebrity and others to join him.

• August 2003: A Steering Group is formed to help transform Central Salford. They believe a design competition is the best way to articulate a vision.

• January 2004: The first-stage brief for the design competition is written.

• 16 July 2004: Expressions of interest returned by competition consortia.

• 27 July 2004: Short-listing of consortia.

• 29 July 2004: Tenders are issued.

• 12 November 2004: Interview and presentation by competition consortia to the judging panel.

• 15 November 2004: Appointment of winning competition consortium.

• Winter 2004 - Autumn 2005: Study to create vision and regeneration framework is conducted. Various stakeholders are consulted.

Source: VivaCity2020

proportion of economic instability, with many residents part of single-parent families (Report of the Leader of the Council, 29 September 2004). Willis's aim for Central Salford was to create a regeneration vision which would solve the problems identified and create a better quality of life for its residents.

• **The Central Salford Process – Timescale: Two Years**

Analysis of the data collected revealed an underlying urban design decision process composed of five stages, representing the early stages of a larger process (see Figure 2.2):

• Early vision development and group formation
• An international competition and first-stage brief
• Entries to the first stage
• Second-stage briefing
• Judging and selecting teams.

Each of the stages is described below:
• *Early vision development and group formation*
A steering group was formed in 2003, comprising representatives from the Regional Development Agency, higher education institutions, government bodies, health care, regeneration partnerships and the private sector. Felicity Goodey, a former BBC personality whom Salford City Council believed could help raise Central Salford's media profile and attract private investors (Senior member of the local authority, September 2005), was asked to chair the steering committee. They had confidence in Goodey, as she had led the development of the Salford Quays area.

The steering group worked together to develop an appropriate vehicle to transform Central Salford. This vehicle, based on guidance from English Partnerships and the Office of the Deputy Prime Minister (ODPM), took the form of a Shadow Urban Regeneration Company (URC), which acted as an interim organisation until a formal application for URC status could be submitted to the ODPM. They felt that the best way to kick-start regeneration in Central Salford was to hold an international design competition, aimed at merging existing and proposed plans and strategies to communicate a holistic vision for the area over 20 years.

• *International competition and first-stage brief*
The international competition began in January 2004, when a first-stage brief was written by Salford City Council. During the first-stage briefing, mention was made that the vision and regeneration framework – outputs from the competition – would need to represent visually the broad design themes intended for the area. Images and other innovative formats could be used to raise expectations and aspirations among the community in Central Salford.

The URC was searching for a design team who could think creatively and use their skills to generate market demand for the benefit of the local community. The design team would need high-level visioning, urban design, presentation and project management skills. They also had to understand the key drivers surrounding sustainable communities. This information was summarised in a brief, and advertised in April 2004 in the Official Journal of the

European Union (OJEU). It appeared that the objective of the brief was to 'sell' Central Salford, with an emphasis on the positive aspects of the area and its potential for transformation through urban regeneration. Deprivation issues, such as crime, social exclusion and poor health, were not covered in the first-stage brief.

• *Entries to first stage*
The international design competition was announced in May 2004 and attracted interest internationally. The URC received expressions of interest from over 50 design teams, and drew up a shortlist of five in July 2004. The shortlisted design teams were then invited to submit their visions for Central Salford, to be judged by a panel in November 2004.

• *Second-stage briefing*
In July 2004 a second-stage brief was released, providing more detailed information to design teams about competition particulars. Again, little mention was made of important sustainability issues affecting the area, such as crime, social exclusion and poor health. The brief stated that the winning design team should be able to develop a vision for the future, based on a critical evaluation of the area. The team should also be able to write a strategic document to inform public and private investment over the next 20 years.

• *Judging and selecting teams*
The visions created by the shortlisted design teams were exhibited to the general public in a Salford shopping mall for two weeks in October 2004. The public were invited to give written feedback on anonymous comment cards about each team's visions. The design teams also presented their visions to a judging panel, composed of members of the

public and private sectors who possessed knowledge of Salford, regeneration and/or planning. The judging panel interviewed each design team, and a decision was made on the team the URC would use to take their vision and regeneration framework forward. The judging panel considered the following criteria when making their decision: the submission of the vision, value for money, and the design team's responses to the interview questions. In addition to these criteria, some of the judging panel members thought about creativity, aspiration, authority, quality of design ideas, economic impact and understanding of regeneration (Judging panel members, 3 December 2004; 9 February 2005).

- **Discussion of sustainability in the urban design decision-making process**

Interviews with members of the URC suggested that they had an advanced understanding of sustainability:

'… sustainability of a neighbourhood is a neighbourhood where it's got a balanced mix in terms of people, in terms of a tenure with education, health and public support systems which mean that the area itself doesn't need any significant public-sector intervention … It can carry on into the future, it has in place all the right characteristics for satisfying living, working and enjoyment, and it doesn't require the local authority to be clearing significant areas or have significant social resources into the area or have support mechanisms.' (Member of the URC, June 2005).

Many URC members stressed economic regeneration when discussing sustainability: that is, harnessing private-sector investment, creating partnerships between the private and public sectors, and improving the skills of the local population. However, they also considered sustainability at a social level, believing that having access to good-quality education, creating goodwill, attracting new people to the area and sufficiently engaging the community would help make Central Salford more socially sustainable:

'… I'm looking for something that offers some hope to the existing population that doesn't just translate new people into the area … The people of Salford appreciate that you don't bring people back to the city by just building more of what you've already got because that's not going to be particularly attractive to people. And it's understanding that and understanding what the benefits are to the local community …' (Member of the local authority, November 2004).

Economic and, to some extent, social sustainability issues were mentioned in many interviews with URC members, but they rarely discussed environmental issues, such as tackling noise, air pollution and unwanted rubbish.

Formal communications with the competing design teams indicated that they needed to consider sustainability, although the concept was not fully explained or described. Consequently, sustainability discussions tended to focus on the economic dimension – the market and 'commercial realities'. The brief raised the concept of sustainability, for example, referring to the desire to 'create a prosperous, attractive and sustainable community', and to develop proposals and activities that 'link together to create a sustainable future'. Again, the

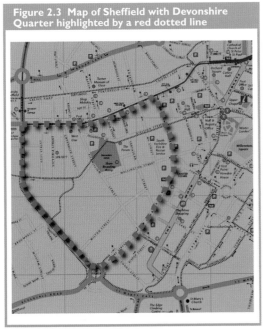

Figure 2.3 Map of Sheffield with Devonshire Quarter highlighted by a red dotted line

Copyright © Sheffield City Council 1997 – 2008

significance of understanding and addressing economic factors was underscored, but little or no specific mention was made of environmental or social issues, and a definition for the term 'sustainability' was not offered.

Finally, the URC's selection criteria to judge design team visions did not explicitly refer to a design team's abilities to recognise and address sustainability issues. Rather, it appears that the URC judging panel's primary concern was with identifying a team of consultants able to think creatively and develop a vision for the area that would attract private investment.

Case Study 2: Devonshire Quarter, Sheffield

Since the collapse of the steel and coal mining industries in the 1970s and 1980s, Sheffield has been in a state of economic recovery, slowly transforming itself into a vibrant, liveable 24-hour city. Improvements in the city centre, in particular, have taken the form of good-quality public spaces, new recreational facilities, small pocket parks, and access

to rivers (Senior Council Officer, 8 June 2005). The Devonshire Quarter is one of the stars of the city centre, boasting a large amount of these improvements. This case study highlights the urban design decision-making process for the Devonshire Quarter, and illustrates the dimensions through which this area is considered, by some, to be a sustainable community.

• Sheffield and the Devonshire Quarter

Sheffield is the fourth largest urban area in England, with a population over 513 000 (HMSO, 2006). Situated in the north-east part of the country, the city has become an important subregional centre (Mackay, 2005) (see Figure 2.3).

Sheffield's current success may be attributable to its ability to search for new ways to sustain itself, following the destruction of the city's traditional economic base. Water-powered industries, cutlery, steel production and coal mining were strong in Sheffield well into the twentieth century. However, technological improvements and economies of scale in steel production meant that the devastation of the steel industry was imminent by the 1970s (Parkinson & Robson, 2000; Mackay, 2005). The late 1980s and 1990s saw an extensive process of urban regeneration, resulting in the demolition of Broomhall Flats, the development of Meadowhall and the Supertram, and the hosting of the 1991 World Student Games. The growth associated with urban regeneration has led to attention being focused on the city centre in the 2000s. One of the city centre's largest areas, the Devonshire Quarter, reflects Sheffield City Council's ongoing commitment to urban design, sustainability and the 24-hour city.

The Devonshire Quarter is a dense, mixed-use area located in the west of the city, on the southern slopes of the high ridge separating the Don and Sheaf Valleys (Sheffield City Council, 2004). The land was used largely for agricultural purposes until the beginning of the nineteenth century, when the area developed quickly in grid-like form, with high-density three-storey terraced housing, small factories and workshops, pubs, shops and churches. Much of the terraced housing and some of the workshops and factories were demolished between the 1920s and 1970s as part of a city-wide slum clearance (CABE, n.d.; Sheffield City Council, 2001, 2004). Despite some improvements to the area in the 1980s, development was slow (Sheffield City Council, 2001), making way for accelerated growth in the 1990s and 2000s. During this time, new housing schemes were adopted, independent shops and restaurants were established, and an attempt was made by Sheffield City Council to connect new retail, housing and late-night entertainment within the area (Sheffield City Council, 2001).

- **The Devonshire Quarter Process – Timescale: 25 Years**

Five key decisions that helped shape the Devonshire Quarter over a 25-year period were designating Devonshire Green as open space and creating an urban park, allowing inner-city housing in the

Brewhouse Yard, London

Devonshire Quarter, opening the Forum, designing and building West One, and forming the Devonshire Quarter Association. These decisions reflect a process of decision-making over time, rather than a prescriptive urban design decision-making process (see Figure 2.4).

Each of the five key decisions is discussed in detail below.
• *Designating Devonshire Green as open space and creating an urban park*
In 1981, based on the advice of the Planning Department, Sheffield City Council took the decision to create Devonshire Green from derelict land. This decision was aided by Urban Programme funding, a national programme designed to assist economic regeneration in disadvantaged areas via industrial, environmental, recreational and social projects (DoE, 1986; Tye & Williams, 1994). At that time, Sheffield did not possess any other green spaces of that size in the city centre. It was presupposed that Devonshire Green would provide a much-needed amenity feature for mixed-tenure houses, flats and the surrounding area.

The decision to keep Devonshire Green as open space was not taken easily, however. Various departments within the local authority wanted to see the land developed differently. Debate between the Planning Department and the City Estates Department was strong, with the latter wanting to build factory units on the land. In the end, the local authority decided to make an urban park, which served as a catalyst for growth in the area. The local authority referred to government guidelines produced for the Urban Programme when designing the area (DoE, 1986; Baldock, 1998; see Tye & Williams, 1994).

• *Allowing inner-city housing in the Devonshire Quarter*
In the mid-to-late 1980s the Housing Department within the local authority gave permission for housing association grants to be used to develop dwellings in the Devonshire Quarter. Key public-sector individuals used their intimate knowledge of the economic climate in the city to maximise the possibility of obtaining funding for affordable housing. They also utilised their knowledge to create a suitable environment for developers to build affordable housing in the city centre. Discussions between the public and private sector were undertaken to persuade the latter group to develop housing in the city centre, rather than develop retail. Creating affordable housing was innovative at the time, as government had neither the policy nor the finances to endorse the idea (housing officials got the idea from an article published by the University of York about creating housing over shops). The Devonshire Quarter area was considered suitable for housing by the local authority because of its size and its access to open space.

• *Opening the Forum*
In 1990 two entrepreneurs decided to open a small café and some shops in the Devonshire Quarter (which was later expanded into a café, restaurant, bar and outdoor terrace). The entrepreneurs chose a building in the heart of the Devonshire Quarter to house the café and shops because of its good location between the city centre and the University of Sheffield. The building's Georgian character also influenced their decision. Moreover, the building was appealing from an investment standpoint because it was cheap to rent or buy at that time. Finally, the entrepreneurs believed that the shops in the building,

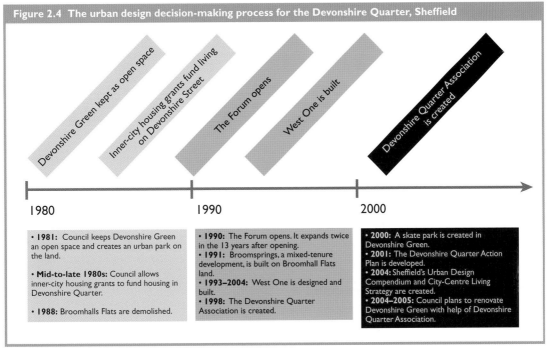

Figure 2.4 The urban design decision-making process for the Devonshire Quarter, Sheffield

Devonshire Green kept as open space

Inner-city housing grants fund living on Devonshire Street

The Forum opens

West One is built

Devonshire Quarter Association is created

1980

1990

2000

- **1981:** Council keeps Devonshire Green an open space and creates an urban park on the land.

- **Mid-to-late 1980s:** Council allows inner-city housing grants to fund housing in Devonshire Quarter.

- **1988:** Broomhalls Flats are demolished.

- **1990:** The Forum opens. It expands twice in the 13 years after opening.
- **1991:** Broomsprings, a mixed-tenure development, is built on Broomhall Flats land.
- **1993–2004:** West One is designed and built.
- **1998:** The Devonshire Quarter Association is created.

- **2000:** A skate park is created in Devonshire Green.
- **2001:** The Devonshire Quarter Action Plan is developed.
- **2004:** Sheffield's Urban Design Compendium and City-Centre Living Strategy are created.
- **2004–2005:** Council plans to renovate Devonshire Green with help of Devonshire Quarter Association.

Source: VivaCity2020

which they named the Forum, could be sublet to independent owners and be utilised as a business incubator for start-up companies in the area.

The decision to open the Forum was based on personal experience with Sheffield city centre and the area over time. The entrepreneurs had visited the area as teenagers, and had knowledge about users of, and visitors to, the area. The entrepreneurs also relied largely on their 'gut feelings' to make their decision, rather than conducting feasibility studies. However, they did visit other cities, such as Dublin and New York, to see how a unique business might operate in a city centre.

• *Designing and building West One*
In 1993 a property investor took the decision to acquire land for West One, which was to become a large, mixed-use development overlooking Devonshire Green. Over the next nine years the property investor acquired more land, eventually taking full possession of the development in 2004.

The specific site was chosen because it was close to the city centre and there was a perceived need for housing in the area. The scheme was originally intended for student accommodation, but this changed because of opportunities in the private rental and sales markets.

The decision to develop West One was guided by market demand more than anything. Understanding the context and how the area might change over time were considered of secondary importance by the property investor. The company was small, and had an 'old-fashioned' feel: thus 'gut feelings for what would work' often prevailed (Private-sector developer, 8 June 2005). The use of published studies, research findings and statistics was minimal. The property investor believed that such tools 'cloud individual judgement' and result in everyone making the same decisions – rather than attempting to be more innovative.

• *Forming the Devonshire Quarter Association*

In 1998 the Devonshire Quarter Association (DQA) was established, with residents, businesses, the voluntary sector, local organisations and students making up the membership. The Planning Division has been able to show the group upcoming planning applications for the Devonshire Quarter. The DQA also has been helpful in establishing a clear identity for those living and working in the area, and in providing an outlet for members of the community to be involved more intimately in the planning and urban design processes.

The decision to form the DQA was predicated on the local authority's commitment to encouraging community consultation. The local authority had previous experience with the formation of groups such as the DQA in the area, and had knowledge of the benefits of community participation.

• **Discussion of sustainability in the urban design decision-making process**

In general, the decisions by the public and private sectors over the past 25 years have contained elements of sustainability that appear to have benefited the Devonshire Quarter. Most of these decisions were made in isolation, rather than as part of a larger, more holistic and sustainable plan for the area. Designating Devonshire Green as an urban park, however, demonstrates the local authority's vision for providing a green space in the heart of the urban centre so that people living and working in the surrounding area would have a refuge from city life. By doing so, Devonshire Green proved to be a catalyst for new, mixed-use and mixed-tenure housing, thus kick-starting a new era for area development.

In most instances, sustainability was not the primary focus of attention in decision-making. For example, the property investor for West One maintained that his company was driven to design and build primarily by the market. The local authority attempted to encourage or ensure that the private sector incorporated sustainability into their developments (e.g., using energy-efficient and soundproof insulation, establishing car-pool incentives). Concomitantly, the local authority at the time was concerned about imposing conditions that might reduce the commercial viability of large developments. This suggests that they perceived some tension between sustainability and commercial viability.

With other decisions, however, issues surrounding sustainability were deemed more important. For example, the Forum sought to give first-time, independent, local retailers an opportunity to open businesses at reduced rents. This decision promotes economic sustainability and may create a culture whereby local entrepreneurs want to stay in the area, rather than move to other areas in the city or outside the city. The Forum also helps to supports a vibrant and diverse culture by offering a range of facilities for users and customers.

Another example of promoting sustainability comes from the DQA. The Association is keen to deal with issues such as crime, keeping the area active when events take place there, improving Devonshire Green, and ensuring that new development in the Devonshire Quarter is sound and sustainable. They will continue to liaise with the local authority and be a key consultation mechanism on area planning matters.

Figure 2.5 Map of London with case study area highlighted by a black dotted line

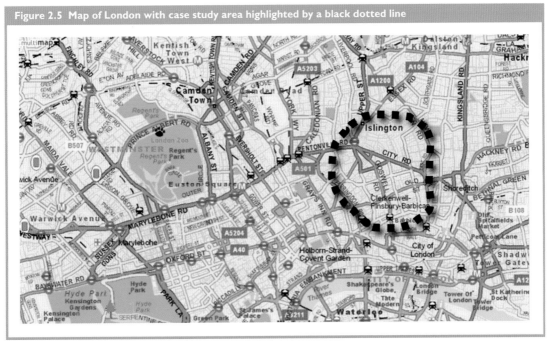

TeleAtlas NV/Crown copyright.
Reproduced from Ordnance Survey mapping with the permission of the Controller of Her Majesty's Stationery Office
© Crown copyright LBI A086452 © Colin Bartholomew Ltd 2008

Case Study 3: The Brewhouse Yard, Clerkenwell, Islington, London

Clerkenwell is located in the Borough of Islington, minutes away from the City of London (see Figure 2.5). Clerkenwell's past as a magnet for monastic life, a beacon for breweries and an attraction for artists has created a unique community of people and places. Within this neighbourhood sits the Brewhouse Yard, an old brewery that has transformed itself over the years into a mixed-use development. Private flats, affordable housing units, offices and public and semi-public spaces dot this urban block and give its users a new twist on Clerkenwell's diversity. This case study highlights the Brewhouse Yard as an example of mixed use in action, and presents the urban design decision-making process for the scheme.

• Clerkenwell and the Brewhouse Yard

Although Clerkenwell's roots lie in the Middle Ages, when London parish clerks performed plays near a well, its present-day landscape owes much to the redesign and reconstruction of older buildings and infrastructure during the eighteenth century. The popularity of the London suburb became even more tangible with the arrival of new merchants and tradespeople, transforming Clerkenwell into a thriving mercantile area. As Clerkenwell modernised in Victorian times, formal factories and workshops were constructed. These new workspaces paved the way for artists to move in throughout the 1980s, and office workers and those wanting to experience loft living in the 1990s. The increased attractiveness of Clerkenwell meant that many of the redundant industrial buildings were converted into offices and apartments (English Heritage, n.d.).

Bevin Court, Finsbury, London

As for the Brewhouse Yard, a brewery has occupied the 1.461 ha site since 1746. Over time, the brewery became known as the Cannon Brewery, and dominated the site. The brewery functioned well into the twentieth century, when bombing during World War II heavily damaged the site. The brewery never fully recovered, and it ceased functioning in 1955 (Islington Council Planning Division, n.d.). In the 1960s the existing brewery buildings on the site – minus three now-listed buildings – were cleared to make way for an eight-storey office building, which remained until the 1990s (Development Control Committee, 1998). Until redevelopment began again in the late 1990s, a large private car park dominated the open spaces on the site (Islington Council Planning Division, n.d.).

- **The Brewhouse Yard Process – Timescale: Ten Years**

From the analysis of the research on the Brewhouse Yard Development, three distinct periods of a larger urban design decision-making process could be identified (see Figure 2.6).

The three periods each have a number of stages – 13 in total – that help to delineate decision-makers, tools and sustainability in the process. They are as follows:
- Period 1 (1995–1998). The Brewhouse Yard is established as a mixed-use site:
  - Creating teams, appraising the situation and forming objectives

  - Designing the development and submitting a report
  - Evaluating and selecting a plan
  - Implementing a plan.

- Period 2 (1998–2000). The stock market fluctuates, residential part sold:
  - Creating teams and forming objectives
  - Modifying objectives
  - Implementing a new plan.

- Period 3 (2000–present day). Commercial part developed, project finishes:
  - Creating teams, appraising the situation and forming objectives
  - Designing the development
  - Adding to the team
  - Submitting a report
  - Evaluating and selecting a plan
  - Implementing and monitoring.

Each of these periods and the stages are described in detail below.
- **Period 1 (1995–1998): The Brewhouse Yard is established as a mixed-use site**

Four stages could be distinguished in this first period of the urban design decision-making process, approximately paralleling those found in the generic urban design decision-making process in Chapter 1.

- *Creating teams, appraising the situation and forming objectives*

This stage of the process occurred between 1995 and 1997, when a private limited company (plc) bought the Brewhouse Yard. Upon purchasing the site, the new owners began creating a team, starting with an architecture firm. The architecture firm first appraised the project site and the surrounding area

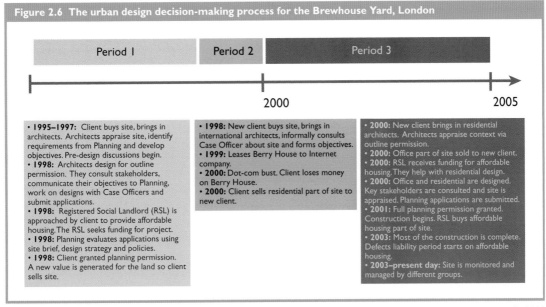

Figure 2.6 The urban design decision-making process for the Brewhouse Yard, London

Period 1   Period 2   Period 3

2000   2005

• **1995–1997:** Client buys site, brings in architects. Architects appraise site, identify requirements from Planning and develop objectives. Pre-design discussions begin.
• **1998:** Architects design for outline permission. They consult stakeholders, communicate their objectives to Planning, work on designs with Case Officers and submit applications.
• **1998:** Registered Social Landlord (RSL) is approached by client to provide affordable housing. The RSL seeks funding for project.
• **1998:** Planning evaluates applications using site brief, design strategy and policies.
• **1998:** Client granted planning permission. A new value is generated for the land so client sells site.

• **1998:** New client buys site, brings in international architects, informally consults Case Officer about site and forms objectives.
• **1999:** Leases Berry House to Internet company.
• **2000:** Dot-com bust. Client loses money on Berry House.
• **2000:** Client sells residential part of site to new client.

• **2000:** New client brings in residential architects. Architects appraise context via outline permission.
• **2000:** Office part of site sold to new client.
• **2000:** RSL receives funding for affordable housing. They help with residential design.
• **2000:** Office and residential are designed. Key stakeholders are consulted and site is appraised. Planning applications are submitted.
• **2001:** Full planning permission granted. Construction begins. RSL buys affordable housing part of site.
• **2003:** Most of the construction is complete. Defects liability period starts on affordable housing.
• **2003–present day:** Site is monitored and managed by different groups.

Source: VivaCity2020

by visiting the site and reading the most current planning brief for the Brewhouse Yard. The plc also asked the architects to identify any requirements from Islington Borough Council, viewed as one of the most important decision-makers for the site. Finally, the architects consulted with local archaeologists, as well as investigating light and lighting issues and so forth. Once the context appraisal was complete, the team gathered and established their principal objective for the Brewhouse Yard: to build a profitable, mixed-use development on the site.

Designing the development and submitting a report
The architecture firm spent most of 1998 designing the mixed-use development. During this stage, the architects often asked themselves: 'What would we like if we lived here?' Answering this question helped them to design spaces with people's needs in mind, moving beyond the form or aesthetics (Architect, personal communication, 16 March 2005).

During this time, the architecture firm consulted with decision-makers and stakeholders about their design ideas (e.g., the local authority and the Clerkenwell Neighbourhood Forum). One of the local authority planning officers was also kept up to date about the team's objectives. Because of the good working relationship between the planning officer and the lead architect, the two were able to develop designs for the Brewhouse Yard together, considering the layout of the site for outline planning permission.[1] Once the designs for the Brewhouse Yard were finished and shown to the owner, the architecture firm submitted ten outline planning applications to Islington Borough Council (four applications for listed building/conservation area consent and six applications for new buildings).

• *Evaluating and selecting a plan*
The Planning Division of Islington Borough Council was responsible for evaluating and selecting a plan (i.e., giving outline planning consent for the Brewhouse Yard). In making their decision, planning

The Triangle, Exchange Square, Manchester

officials considered the amended 1990 planning brief for the site, experiences of planning officers who had written briefs before, information gathered in the area, an understanding of Clerkenwell's history, and a design strategy written for the Brewhouse Yard. An important tool used in decision-making, the design strategy contained a number of goals that addressed masterplanning in the area, including developing a balanced and sustainable economic community, increasing the amount of housing and ensuring that a large part of this was affordable housing, creating safe, attractive and accessible public spaces, and providing opportunities for new businesses (Islington Council Planning Division, n.d.).

Once decisions were made on the planning applications for the Brewhouse Yard, the local authority wrote a report, granted outline planning permission, and gave it to the owner. The report also stated that the local authority had considered issues of sustainability in their decision-making (e.g.,

permeability, safety, maintaining pedestrian character with the surrounding area, having interconnected car-free spaces and green links to surrounding pathways and open spaces). Furthermore, the local authority believed that improving the flexibility of the commercial part of the site could be advantageous: 'This flexibility would in turn activate stronger demand and increase the likelihood of successful redevelopment' (Development Control Committee, 1998: 31).

• *Implementing a plan*
Once the client gained outline planning permission in late 1998, the Brewhouse Yard generated a new land value. Instead of progressing to a more detailed design stage, the owner decided to sell the property. The new owner changed the direction of the design process by choosing a new 'team' and re-forming the objectives for the site.

• **Period 2 (1998–2000): The stock market fluctuates, residential part sold**
Three stages are identified in the second period, one of which corresponds to the generic urban design decision-making process in Chapter 1. The introduction of an external event to this process (i.e., fluctuations in the stock market) influenced the direction of the process and the decision-makers involved.

• *Creating teams and forming objectives*
In late 1998 the new owner of the Brewhouse Yard and a developer/part-owner began to assemble a team to produce a detailed design for the site. The developer/part-owner appointed an international architect who was known for his modern designs. Hiring a high-quality, international architect early in the process, in addition to holding informal meetings with a local authority design officer about design quality and having enthusiasm for the site and Clerkenwell, helped to generate design objectives. These design objectives highlighted the idea of 'mix': mixed-use, mixed tenure, and a mix of contemporary and historic architecture.

• *Modifying objectives*
At the height of the dot-com boom in 1999, the developer/part-owner leased two floors of a listed building to an Internet consulting company. The developer/part-owner and the Internet company spent a lot of time and money retrofitting the listed building to enable 'dot-com activity'. In 2000, however, the dot-com bubble burst, which had negative economic consequences for Clerkenwell, a noted hotbed of dot-com activity (Dodson, 12 February 2004), and for the developer/part-owner of the Brewhouse Yard and the Internet company. As a result, the owner's overall objectives needed to be modified.

• *Implementing a new plan*
In response to losses from the dot-com bust, the developer/part-owner sold the residential component of the Brewhouse Yard to another company that specialised in home design and development. As had been the case in 1998, a new part-owner meant that the direction of the process and the design would change again. Fortunately, because outline planning permission was vague, the architects and designers could easily modify the plans, for example in terms of massing, height and so forth.

• **Period 3 (2000–present day): Commercial part developed, project finishes**
Six stages of the process have been identified in the third period. Four of the stages correspond to stages found in the generic urban design decision-making process from Chapter 1.

• *Creating teams, appraising the situation and forming objectives*
The new owner of the residential component of the Brewhouse Yard began work in 2000, assembling a team to produce detailed designs. An architecture firm was hired, based on their ability to design high-quality residential spaces that did not compromise on profit. The architecture firm used the contents of outline planning permission to appraise the site and the surrounding area. The new owner's objective was always in the architects' minds: maximise profit.

While the new owner was taking over the residential component of the Brewhouse Yard, the office component was sold to a property trust. The property trust decided to keep the international architect, commissioned in 1998, and allow him to design the office component.

• *Designing the development*
Between 2000 and 2001 the two architecture firms individually designed the office and residential components of the Brewhouse Yard. The residential architects accomplished a number of tasks as part of their design work (e.g., consulting the Planning Division in Islington Borough Council and the Clerkenwell Neighbourhood Forum, and using the international architect's designs for the residential component of the Brewhouse Yard as a starting point for their designs).

The Triangle, Finsbury, London

From the initial designs, the residential architects re-examined their context appraisal in terms of site, location, constraints and opportunities. They produced many diagrams to elucidate the various issues, forming a 'design story'. To complement the 'design story', the architects drafted a list of options and alternatives, considering the Clerkenwell context, cost, and how their designs would need to integrate with the rest of their team. The architects then held an internal design review meeting to allow other members of their firm to critique the work. Using a checklist-type tool, the firm's members assessed the designs and offered advice about the relationship between the site and the surrounding area.

• *Adding to the team*
Landscape architects were added to the team to help with detailed landscaping design. A provider of affordable housing also joined the team. Their joining was predicated on the owner of the residential component of the site receiving a grant from the Housing Corporation to build affordable housing. Through the owner, the affordable housing provider worked with the architecture firm on the affordable housing design. Using their previous knowledge of people's needs in affordable housing, the affordable housing provider was able to appraise the design drawings, give input about the layout of affordable housing units and the mix of units, and help to make decisions about interiors and finishes.

The affordable housing provider used Housing Corporation guidelines for scheme development standards to make design decisions with the architects. They also referred to an internal company design brief that specified design guidelines for affordable housing. Once designs neared completion, the affordable housing provider submitted a report to an internal development committee who evaluated the site. Evaluations were based on cost, social issues, and how the designs integrated with the organisation's remit.

• *Submitting a report*
The architects submitted their applications for full planning permission in September 2000. The office component of the Brewhouse Yard was viewed as quite radical and contemporary for historic Clerkenwell, the design calling for large glass boxes and copper siding. The lead architect involved in the site from 1995 to 1998 speculated that it might have been easier to produce such radical designs because many issues, such as height, massing and rights to light, had already been negotiated at the outline planning stage (Architect, personal communication, 16 March, 2005).

• *Evaluating and selecting a plan*
As with outline planning permission, the Planning Division of Islington Borough Council was responsible for evaluating and selecting a plan for full planning permission. The amended 1990 planning brief was used again by the planning officials in decision-making. Additional tools included national policy, Islington Borough Council's then-current Unitary Development Plan, the design strategy for the site, holding discussions with the

owners' teams prior to planning application submission, visiting and talking with the local community, and using knowledge from university-level urban design courses.

• *Implementing and monitoring*
Islington Borough Council approved the planning applications for the Brewhouse Yard in January 2001. With consent given, the architects' designs were implemented and the construction of the office, residential and affordable housing components began.

In 2003 most of the construction had finished. The affordable housing component of the Brewhouse Yard was then evaluated during a defects liability period, which lasted for approximately two years. As of 2005, the affordable housing provider acted as a management company for the affordable housing accommodation, along with a housing ownership team for shared ownership premises. The client who owns the residential component of the Brewhouse Yard monitors the private accommodation, visiting every three months and liaising with residents about their concerns.

• **Discussion of Sustainability in the Urban Design Decision-Making Process**
The case study suggests that key decision-makers and stakeholders considered sustainability to some degree throughout the process, focusing primarily on social and economic qualities. Furthermore, sustainability appears to have been considered at the outset of the process, when the plc in Period 1 wished to have a mixed-use development in the form of residential with some commercial. This type of development meant that people who lived and worked on and around the site would be better equipped to police the area visually, as well as have more opportunity to get to know their neighbours. Being close to nearby shops and the City also meant less reliance on private automobiles for travel.

Warner Street, London

However, consideration for sustainability in Period 1 was bound by what the architects thought they would like, if they lived in the Brewhouse Yard. This might be problematic, as design professionals may not be representative of new residents. Ideally a proper requirements-capture process should be conducted to understand who the residents are, and their needs.

Less attention was paid to sustainability later on in the development project. After the first owner sold the property in Period 1 and the dot-com bust occurred in Period 2, some of the sustainability principles were abandoned. Particularly in terms of the private-sector decision-makers in Period 3, maximising profit was seen as the most important objective. For example, the new owner in Period 3 wanted to create a gated development with no access routes, thus reducing permeability and social connectedness. Moreover, the residential architecture firm hired in Period 3 did not consider sustainability – particularly environmental sustainability – in their internal design review checklist, and sustainability was not part of the architecture firm's overall mission, even though they 'had a sustainability page in … the corporate brochure' (Architect, 25 April 2005).

Bentley House Estate, Hulme, Manchester

In comparison with the private sector, the local authority did more to consider the social, economic and environmental dimensions of sustainability in decision-making. This may be due to the local authority's greater interest in working towards government targets on sustainability compared with the private sector.

Comparing the urban design decision-making processes

Comparisons across the three case studies presented in this chapter reveal interesting insights about the urban design decision-making process, sustainability and tools and resources used in decision-making. Each of these issues is discussed below.

The urban design decision-making process

In all three case studies, it appears that decision-makers did not follow an explicit urban design decision-making process (i.e., written down, visualised and/or in tabular form), such as the generic urban design decision-making process in Chapter 1. Instead, decision-makers employed tacit or ad hoc processes, influenced by their knowledge, by past experiences and – as with the London and Sheffield case studies in particular – by policy, public-sector planning and private-sector desires. These ad hoc processes were more or less implicitly shared within

individual organisations (e.g., registered social landlord), but required explanation and understanding when decision-makers from different organisations became involved (e.g., local planning authority and landscape architecture firm).

If we compare the Central Salford process with the generic urban design decision-making process identified in Chapter 1, several activities appear to conform, particularly the activities in the first stage of the generic urban process (Boyko *et al.*, 2005) (see Figure 2.2). For example, a team was established, in the form first of a steering group and later of a URC; the URC appraised the area in terms of problems, issues and opportunities; they formed goals for the urban regeneration project; they acquired funding to look for an appropriate vehicle for urban regeneration in the area and to hold an international design competition; and they communicated their aims for Central Salford's urban regeneration in the form of a brief to design teams.

There are some minor variations from the process described in Chapter 1. For example, the brief was produced earlier in the process, and the URC's objectives continued to be developed for a longer period of time. In addition, the URC engaged in other activities during the early stages of the process, such as exhibiting design teams' visions in a shopping mall in Salford as part of public consultation. The URC also added a stage in which they judged and selected a design team to take their vision forward.

A major departure from the generic urban design decision-making process in Chapter 1 was that the design teams were not able to capture the requirements and understand the needs, problems and issues of the area. Boyko *et al*. (2005) suggest that this activity should occur in the first stage of the urban design decision-making process. The competition teams were also not made fully aware of the crime and health issues, possibly for fear of undermining the URC's efforts to attract private investment. Thus the design teams' visions, as seen by the URC and the public, were not based on a detailed understanding of the contextual social, economic and environmental requirements. Once the URC had selected the design team, however, the process of understanding requirements, needs, problems and issues commenced through the development of a more detailed vision.

The Devonshire Quarter's process clearly contrasts with the urban design decision-making process in Chapter 1. The former may be better represented as a cycle of development, decline, demolition and regeneration. Within this cycle, five key decisions could be identified. Viewing the urban design decision-making process in this way may be due in part to the 25-year timescale and the number of key development projects. It may be easier to remember key decisions made during this time, rather than the details of how individual projects were set up and run.

Finally, in comparison with the generic urban design decision-making process in Chapter 1, the London case study comprised three distinct periods along with 13 stages. It demonstrates that urban design and development projects do not necessarily follow a linear process. Rather, development projects begin, may be abandoned prior to completion for a variety of reasons (e.g., the stock market crash), and restart. Some aspects of projects are conducted over again (e.g., creating teams) whereas other aspects are modified (e.g., establishing objectives) and some are not undertaken at all (e.g., designing a gated community).

Sustainability

In each of the case studies, decision-makers and stakeholders considered sustainability when making urban design decisions. However, sustainability differed according to how it was defined, the stages in the process at which it was considered, who was making decisions, and the size, type and scale of the urban design and development projects.

The local authority planning departments generated the most interviewees who had considered sustainability. Private-sector property developers and architects also contributed to sustainable decision-making to some degree. Depending on the decision-maker, sustainable urban design decisions were made during brief preparation, when designing and developing schemes, and while evaluating and selecting a design for planning consent. These stages correspond to stages found in the generic urban design decision-making process identified in Chapter 1 (Boyko *et al.*, 2005).

Interviewees also consistently emphasised various environmental, social and economic aspects when discussing sustainability. Conversations frequently centred on environmental improvements that could be made to the design of projects, the use of more sustainable materials during the construction phase, the significance of public consultation, and the need to reduce crime (the latter two issues were more often cited by the public sector). When talking about economic sustainability, the private-sector developers, clients and landowners indicated that the potential return on investment on their urban design and development projects was a priority for them. In contrast, when interviewees from the public sector mentioned economic sustainability, they looked at more macro-scale issues, such as the notion that a local economy could thrive and be diverse owing to the creation of urban development projects (see ODPM, 2003; CLG, 2007).

Perhaps one reason why interviewees highlighted the environmental dimension of sustainability was that climate change, global warming and recycling were – and continue to be – commonly cited in the media. Social issues surrounding the fear of crime and the need to consult stakeholders in design and development projects were also emphasised in the media and in government policy. In terms of the economic dimension of sustainability, the private sector's reference to return on investment is sensible, given their need to make profits in order to survive. The public sector's emphasis on the economic sustainability of neighbourhoods and cities also makes sense, as the national government continues to promote its sustainable communities agenda through local authorities. However, whereas most of the private-sector decision-makers interviewed for all three case studies mentioned return on investment, the idea of creating economically sustainable communities on a more macro scale was described only in the Greater Manchester case study. One reason for this could be that the size and type of the urban design and development project in Greater Manchester required decision-makers to 'think big' about economic sustainability (i.e., a large urban area that was being recently regenerated using a vision and regeneration framework). In contrast, the projects in London and Sheffield were smaller in size and type, and therefore interviewees considered other, more relevant, sustainability issues.

In London, local government policy, guidance and planning briefs mentioned sustainability. Planning and design officers in the local authorities also considered sustainability when writing reports to give to the Planning Board, who gave approval for planning applications. The planning and design officers involved in Brewhouse Yard disclosed that they considered sustainability, but it was not fully enforced through the planning system at the time. For example, incorporating environmental sustainability into the design of Brewhouse Yard (e.g., grey water recycling) – which one of the private-sector architects wanted to see as part of the site – was not a major concern at planning application meetings between one of the site owners and the local authority planners.

In Sheffield, interviewees asserted that sustainable design decisions were not influenced greatly by local policy at the time. Nonetheless, local authorities and the private sector made decisions in the development of the Devonshire Quarter that emphasised elements of sustainability. The decision by the local authority to designate a park as urban open space, rather than develop on the land, has its roots in environmental sustainability (e.g., the park provides a green oasis in a dense, urban space) and social sustainability (e.g., the park is an amenity for neighbouring residents). Furthermore, the decision by the entrepreneurs of the Forum to create a mixed-use space for independent retail operators and for leisure activities (e.g., bar, café, restaurant) promotes economic and social sustainability. Other decisions in the case study site – allowing inner-city housing,

Table 2.3 Tools and resources used across the three case studies

Greater Manchester	Sheffield	London
• Visionary leadership • Strong conviction • Able to take things forward with 'the right team' • Shared value system • Consulting past briefs and experiences	• Government guidelines • Holding ongoing discussions between public and private sectors • Having an intimate knowledge of economic climate • Reading academic journals and magazines on housing • Travelling to other cities for inspiration • Consulting past experiences • Knowing who uses the area • Maintaining good relationships with people in the area • Not using common research studies	• Good-quality brief • Good planning officers who work well with applicants and who have prior knowledge of the area • Having the 'right kind of team' • Having time to appraise the context • Creating a design strategy for the site • Examining appropriate policies • Holding discussions with applicant teams prior to submitting planning applications • Having internal design reviews before submitting planning applications

creating a mixed-use site of office, retail and residential at West One, and establishing the Devonshire Quarter Association – accentuate the importance of social and, to some extent, economic sustainability.

In the Greater Manchester case study, sustainability was mentioned in the first- and second-stage briefing documents. However, it was not defined, nor was there any information about how to consider sustainability in the design competition. Furthermore, sustainability was not one of the criteria used by the judging panel for the international design competition; rather, cost and creative thinking were seen as more important.

In terms of addressing sustainability explicitly in the urban design decision-making process, these case studies reflect the change in attitudes over time. They move from a situation where addressing sustainability arose from a genuine understanding of well-being and quality of life by specific individuals (e.g., the need for green space in the centre of Sheffield by the Planning Department) to a more directed approach resulting from the emergence of

specific sustainability policies and agendas. Nonetheless, it is clear that sustainability is a complex concept, composed of many dimensions, and is subject to the intentions and agendas of the myriad decision-makers. Today, we are more aware of these dimensions, yet it is still to be determined how much decision-makers objectively address all of the dimensions of sustainability and, indeed, whether they are able to do so. The remaining chapters of this book investigate this phenomenon.

Tools and resources used in decision-making

The tools and resources used by decision-makers varied across the three case studies (see Table 2.3). When asked in the interviews, people rarely mentioned a tool or resource by name (e.g., Enquiry by Design for community consultation). Rather, they tended to think of personality traits, interpersonal skills, general guidance from all levels of government, planning documents, and temporal/structural issues.

In Greater Manchester, the local authority's recent decision to regenerate the area of Central Salford meant that many of the tools and resources used to make decisions were based on people and characteristics. Because decision-makers were beginning a process, they concentrated on creating teams and forming goals. To do so required thoughtful consideration about leadership, team members, desired qualities and value systems, and what the team wanted to achieve. Central Salford had a visionary leader, in the form of the Chief Executive of Salford City Council. He possessed strong conviction and passion to take forward a vision for urban regeneration in the area. He knew that the vision would not be realised unless he surrounded himself with the 'right' team. Thus he hired Felicity Goodey, a well-known BBC presenter, who also was passionate about Salford. Together, they gathered a team of people who had vast experience in regeneration, planning, brief writing, government, business, academia, and the city itself. They held a shared value system in wanting to increase quality of life in the area.

In Sheffield, the tools and resources used were more diverse than in Greater Manchester. Although government guidelines about sustainability were non-existent at the time, the local authority still referenced governmental policies and programmes when making decisions (e.g., guidance on the Urban Programme). They also took the time to read academic journals and trade magazines about issues, such as housing in city centres. Finally, the local authority possessed an intimate knowledge of the economic climate of Sheffield, which they used when making decisions about where and when to create new development opportunities.

The tools and resources used by decision-makers in the London case study were both human centred and policy and planning centred. The public-sector planners believed that having the right team, particularly good-quality planners, to take a local authority's goals forward was important in day-to-day operations. Members of the team should also be able to write briefs and design strategies well, examine the appropriate government policies when necessary, and know the historical and planning

Catherine Griffiths Court, Clerkenwell, London

contexts of their area. Moreover, local authority planners were encouraged to hold meetings with planning applicants prior to the submission of applications, not only as a way to iron out planning-related issues, but also to develop a good working relationship with applicants in the long term. Having internal design review meetings was perceived to be very important on the private-sector side, especially with the architects, who wanted constructive and informed critiques from their colleagues before taking designs to the client team.

Like the local authority, private-sector decision-makers (e.g., developers, architects) utilised their knowledge – as well as prior experiences in the city – to find the best development opportunities for them. They did not use common research studies to make decisions, but instead relied on their 'gut feelings' about places. Moreover, regardless of their feelings about the planning system, private-sector decision-makers attempted to maintain a good working relationship with public-sector planners. One way of doing this was to hold discussions often with the planners – for example, through pre-planning and planning application meetings – to understand what local and national government were saying about different planning-related issues.

The research team was specifically interested in the plethora of computer-based support; however, rarely did the interviewees refer to such systems. It would appear that their use and existence are still emerging, often relegated to technical support. Decision-makers use them only in a secondary capacity. However, the increasing sophistication of such tools means they may have a critical role in providing verified evidence upon which increasingly reliable decisions can be made.

Conclusion

The case studies presented in this chapter illustrate different approaches to urban design and development over various timescales in three UK cities. Analysis of the case studies has revealed the similarities and differences between these three processes and the generic urban design decision-making process identified in Chapter 1. The content and activities of each process also reveal the degree to which sustainability was addressed, and how various tools were used in decision-making. It is clear that sustainability and the process are both ill defined and rather random in approach and use. Therefore Chapter 3 will go on to discuss how to improve the urban design decision-making process so that sustainability is seen as an integral part of decision-making for 24-hour cities.

References

Baldock, R. (1998) Ten years of the Urban Programme 1981–91: the impact and implications of its assistance on small businesses. *Urban Studies*, **35** (11), 2063–2083.

Boyko, C. T., Cooper, R. & Davey, C. (2005) Sustainability and the urban design process. *Engineering Sustainability*, **158** (ES3), 119–125.

CABE (n.d.) The Devonshire Quarter, Sheffield, *Case Studies*, http://www.cabe.org.uk/default.aspx?content:temid=1289&aspectid=23

CLG (2007) *Consultation paper on a new Planning Policy Statement 4: Planning for sustainable economic development*. London: HMSO.

Development Control Committee (1998) *Development Control Committee Report, 06/10/1998, Agenda No. B4, Former Allied brewery site, 148–176 St John Street, EC1*. Islington, London: Development Control Committee.

Dodson, S. (2004) A place to hang on the web. *The Guardian*. Retrieved 2 August 2005 from http://arts.guardian.co.uk/features/story/0,11710,1145890,00.html.

DoE (1986) *Evaluation of environmental projects funded under the Urban Programme*. London: HMSO.

English Heritage (n.d.) *Current projects: Clerkenwell*. Retrieved 17 August 2005 from http://www.english-heritage.org.uk/server/show/nav.1651.

HMSO (2006) *Population of Sheffield from the 2001 Census*. Retrieved 11 October 2006 from http://www.statistics.gov.uk/census2001/pyramids/pages/00cg.asp.

Islington Council Planning Division (n.d.). *Allied Domecq Site, Clerkenwell, Nos 148–180 St John Street: Design statement*. London: Islington Borough Council.

Mackay, L. (2005) VivaCity 2020: Shopping and crime in Sheffield. Unpublished report, University of Salford, Salford.

ODPM (1998) *Planning permission: A guide for business*. London: Office of the Deputy Prime Minister.

ODPM (2003) *Sustainable communities: Building for the future*. London: ODPM.

Parkinson, M. & Robson, P. (2000) *Urban regeneration companies: An evaluation*. London: DETR.

Report of the Leader of the Council (2004) *Submission for Urban Regeneration Company (URC) status for Central Salford*. Salford: Salford City Council.

Salford City Council (2004) *Frequently asked questions*. Retrieved 11 August 2004 from http://www.salford.gov.uk/living/yourcom/salfordlife/regeneration/central-salford/regeneration.

Sheffield City Council (2001) *Devonshire Quarter Action Plan*. Sheffield: Sheffield City Council.

Sheffield City Council (2004) *Sheffield city-centre urban design compendium*. Sheffield: Sheffield City Council. Retrieved 29 June 2005 from http://sccplugins.sheffield.gov.uk/urban_design.

Tye, R. & Williams, G. (1994) Urban regeneration and central–local government relations: the case of New East Manchester. *Progress in Planning*, **42** (1), 1–97.

Footnote

1 Outline planning permission is a local authority consent that approves a development 'in principle', giving an indication of whether or not a proposed development is likely to be granted full, or detailed, planning permission in the future. Once outline planning permission has been given, full planning permission must be sought for the approval of reserved matters, or details. Outline planning permission is valid for up to five years, but a full planning application must be submitted within three years (ODPM, 1998).

CHAPTER 3

THE URBAN DESIGN DECISION-MAKING PROCESS: A NEW APPROACH

Christopher Boyko and Rachel Cooper

This chapter builds on the previous two chapters by discussing the need to reconceptualise the urban design decision-making process. Based on the generic urban design decision-making process (see Chapter 1) and the three in-depth case study urban design processes (see Chapter 2), we found that sustainability was not considered consistently in process stages. Furthermore, there was little understanding of who makes sustainable urban design decisions and when these decisions could be made. Comments from a panel of experts validated the above issues and suggested ways to improve the process.

A discussion of the issues brought forth by the expert panel concerning the urban design decision-making process begins the chapter. With these comments in mind, a visual reconceptualisation of the process is offered. The new stages, tasks and reviews of the reconceptualised urban design decision-making process are then explained, with particular attention paid to decision-makers and how sustainability is to be considered throughout the process.

Validation of the urban design decision-making processes

Once the case studies in Chapter 2 were completed, they were shown – along with the generic urban design decision-making process – to a panel of experts who were external to the VivaCity2020 project. The experts worked in both the public and private sectors within a range of relevant fields and disciplines, including urban planning, design, development, regeneration and community consultation. Thus the panel had both the experience and the knowledge to comment on the validity of the processes and indicate possible ways to improve the process for urban design decision-making in general.

Upon listening to presentations of the generic process and the case study processes, the experts validated the processes and acknowledged the legitimacy of the generic urban design decision-making process. There were some issues, however, that the experts felt were necessary to raise in order to help enrich the process.

First, the process could benefit from having a timeline. A timeline could show how long each stage takes to complete before moving on to another stage. It also could be used to demonstrate that the stages are not equal in terms of the time it takes to complete them. Finally, having a timeline as part of a diagrammatic process could help to avoid the misunderstanding that the entire process takes a relatively short time to realise.

Second, the panel wanted the process to reflect the non-linear nature of urban design decision-making. Many of the tasks within the process stages did not necessarily follow a prescribed order. Instead, tasks and stages sometimes blurred together as different decision-makers and stakeholders transitioned from one task or stage to another and back again. Being able to visualise the non-linearity of the urban design decision-making process may be beneficial for the myriad people involved in the process, as they may be able to better understand the complexity – and the potential flexibility – associated with urban design decision-making.

creating a legacy archive of decisions, the time it takes for tasks and stages to be completed could be recorded however. Thus decision-makers and stakeholders could revisit past urban development projects as they become involved in new, similarly scaled projects, which could help them to better understand time frames and timelines.

The reconceptualised urban design decision-making process

The reconceptualised urban design decision-making process takes its form principally from the generic urban design decision-making process in Chapter 1, and is informed by the case study processes in Chapter 2 and the expert panel comments. The generic process had four main stages:

- Creating teams, appraising the situation and forming goals
- Designing and developing
- Evaluating, selecting and creating a plan
- Implementing, monitoring and following up

and four transition stages:

- Continuing to understand the context
- Continuing to think about alternatives
- Re-creating a plan
- Continuing the process.

Third, the panel felt that although community engagement in the urban design decision-making process is important, it may be difficult to implement in practice. Local residents, particularly those who have lived through previous, unsuccessful regeneration projects, may remain unconvinced of urban development when changes are not seen quickly enough, or are not sustained. Thus having a variety of different strategies to actively engage the community throughout the process – particularly in the early stages with the exploration of the urban development project – would be advantageous.

In developing the reconceptualised urban design decision-making process, we were able to incorporate two of the panel's suggestions: visualising the non-linear nature of the process, and doing a more effective job of incorporating the local community into the process stages (see next section for more detail). The remaining suggestion, that of having a timeline alongside the process, is more difficult to include because the reconceptualised process is generic in scope. Decision-makers and stakeholders involved in a range of urban developments, from smaller-scale (e.g., urban block) to larger-scale (e.g., city-wide) projects, should be able to look at the process and loosely follow the tasks and stages. Having timelines and approximations for how long each stage takes would therefore not be helpful, and might possibly give a false impression of when stages begin and end. By

Although useful as a baseline from which to compare urban design decision-making in practice, there were some discrepancies between the generic process and the case study processes that needed to be resolved when developing the reconceptualised process. One discrepancy was that the transition stages were not followed in any of the case study processes. This could be because decision-makers just did not undertake the transition stages. However, a more plausible reason is that decision-makers recognised the transition stages as being an implicit part of the process, and therefore did not feel they needed to be separate from the other tasks and stages. As a result, the reconceptualised process streamlines the stages and transition stages, creating five new stages that better reflect the process for urban design decision-making (see next section).

A second discrepancy between the generic process and the case study processes was that explicit reference was not made to the different decision-makers. An earlier idea, based on the work of Woodhead (2000), was to categorise decision-makers into four different groups: decision-approvers, decision-takers, decision-shapers and decision-influencers. However, these categories did not take into account the potential fluidity of people to be different types of decision-maker throughout the process (e.g., to change one's role from someone who influences the development of a proposal – a decision-influencer – to someone who develops a proposal to be evaluated by others – a decision-shaper). Furthermore, it may not make sense to ascribe specific decision-making roles to specific people or occupations (e.g., architects are always decision-shapers), as the situation may be different with each urban development project (e.g., architect may shape proposals, but also approve proposals). Thus the reconceptualised urban design decision-making process divides decision-makers into two groups – the project sustainability group and the development team – and the issue of decision-making is left to the two groups to determine who will make, and who will contribute to, decisions.

A third discrepancy found when comparing the generic process with the case study processes is that specific decision-making tools, techniques and resources were not explicitly mentioned. As with

Deansgate, Manchester

defining the decision-makers in the process, it was felt that it would be better not to list specific tools to use during each task. Having such a list might limit some decision-makers' and stakeholders' creativity and innovativeness to use new tools when making decisions (e.g., mobile technology, virtual reality). Rather, throughout the remaining chapters of this book, we shall describe some innovative tools to use in sustainable urban design decision-making. It will be up to the decision-makers when best to use them throughout the process.

A final discrepancy between the generic process and the case study processes was that sustainability was not addressed nor considered consistently. A variety of decision-makers made decisions regarding the sustainability of urban development projects – or elements of urban development projects (e.g., the use of sustainable urban drainage systems) – but there were few points in the processes where these sustainability issues were repeatedly discussed. For their part, the public sector used guidance and policy about planning and sustainability to evaluate planning applications and inform pre-planning application meetings. However, this did not always happen, as other issues were perceived to be important at the time (e.g., economic growth). Moreover, sustainability was rarely considered in a holistic manner when making decisions. That is, decision-makers mulled over one or two sustainability issues – the most frequent being environmental issues, such as the reuse of building materials – but proposed urban development projects were rarely assessed on the basis of a more thorough examination of the social, economic and environmental dimensions of sustainability. The reconceptualised urban design decision-making process has incorporated consideration of sustainability at each stage (via sustainability tasks and sustainability reviews: see next section), and compels decision-makers and stakeholders to look at the trade-offs and negotiations associated with the three dimensions of sustainability.

The reconceptualised urban design decision-making process in greater detail

The reconceptualised urban design decision-making process is characterised as a series of five stages, four sustainability tasks and four sustainability reviews. A legacy archive is also apart of the process, used as a means of storing knowledge, information and recorded decisions produced throughout the urban design life cycle (see Chapter 1). This provides a legacy of information and decisions for use both on the current project and on future projects.

Each stage, task and review will be described in turn, followed by a general discussion of the process (see Figure 3.1).

Stage 0: Need/opportunity identification

In Stage 0, an individual or team (e.g., local authority, landowner) identifies a need (e.g., more doctors' surgeries in an area) or an opportunity (e.g., new homes in Thames Gateway) for an urban development project. This is coupled with an identification of a potential location for the urban development project and an exploration of potential partnership opportunities.

Why is this stage important? It is important for the individual or team to consider social, economic and environmental sustainability factors as early as possible when making decisions about the urban development project, because the critical factors will emerge and can be used to highlight the principal trade-offs, to which the individual or team will return throughout the project.

Stage 1: Exploration

In Stage 1, a development team is normally formed to explore the urban development project from all perspectives (e.g., architecture, context, finances, sustainability).

At this point, a project sustainability group also should be formed, comprising individuals who are able to work throughout the lifetime of the urban development project (e.g., local authority staff, developers, financiers/investors, those in the construction industry, residents). In some cases, particularly when the urban development project is small and/or the identified need or opportunity is still being investigated, the group may consist of only one or two individuals, rather than an entire team. Furthermore, a leader should be appointed who has the appropriate skills to chair the group.

The development team will take forward the urban development project. While this is occurring, the project sustainability group will ensure that the dimensions of sustainability are considered and included throughout the process. The leader of the group will (re)assess the members throughout the lifetime of the urban development project to ensure that new expertise is brought on board when needed, and/or to give existing group members an opportunity to take a less active role if necessary.

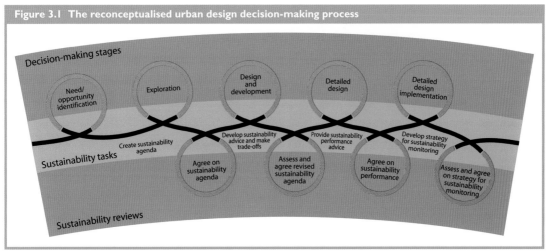

Figure 3.1 The reconceptualised urban design decision-making process

Source: VivaCity2020

Both teams will take the initial ideas from Stage 0 and begin to formalise them into a sustainability agenda.

Why is this stage important? If the teams understand the basic principles of sustainability and work together to explore the project and the sustainability agenda, they are more likely to progress through the process without encountering major hurdles.

Sustainability tasks

Between Stage 0 and the first sustainability review (see below), a sustainability agenda is created by the project sustainability group – yet held by the local authority – from knowledge, information and recorded decisions in the legacy archive. The sustainability agenda outlines what sustainability issues, ranked in order of importance in each context, are deemed important throughout Stages 2 (Design and development) and 3 (Detailed design) of the urban development project. The project sustainability group contextualises the urban development project, based on planning documents (e.g., past planning applications for the site), local plans (e.g., Local Development Framework), sustainability policy (e.g., ODPM's 2006 report, *Securing the future*), maps (e.g., GIS maps with layered information about housing, school locations, demographics), and so forth.

The development team may also help to inform the sustainability agenda by using various tools to examine sustainability within the urban development project (e.g., Arup SPeAR, crime data, IT). One 'tool' that the development team should consider is consultation with the numerous stakeholders who will be affected by the urban development project. Time should be spent up front to contemplate carefully how best to engage with stakeholders throughout the project, and what tools should be used to maximise input from stakeholders (e.g., Enquiry by Design, walkabouts using disposable cameras and uploading the images onto a Participatory GIS map). Stakeholders should also be (re)assessed throughout the team's involvement in the project to ensure that there is good stakeholder representation, and that people do not experience 'consultation fatigue'.

Why is this task important? The sustainability agenda sets in writing how the teams understand the various sustainability issues surrounding a specific urban development project. This agenda will be revisited and modified throughout the process,

Carver Lane, Sheffield

providing a live document with which to benchmark achievements and negotiate sustainable decisions.

Sustainability review
Before the development team begins designing and developing their plans for an urban development project, they must agree the sustainability agenda with the project sustainability group.

Why is this review important? This review allows both teams the opportunity to consider the most important sustainability issues within the context of the project, and to negotiate the terms of the agenda.

Stage 2: Design and development
Stage 2 of the process corresponds to stages or phases within traditional construction management and architectural processes, such as Phase 4 (Outline conceptual design) of the Process Protocol (www.processprotocol.com) and Stage C (Outline proposals) of the RIBA Plan of Work. However, it should be recognised that the development team working on design and development ought to consider the larger scale of urban development projects rather than only smaller-scale design and construction projects.

Why is this stage important? This stage allows the development team to begin designing the urban development plan, and to consider design and development issues relating to sustainability.

Sustainability tasks
Between the first and second sustainability reviews – and often during Stage 2 – the project sustainability group and the development team develop sustainability advice from an ongoing series of trade-off discussions (e.g., as part of pre-planning application meetings). Both teams give and seek advice regarding the sustainability of the urban development project, explaining and negotiating sustainability trade-offs where necessary. Recourse to sustainability tools, techniques and knowledge is taken at this point. As a result of the trade-off discussions, revisions will be made to the prioritisation of sustainability issues, and the revised sustainability agenda will be presented at the second sustainability review.

Why is this task important? Sustainability advice gives both teams involved in the urban development project an opportunity to share information and knowledge about sustainability and the progress of the project.

Sustainability review
The project sustainability group discusses and agrees the re-prioritisation of the sustainability agenda with the development team. This ensures that both teams are kept informed of the role of sustainability in the project. The project sustainability group also agrees on the preliminary designs created by the development team.

Why is this review important? Trade-offs involving sustainable decision-making will be highlighted, and the result of such negotiations will further update and inform the sustainability agenda.

Stage 3: Detailed design

Stage 3 of this process corresponds to stages or phases within traditional construction management and architectural processes, such as Phase 5 (Full conceptual design) of the Process Protocol (www.processprotocol.com) and Stages D and E (Detailed proposals and Final proposals, respectively) of the RIBA Plan of Work. However, it should be recognised that the development team working on design and development ought to consider the larger scale of urban development projects rather than only smaller-scale design and construction projects. Unlike the process protocol, the detailed design of the urban development project should be created before submission of a planning application(s) for approval.

Why is this stage important? This stage allows the development team to progress in more detail with the designs of the urban development plan, offering an in-depth understanding of design and development issues relating to sustainability.

Sustainability tasks
Between the second and third sustainability reviews, the two teams can elicit and provide sustainability performance advice as part of pre-planning application meetings. This task gives both teams the opportunity to discuss the proposed performance of the urban development project design, and to give initial feedback before the formal performance assessment occurs at the third sustainability review.

Why is this task important? Sustainability performance advice gives both teams involved in the urban development project an opportunity to share information and knowledge about the design, and how it is likely to perform in terms of sustainability.

Sustainability review
Once the development team has created a detailed design for the urban development project and sought advice from the project sustainability group about sustainability performance, the project sustainability group assesses the performance of the design against the sustainability agenda. Compliance between the detailed design and the sustainability agenda provides the impetus for the submission of a planning application(s) for approval. Non-compliance means that the two teams will have to refer back to the sustainability advice given, and will have to continue to negotiate the sustainability trade-offs.

Why is this review important? Complying with sustainability performance provides the development team with a 'go/no go' decision for planning application submission. Without this stage, the development team may not be as confident about submitting their planning application (i.e., they will not know whether their project 'stands up' to the sustainability agenda and the sustainability advice given).

Stage 4: Detailed design implementation

Stage 4 of the process corresponds to stages or phases within traditional construction management and architectural processes, such as Phase 6 (Coordinated design, procurement and full financial authority) of the Process Protocol (www.processprotocol.com) and Stages F to L (Production information, Tender documents, Tender action, Mobilisation, Construction to practical completion and After practical completion) of the RIBA Plan of Work. The content within this phase should be followed with a view towards urban development projects (i.e., both buildings and the spaces between the buildings).

Why is this stage important? Once planning permission has been sought, this stage allows for the urban development project to be built via the construction process.

Sustainability tasks

Once the urban development project has been built, the project sustainability group and the development team will agree on a strategy for sustainability monitoring. The strategy may include a timeline, budgets, and statements about who will manage and maintain the project during its lifetime.

Why is this activity important? The strategy for sustainability monitoring gives both teams a plan of how to take care of the urban development project once it is built, in both the short and the long term. The strategy should also consider the surrounding area within which the project is situated, as decisions about sustainability for the project may impact on the sustainability of the neighbourhood, city and region.

Sustainability review

Once the strategy for sustainability monitoring has been developed by the two teams, it is reviewed and assessed to ensure that whoever is assuming the curatorial role is able to manage and maintain the urban development project in the short and long term. The information from the legacy archive and the project sustainability reviews will be used to guide the assessment.

Why is this review important? The assessment of the strategy for sustainability monitoring provides a formal benchmark against which future urban design decisions about sustainability can be compared and evaluated.

Summary

The reconceptualised urban design decision-making process presented in this chapter illustrates the culmination of effort on the VivaCity2020 project – from the generic urban design decision-making process from Chapter 1, to the case studies in Chapter 2, and finally to the expert panel comments discussed earlier in this chapter – to develop a process for urban design decision-making that explicitly shows when and how sustainability should be considered. Each stage of the process corresponds to specific sustainability tasks and sustainability reviews that allow decision-makers and stakeholders to evaluate, holistically, the sustainability of an urban development project and its component parts. Trade-offs and negotiations concerning sustainability are clearly highlighted at different stages, and the legacy archive captures this information for use later on in the project or on new projects. Finally, there is enough detail written into the process to let decision-makers know what actions need to be taken, yet the detail is not so meticulous that it limits flexibility.

With this reconceptualised and improved urban design decision-making process in mind, the next set of chapters will introduce the various sustainability issues that make up the VivaCity2020 project.

References

ODPM (2006) *The Office of the Deputy Prime Minister's sustainable development action plan. Securing the future: Delivering UK sustainable development strategy.* London: TSO.

Woodhead, R. M. (2000) Investigation of the early stages of project formulation. *Facilities,* **18** (13/14), 524–534.

SECTION OVERVIEW

This section began with a discussion and definition of urban design, highlighting the idea that urban design is both a dynamic art and a process. The notion of process was explored further through the development of a generic urban design decision-making process that is based on the relevant literature (see Chapter 1). This generic process was then used to compare processes from three case studies of urban design and development projects in the UK as part of the VivaCity2020 project (see Chapter 2). The comparison between the processes yielded new insights into what was absent from the process, and what was needed to improve the process for urban design decision-making (i.e., making more socially responsible and sustainable urban design decisions).

Both the generic process and the case studies revealed that sustainability was not considered consistently at each stage, and that the activities within each stage were not 'hardwired' to allow for proper reflection about sustainability. Furthermore, specific tools and resources were not consistently used by decision-makers when making urban design decisions (or were not mentioned, as found in the generic process). The tools and resources employed most frequently, in fact, were more human-centred (e.g., spending time to find the 'right' team), but many decision-makers also found planning policy and guidance to be very beneficial in their strategic and daily decision-making. Finally, the case studies revealed that a diagrammatic or visual process was often not followed, with decision-makers preferring to use past experiences and knowledge to move from one activity to another. Doing so may not give decision-makers the opportunity to reflect critically on their decisions, or understand how earlier decisions could impact on later decisions.

Taking these issues into consideration, the reconceptualised urban design decision-making process in Chapter 3 offered an alternative. This new process promotes thinking and decision-making about sustainability at all process stages through the use of sustainability tasks (activities, such as creating a sustainability agenda, that oblige decision-makers to consider the contextual dimensions of sustainability associated with their urban design and development project) and sustainability reviews (points in the process whereby decision-makers agree on the contextual dimensions of sustainability before moving on to the next stage, similar to a 'gate'). It also suggests that two different teams be involved in decision-making: a development team (decision-makers who want to develop a project) and a project sustainability group (decision-makers who will be around for the lifetime of the project). These two teams incorporate as many of the decision-makers and stakeholders on a project as would like to be involved. Moreover, the project sustainability group brings a potentially diverse collection of people together (e.g., local authority, financiers, residents), creating the occasion for a more holistic approach to working on a project. That is, rather than staying in disciplinary silos and working on separate issues, the group will work together on cross-cutting issues.

SECTION 2
ENVIRONMENTAL SUSTAINABILITY AND CITY-CENTRE LIVING

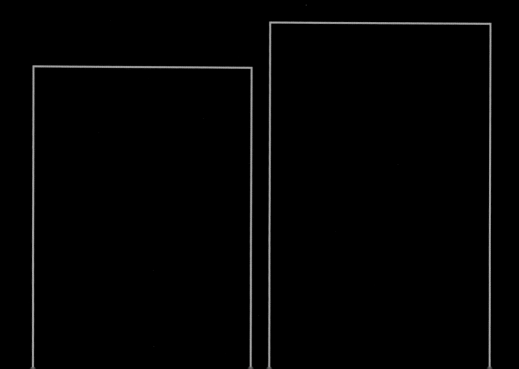

ENVIRONMENTAL SUSTAINABILITY AND CITY-CENTRE LIVING

This section reviews the environment, and more specifically environmental sustainability, as it relates to city-centre living and urban design.

Environmental sustainability is a vast topic, ranging from environmental economics to environmental justice and quality of life. This section does not attempt a comprehensive approach to the subject. Rather, it is concerned with the relationship between two environmental dimensions: noise and pollution. It explores how noise and pollution are measured, how individuals living in the city perceive them, and how the design of the environment contributes to negative and positive aspects of these environmental dimensions.

We do this to illustrate how decision-makers can make evidence-based decisions informed by individuals and the community, which can contribute to improved sustainable design decisions for the urban environment. In Chapters 4 and 5 we illustrate the complex relationship between environmental quality, perceptions of quality and residents' context-specific experiences. We identify the impact of our experience of using the city on our senses, both positive and negative. These issues can be at the macro scale and require significant design, policy and planning intervention. For example, the relationship between transport infrastructure, economy and residential property can have a great impact on levels of traffic, pollutants and noise. However, there are also micro-scale issues that appear to have as great an effect as the macro issues on our perceptions of the city experience. One such issue is the human need to urinate and defecate. This concerns everyone, yet little advice is available on the provision of toilets.

Accessibility and provision of public conveniences have a significant impact on the fabric of the city, the environment, and overall citizen well-being. Chapter 6 illustrates that the design of the urban environment at a micro level is just as much a matter for concern for residents, businesses and local government as is the wider design of the general urban scale (i.e., the buildings and infrastructure). Thus it is critically important that decision-makers consider carefully the design and provision of accessible toilets in the urban design process, ensuring the inclusion of all members of society in 24-hour city living.

CHAPTER 4

URBAN ENVIRONMENTAL QUALITY

Gemma Moore, Mags Adams, Mohamed Refaee, Trevor Cox,
Ben Croxford and Steve Sharples

'The qualities of urban living in the 21st century will define the qualities of civilisation itself.'

(Harvey, 1996)

Here we present an overview of urban environmental quality based on a review of the literature and then findings from the VivaCity2020 project itself. Much existing research tends to focus on either, outdoor or indoor, and either objective or subjective measurements. The aim of VivaCity2020 was to explore both measurements and perceptions of indoor and outdoor environmental quality.

The chapter is split into sections on the outdoor and indoor environment and includes data gathered and quotes taken in interviews from the three case study cities: Sheffield, Manchester and London. Chapter 5 explores sensory perception in more detail.

Overview of urban environmental quality

Because of the many specific criteria for assessing and measuring environmental quality there is no established protocol: quality is often measured for specific purposes rather than developing a general index. The term 'quality' can encompass a wide range of variables, and there is a complex interplay between them. Pirsig (1976) is one of many who have grappled with the term 'quality':

> '… you know what it is, yet you don't know what it is. But that is self-contradictory. But some things are better than others, that is, they have more quality. But when you try to say what quality is, apart from the things that have it, it all goes poof!'

Any attempt to 'measure' environmental quality will experience difficulties in encompassing all the possible influential and intertwined factors. Van Kamp et al. (2003) state that 'objective conditions (alone) do not convey true quality', enforcing the impression that it is necessary to link different forms

and types of knowledge in the assessment of quality. For instance, while physical measurements yield quantitative data, the richest perceptual datasets are qualitative. Any investigation requires numerous environmental aspects to be explored and examined, alongside the perception of those factors. However, a common difficulty to be overcome is in ensuring that all perceptual and physical data are co-located and measured simultaneously.

The perception of urban environments has been explored in many research disciplines, including urban studies, geography, planning, and psychology, and can range in scale from city, through neighbourhood, to home, and also to the perceiver, residents, workers or tourists (e.g. Ellaway et al., 2001; Parkes et al., 2002). In general, in the investigation of urban environments, the focus has been on negative environmental and social aspects; few studies have looked at factors that promote greater satisfaction. This is perhaps surprising, as an insight into the positive aspects associated with living in urban neighbourhoods is necessary for a detailed understanding of city-centre living for both researchers and policy-makers. Tallon and Bromley (2004) investigated both the positive and negative aspects of living in the centre of two provincial

British cities (Bristol and Swansea). Over 500 residents were surveyed to gain a broad picture of the advantages and disadvantages of city-centre living. Tallon and Bromley's findings indicate that it is the practical, mundane and routine aspects of city-centre living, such as proximity to points of employment and consumption, that are its key attractions. These factors were considered more important than lifestyle or cultural attractions, which are commonly emphasised in the urban gentrification literature. Environmental issues of noise, pollution and traffic were all mentioned as disadvantages of city-centre living.

Studies tend to explore people's perceptions of their environment through questionnaire surveys, developed to gauge opinion and establish indicators. However, there are evident limitations with this method. Questionnaires and scoring systems limit opportunities for research participants to explain their answers in depth (e.g. providing further social–spatial information), which would allow for a more detailed understanding of the perception processes. In addition, this narrow, prescriptive approach means that the variables explored are determined solely by the researcher (who has designed the questionnaire), and thus it neglects other factors that might influence the findings.

Other urban environmental quality research has tended to focus directly on issues that are thought to impact upon the quality of environment and life, such as noise and air pollution.

It has been argued that most urban environmental problems are now under control, with the exception of the persistent problems of noise and air pollution (de Hollander & Staatsen, 2003). Both noise and air pollution depend on many factors, but they are widespread and unavoidable, affecting everyone. Densely populated, congested urban areas are hot spots for both problems, with the main source in most cases being road traffic.

A vast amount of research has included measurements of environmental variables such as noise and air pollution, and of the physical processes taking place in the urban environment (e.g. Onuu, 2000; Kaur et al., 2005,). Researchers have also studied the public's response to traffic and pollutants, exploring their perceptions and attitudes (e.g. Klaboe, 2000; Bickerstaff & Walker 2001).

Many researchers have recommended a more integrated approach to environmental research. For instance, in the case of air quality, policy developments in the UK have urged local authorities to engage with the public on air quality management issues alongside physical monitoring to gain support and implement policy procedures. Bickerstaff and Walker (2001) assert that involving the public is central to the delivery and success of air quality objectives, as personal responsibility and individual action will allow the necessary steps to be taken to improve air quality.

Indoor environments and environmental quality

Mention environmental quality and people will often think of the external environment: cities are perceived as being noisy and polluted. Our perception of the outdoor environment is important; however, in the UK people spend far more of their time indoors. Saunders (2002) quotes a figure of 85% for the percentage of time people spend either indoors or in a vehicle conveying them

Chorlton Road, Hulme, Manchester

from one building to another. An equivalent US estimate is 69% at home indoors and 18% spent in other indoor locations (Klepeis *et al.*, 2001). So, while perception of city environments may focus on the outdoors, the indoor environment is important to quality and the public's health.

A study by Carrer *et al.* (1997, as cited in Carrer *et al.*, 2001) showed that the concentrations of many air pollutants were higher indoors than outdoors in an urban environment. Pollutants found indoors include CO and NO_2 as well as dust, volatile organic compounds (VOC), radon and indoor noise. The sources of these pollutants vary depending on the type of pollutant, but studies have shown that common sources can be heating appliances, cookers, boilers and fires, the external environment, building materials and household products. Other work has highlighted the public health risks of mould growth and damp (Mudarri & Fisk, 2007). Approximately 20% of all dwellings in England suffer from mould growth and dampness to some degree (Oreszczyn & Pretlove, 2000). The UK Building Regulations cover aspects of the indoor environment, with Part F covering ventilation requirements and Part E covering acoustics issues (CLG, 2006). However, most homes in the UK were built before the current Building Regulations came into force.

The major source of pollutant exposure for many is smoking. Currently, smokers number 24% of all UK adults (ONS, 2005). There are no regulations regarding smoking in the home, and smoking-related disease is the highest cause of mortality in the UK.

Recent trends have seen increasing market penetration of double glazing and draughtproofing. Both are assumed to lead to reduced ventilation in homes, and thus to an increase in the significance of indoor sources for overall pollutant exposure. For instance, a pollutant inside homes that is currently raising concern is formaldehyde. This is a probable carcinogen, present in glue used in many types of processed wood, such as new pressed wood flooring (EPA, 2007a). Changes in ventilation with double glazing are also likely to affect noise exposure, with less outside noise entering the home, and a consequent rise in the importance of noise sources within the building, including neighbour noise.

It would be wrong to assume that, overall, Britain is becoming a noisier place. Average noise levels in recent decades have not changed by very much (DEFRA, 2002a). Sound sources, particularly motor vehicles, are becoming quieter, but there are many more vehicles on the road. So current trends are for fewer periods of quiet, and this is why the preservation of tranquillity in the countryside and relative quiet in urban areas has become an increasingly important campaign, research and policy issue. Air traffic has increased, and the spreading-out of flight paths has meant that more people are exposed to increasingly frequent noise, even though those who were previously exposed to very high noise levels from aircraft have a slightly reduced exposure when averaged over a year.

Within urban areas many people live in flats and houses in mixed-use areas, where poor external sound insulation and poor insulation between properties are common. A cacophony of sounds can be heard in the urban environment. Choice and control over the noises that people hear while in their homes is something that many desire. Grimwood (1997; see also DEFRA, 2002b) found that the main noises heard between properties included music, TV, radio, voices and banging doors. Noise may deter people from sleeping, discourage people from using certain rooms in their property, and prevent them from opening windows (which in turn limits ventilation and influences indoor air quality). Indoor noise nuisance can often lead to problems and disputes between neighbours. Grimwood's study revealed that some people were dissatisfied with indoor noise levels even when their homes met the standards imposed by the Building Regulations, because these did not control noises such as banging doors. As well as the government's proposal to meet the Decent Homes standard by 2010, a new Housing Health and Safety Rating Scheme (HHSRS) has been proposed that aims to deal with the issue of indoor noise (GLA, 2004).

Rochdale Canal, Manchester

Perception of the urban environment

The environment is experienced through all our senses, and yet often more attention is paid to the visual experience than to what is perceived through the other senses. We perceive noise and pollution, but often subconsciously. For example, a busy road may be noisy all the time, but it is only when you are making a mobile phone call that you suddenly realise the ambient noise level makes it difficult to hear.

Even in the city it is possible to hear nightingales or seagulls, which can both be quite loud, but the perception of even these two different sounds can be very different, depending on the person. Some noises are perceived as pleasant by some people, whereas others cannot stand them. This perception can be affected by many things, including the time of day, the context, and the personality of the listener. In the following paragraphs we discuss the varying perceptions of different types of noise. Some people love the throaty roar of a big motorbike, but very few would like to be woken by scooters being raced outside their window late at night.

Bröer (2002) hypothesises that the political context in which people live has a big effect on their attitudes to noise. If people feel that they are involved in local political processes, and that their input has some effect on the source of a noise that annoys them, then this may reduce some of the annoyance they might feel about that noise.

In her comprehensive paper on acoustics environments and living spaces, Schulte-Fortkamp (2002) points out that noise can produce several social and behavioural effects as well as annoyance. These effects are often complex, subtle and indirect, and many effects are assumed to result from the interaction of various non-auditory variables. Equal levels of the various traffic and industrial noises cause different magnitudes of annoyance, because annoyance in populations does not only vary with the characteristics of the noise, including the sound source, but also depends largely on many non-acoustical factors of a social, psychological, or economic nature.

Lercher *et al.* (1999) found that 'noise sources interact with the specific acoustic and environmental make-up (topography, meteorology, land use pattern and lifestyle)'. They claim that the dissatisfaction people feel about their environment is related to the amount of control they have over the source of noise in the environment, and it can be high even when they are generally satisfied with the quality of their personal life.

Maffiolo (1999) says that subjective evaluations of landscapes integrate visual contributions, and that a positive evaluation of the landscape reduces annoyance of the soundscapes, whereas a negative opinion increases annoyance. In discussing research on annoyance, Schulte-Fortkamp (2002) states that assessments of the quality of an environmental area depend on several factors: how long people have lived there, how they define the place in relation to the surrounding infrastructure, how involved they are in the social life of the area, and how integrated they feel in their neighbourhood. As she says:

> *'The factors here – as interactions of people and sound, the ways people are consciously perceiving their environment, habits towards natural and self-produced sounds, the context, the focus of attention, and personal knowledge/experience, background factors which influence reaction to noise, topography, meteorology, land use pattern, visual contributions, landscape evaluation – show the close relationship of perceived environmental sounds and the context of experienced soundscapes.'*

Zannin *et al.* (2002) describe reactions to a variety of neighbourhood noise by residents of the city of Curitiba, Brazil. They classify neighbourhood noise as the collective of noise from neighbours, animals, sirens, civil construction, religious temples, nightclubs, toys, fireworks and domestic electric appliances. They show that the effects of exposure to these noises include irritability, difficulty in concentrating, sleeping disorders and headaches. They identify traffic sounds as the biggest annoyance, followed by neighbour noise, and identify the distinction between continuous and non-continuous noise (Zannin *et al.*, 2001). When these noise sources are classified separately, non-continuous neighbourhood sounds take on a more significant role in the public's perceptions of noise on their street. The authors conclude that allowing for subjective input from respondents produces a more accurate understanding of the effects of noise in urban residential areas.

Volz (2002) demonstrates the relationship between the visual and the auditory in relation to the urban environment by using a video installation of two urban scenes (one a quiet urban park, one a busy street with traffic) and transposing the soundtracks of the scenes. He observed that the auditory environment was more important than the visual picture for the pleasant quality in the whole scene. This contrasts with results from Maffiolo's (1999) study, which asked people what they appreciated about public gardens. Fifty per cent of respondents mentioned the visual modality, with between 20% and 35% mentioning the auditory modality: the variation depended on whether people were in a public garden at the time. This demonstrates the importance of context when talking to people about how they value their urban environment.

Schulte-Fortkamp (2002) draws attention to several studies in this field, including a questionnaire survey conducted in Kyoto, Japan, by Hiramatsu & Minoura (2000). They found that response to sound is related to the listener's mental, social and geographical connection with the sound source. Schulte-Fortkamp (2002) links this to the work undertaken by Berglund (2001), who proposed structured walks where residents identified sounds discerned in the soundscapes of their residential area, indoors and outdoors. Listening places were selected where people had to scale the total loudness, and loudness from specific sources (such as traffic noise). The participants in Berglund's study characterised the residential soundscapes under four dimensions: adverse, reposing, affective, and expressionless. Schulte-Fortkamp reports on a highly structured exercise carried out in Berlin, where respondents had to evaluate their noise and visual impressions at five locations. The evaluation tasks utilised various approaches, including photo-documentation, noise recording and loudness scaling. Others in acoustics have conducted more subjective research into environmental quality. Fyhri & Klaboe (1999, as cited in Schulte-Fortkamp, 2002) consider a subjective sound or urban scape that is dependent on which parts people relate to and how they relate to them.

When noises from different sources have to be judged, more difficulties arise. Schulte-Fortkamp (2002) reports that although there have been various attempts to solve this problem of measurement, so far no model or measurement has definitively defined the procedure (Gjestland, 1999). Schulte-Fortkamp says that for the estimation of combined effects to be effective, there needs to be a better map of the relevant psychological variables, and more precise indicators of both acoustic and non-acoustic environmental factors. This embodies a very deterministic approach to understanding the soundscapes of urban areas.

As demonstrated by the literature, the concept of noise and annoyance needs to be broadened to an integrated environmental, psychosocial, and socio-economic assessment of the community situation. This may lead to a more realistic basis for environmental impact and health risk assessments. Schulte-Fortkamp (2002) advocates that acoustics, physics, psychology, medicine and sociology need to work together in surveys on the perception of acoustic environments.

Environment and health

The UK's Committee on Medical Effects of Air Pollutants (COMEAP) has reviewed the links between outdoor air pollutant concentrations and health effects (DH, 2007), and has concluded that particulate matter, carbon monoxide, oxides of nitrogen, ozone and sulphur dioxide can all affect health. Increased mortality is linked to increased levels of background pollution, particularly fine particulate matter (PM). Respiratory problems are linked to oxides of nitrogen and sulphur, and also to ozone. Cardiovascular disease is linked to carbon monoxide exposure.

Pollution is just one factor that can affect health: to prove the link, large numbers of people must be studied so that the analysis can consider the

Devonshire Green, Sheffield

confounding effects of other factors, such as poverty, smoking, housing conditions, and stress. Most of the research underlying the COMEAP recommendations is based on epidemiological studies of populations and average background pollutant concentrations for those populations: more detail can be found at the Department of Health website (DH, 2007). COMEAP also recommends that concentrations and averaging times that are used to regulate outdoor air quality should also be used as guidelines for indoor air quality.

Noise has also been linked to health effects. The simplest case is that of sleep disturbance, which leads to increased stress levels, which in turn can lead to high blood pressure (hypertension) and related illnesses. Recent research by WHO has suggested that 3% of deaths from heart diseases are due to environmental noise. Another effect of noise is impaired cognition: for instance, noise has been linked to impaired performance by children in schools. A summary of the effects of noise on health can be found on the WHO website (WHO, 2007a). But perhaps the most obvious effect of unwanted noise is that it contributes to a reduced quality of life.

The case studies

Case studies were undertaken in three UK city-centre areas: London (Clerkenwell), Sheffield (Devonshire Quarter) and Manchester (city centre). As the project concentrated upon the experiences of city-centre living, the areas targeted for study were mixed-use areas with housing located near the main daytime and night-time commercial and leisure activities. Within each case study area there are a variety of amenities (shops, offices, entertainment facilities) located within close proximity to residential areas, which themselves are varied, incorporating social housing, privately owned flats and houses. The environmental conditions were also rather varied, with mixed traffic and pedestrian levels and a number of small open spaces within each case study.

The schedule undertaken was as follows:
Winter 2004   London, winter (Round 1)
Summer 2005   Sheffield, summer (Round 1)
Late summer 2005   London, summer (Round 2)
Early winter 2005   Manchester, winter (Round 1)
Winter 2006   Sheffield, winter (Round 2)

Project methodology
An innovative multi-method approach combining qualitative and quantitative data collection techniques was developed and employed in this project (Moore *et al.*, 2006). The methodology can be divided into three fundamental components that link with the three key aspects of the project:
• outdoor environmental quality
• indoor environmental quality
• the experiences of city-centre dwellers (perceived environmental quality).

Table 4.1 Summary of data gathered during Designing Environmental Quality in City-Centre Living work package				
Case study area	Semi-structured participant interviews	Photo surveys: (photos taken)	Sound walks: (recordings)	Outdoor monitoring, kerbside: winter (W) summer (S)	Indoor monitoring: homes monitored winter (W) summer (S)
London Clerkenwell, located in north-east of city centre within borough of Islington	34	773	32	7 (W) 3 (S)	30 (W) 20 (S)
Sheffield Devonshire Quarter, located to west of city centre	20	481	11	3 (W) 5 (S)	20 (S) 20 (W)
Manchester City centre, area within the ring road	30	640	29	4 (W)	30 (W)
Totals	**84**	**1894**	**72**	**22**	**120**

Table 4.1 and Figure 4.1 summarise the measurements made at the case study sites. Figure 4.2 illustrates the range of data gathered in one case.

Outdoor environmental quality (OEQ)
The outdoor environmental monitoring involved the intensive monitoring of an urban road system at a number of locations (kerbside) within each city centre. Noise levels (dB(A)), carbon monoxide (CO, ppm), temperature (°C) and particulate matter (TSP, PM2.5) were monitored at various sites within the case study areas over a summer and a winter period.

The monitoring sites were chosen near the residential premises of participants, to allow comparisons between the data. Other considerations for the location of the monitoring equipment included the practicalities of installation, the threat of vandalism, and how representative the site was of the surrounding area. The monitoring sites provided a range of conditions (high and low levels of traffic and pedestrians, and mixed land use).

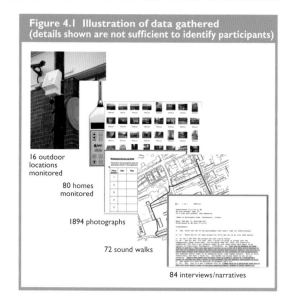

Figure 4.1 Illustration of data gathered (details shown are not sufficient to identify participants)

16 outdoor locations monitored

80 homes monitored

1894 photographs

72 sound walks

84 interviews/narratives

A specially designed noise and air quality monitor, a variation of the Streetbox developed by Learian ltd (now Routesafe, www.routesafe.co.uk), was developed and used: a sound level meter was incorporated into a standard carbon monoxide Streetbox to allow the continuous monitoring of noise and air quality simultaneously (see Croxford & Penn, 1998, for more information on the Streetbox). A Met One E-Sampler (light scatter

Figure 4.2 An example of mapping of photos taken by residents with some pollution information

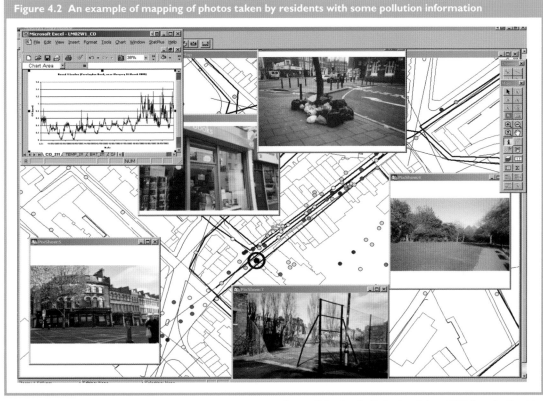

Source: Reproduced with the permission of WIT Press, Southampton

aerosol monitor) was used to monitor the particulate matter (www.metone.com/documents/esamplerParticulate.pdf). Average temperature, CO and PM levels were collected at 15-minute intervals, but average noise levels (Leq,A) were collected at differing intervals (15min, 3min or 1min), depending on the Streetbox used.

Indoor environmental quality (IEQ)
The indoor environmental monitoring involved the measurement of various environmental parameters within each participant's home. A portable Quest AQ5000Pro monitor was used to monitor levels of carbon dioxide (CO_2), carbon monoxide (CO), relative humidity (%) and thermal conditions (°C) (Quest Technologies; http://www.quest-technologies.com/IAQ/aq5000.htm). A HOBO U12-012 (Onset Computers; http://www.onsetcomp.com/node/2250)

was used to measure light intensity. Respirable-size particle counts (0.5 to 5μm) were determined using a portable laser diode particle counter (Met One model 227A; www.metone.com). In addition, noise levels were recorded by using a Quest 2900 Integrating/Logging sound level meter (Quest Technologies; http://www.quest-technologies.com/Sound).

All equipment was placed in the living room of each home, specifically in the breathing zone of a person sitting on a sofa (approximately 1.5m above the floor level) and away from open windows and heat sources. Each participant was asked to complete a daily log sheet, recording certain behaviours (occupancy, smoking, cooking, opening windows) and their approximate time of occurrence. These measurements were taken during a summer and a winter period within each home, with data collected for a period of between two days and one week, depending on the home monitored.

The objective of monitoring indoor air quality was to gain an insight into conditions within residents' homes, and to facilitate comparisons between homes and the outdoor data collected. A 24-hour indoor air quality investigation was carried out within each participant's home during the period from 28 June 2004 to 1 July 2004. Each of the four homes was naturally ventilated, and the occupants had the option of opening or closing windows when they felt appropriate.

Perceived environmental quality (PEQ)
The means of recruitment is key to engaging a diverse range of participants. A strategy was developed that incorporated several different techniques: flyer distribution within the local vicinity; targeted recruitment at residential blocks and community facilities; a press release; information posted on local websites; and the utilisation of local authority and community organisation contacts.

Contact details of a project researcher were given on the flyer, with several contact options (email, telephone and mobile) to provide more opportunities for response. Those contacting the researcher were given information about the project and the processes involved. Respondents were also vetted to see whether they were suitable participants (e.g. whether they lived in the study area, and whether they had lived in the area for over 12 months). The target recruitment number was 30 residents within each case study area. To ensure anonymity each participant was given a reference identification code.

Corporation Street, Manchester

Lexington Street, London

Approximately two weeks before each scheduled interview date a disposable camera (27 exposures, 35 mm film, 400 ISO with flash), a log sheet, prepaid envelope and instructions were sent to the participants. They were asked to take photographs of their local area, noting the time, date, location and a short description of the photograph on the log sheet. We did not want to be too prescriptive in telling participants what to photograph, so the instructions simply stated: 'We would like you to take photos that record both the positive and negative aspects of your area. Please bear in mind how things sound and smell when taking the photos as well as what they look like.' They were given approximately one week to take photographs before sending the camera back to a researcher in the prepaid envelope. The photographs were developed and numbered, and brought to the scheduled interview.

Prior to the start of the interview, participants were asked to complete a short questionnaire (on personal data, household characteristics and local information), and to mark a five to ten-minute walking route around their local area on a map. This walk was undertaken by a researcher and the participant, and recorded with a DAT recorder. Participants were asked not to talk during the walk, but to listen and observe.

On return to the participant's home the photos and the sound walk were used to help direct a semi-structured interview. The interview was based upon general questions about the urban environment, made specific to the resident's locality. The questions were open to interpretation. They included: How would you describe your urban environment? What do you think the air is like outside your home? How would you describe the sound of the area you live in? How would you describe the environmental quality of this area? Participants were asked to refer to their photographs and to the sound walk at any stage during the interview. Details of this multi-method approach can be found in Adams *et al.* (2006) and Moore *et al.* (2006, 2008).

Measurements of outdoor environmental quality
During the VivaCity2020 project, outdoor noise and pollution measurements were undertaken in 16 outdoor locations in three city centres in summer and winter. Carbon monoxide concentrations and noise levels (Leq,A) were measured. Fine particulate matter concentrations (PM2.5) were also measured in one location in each city centre.

In all cases, carbon monoxide levels were well below UK guideline levels (DEFRA, 2003). Carbon monoxide concentrations in the UK tend to be well below UK air quality objectives, with peak levels of about 1–3 ppm compared with an eight-hour WHO guideline level of 8.6 ppm (WHO, 2007b).

cold air above the city can trap warmer, polluted air at low levels, and there is little or no dispersion. The US EPA lists some examples of 'pollution episodes' occurring with temperature inversions (EPA, 2007b). The great smog of London in 1952 also occurred during a temperature inversion (LSHTM, 2007).

Measurements of indoor environmental quality

The average indoor CO_2 levels measured in homes during the study were all below 1000 ppm, which indicated sufficient ventilation. Time series measurements of indoor CO_2 levels were often seen to rise during lunchtime and drop afterwards, later rising and falling at dinner time and again at breakfast time. No clear differences in CO_2 levels were found between smoking and non-smoking homes. Older homes are likely to have greater infiltration from the outside environment and thus lower CO_2 levels, though in areas with higher outdoor levels of air pollution this could increase the concentrations of some pollutants.

Levels of carbon monoxide were within guideline levels for outdoor CO, as mentioned in the previous section. Time series measurements show rises of background levels with outdoor traffic fluctuations, and also occasional peaks due to indoor sources such as gas cooking or unvented heaters.

The mean value of indoor temperatures for most homes complied with comfort guidelines of 21–23 °C: summer temperatures were higher on occasions and winter ones lower. The recorded measurements complied with CIBSE (Chartered Institute of Building Services Engineers) standards for peak summer temperatures in naturally ventilated buildings. Indoor temperatures are affected by outdoor temperature fluctuations. Indoor temperatures were found to be higher than outdoor temperatures, owing to heat retention properties of the buildings, internal heat gains, and occupant behaviour or choice.

The mean PM2.5 concentrations were between 12 and 27 $\mu g/m^3$, with London the highest and Sheffield the lowest. These levels are around the WHO guideline values, and are perhaps a cause for concern: guideline values are an annual mean of 10 $\mu g/m^3$ and a 24-hour running mean of 25 $\mu g/m^3$. High levels of particulate matter are linked to mortality: the smaller the particles, the deeper they are inhaled into the lung, and current thought is that fine particles formed from fossil fuels consumed by vehicles are the most harmful to human health (WHO, 2006).

Noise levels (Leq 5 minutes[1]) varied from a very low 30 dB(A) at night in quiet streets to over 85 dB(A) in busy main road locations during the day. These highest levels are well above the WHO guidelines of 55 dB(A) (WHO, 2000), but most people will not be exposed to levels above 55 dB(A) for 16 hours, unless they live very close to a main road.

During the measurement campaigns outdoor levels of both noise and pollution were generally within guidelines; exceptions were noise levels on the busiest roads, and fine particulate concentrations in London.

Pollution and noise vary with traffic levels, but the day-to-day and even week-to-week variations that occur with economic activity and school and other holidays are often small in comparison with those caused by changes in weather conditions. For example, high-pressure zones with low wind speeds and temperature inversions prevent pollutant dispersion, and so concentrations build up over time. This is sometimes exacerbated by the topology of cities, which are very often in river valleys, so the

Indoor relative humidity measurements were generally within guidelines for comfort (CIBSE, 2006). Relative humidity falls as air temperature rises, so minimum values were recorded at maximum temperature. Homes with the highest relative humidities had high moisture generation and low ventilation. When relative humidity (RH) is over 70%, mould is likely to form on surfaces.

In conclusion, indoor environmental measurements for city-centre homes were generally within guidelines and not a cause for concern. It is possible to see an effect on carbon monoxide concentrations due to external influences, but the concentrations are well within guideline levels. Homes in cities can have high levels of particulate matter, again depending on ventilation by occupants, outdoor concentrations of particulates and infiltration.

Recorded perceptions of the urban environment
Interviews
The city-centre residents took a broad definition of environmental quality. They commented on a range of issues that affect the comfort and advantages of living in the city centre, including noise, air pollution, rubbish, vandalism, fly-tipping, street vomiting and street urination. For some these issues overshadowed life in the city, but others recognised that these negative aspects were only one facet of life in the city.

In providing detailed, rich descriptions of the quality of the environment, the residents highlighted the complexity of these issues. They commented on the discrepancies in the quality of the environment over different spatial scales (certain locations, streets) and temporal scales (times of day, seasons), and between social groups (young people, residents within social housing). The spatial contrasts were evident through residents' descriptions of their urban environment.

Broom Field, Sheffield

The following quote from participant L17, a 30-year-old male resident living in the heart of Clerkenwell, London, expresses this when he was asked to describe the area:

L17: *'Yeah, and there are lots of little hidden areas like that which are really nice in Clerkenwell. But then you sort of, it almost makes it worse when you kind of emerge from those lovely quiet areas and go onto the main, big two big main roads, Clerkenwell Road and Farringdon Road, and then it's sort of – oh God – and there's all these lorries and buses.'*

Most residents interviewed reflected upon the contrasts in conditions and levels of pollution experienced within their local area. Comparisons were particularly evident when participants talked about the air quality: when asked 'What is the air like outside your home?' most residents answered by evaluating the air on their street against other locations both within and outside their neighbourhood. The quote below illustrates this: when asked about the air quality outside their home, participant S32 compared the street (which is located within the Devonshire Quarter, Sheffield) with other parts and streets within the city centre. The participant, either consciously or unconsciously, used certain criteria to assess the quality of the air:

Interviewer: *'What's the air like outside your home?'*

S32: *'I think it's pretty good. There are parts of the city centre where I don't even want to breathe, but I don't get that sense around here. I noticed it a little bit, we were coming back onto West Street, and I certainly notice it when I'm walking round Castle Market, that area, just, you can just smell the fumes. But not round here, I don't notice that. And I think partly that is because there are trees and there's the green space, so whether that's a psychological aspect to the, to the air that we think we're breathing, but I don't feel it's, it's too bad.'*

Most residents who were interviewed undertook this process of deliberation: comparing and assessing the conditions of the environment. These assessments were not only based on the variety of conditions experienced within the local area; residents also made comparisons with other geographical areas (different neighbourhoods, cities and countries) and other, past times. For instance, one elderly resident, L13, who had lived in Clerkenwell, London, all his life, remarked upon his experience of the great smogs in the late 1950s, caused by air pollution:

Canal Street, Manchester

L13: *'I was in London when we had the smog. It was four days thick. It was like continual night it was, you went out and you, like walking through a fog it was.'*

Interviewer: *'So even here in Clerkenwell?'*

L13: *'All, we had it yeah. Walking, you had to look to see what was across the road before you attempted to cross.'*

Interviewer: *'So when was that?'*

L13: *'In 1957, something, something like that. Four days solid. That brought in the Clean Air Act.'*

Interviewer: *'So you can compare for me the air then and the air now. What comparison would you make between how the air was then and how the air is now?'*

L13: *'Well I'll give you an idea as well. Walking up Farringdon Road, but coming up from the station, you know we walked down and turned off, coming up from the station all them shops and houses coming up there were black...'*

Residents' assessments of the quality of the environment relied on local and personal indicators. References were made to visual markers (e.g. rubbish in the street or graffiti on a building), auditory markers (e.g. hearing traffic noise), smells markers (e.g. smells from diesel fumes, urine or rubbish) and personal markers (e.g. impacts on individuals' health or well-being). Concentrating on air quality, the quotes below by two city-centre residents, one living within Clerkenwell, London (L4), the other within Manchester city centre (M23), illustrate this point:

Interviewer: *'What's the air like outside your home?'*

L4: *'It seems, the air seems alright, but I know it's not.'*

Interviewer: *'Tell me about that.'*

L4: *'Well, because I'm asthmatic you pick up, you pick up on, on the air quality. There might be some mornings where I'll be all right. Other mornings I go out and I'm feeling breathless. And that's, when I go out for a walk part, well I think it's partly, well wholly due to the traffic pollution because we're on a major road, which is Goswell Road leading to City Road, which sees a volume of traffic there.'*

Table 4.2 Analysis of subjects depicted in photos recorded by project participants

Photo code	Total	London	Sheffield	Manchester
Local facilities and amenities	575 (30.4)	243 (31.4)	130 (27)	202 (31.6)
Built environment	306 (16.2)	131 (16.9)	59 (12.3)	116 (18.1)
Views	182 (9.6)	72 (9.3)	53 (11)	57 (8.9)
Transport	160 (8.4)	52 (6.7)	37 (7.7)	71 (11.1)
Open space and urban nature	158 (8.3)	79 (10.2)	38 (7.9)	41 (6.4)
Combination	146 (7.7)	54 (7)	36 (7.5)	56 (8.8)
Environmental issue	138 (7.3)	77 (10)	28 (5.8)	33 (5.2)
Social issue	94 (5)	45 (5.8)	27 (5.6)	22 (3.4)
Missing (category unknown)	87 (4.6)	11 (1.4)	47 (9.8)	29 (4.5)
Management	36 (1.9)	8 (1)	19 (4)	9 (1.4)
Crime and antisocial behaviour	12 (0.6)	1 (0.1)	7 (1.5)	4 (0.6)
Total	**1894**	**773**	**481**	**640**

Interviewer: *'What's the air like outside your home?'*

M23: *'It's fine. It just, you know, I don't really, I mean I don't … I can presume that it's not very healthy right, based on the dust I can see collecting now at my windows I think it's probably quite bad. But I don't really, I don't feel it, you know I, I can't make you know any … I don't think I can really sense it though.'*

It is evident that people's perception and understandings of pollution are embedded into their individual experiences, often from local knowledge and encounters. The impact of environmental factors on the overall perception of the quality of the environment should not be neglected. A holistic approach needs to be taken when looking at urban sustainability, focusing on the wider relationships and connections between the environment, society and the economy. Negative evaluations of the quality of the environment could reflect a person's overall dissatisfaction with their neighbourhood; alternatively, satisfaction with a residential area or neighbourhood may lead to a downplaying of any negative aspects of the quality of the environment. When people were asked whether they liked the area they lived in, most stated that they really enjoyed living in the city centre: the

benefits of living there (e.g. accessibility, amenities, vibrancy and transport connections) outweighed the negatives (e.g. pollution and crime). This was succinctly described by L41, a mother of one living on Clerkenwell Road, the main access route into Clerkenwell, London:

Interviewer: *'How would you describe your urban environment here?'*

L41: *'Um, I think it's quite a, it can be a little raw in terms of the pollution and the traffic because we live on the main road. But in general I perceive it as um, quite positively. Because I suppose its amenities and its proximity to the West End.'*

Accessibility was often seen as a positive aspect of life in the city centre: residents frequently commented on the proximity to other areas within the city, and the benefits this brought them. They remarked on the wider spatial connections of their local area: intriguingly, this emphasises that people do not see their local area in isolation, but as part of a wider system with wider interactions and trade-offs. These comments are marked by a tolerance of the negative aspects of city-centre living (such as pollution). The quote about traffic noise by participant L1, an elderly man living on one of the most congested roads within Clerkenwell, London,

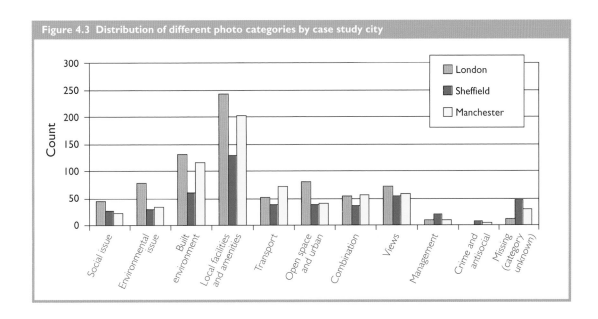

Figure 4.3 Distribution of different photo categories by case study city

echoes what many residents said about the negative aspects of living in the city: 'I mean it's a terrible thing to say but you just get used to it.'

The level and scale of information provided from objective and subjective accounts of environmental quality are obviously different, from the general to the local, from individual experiences to the measured. Residents identified disparities they had experienced in the environment (e.g. quiet/loud areas), and explained daily encounters with these issues. These subjective accounts are very different from the monitored data obtained from objective recording of the conditions at various sites. But, combined together, they provide detailed knowledge of the environmental conditions in the case study area, documenting the spatial nature of air and noise pollution to differing extents.

Residents' photographs

In total, 1894 photographs were taken by participants during the case studies. Table 4.2 and Figure 4.3 present the main contents of all the photographs, coded across various categories, for the three cities. Each code encompasses a range of

features of the urban environment: for instance, 'Built environment' includes landmarks, architectural features and street furniture.

In addition to being used within the interviews, the photographs were also analysed to explore what factors, both positive and negative, contribute to residents' experiences of the urban environment (the participants had been instructed to take photographs of the positive and negative aspects of living in the city). Details of the photo coding and the methodology can be found in Moore *et al.* (2006, 2008). Despite its limitations, the coding has enabled the data to be used to identify general trends and patterns.

All factors represented in photographs are those that residents feel influence the quality of the urban environment that is also their residential environment. Key aspects of the urban environment that occur in residents' photos are 'local facilities and amenities', the 'built environment' and 'views', demonstrating their potential importance for an

Glossop Road, Sheffield

for their input. However, this necessitates the use of targeted recruitment and public engagement practices. Recruitment is a time-consuming process, but with effort a diverse range of participants can be mobilised. We argue that the use of a qualitative methodology would give urban designers a better understanding of local communities.

It is clear from the interviews that residents' perceptions of their urban environment may be significantly improved at the design stage by addressing 'doorstep' issues such as litter, graffiti and fly-tipping, so as to provide mechanisms to prevent or minimise the impact of such issues. The provision of suitable infrastructure to enable more sustainable behaviour, such as recycling provisions, should also be incorporated at the design stage.

understanding of environmental quality. Local facilities and amenities were a predominant code in each city, covering approximately a third of all photos taken. Having accessibility to a wide range of shops, cafés and restaurants close to people's homes is a key feature of city-centre living.

Design impact on urban environmental quality

A user-led framework has been used to gather data on the urban environmental experience. This provides access to an excellent knowledge base, and a more detailed understanding of environmental quality.

Often, key deliberations about urban design do not adequately involve local people. In the interviews we have found that many are unaware of the timing of planning decisions, and of their scope for involvement. Local residents have valuable understandings of their local environment that would be beneficial to urban designers if they were listened to. Even people who are not actively involved in their communities, and could not be described as community activists, can be targeted

By monitoring sound levels and air quality continuously at the street scale it is possible to highlight trends and spatial variations that can be used by urban designers when considering the layout of new developments or regeneration projects. This raises questions as to how this information and data are communicated to residents and local people in a format that is accessible and clear.

There are implications for urban design if one attempts to design to a measurable noise level. For example, who can legitimately decide what is valued, and how decisions can be reached regarding what sounds are positive and negative, and what should be preserved?

There are clear, strong links between environmental quality and other sustainability issues (crime, social, economic, urban regeneration and renewal): this clearly illustrates that an integrated approach to urban design is required. Once a particular design becomes part of a hardened network of practices, institutions, norms and values, it will be difficult to change.

URBAN ENVIRONMENTAL QUALITY 73

From the research we find that the practical, mundane and routine aspects of city-centre living (e.g. proximity to points of employment and consumption) are often its key attractions. These factors were considered more important than lifestyle and cultural attractions, which are often commonly emphasised within the urban gentrification literature. Environmental issues of noise, pollution and traffic were all mentioned as disadvantages of city-centre living.

Designers should consider how a project improves both indoor and outdoor environmental quality. They should consider positive sounds, good views, reduced air pollution, increased social interaction, and reduced litter and graffiti, enabling good environmental management procedures to be easily implemented.

References

Adams, M., Cox, T., Moore, G., Croxford, B., Refaee, M. & Sharples, S. (2006) Sustainable soundscapes: noise policy and the urban experience. *Urban Studies*, **43** (13), 2385–2398.

Berglund, B. (2001) Perceptual characterization of perceived soundscapes in a residential area. *Proceedings of the 17th International Congress on Acoustics*, Rome, Italy, Vol. 3 (CD-ROM).

Bickerstaff, K. & Walker, G. (2001) Public understandings of air pollution: the 'localisation' of environmental risk. *Global Environmental Change*, **11** (2), 133–145.

Bröer, C. (2002) Sound, meaning and politics: the social construction of aircraft noise annoyance. *Proceedings of Forum Acusticum 2002*, Sevilla, Spain (CD-ROM).

Carrer, P., Maroni, M., Alcini, D. & Cavallo, D. (2001) Allergens in indoor air: environmental assessment and health effects. *The Science of the Total Environment*, **270**, 33–42.

CIBSE (2006) *Guide A: Environmental design*. London: CIBSE.

CLG (2006) Building regulations. Retrieved 2 February 2007 from http://www.planningportal.gov.uk/england/professionals/en/4000000000001.html

Croxford, B. & Penn, A. (1998) Siting considerations for urban pollution monitors. *Atmospheric Environment*, **32** (6), 1049–1057.

DEFRA (2002a) *The UK National Noise Incidence Study (NIS) 2000/2001*. London: DEFRA.

DEFRA (2002b) *The UK National Noise Attitude Survey (NAS) 1999/2000*. London: DEFRA.

DEFRA (2003) UK air quality national objectives. Retrieved 2 February 2007 from http://www.defra.gov.uk/environment/airquality/strategy/addendum/pdf/aqs_addendum.pdf.

DH (2007) Committee on the Medical Effects of Air Pollutants. Retrieved 7 February 2007 from http://www.advisorybodies.doh.gov.uk/comeap/state.htm.

Ellaway, A., Macintyre, S. & Kearns, A. (2001) Perceptions of place and health in socially contrasting neighbourhoods. *Urban Studies*, **38** (12), 2299–2316.

EPA (2007a) Basic information: formaldehyde. Retrieved 7 February 2007 from http://www.epa.gov/iaq/formalde.html#Health%20Effects.

EPA (2007b) Origins of modern air pollution regulations. Retrieved 7 February 2007 from http://www.epa.gov/apti/course422/apc1.html.

Gjestland, T. (1999) Assessment of annoyance in a multi-source noise environment. *Proceedings of Internoise '99*, Fort Lauderdale, FL, USA, pp. 1297–1298.

GLA (2004) *Sounder city: The Mayor's ambient noise strategy*. London: GLA.

Grimwood, C. (1997) Complaints about poor sound insulation between dwellings in England and Wales. *Applied Acoustics*, **52** (3–4), 211–223.

Harvey, D. (1996) Social justice, postmodernism and the city. In C. Hamnett (ed.), *Social geography: A reader*, pp. 291–308. New York: John Wiley & Sons.

Hiramatsu, K. & Minoura, K. (2000) Response to urban sounds in relation to the residents' connection with the sound sources. *Proceedings of Internoise 2000*, Nice, France (CD-ROM).

Hollander, A. de & Staatsen, B. (2003) Health, environment and quality of life: An epidemiological perspective on urban development. *Landscape and Urban Planning*, **65** (1–2), 53–62.

Kamp, I. van, Leidelmeijer, K., Marsman, G. & de Hollander, A. (2003) Urban environmental quality and human well being – Towards a conceptual framework and demarcation of concepts: a literature study. *Landscape and Urban Planning*, Schulte-Fortkamp, 5–18.

Kaur, S., Nieuwenhuijsen, M.J. & Colvile, R.N. (2005) Pedestrian exposure to air pollution along a major road in Central London, UK. *Atmospheric Environment*, **39**, 7307–7320.

Klaboe, R. (2000) Analyzing the impacts of combined environmental effects: can structural equitation models (SEM) be of benefit? *Proceedings of Internoise 2000*, Nice, France (CD-ROM).

Klepeis, N.E., Nelson, W.C., Ott, W.R., Robinson, J.P., Tsang, A.M., Switzer, P., Behar, J.V., Hern, S.C. & Engelmann, W.H. (2001) The National Human Activity Pattern Survey (NHAPS): a resource for assessing exposure to environmental pollutants. *Journal of Exposure Analysis and Environmental Epidemiology*, **11**, 231–252.

Lercher, P., Brauchle, G. & Widmann, U. (1999) The interaction of landscape and soundscape in the alpine area of the Tyrol: an annoyance perspective. *Proceedings of Internoise 99 (28th International Congress of Noise Control Engineering)*, Fort Lauderdale, FL, USA, pp. 1347–1350.

LSHTM (2007) The Big Smoke: Fifty years after the 1952 London smog – a commemorative conference. Retrieved 7 February 2007 from http://www.lshtm.ac.uk/history/bigsmoke.html.

Maffiolo, V. (1999) *De la caractérisation sémantique et acoustique de la qualité sonore de l'environnement sonore urbain.* Unpublished PhD thesis, Université du Maine, Le Mans, France.

Moore, G., Croxford, B., Adams, M., Cox, T., Refaee, M. & Sharples, S. (2006) A multi-method approach to extracting objective and subjective accounts of road traffic related noise and air pollution. *Proceedings of the Second Environment & Transport Conference*, Reims, France (CD-ROM).

Moore, G., Croxford, B., Adams, M., Cox, T., Refaee, M. & Sharples, S. (2008) The photo-survey research method: capturing life in the city. *Visual Studies*, **23** (1), 50–61.

Mudarri, D. & Fisk, W.J. (2007) Public health and economic impact of dampness and mold. *Indoor Air*, **17**, 226–235.

ONS (2005) Cigarette smoking. Retrieved 2 February 2007 from http://www.statistics.gov.uk/cci/nugget.asp?id=866.

Onuu, M.U. (2000) Road traffic noise in Nigeria: measurements, analysis and evaluation of nuisance. *Journal of Sound and Vibration*, **233** (3), 391–405.

Oreszczyn, T. & Pretlove, S. (2000) Mould index. In J. Rudge & F. Nicol (eds), *Cutting the cost of cold*, pp. 122–133. London: E & FN Spon.

Parkes, A., Kearns, A. & Atkinson, R. (2002) What makes people dissatisfied with their neighbourhoods? *Urban Studies*, **39** (23), 2413–2438.

Pirsig, R. (1976) *Zen and the art of motorcycle maintenance.* London: The Bodley Head.

Saunders, T. (2002) *The boiled frog syndrome: Your health and the built environment.* Chichester: Wiley-Academy.

Schulte-Fortkamp, B. (2002) Soundscapes and living spaces: sociological and psychological aspects concerning acoustical environments. *Proceedings of Forum Acusticum 2002*, Sevilla, Spain (CD-ROM).

Tallon, A.R. & Bromley, R.D.F. (2004) Exploring the attractions of city-centre living: Evidence and policy implications in British cities. *Geoforum*, **35**, 771–787.

Volz, R. (2002) Interaction between picture and sound on the perception of an observer: a video installation. *Proceedings of Forum Acusticum 2002*, Sevilla, Spain (CD-ROM).

WHO (2000) Guidelines for community noise. Retrieved 21 March 2007 from http://www.who.int/docstore/peh/noise/guidelines2.html.

Great Windmill Street, Soho, London

WHO (2006) Air quality guidelines: global update. Retrieved 21 March 2007 from http://www.who.int/mediacentre/factsheets/fs313/en/index.html.

WHO (2007a) Noise and health. Retrieved 21 March 2007 from http://www.euro.who.int/Noise.

WHO (2007b) Environmental health criteria 213: Carbon monoxide. Retrieved 21 March 2007 from http://www.inchem.org/documents/ehc/ehc/ehc213.htm.

Zannin, P.H.T., Diniz, F.B., Calixto, A. & Barbosa, W.A. (2001) Environmental noise pollution in residential areas of the city of Curitiba. *Acustica Acta*, **87** (5), 625–628.

Zannin, P.H.T., Diniz, F.B. & Barbosa, W.A. (2002) Environmental noise pollution in the city of Curitiba, Brazil. *Applied Acoustics*, **63** (4), 351–358.

Footnote

1　The equivalent average continuous noise level that has the same power as that actually measured over the time interval.

CHAPTER 5
THE SENSORY CITY

Mags Adams, Trevor Cox, Ben Croxford, Gemma Moore,
Steve Sharples and Mohamed Refaee

Henrietta Street, Hulme, Manchester

This chapter[1] focuses on residents' sensorial experiences of the 24-hour city, highlighting the interaction between the physical environment and the emotional and sensorial responses of the people within it, that together co-produce the sensory 24-hour city. As Irving states, 'the city is not simply architecture alone, but a curious melding of "flesh and stone"' (Irving, 2004, citing Sennett, 1994), and it is this melding of flesh and stone that is considered in this chapter – the physical and sensual relationship that residents of the city have with where they live. While literature on the 24-hour city has focused on specific aspects of city development and management, such as the effects of alcohol on crime rates and behaviour, it has so far neglected the senses as a means of understanding and organising the city. The academic field of sensory cities is a developing one, and there is a burgeoning literature on sensory urbanism. However, these studies tend to focus on historical cities or on specific (usually minority) groups' sensory engagements with particular cities.

VivaCity2020 starts to bridge this gap between the more policy-driven knowledge and understandings of 24-hour cities and the more subjective familiarity and experience of sensory cities, by using the theoretical ideas of sensory urbanism as tools for identifying residents' use of and engagement with the city. With reference to the theoretical concepts of emplacement and displacement (Howes, 2005) and VivaCity's empirical work with city-centre residents, this chapter concentrates on the sensory dimensions of being a resident in the 24-hour city. Furthermore, the chapter is used as a platform for raising some key issues that need to be addressed in the further development of 24-hour city centres. Data were gathered from residents in the cities of London, Manchester and Sheffield through the media of sound walks, interviews and photo surveys, and their voices are used to argue that the 24-hour city is a place rich with sensual encounters, and that these are highly significant components of people's everyday urban experience. Ultimately it is argued that designing the 24-hour city necessitates an awareness of this sensory human engagement with the city.

A sense of belonging

Sensory engagement with the city is aptly described by Pallasmaa (2005: 40), who argues against the hegemony of the visual:

> 'I confront the city with my body; … I experience myself in the city, and the city exists through my embodied experience. The city and my body supplement and define each other. I dwell in the city and the city dwells in me.'

The materiality and sensoriality of the city are one through the medium of personal bodily experience; the city is a domain of sensory opportunities that change according to time, space, culture and traditions, and which the individual interacts with in the context of defining their own place within it.

Many commentators (Picker, 2003; Howes, 2005; Drobnick, 2006; Landry, 2006) have engaged with the subject of sensory cities, cumulatively illustrating how the sensory mix of urban culture is politically and socially influenced. For example, Picker (2003), in chronicling changes in the Victorian soundscape, emphasises the many sensorial influences experienced by Londoners in the Victorian era: 'During a period, in fact, when complaints surged against the stink of the Thames and smoky London air, street sounds also came to be represented as threatening pollutants with noxious effects' (p. 66).

At this time the street organ was vilified as 'a nuisance' by middle-class professionals, particularly those working from home. They presented street music as 'horrible sounds' (p. 62) and 'a kind of bodily infection' (p. 67), and applied pressure politically until an Act of Parliament was passed that enabled residents to ask street musicians to move on if they were disturbing 'the ordinary Occupations or Pursuits of any Inmate of such House, or for other reasonable or sufficient Cause' (p. 63 and fn 74). Picker demonstrates that by attempting to control the auditory realm to meet their own sensibilities, the Victorian middle classes were asserting and establishing themselves as a formidable social presence. He advises caution, however, in being too hasty in judging or denouncing the responses of those Victorian professionals, by raising a contemporary analogy with the modern phenomenon of telecommuting, stating that with the 'newer auditory challenges of accelerated technology – the bleeps and blare of cell phones, car alarms and superhighways – battles continue for spaces to concentrate and to write' (p. 81). Many of the tensions of working at home may be as apparent today as they were in the Victorian era, albeit with different causality. When the home is in a mixed-use area of a 24-hour city, the sources of these tensions may be manifold.

The Victorian city was a place of sensory constraints and restrictions imposed by a burgeoning middle class whose philanthropic motives, directed towards creating a better society for everyone, sat alongside their struggle to assert power and authority. Picker observes that 'many scholars have noted the sensory elements of social reformers' growing fascination with urban others' in the Victorian era. He emphasises Stallybrass and White (1986), who write of the 'transformation of the senses' that Victorian policing policy enacted, arguing that an 'increased regulation of touch' arose between lower and middle classes during the period, as well as a new emphasis on visual and olfactory senses (as in The Great Stink of 1858) (p. 147, fn 81).

The parallel with the 24-hour city is the contemporary enactment of regulations that censor and transform the senses, including: the noise laws that reduce sound to deliberations about sound levels (see Adams et al., 2006, for a discussion of how deterministic approaches to noise in terms of sound levels might homogenise city soundscapes); the drinking laws that restrict social interaction on the street and other public spaces; and the entertainment laws that regulate the performance of live music. These may be endorsed in good faith, or by legal requirement, by local authorities intent on making cities better places for everyone, but they highlight the struggle between creating a moral order and asserting power and authority. Ultimately the effect may be a sanitising of the city and a transformation of the senses – indeed, a sensory censorship.

Utilising Howes' (2005) concept of emplacement helps to clarify this sensory transformation, the sensuous interrelationship of body, mind and the environment which ultimately brings about the residents' urban experience – their feeling of 'home' and belonging (p. 7). In contrast, the counterpart concept of displacement acknowledges discordance between people and places, a feeling of homelessness and being disconnected from one's physical and social environment (p. 7). These tensions between emplacement and displacement are symptomatic of city life.

Narratives and practices of 24-hour city residents were gathered during the VivaCity2020 project in London, Manchester and Sheffield by means of sound walks, photo surveys and semi-structured interviews (see Adams et al., 2008, for full details of the methodology used), and it was found that the tensions between emplacement and displacement resonate in the associations that inhabitants have with the physical and social space surrounding their homes. Of course, the city itself has multiple identities, as a residence for some and a destination for others. The research presented here focuses purely on experiences of the resident, not the visitor.

While others have focused on mobility in and through the city (Sheller & Urry, 2000; Pooley et al., 2005), gentrification of the city centre (Smith, 1987) and attitudes towards city living (Heath, 2001), they have not engaged in the multisensorial culture within which these are embedded. The Western bias of this study (in terms of both location and entrenched epistemological perspectives) encourages a focus on the five senses as determined by Aristotle (see Synnott, 1993, cited in Zardini, 2005, for a discussion of the reduction of the sensorium into five senses). However, following Howes (2003), who criticises the practice of studying the senses in turn without

exploring their interactions, attention is turned to the sensory interactions occurring within the city, thereby identifying a hotbed of stimuli where the co-presence of sensory inputs is considerable. By focusing on narratives of the sensory practices and values of residents within their city, we can better understand the organisation of the urban spaces (both physical and social) they live within, and start to understand what constitutes the 24-hour city.

Sensing the 24-hour city

A salient feature of sensory experience is that it provides a strong sense of place and belonging. In *Village Bells*, Corbin (1999) investigates the fundamental role of sound as a means of communication in the lives of ordinary people. While his study is of the French countryside rather than the urban environment, he emphasises the important point that sensory influences have both political and cultural dimensions, and that they are situated historically. The traditional peal of bells as a call to prayer was only one function of a system that reinforced the physical geographical boundaries of parishes and the political tensions between them, demarcating them through auditory means. Similarly, Law (2001) links sensory experience to urban culture and power relations. In the city of Hong Kong she examines the spaces of the city where Filipino domestic workers engage in mass leisure activities, and she exposes the relationship between space, bodies and sensory experience. By examining the consumption of Filipino food in Hong Kong she provides 'a salient example of how everyday experience can become a performative politics of ethnic identity' as she demonstrates that the 'sensory landscapes of cities suggest less conventional forms of ethnic politics, and reveal how diasporic populations find original ways of engaging with urban life' (p. 278). Within a given city, certain (often minority) groups establish their own sensory landscapes, which shape and reinforce their position within that city and culture and contribute towards broadening the identity of the city itself.

While these studies reveal political, cultural and historical aspects of the role of senses in the city, none of them engages with the contemporary 24-hour city as a locus of sensory investigation, or the connections between the material and sensorial engendered by it. With this in mind, and considering the tensions between emplacement and displacement, it is to the physical and social urban environment, the liveability of 24-hour cities, that we now turn. What we find is that feelings of emplacement work at many levels, not just at the neighbourhood level, and that in the 24-hour city residents' feelings of emplacement may be the result of their social and cultural interactions, which are often spatially distant and not part of their everyday interactions within their local community. As a consequence, a sense of displacement may exist at the local level, where people feel disconnected from their physical and social environment, but this may not necessarily result in a sense of social marginalisation.

In this section, the narratives of the residents themselves are used to discuss the sensing of the 24-hour city. Participants are referred to by a unique ID number that was assigned to them to ensure anonymity throughout the project and their city of residence.

The city from a height

De Certeau (1984) suggests that it is only with height and distance that the observer really sees the city – 'his elevation transfigures him into a voyeur' (p. 92) – and that at ground level 'the ordinary

Moor Shopping, Sheffield

practitioners of the city live "down below", below the thresholds at which visibility begins' (p. 93). This is undoubtedly accentuated at 110 storeys, where de Certeau's observer is located, but is also relevant to the resident of the city living on the fifth, sixth or seventh floor of an apartment block. The resident is a voyeur from his or her little window up above the city, but at street level he or she becomes the 'ordinary practitioner' (p. 93) experiencing everything in close proximity. It is this contrasting experience we are concerned with here.

At street level the city is experienced at full scale, in immediate contrast with the elevated voyeur's position, which provides a distance and perspective unobtainable from the ground. From above, sight is indeed the prevailing sense as others' activities are observed at a distance down below, giving the resident a familiarity with everyday occurrences within the wide view afforded by their window:

> '… I like looking over the cityscape … One advantage of living in a high-rise block of flats I think you get a good view … I enjoy it, it's nice to sit out there, have a look' (S3, Sheffield)

and enabling them to keep an eye on things:

> '… it is a very good view. [My children] sometimes panic a bit because I can see them sort of from every angle now [in the playground]. I've got a balcony, so it enables me to go out onto the balcony and if I look say to my left I can see … if they're coming down, coming out of the playground … And

Leather Lane, Clerkenwell, London

then from my bedroom window there's another angle looking to your right, so in all sorts of directions.' (L23, London)

At height, an impression of order is implied that is belied by a more intimate familiarity with the same spaces, an intimacy enabled by the descent to street level, allowing navigation of and interaction with the city and augmenting sensorial experiences. These more personal, bodily encounters with the city disrupt the image of order as the city proffers full auditory, olfactory, gustatory and tactile experiences at this level.

The city at street level
At street level sights, sounds, smells, tastes and touches are encountered directly and immediately, again in contrast to experiences from above street level, where, although sight remains constant, sounds and smells waft past the 'elevated voyeur', making their origins difficult to pinpoint. At street level the street corner is a sensory boundary, filtering, insulating, even masking sensorial experiences.

Simply turning the corner can result in significant changes in auditory experience:

> '… the other thing on noise is that there are very quiet areas. I mean when we walked up Cowcross Street I always think it's amazing how quiet that is …'.

Pockets of relative tranquillity exist, affording the urban resident routes through the city that provide some respite from the main arterial routes:

> '… it almost makes it worse when you kind of emerge from those lovely quiet areas and go onto the main, big two big main roads, Clerkenwell Road and Farringdon Road, and then it's sort of – oh God – and there's all these lorries and buses.'

Suddenly the sensorium is bombarded again by the sight, sound, smell and taste of the traffic as it services the machine of the city. The quiet areas are appreciated. They constitute a haven, and give the city a feel that, in Tuan's words, 'eludes analysis' (Tuan, 2005: 78) and is not quite definable:

> '… and it feels really sort of really lovely, … there are lots of little hidden areas like that which are really nice in Clerkenwell'. (L17, London)

The 'tranquil' city
Another potential site of tranquillity in the 24-hour city is the public park, or green space, providing both a haven and a rich sensory environment. As a haven, the green spaces provide locations that enable auditory experiences that contrast starkly with the 'low fi' soundscape of the city, areas where ambient noise levels are low and where discreet sounds may, at least sometimes, be heard clearly (see Schafer, 1994 for a clear exposition on the move from hi-fi to low-fi sonic environments). Thus, for the resident, green spaces can be enticing, inviting to office workers at lunch, to parents with young children and to teenagers as a spot to hang out. And yet it can also be repelling, affording refuge to drug dealers

and drinkers, and becoming the site of other 'unsanctioned' activities. The tranquil space is a place of contrasts with spatial, temporal, and seasonal variations.

Of course, urban green space does not consist of parks alone, but encompasses canal towpaths, abandoned plots, allotments and other spaces. Both Manchester and London have networks of canals running through the city, which are used by residents as pedestrian thoroughfares:

'… the canal walk's actually quite, quite good. You can walk all the way down to Castlefield from here, can't you, so that's quite a nice walk.' (M14, Manchester),

and as displacement from the auditory overload of the city:

'The canal's a lovely place, it's a beautiful place … It's very tranquil. You can't hear traffic, you've just got the calmness of the water … just to stand there and listen to these little narrow boats chugging along … a little chug chug chug chug.' (L4, London)

The experience of using the canal can be highly sensory, heightening awareness of proximity to others, of the gradual accumulation and slow decay of carelessly disposed rubbish:

'… there's all litter just flowing down the canal again, brought on because there's no bins anywhere along the whole canal.' (M16, Manchester)

and the smells that ensue, of the 'unsanctioned' uses of the space that make it inviting to some and uninviting to others:

'It's a cruising ground so, so I'd probably be quite out of place with loads of gay men.' (M12, Manchester)

The allure of designated city parks themselves may change over time, at one time affording sanctuary to illicit activities:

'… that was a shocking place that Devonshire Green really, people on drugs and such and needles all over the place, it wasn't a safe place to go.' (S1, Sheffield)

and at another time, changing to provide safe community spaces where children play and people walk:

'… I feel comfortable walking round here [now], no problem at all.' (S1, Sheffield)

'… if you go in the summer there tends to be lots of students down there, go down and kick a football around, whatever, have a picnic, have a few drinks I think I dare say. You sometimes see people with musical instruments down there playing. It's quite nice.' (S3, Sheffield)

'Since it's started to get nice weather it's just, it's been really well utilised, there's always people playing football and the skate park is busy all year round … And the weekends it gets very busy with kids.' (S5, Sheffield)

However, the drugs and the needles in a public park conjure up images of two distinct, haptically charged scenarios: the drug user getting their fix, their sensory focus on the immediacy of their created euphoria; and in direct contrast the child finding the abandoned needle, touching it, picking it up, asking 'What is this?' To the child the park is a sensually engaging play space, along with everything contained within it, but to an accompanying adult numerous dangers lurk in the shadows: the needles, the dog mess, the broken glass.

The night-time city

As day morphs into night, realms of the city change: footfall on the street increasingly becomes that of the entertainment seeker; the babble of voices and smell of smoke and beer emanate from the pubs or, with a smoking ban now in place, the pub itself merges with the street as benches are set outside to aid smoking customers; rich, enticing aromas waft from the city restaurants; and the sound of music emerges from clubs and pubs as the doors swing open to allow in customers. Living in close proximity to (and sometimes on top of) such establishments ensures the city resident partakes in the ensuing auditory and olfactory occurrences, at least passively if not actively, while simultaneously being free to elect whether to engage haptically and gustatorially, and whether to view from the inside or the outside.

Passive engagement includes pleasurable as well as offensive stimuli. Smells that can 'evoke strong emotional responses' (Classen *et al.*, 1995) entrance, allure, repulse and unnerve. When walking through the city at night, awareness of concealed doorways and entrances is heightened, an unexpected shuffle, a voice, a repugnant smell can all be alarming. The doorway and the alleyway play host to the activities of those who cannot, or will not, wait until they find the privacy of their own space:

> *'On the way to Spar, down that road we walked, there was two guys shagging in a doorway and as they heard me coming by there was like rustling of belts and stuff, but yea I mean, I'm gay so I know, you know I know what goes on … I mean I must admit it's not particularly nice having it on your doorstep.'* (M14, Manchester)

and those who find that their own bodies cannot hold onto the quantities of liquid that have been consumed:

> *'[People] often urinate in the corners and down the streets – you often get kind of, you know, streams of urine coming down these back streets, which is not very nice.'* (L17, London)

The smell of urine is the smell of weekend mornings:

> *'… the other joy is of course on a Saturday morning when you get up early and go to the gym round the corner it, it stinks of piss.'* (M5, Manchester)

Negotiating the nocturnal city brings with it a visceral engagement with the activities of others.

Claremont Close, Finsbury, London

While some local authorities address this situation with urinals that pop up in strategic places:

> *'I notice that they've put some, some of those portable urinals by the main bus station and personally I think we could do with some more round other busy kind of areas.'* (M14, Manchester)

they cater only for the desperate male, the female reveller being left to seek out more secluded, but still public, spaces:

> *'We used to get quite a lot of people urinating in the doctors' car park opposite … [it's] summertime and it certainly happens more. And it's not just men either, it's girls as well.'* (S4, Sheffield)

But despite these rather odious sensory associations, a more active engagement is the absolute raison d'être for city-centre living for many of its dwellers who themselves contribute to the hoards of entertainment seekers indulging in the city's sensorial offerings in the evenings. In the city, the delights of eating out are pandered to, a range of palates are catered for, and it is possible to eat food from practically any nationality on earth:

> *'You know it's gastro pub city round here basically. I mean it's, the choices in restaurants is just amazingly good.'* (L24, London)

> *'If you walk, turn out and turn right, the first place, which is a really cheap place, is a pasta place … I then move onto a Clerkenwell restaurant which is*

really nice, and then there's a Michelin Star, Club Gascon, around Smithfield, which is spectacularly good food ... Turnmills does quite a good fish menu ... And pasta joints, Thai restaurants, oh you have just a fantastic choice.' (L36, London)

The resident of the 24-hour city lives in a cosmopolitan world where the cultural offerings are aplenty. Access to theatres, art galleries, cinemas, pubs, music, everything is on the doorstep:

'There are theatres, there are art galleries, there are cinemas, but I have very little to do with them although I'm led to believe they're among the best you can get. I mean very occasionally we will go and see a foreign film at the Cornerhouse ... But my personal involvement in the local culture is very much in music ... [this] is Night and Day, which is my favourite music venue in the city, which is about ten minutes walk from here ... and again it's somewhere I feel at home.' (M3, Manchester)

Crucially, however, not all want to live right on top of it all; just round the corner, tucked away slightly is perhaps better:

'I really love the city but, but where I live I want it to be private and quiet, but then I can go to the bars, I can go to the theatre, I can go to the noise if I want to, I can go to the mayhem. I like the mayhem of the metropolis but I don't want to live in it, well I want immediate access to it so I want to live in a city, but I want to live in a quiet street.' (L19, London)

Proximity is key: close enough to engage with, but not so close that it intrudes. People enjoy being able to indulge a passion, whether for music, art, theatre with other like-minded people, all at a short distance from home:

'... it's seven minutes. You can still hear The *Archers and be there in time for the performance, and I like that.'* (L37, London)

but they also want sensory respite, the quiet haven of home.

Sensory conflict in the city

As we have illustrated, one of the big attractions of living in the city centre is the sheer variety of activities on offer: the abundance of eating establishments panders to any whim and every pocket; the range of theatres, cinemas and galleries facilitates a cultural immersion unattainable outside the city; the variety of music on offer caters for diverse musical tastes. The 24-hour city resident can consume them all. However, this raises another key issue that runs through the residents' narratives recounted above. With activities taking place throughout the day and night there will of course be conflict. The infrastructure that facilitates and supports the attractions of the city must also be considered in order that the 24-hour city be a functional, liveable city. The sensorial stimuli of the city include the smell and taste of pollution, the noise of buses, cars, horns and sirens, the sound of people coming and going at all hours, the sight and smell of vomit and urine. These negative sensory stimulators are brought about, quite simply, because of the positive ones, and this co-production of the positive and negative can bring about conflict as some people enjoy the positive production while others experience the negative aftermath. Of course, many people experience the positive and the negative together.

Developing this point further, perhaps the greatest challenge to the future of the 24-hour city is working out how to facilitate the maximisation of the positive sensory characteristics of residing in the city, while reducing or minimising the negative ones; maximising emplacement while minimising displacement. This might be achievable through design-led interventions, including building design that acknowledges the transmission of sensory

Margery Street Estate, Clerkenwell, London

information, insulating against the negative impacts and enabling choice over those considered positive. Orientation of building facades, uses of spaces within buildings, and juxtaposition of living and commercial premises are all significant in this regard. However, it is essential that decision-making processes concerning city-centre development respect subjective sensorial diversities alongside any technological or design-led interventions, if the ultimate goal is liveable 24-hour cities.

Diversity and liveability in the 24-hour city

The 24-hour city as a concept has been utilised to market the expansion of city-centre areas to accommodate residents in mixed-use developments where they will live in close proximity to retail, commercial and entertainment facilities. This urban renaissance is presented as a dynamic means of meeting sustainability objectives for urban areas that include high-density, compact and well-connected centres. What are not generally considered are the diversities that make up these 24-hour cities, the individuals that frequent the spaces, the variety of uses to which individual spaces are put, and the requirements of different sectors of the community when living in close contact in high-density spaces. We have now established the multiplicity of sensorial experiences in the city and the significance of these diverse stimuli to residents' everyday lives. While it is often argued that diversity is essential to vibrancy in the city, we have demonstrated that the 24-hour city creates sensorial diversities that bring about conflict, and that there is a need to acknowledge and manage them.

We have demonstrated the complexity of the 24-hour city in the diversity of activities that take place within the city. Not only is the city a home for the resident, it is their shopping centre, their green space,

their playground. The same public space (for example the public park) may attract different groups of people at different times: families playing games; friends picnicking; office workers eating; people drinking; and drug users. It may temporarily be utilised to hold concerts or festivals, or may simply be a passing place, a route to somewhere else. For the resident living close to such a space each of these activities will have a different sensory impact and will shape how they feel about residing in their home; they may be active participants in some of the activities and passive bystanders for others.

By exploring such a space from a sensory perspective it is possible to start to understand some of the tensions that exist within the space, and the planning and design issues that might ensue. A key issue for developers therefore is designing spaces that accommodate these alternative uses (and determining which uses should be accommodated), while at the same time enabling the resident to exercise choice over their participation.

In an era where mixed use is heralded as the design solution to city-centre living, more attention needs to be paid to the scale at which mixed use is workable. This entails questioning whether it is at the building level (with a mini supermarket or pub at ground level, for example), at the level of the block (with pubs adjacent to residences and retail outlets), or within some geographical area (such as Clerkenwell in London) that mixed use is successful. Unless there is a specific development aspiration for a city centre as a whole, it is difficult to create a level of mixed use beyond the building level: for instance, there has to be some way of acknowledging and integrating current patterns of use into the design of regenerated areas. Exploring the city from the resident's sensorial perspective helps in generating an understanding of the physical and sensual relationships within the city – we can begin to understand what works, and for whom, and build these into the design and regeneration process.

Recommendations

We conclude by raising a number of key issues that need to be addressed in the further development of 24-hour city centres:

- the need to design city spaces for simultaneous and yet diverse uses
- the co-production of positive and negative sensory stimuli, and the conflict this can engender
- the need to design city spaces that incorporate multisensory experiences
- the challenge of maximising the positive sensory characteristics while minimising the negative ones
- the challenge of introducing research methods that provide sensory evidence to design decision-makers, along with an understanding of how this evidence might be utilised in the design process.

References

Adams, M., Cox, T., Moore, G., Croxford, B., Refaee, M. & Sharples, S. (2006) Sustainable soundscapes: noise policy and the urban experience. *Urban Studies*, **43** (13), 2385–2398.

Adams, M., Moore, G., Cox, T., Croxford, B., Refaee, M. & Sharples, S. (2008) Environmental quality, housing and city residents: a sensory urbanism approach. In P.J. Maginn, M. Tonts & S. Thompson (eds), *Qualitative housing analysis: An international perspective*, pp. 187–210. Bingley, UK: Emerald.

Certeau, M. de (1984) *The practice of everyday life*. Berkeley: University of California Press.

Classen, C., Howes, D. & Synnott, A. (1995) *Aroma: The cultural history of smell*. London: Routledge.

Corbin, A. (1999) *Village bells: Sound and meaning in the 19th-century French countryside* (M. Thom, trans). London: Papermac (Macmillan).

Drobnick, J. (ed.) (2006) *The smell culture reader*. Oxford: Berg.

Heath, T. (2001) Revitalizing cities: attitudes toward city-center living in the United Kingdom. *Journal of Planning Education and Research*, **20** (4), 464–475.

Howes, D. (2003) *Sensual relations: Engaging the senses in culture and social theory*. Ann Arbor, MI: University of Michigan Press.

Howes, D. (ed.) (2005) *Empire of the senses: The sensual culture reader*. Oxford: Berg.

Irving, A. (2004) Cities: an anthropological perspective. *Anthropology Matters Journal*, **6** (1), Introduction.

Landry, C. (2006) *The art of city making*. London: Earthscan.

Law, L. (2001) Home cooking: Filipino women and geographies of the senses in Hong Kong. *Ecumene*, **8** (3), 264–283.

Pallasmaa, J. (2005) *The eyes of the skin: Architecture and the senses*. Chichester: Wiley-Academy.

Picker, J.M. (2003) *Victorian soundscapes*. Oxford: Oxford University Press.

Pooley, C.G., Turnbull, J. & Adams, M. (2005) Kids in town: the changing action space and visibility of young people in urban areas. In A. Schildt & D. Siegfried (eds), *European cities, youth and the public sphere in the twentieth century*, pp. 90–109. Aldershot: Ashgate.

Schafer, R.M. (1994) *The soundscape: Our sonic environment and the tuning of the world*. Rochester, VT: Destiny Books.

Sheller, M. & Urry, J. (2000). The city and the car. *International Journal of Urban and Regional Research*, **24** (4), 737–754.

Smith, N. (1987) Of yuppies and housing: gentrification, social restructuring and the urban dream. *Environment and Planning D*, **7**, 151–172.

Stallybrass, P. & White, A. (eds) (1986) The city: the sewer, the gaze and the contaminating touch. In *The politics and poetics of transgression*, pp. 125–148. London: Methuen.

Tuan, Y.-F. (2005) The pleasures of touch. In C. Classen (ed.), *The book of touch*, pp. 74–79. Oxford: Berg.

Zardini, M. (ed.) (2005) *Sense of the city: An alternate approach to urbanism*. Montréal: CCA and Lars Müller.

Footnote

1 This chapter is an adapted version of a paper published in *Senses and Society*, **2** (2), 201–215. Reproduced with permission from Berg Publishers.

CHAPTER 6

INCLUSIVE DESIGN OF 'AWAY FROM HOME' TOILETS

Jo-Anne Bichard and Julienne Hanson

Clerkenwell Road, London

Introduction

This chapter reports findings from research conducted in London, Manchester and Sheffield city centres that studied the design of the 'accessible' toilet cubicle, which should be provided for customer or public use wherever there is standard toilet provision. The term 'accessible toilet' refers to a purpose-designed cubicle provided for use by disabled people. It is large enough to accommodate a wheelchair user or someone who needs assistance in order to use the toilet, thereby creating inclusive toilets for all. The location and design of accessible toilet facilities merit scrutiny, because it is essential to provide these and to design them correctly, so that disabled people can participate in every aspect of city life on equal terms to able-bodied people. Since its introduction in the 1970s, the unisex accessible toilet has become one of the central symbols of an accessible environment.

At a practical level, good 'away from home' toilet provision is essential to urban sustainability because it makes cities accessible to a wide range of users, including women, children, disabled and older people. Public toilets[1] are necessary if walking and public transport – modes of transport that are more sustainable than the private car – are to be encouraged within the city centre. Finally, good

public toilet provision improves the visual and sensory urban realm and reduces environmental degradation, factors that lead to a more sustainable urban environment. However, in order to be sustainable, toilet provision needs to be located so as to fit into the way the city is actually used, and in ways that support environmental balance and water conservation, reduce sewerage and pollution and eliminate street urination.

The UK's first modern public toilets opened on 14 August 1852, opposite the Royal Courts of Justice in Fleet Street, London. Their purpose was to combat the spread of disease, which was attributed to street fouling (London Assembly Health and Public Services Committee, 2006). Under the 1936 Public Health Act local authorities were given the right to build and run public toilets, but the provision of public toilets has always been discretionary, and no statutory duty has ever been placed upon local authorities to provide them. Public toilet provision therefore falls outside normal urban design decision-making processes and, from the perspective of VivaCity2020, the topic affords an opportunity to study a grass-roots issue that is not recognised by the sustainability agenda, but which nonetheless may contribute substantially to urban sustainability.

Toilets house an apparently mundane activity, but the public toilet is a highly contested 'site'. It shelters a very intimate activity that takes place in public space, in proximity to complete strangers. Public toilet provision therefore provides a graphic illustration, at a scale that can be grasped, of how conflicting issues can impact on design within the context of the 24-hour city. Differential provision has always existed for men and women. Usually equal floor areas are allocated to male and female toilets but, because male urinals take up less space than a WC cubicle, the number of actual facilities provided for men tends to be greater. This gender discrimination may not have been challenged because women are largely unaware of the number of public facilities, particularly urinals, that are provided for men. Moreover, while under the terms of the 1936 Public Health Act it is lawful for a local authority to charge an entrance fee for the use of a public toilet, it is unlawful to charge a fee to use a male urinal.

At present, many of the public toilets that do exist are not accessible to people with physical, sensory or cognitive impairments or limitations. Their unavailability severely limits disabled people's access to the city and its resources at all times of the day and night. Disabled people are therefore being denied opportunities to lead independent lives because the poor design of cities and urban centres poses barriers to accessing suitable housing, public transport, public spaces and buildings. However, the implementation in October 2004 of Part III of the Disability Discrimination Act (DDA): Access to Goods, Facilities and Services (2002) addressed the design of physical features within the built environment that are a barrier to access. This included the provision of, and access to, suitable toilet facilities. In this respect, design has the potential to redress a historic imbalance and, following the enactment of Part III of the DDA, many private providers have taken steps to make toilets for customer use accessible, thus bringing about a shift in the overall balance of provision from the public to the private sector.

The promotion of the 24-hour economy in recent years has fuelled alcohol-related evening and night-time activity in city centres. This appeals to a narrow 18–30 age group, in consequence of which older and disabled people can often feel excluded from

Brown Street, Sheffield

the city centre at night, and especially at the weekend. The needs of late-night 'binge' drinkers often compete for resources with those of daytime shoppers, and public toilets are often colonised at night by unplanned uses such as vandalism, drugs or sex, which make the environment unattractive or even dangerous for ordinary members of the public. This has led to a conflict between toilet users, who require easy access, and toilet providers, who aim to defend the facilities like a fortress (Greed, 2003) in order to deter unwanted uses.

Research by the British Toilet Association, an organisation that campaigns for better toilet provision within the UK, has indicated that fewer than three in every ten public toilets remain open at times that serve the expanding night-time economy (Chisnell, 2003). Some local authorities feel that it is preferable to deal with late-night street urination rather than to manage the potential consequences of crimes that may occur in unattended public toilets. Most have no plans to improve their local public toilets in the foreseeable future, as there is a widespread perception that this will not encourage more people to use the town centre at night (Mummery, 2005).

Where they do provide facilities, local authorities tend to be most concerned about street urination, and in this respect several innovative products such as 'pop-up' or portable urinals have been installed at known urination 'hot spots'. One council, Westminster, a participant in the research, provides temporary urinals in the West End at weekends. It is estimated that this measure alone prevents more than 10000 gallons (45000 litres) of urine from being deposited in alleyways or against buildings each year, at great cost to the cleansing services. However, while public urinals serve the requirements of the youth-orientated night-time economy, the current designs have obvious limitations in respect to females and disabled men, and arguably they divert resources away from general toilet provision that would benefit society as a whole.

Conflicting needs such as these, and dimensional 'dissonances' between different user groups, affect just about every design feature of the accessible toilet, so it is simply not possible to optimise the design to suit everyone: someone will always be inconvenienced or excluded. From a design perspective, the accessible toilet cubicle is not so much the 'smallest room' as the 'most complex building'. It is this complexity that the VivaCity2020 research project set out to investigate, in order to make recommendations about how accessible and inclusively designed 'away from home' toilets contribute to environmental, economic and social sustainability in the 24-hour city.

Barriers to access in city centres

It is estimated that the average person goes to the lavatory between five and eight times a day, and people with chronic health conditions and disabilities may need to use the toilet even more frequently. During periods away from home people rely on toilet provision offered by a number of service providers. Some areas of the city may have public toilets provided by local authorities, whereas others may have no public toilets, leaving people to rely on the toilets provided for customers by local businesses such as cafés, bars, pubs and fast-food restaurants.

People who require more space than is normally provided in an ordinary toilet cubicle, or who need the assistance of grab rails when toileting, may therefore find it difficult to identify a facility in the city centre that meets their requirements. This can become a real barrier to disabled people's participation in mainstream society. Previous research (Kitchin & Law, 2001) has reported that the dearth of accessible toilet provision requires many disabled people to restrict their visiting patterns to areas of the city where they know there is an 'away from home' toilet that meets their needs. They use the graphic metaphor of 'the bladder's leash' to describe the restrictions that this places on disabled people's freedom to explore the urban environment.

The most recent major audit of UK public toilet provision carried out by the Audit Commission in 1996 found that of 10000 public conveniences provided by local authorities, only 3500 had facilities accessible by disabled people. In addition, only 1330 had adequate baby-changing provision. Prior to the introduction of Part III of the Disability Discrimination Act (DDA) in October 2004, many local authorities around the UK closed their public toilets. Accurate statistics are notoriously difficult to come by, but the numbers of toilets closed by local authorities have been estimated at anything between 10% for the country as a whole between 2000 and 2004, and as much as 40% in London since 1999 (London Assembly Health and Public Services Committee, 2006). In the first quarter after the DDA was introduced, many more facilities were closed in the UK. Although repeated problems with vandalism and antisocial behaviour, coupled with the

Chorlton Road, Hulme, Manchester

cost of repairing damage to the facilities, were often held to blame for these closures, the perceived and actual cost of making local authority provision accessible under the remit of the DDA has also been given as a reason for withdrawing the service. Ironically, legislation intended to widen access to the built environment may inadvertently have reduced it in this one important respect.

Figures representing the number of people affected by toilet closures vary widely depending on the source, but what can be inferred from the available data is that a significant percentage of the population may be considered (by themselves or by the definitions found in various models) to have an impairment that 'has a substantial and long-term effect on [their] ability to carry out normal day-to-day activities' (Disability Rights Commission, 2002: 119). In 2001, the Office of National Statistics reported that 8% of adults recorded having difficulties going out-of-doors (ONS, 2002). A conservative estimate in 2002 reported that 12–13% of the population has some form of impairment (Oxley, 2002), while a current estimate by the Disability Rights Commission suggests that one in five adults in Great Britain is a disabled person (Disability Rights Commission, 2002). Of these, 5% are estimated to require the use of a wheelchair.

Whitfield (1997) suggests that the 1.6 million people who have continence concerns would benefit from improved access to public toilet provision. The needs of all those who have at some point been diagnosed with cancer are now protected under the DDA's remit. People who use urostomy and colostomy bags have particular concerns, as their disability is centred on toileting, often involving a frequent and urgent need to use a toilet to empty or change their bag. Many people within this group of users have full physical mobility. Because they do not 'look disabled' their need for well-designed and accessible facilities is often ignored.

Further breakdowns of the relevant figures reveal that two-thirds of disabled people are aged over 60 years. As a result of the fact that there are twice as many women as men in this age group within the population at large, the majority of older disabled people are female. With the demographics of ageing predicted to shift progressively over the next 30 years, current estimates suggest that by 2030 the population aged over 65 will have doubled, while those in the population aged over 80 will have trebled (Atkins, 2001; Frye, 2003). These figures suggest not only that a large proportion of the population may currently experience difficulty in gaining access to many aspects of the built environment owing to the wide array of explicit and unseen barriers to access that currently exist, but also that, unless the issue of accessible toilet facilities is addressed now, the problem is set to increase as a consequence of the 'age shift' that will impact on society in the years to come.

Deficiencies in standard and accessible toilet provision

Even standard toilets cannot be considered to meet the needs of the majority of potential users, as most ordinary provision is not well designed, and may disadvantage or embarrass many able-bodied users. For example, the size of a standard toilet cubicle is inconvenient for many able-bodied users. Those who are particularly disadvantaged include pushchair users, who often have to choose between leaving children outside or folding the pushchair up and carrying it and the child (or children) into a tiny WC compartment. Previous research by Goldsmith (1997) found that many parents were unwilling to leave their children outside the toilet while they used the facility themselves. The alternative of including the child and leaving the pushchair outside the cubicle was considered risky, while attempting to fold it up and bring both it and the child into the cubicle with them was time-consuming and inconvenient. Wheelchair users, those who require a walking aid, less agile or older people and those who are encumbered by luggage all may find it difficult to squeeze into a standard cubicle.

Difficulties do not stop at the toilet door. An essential feature of male toilets that suffers from poor design is the urinal, which is often set at a height that is inconvenient for many men and boys to use. Likewise, in women's facilities there is rarely a lower WC pan set at a height that is suitable for young girls. Hand-washing facilities in both the men's and women's facilities are often set too high for children to use without being lifted by an adult. WC pans in standard toilets are often set too low for people with hip, knee or back problems. These people may not consider themselves to be disabled, but they could benefit from a higher WC pan, and by the inclusion of grab rails within the cubicle. However, such fixtures and fittings rarely form part

of standard male and female toilet provision. Many people would benefit if standard provision was better designed and had improved wayfinding, colour contrast and signage.

Finally, most toilet facilities are provided on an equal basis for men and women, yet research suggests that women take twice as long as men to use the toilet. Many men's facilities may have more than the equivalent provision for women, as urinals take up less space than cubicles. The resulting effect is a gender inequality within standard toilet provision, with men taking half the time and having as much as double the provision, which usually results in women being obliged to queue to use the toilets.

Even where standard facilities are provided, people are understandably reluctant to use them if they are perceived to be inadequate, either because they are dirty or because the facilities are located away from main areas of city life – down side streets, in underground subways, in uninhabited and unsupervised city parks – thus raising concerns about personal safety. Personal safety is also a major concern among teenagers, who report knowing where the public toilets are in their city centre but avoid them owing to their poor reputation as places where one may be attacked.

Many disabled people require assistance from a caregiver of the opposite gender and prefer to use a 'unisex' accessible cubicle, as this does not embarrass their caregiver. However, independent people with disabilities who do not require such assistance may prefer to use the standard facilities located within gender-specific provision. Indeed, some disabled people regard the very existence of the 'unisex' cubicle as a hangover from an era when designing for special needs rather than social inclusion was taken for granted. In some cases, people with visible disabilities have been known to challenge the rights of people with a 'hidden' disability to use the accessible toilet. Ideally, therefore, both accessible cubicles in the men's and women's toilets and a 'unisex' accessible cubicle for wheelchair users and those who require assistance from a caregiver should be provided, to meet everyone's needs.

This is not the only bone of contention, and opinions differ on many other aspects of both standard and accessible toilet design, such as where an adult and baby room should be provided. While some advocate that this should be placed within the accessible toilet, the majority of experts and disabled users assert that a separate adult and baby room should be located in both the men's and the women's toilets. Moreover, people with different medical conditions require different detailed design features within the WC cubicle itself. The most fundamental challenge to dimensional coordination is the actual size and overall dimensions of the WC compartment, since these affect people's ability to access the WC in the first place.

Toilet cubicles specifically designed for disabled people do not necessarily cater for the wide spectrum of disabilities among potential users. For example, the current size of the accessible cubicle may be suitable only for wheelchair users who have a standard self-propelled or pushed wheelchair. Since the accessible toilet was first introduced, wheelchair design has improved to enable many more people to live independently, but toilet design has not kept pace with these changes. Many of today's powered wheelchairs are also larger than the standard wheelchair that the accessible cubicle was originally designed to accommodate. This has not been reflected in the design of accessible facilities, which may therefore be too small for users of large powered wheelchairs and their caregivers to access.

Disabled people cannot even rely upon being able to use a toilet that is designated as accessible, even if they are fortunate enough to locate one close to the area of the city that they are visiting. Despite the fact that the unisex accessible toilet is arguably one of the most tightly specified architectural environments imaginable, providers generally do not follow the recommendations and guidelines that are provided to ensure that the facility really *is* accessible. Even providers such as chain stores and multiples, whose premises tend in other aspects to be highly standardised, have accessible customer toilets that reflect local circumstances. Thus a disabled user who relies on past experience, and assumes that the premises of a familiar service provider will be accessible when visiting an unfamiliar town or city, could discover that the cubicle in that location is not of an adequate size, or does not contain essential fixtures and fittings.

Addressing the design of toilets within VivaCity2020

Well-designed toilets for customer use are an important amenity within any building or urban environment, and the way they are designed should meet everyone's needs, yet users have rarely been consulted regarding the design of these facilities. This absence of user consultation has been addressed in VivaCity2020 projects by holding focus groups and interviews with representatives from many different user groups. These included members of support groups for people with disabilities and chronic health conditions, families with young children, young people, older people, and members of different faith communities. The research reported here was conducted over a three-year period from September 2003 to August 2006, and traced the impact of the introduction of Part III of the DDA, which required service providers to make buildings accessible to disabled people, on the amount and standard of 'away from home' toilet provision. The main objective of the project was to involve disabled users in making design recommendations to architects, designers, planners, manufacturers and providers of 'away from home' toilets.

Street surveys

To arrive at a better understanding of the issues involved, early on in the project street surveys were conducted in the case study areas of Clerkenwell (and Westminster) in London, and in Manchester and Sheffield city centres. In all, 211 able-bodied people – 87 men and 124 women – agreed to be surveyed and answered a short questionnaire. Their ages ranged from 16 to over 65. When asked 'Do you know where the nearest public toilet is?' 59% of respondents answered 'Yes'. However, 75% of respondents in Westminster knew where their local toilets were, compared with only 32% of respondents in Clerkenwell. This may reflect the level of provision in each location, as Westminster is widely regarded as having exemplary provision while Clerkenwell is noted for its lack of public toilets.

Only 33% of all those questioned reported that they had actually used the public toilets that had been provided in the relevant locality. Again, the highest response was in Westminster, with 51% of all interviewees admitting to using their local public toilets. Only 39% of those asked in Manchester said they would use their local toilets. In Sheffield and Clerkenwell less than a quarter (23% and 22%, respectively) would use public facilities. Of all respondents, 63% of men and 69% of women reported that they did not use public toilets. Even so, when people were asked whether there should be more public toilets, over 80% (90% of men and 80% of women) answered 'Yes'. Over 75% of respondents of all ages in all areas involved in the case studies also thought there should be more public provision. Users clearly expressed a need for these facilities, but that provision is only the first step.

Public toilets need to be well designed and well maintained if they are to be well used. When asked to report on the condition of their local toilets, 48% replied they did not know this as they avoided the facilities altogether. About a quarter of all respondents (24%) described the condition of their local toilets as 'Bad', 16% as 'Adequate' and only 13% as 'Good'. The lowest score for respondents' not knowing the condition of their local toilets was in Westminster, where just 23% answered 'Don't know'. Yet Westminster was also the area where the most respondents (49%, or nearly half of all those asked) considered the toilets to be 'Bad'. This rather surprising result seems to be related to the fact that more of the people we spoke to in Westminster knew about and used public facilities, and so they felt better informed and more confident when making a judgement, albeit negative, about their condition.

Given the lack and notoriety of public toilet provision, we asked people, 'Do you prefer to use "private" provision?' such as toilets in cafés, supermarkets, etc. In all, 82% reported 'Yes'. There was no major gender difference in this preference, with 79% of men and 83% of women preferring to use toilets operated by businesses. The area with the highest preference for private toilet provision was Sheffield, with 92%. Westminster scored the lowest, with only 8% reporting that they preferred to use toilets offered by local businesses.

When asked whether they came to the city centre in the evening, this resulted in a clear difference between those age groups who used the city centre at night and those who did not: 70% of those under 44 reported that they came to the city centre in the evening. However, 74% of those aged over 45 said they did not come to the city centre in the evening. When people were asked whether they felt there was adequate toilet provision in the evening, 77% of respondents reported 'No'. Over 70% of men and women of all age groups and in all city centres involved in the study felt that current evening toilet provision was inadequate. These results are in line with the research on local authority provision for quality and diversity in the evening and night-time economy that was reported earlier (Mummery, 2005).

The issue of street urination was explored, with 52% of respondents considering it to be a problem. In many city centres the automatic public convenience (APC) has become a familiar sight, and our survey asked respondents whether they ever used them. Overall, 60% reported that they did not use APCs. However, it appeared that people's attitudes towards this form of provision differed between areas. In Manchester, where APCs form the bulk of public toilet provision, 71% reported that they did use these facilities. By contrast, only 14% of respondents in Westminster used APCs. A clear gender difference emerged, with 64% of women reporting that they would not use APCs, while only 53% of men answered 'No'. Less than a quarter (22%) of those over 65 said they used APCs, and in Clerkenwell no women over 65 used this provision.

Beehive Works, Sheffield

GREGORY FENTON LTD
BEEHIVE WORKS

TO LET
SMALL OFFICES
WORKSHOPS
STORAGE AREAS
RING 0114 272 4525

TO LET
SMALL OFFICES
WORKSHOPS
STORAGE AREAS
RING 0114 272 4525

BRUNCH
BOX
Tel / Fax: 276 2666

BEEHIVE WORKS

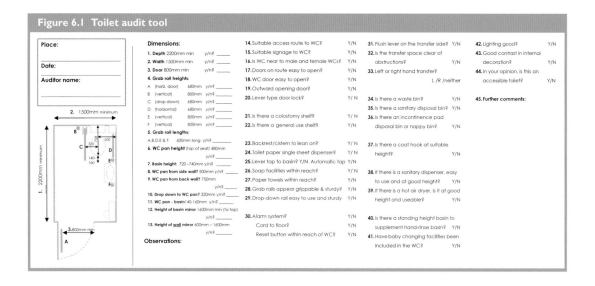

Figure 6.1 Toilet audit tool

During the course of the study, longer and more exhaustive street surveys were conducted with a further 89 people who identified themselves as having mobility concerns. We found that 72% of those people who considered themselves to have some form of disability would use a public toilet if one were available. However, 58% described the condition of public toilets as 'bad', and 73% did not find public toilets comfortable to use.

Nearly nine out of ten (89%) disabled respondents reported a preference for using private provision (customer toilets) in businesses such as supermarkets, cafés and the like. Even more disabled people (91%) felt that there was inadequate provision in the evening, which limited not only their access to the city centre but also the times of day when they could be away from home. For these people, the lack of adequate provision effectively placed a curfew on their use of the city centre. The issue of adequate provision often made people with disabilities think twice about leaving home: 30% reported that a lack of adequate toilets prevented them from going out, while 28% reported that a lack of provision sometimes prevented them from being away from home for as long as they would like.

It was reported earlier that APCs have become a popular response by local authorities to the need for evening provision of toilets, but many of the disabled people who took part in our street surveys found them to be inaccessible: 83% of people with mobility concerns reported they would not use an automatic public convenience. Many disabled respondents said they would rather go home or attempt to use the toilets on the top floor of a department store, than use an on-street APC.

Over half of disabled respondents (57%) did not have a RADAR key,[2] and 61% felt that accessible toilets should not be locked. Thirty-seven per cent of disabled respondents reported preferring the unisex cubicle. As well as catering for the needs of a caregiver of the opposite sex, women with disabilities said they preferred unisex provision as they normally did not need to queue to use the facility. However, 63% of respondents said they would prefer accessible toilets to be available within gendered provision. By contrast with female respondents, some male respondents preferred an accessible cubicle within the men's toilets because they had experienced having to queue for the unisex facility.

Figure 6.2 The accessible toilet that scored the most points of those audited using the toilet audit tool

When respondents were asked whether there were any features of the design of the accessible toilet that they found problematic, many issues were brought to light, and 85% described at least one feature of the toilet that was difficult to use. Nearly half of all wheelchair users (48%) reported that the cubicle lacked adequate turning space for their wheelchair, and a quarter said that the cubicle was too small to accommodate their caregiver. With respect to the height of the toilet seat, 38% of disabled people said they had problems with the recommended seat height of 480 mm, but while 17% found the seat too high another 21% said it was too low. The same proportion of respondents reported difficulty in flushing the toilet, using the toilet paper dispenser, and locking the toilet door.

With respect to other design features, 36% reported problems using taps and coat hooks, 34% reported difficulties using hand-drying equipment, 33% reported difficulty using the soap dispenser, and 30% found grab rails difficult to use. Other problems were reported with disposal bins (29%), door handles (27%), transfer preferences (26%), heavy doors (26%), wash hand basins (25%) and door opening widths or the absence of a shelf (21%). Ninety-seven per cent of disabled respondents to the street survey felt that baby changing should be provided in a separate facility.

Toilet audit tool

In light of disabled users' concerns about the design of the accessible cubicle, and in order to determine how accessible 'away from home toilets' really were, the VivaCity2020 research team, with the help of an access auditor,[3] developed a tool based on the design guidance set out in the British Standard BS 8300 (BSI, 2001) and Approved Document M of the Building Regulations (2003) with which to audit

accessible toilet cubicles in city centres (see Figure 6.1). The tool comprised 44 questions that required a 'Yes' or 'No' answer, and recorded 50 different points of design, layout and fittings guidelines that should be found in all accessible toilets.

One hundred and one accessible toilets around the UK were then audited, mainly but not exclusively from the three fieldwork areas of Clerkenwell in London,[4] Manchester and Sheffield. The vast majority of these toilets (85%) were located in private premises that were open to the public, such as retail outlets, shopping centres, bars and restaurants, transport interchanges and buildings for cultural and leisure activities, in which toilets were provided for customer use, and only a small minority (15%) comprised 'on-street' provision managed by local authorities. This ratio reflected the sharp decline that has occurred in the number of local authority owned and run public toilets in recent years.

Toilet audit tool findings

Of the 101 toilets audited during the course of the research, not one had incorporated all of the design features noted in the toilet audit tool. The accessible toilet that scored the most points offered right-hand transfer[5] and included only 32 out of the possible 50 design features (see Figure 6.2). These included meeting the recommended minimum dimensions for the cubicle's depth and width,[6] and having a WC pan installed at the correct height of 480 mm and a wash hand basin installed at the correct height of 720 mm. The flush was installed on the transfer side of the cistern, and four of the six recommended grab rails were set at the correct heights.

However, areas of design where this particular top-scoring facility could have been improved included eliminating an observed height discrepancy of 30 mm between the drop-down rail and the horizontal wall rail, as having the two rails set at different heights may be awkward for some users when transferring on and off the WC pan. Also, the wall mirror was found to be too high to be used by a person seated in a wheelchair. The toilet paper was not housed in the recommended dispenser, despite the fact that toilet rolls may be difficult for some disabled people to use, as they require grip and strength to access. The soap dispenser was within reach but not fixed, presenting the possibility that it could fall or spill on the floor, becoming a slip hazard. The alarm cord was set on the transfer side of the WC pan, whereas guidance suggests that it should be located near the horizontal wall rail. If the location is as shown in this facility, the cord can obstruct a person transferring from the wheelchair to the WC pan. Moreover, the cord was not long enough, and did not reach 100 mm from the floor. Finally, a bin obstructed the transfer space and the cubicle included a baby change unit, a feature that is regarded as acceptable by some, but which is generally considered to fall short of best practice.

The most accessible toilet in the sample illustrates common design faults that were found in many of the toilets audited, and also some of the requirements that were well understood and so more often correctly installed. The most common feature to have been included in the sample of accessible cubicles audited (98%) was a lever-operated mixer tap that could be operated by anyone with limited manual dexterity or grip. However, in many facilities the taps were placed either in a central position or on the side of the basin furthest from the WC pan, which might mean that the tap would be out of the reach of any users who needed to wash their hands while seated on the WC pan. The fixture that was most often missing from accessible toilets (97%) was a colostomy shelf. This may be due to providers' reluctance to include a flat surface within the cubicle that could be used to take illegal substances.

Aside from installing lever-operated mixer taps, the audit found that the grab rails in 95% of the accessible cubicles were adequately fixed to the wall. Even though they may not have been placed in the correct position, most providers had realised that the rails were intended to support full body weight and needed to be sturdy and reliable. Ninety-three per cent of cubicles were not being used for storage but for their intended purpose, and 92% of cubicles included either a left- or a right-hand WC transfer space so that a wheelchair user could make use of the facility. Nine out of every ten accessible cubicles audited had a clear door opening of 800 mm, so that a wheelchair user could enter the compartment, and 83% of cubicle doors opened outwards, so that in the event of someone collapsing against the door it could still be opened by a caregiver. The same proportion of cubicles had a WC door that was sufficiently lightweight to be used by a person in a wheelchair or with limited strength.

Eighty-three per cent of accessible toilets had an access route that was sufficiently wide for a wheelchair to use and that was not blocked, and the same proportion of routes to the accessible toilet either did not have doors or had installed doors of

Figure 6.3 Example persona

Ileostomy / Colostomy	Persona - Terry

Terry is 55 and has taken early retirement on grounds of ill health. He likes to visit the city centre for shopping and special events at galleries. Yet he has difficulty being away from home for any length of time due to the lack of toilet facilities that cater to his need

Terry has short bowel syndrome caused by the removal of his small intestine during surgery, and now he has to wear an ileostomy pouch. His ileostomy pouch can fill up very rapidly which means he sometimes requires toilet facilities urgently.

To empty his ileostomy pouch Terry has to kneel on one knee in front of the WC pan. He also needs access to a wash basin in order to wet some tissue that he uses to clean the opening of his ileostomy pouch after emptying it. Being able to access tissue for cleaning and drying his pouch is extremely important to him, as is having a clean dry floor to kneel on.

When out in the city centre, Terry relies on the toilets located in department stores, as there are no longer any local authority operated public toilets open. Although he finds the department store toilets to be immaculate, he also tires of having to rely on them and sometimes feels 'chained' to one area of the city. Terry feels there is quite a variety of standards in design and management of away from home toilets, which he finds frustrating. His local shopping centre has toilets that are located on an upper floor and are difficult to reach in a hurry.

In addition, the toilets at the local bus station often have wet floors and poor standards of hygiene. A clean toileting area is extremely important for Terry as if his stoma is not cleaned adequately he can develop health problems.

Terry sometimes limits the amount of time he is away from home, to avoid having to empty or change his pouch in public facilities, especially as he often finds even the 'disabled' toilet does not adequately cater for his specific needs. Terry requires a clean shelf to set out his ostomy supplies, as well as access to hot water. All too often he finds that only cold water is available. Terry also requires the appropriate bin to dispose of his pouches. He often finds that such a bin is not provided in toilets and then he has no resort but to leave his soiled pouch in a disposal bag on the floor. Terry also requires a full length mirror so that he can check that his clothing is appropriately adjusted after changing or emptying his pouch. Terry has a RADAR key but often finds even locked toilets are poorly maintained. Terry has also experienced problems if baby change facilities are included in the accessible toilet, as he has been challenged by mothers for using the facility. This is because Terry's disability is invisible and hidden under his clothing. Terry has found these situations extremely distressing and now tries to avoid accessible toilets that include baby changing fixtures.

Design Wish List

A clean shelf to lay out ostomy supplies.

Appropriate bin for ileostomy pouch disposal.

Full length mirror to check clothing after changing pouch.

Separate facilities for baby changing.

Coat hook.

Planning Wish List

More accessible local authority public toilets.

Separate facilities for baby changing.

Management Wish List

Toilets kept clean, with dry floors, a good supply of toilet paper that can be easily reached and a supply of hot water.

Toilets located in accessible areas that can be reached quickly in an emergency.

A clean shelf to lay out ostomy supplies.

Appropriate bin for ileostomy pouch disposal.

Air hand dryers in good working order.

Terry was created in co-operation with members of:
The British Colostomy Association and The Nottingham CIU Group

a suitable weight, dimensions and clearances to make them easy for people with limited strength to open. The last of the top ten features that were most often installed correctly was the alarm system, with 81% of accessible cubicles having a suitable emergency alarm.

However, over a fifth (22%) of the accessible cubicles that were audited were not of the recommended minimum depth (2200mm) or width (1500mm), making them too small for the users they were primarily designed to accommodate. Small wonder, then, that nearly half the wheelchair users who were interviewed during the course of the research (48%) found that the accessible cubicle lacked adequate turning space for their wheelchair. Only 6% of

cubicles had the correct configuration of grab rails fixed according to the recommended measurements set out in the regulations. This may explain the finding that 30% of the users consulted by the research team reported that the grab rails in accessible toilets were difficult to use.

In 87% of the accessible cubicles, coat hooks had either not been included or had been placed at a height that a seated user could not reach. Over a third of the users surveyed (36%) reported that they had experienced these difficulties with coat hooks in respect of accessible cubicles. In 80% of the accessible cubicles that were audited, the

St Mary's Parsonage, Manchester

recommended single-sheet toilet paper dispenser[7] had not been installed. In many cubicles a large-roll toilet paper dispenser had been used, which many able and disabled people find difficult to use. Nearly 40% of the users surveyed reported that they had difficulty accessing toilet paper when using the accessible cubicle, because the toilet paper dispenser either was out of reach or was not the recommended design.

Other features of the accessible cubicle that were often installed incorrectly or omitted altogether included the fact that only 17% of cubicles had provided the correct distance of 140–160mm between the WC pan and wash basin, just 14% of cubicles had the alarm reset button in the correct position next to the WC pan, and only 13% of cubicles had coat hooks set at a height that was accessible to a wheelchair user. Eighty-eight per cent of accessible toilets did not provide paper towels or a suitable wall mirror, and only one in ten cubicles had a general shelf. Fewer than one in ten female

cubicles had provided a sanitary towel or tampon dispenser. The toilet audit conclusively demonstrated that very few supposedly 'accessible' toilets conform to the specification required for inclusive access.

Personas

An important output from the research was the development of 'personas' as a tool to communicate disabled people's needs to architects, designers and toilet providers. The personas, an example of which is provided in Figure 6.3, can be used to assist service providers and design professionals when assessing how current and future 'away from home' toilet provision may be improved to cater for everyone's needs. The personas articulated the varied needs of our informants, describing their lifestyles and aspirations in a holistic way that did not reduce them to a stereotype. The personas were designed from detailed interviews, conducted by telephone, in person and through focus groups.

Nearly 250 people contributed to the 42 personas that were developed during the course of the research.[8] These personas represented a range of ages, abilities, faith and gender concerns regarding toilet facilities. The needs of people who required space for adult changing, families visiting the city centre and individuals who required assistance from a caregiver (as well as the caregiver's own needs) and the concerns of young people when using away from home toilets were all addressed by creating personas to articulate their requirements.

Participants in focus groups and interviews were asked what they liked to do in the city, and how the lack of adequate toilet provision became a barrier that inhibited or prevented access to the city centre.

Interviewees were asked about each aspect of the design of an accessible toilet that was recorded on the toilet audit tool, from the entry and exit to the signage, the height of the WC pan, the soap dispenser and people's preferences in respect of the toilet paper dispenser and hand-drying facilities.

Interviewees revealed that they experienced the most problems with the physical design specification for the accessible toilet cubicle. A total of 315 items were mentioned by the 42 personas, which is an average of 7.5 items per persona. Altogether, the personas raised 77 separate issues that they wished to see included or improved in respect of toilet design. The top 12 items mentioned most often by the personas were:
- non-slip flooring (17 mentions)
- larger standard cubicles (15)
- good, bright lighting (13)
- a paddle flush on the transfer side of the toilet (13)
- provision of a shelf in the cubicle (12)
- provision of a coat hook (11)
- the hand wash basin and other fixtures set at the correct distance and height in relation to the WC pan (11)
- good-quality door locks (10)
- larger cubicle that included hand wash provision (9)
- larger cubicle that included a hose or tap for ablution (9)
- locks that were easy to open (9)
- lever action mixer taps (9).

Several of these requirements are not included in current design guidelines or standards.

Eight personas would like to see better ventilation provided in public and customer toilets, a good secure seat on the WC pan, a mirror to check clothing after toileting, and a lightweight, outward-opening door. Seven mentioned the need for a suitable bin for the disposal of changing pads, cubicles that were of a standard design, a level entrance, a preference for a fully enclosed cubicle, a plentiful supply of paper towels, and a soap dispenser that could be operated with one hand.

Relatively small numbers required all the recommended grab rails to be installed and to be placed at the correct height. Other items mentioned by just a few personas included good-quality urinals that offered a choice of heights, and a WC pan that was at least 480 mm high. The issue of a height-adjustable changing bench was also mentioned by several personas, as was the need for grab rails to be installed in some standard cubicles. A few personas expressed a specific preference for unisex facilities. Also mentioned were the need for a good-sized basin in the facility that was suitable for washing items such as colostomy bags, the need for a key scheme or smart card to control access, and for privacy screens to be erected around urinals. A small number of personas required a hoist or a free-standing, height-adjustable changing bench, family toilets, a plentiful supply of hot water, a WC pan at a height that was suitable for children, taps and basins so designed that they did not splash onto the floor, and a single-sheet toilet paper dispenser.

Some suggestions were related to the sensory environment of the toilet, including the need for a low-stimulation environment, fixtures and fittings that were obvious and intuitive to use without instructions, glare-free fixtures and fittings, and background music to mask the sounds of toileting.

Several items were raised in relation to children. These included safe storage for pushchairs, child seats to be available in the male and female toilets, baby-changing facilities in the men's toilets, and a larger changing table that was suitable for toddlers.

A total of 182 items were mentioned by personas in respect of management, 4.3 per persona, in relation to 21 different management-related issues. The top management issues included:
- regular cleaning (34)
- well-stocked soap dispensers (27)
- well-stocked toilet paper dispensers (26)
- well-stocked paper towel dispensers (17)
- the provision of bins for disposable pads, gloves, towels, etc. (11)
- locks that are well maintained and kept in good working order (10).

Smaller numbers of personas mentioned that disposable wipes should be provided, or stressed the benefits of providing strong, secure toilet seats. Other issues relating to management included the need for a good supply of warm water, good lighting, air hand dryers that were kept in good working order, wide tear-off paper to be provided, the need for dry floors, and for bins to be kept out of the transfer space. Some would also have liked dispensers that showed the level of stock remaining, and it was also mentioned that good ventilation and temperature control were needed in accessible toilets. Some of these management issues overlapped with the design issues previously discussed, so need to be addressed by both architects at the design stage and facilities managers when the premises are in use.

Though the planning authorities do not have a statutory duty to provide public toilets, several planning items were mentioned by our personas. However, these items were less numerous than either design or management, with 74 items raised

altogether, representing an average of 1.8 items per persona. These related to 12 distinct planning issues. Each persona raised only one, two or three issues.

The most important space planning issue, with 15 mentions, was the need for increased provision. Fifteen personas also raised issues at the interface between planning and design, such as ensuring that there is more choice in the range of toilet cubicles provided. The next most important planning issue, with nine mentions, related to the need for more evening provision, while seven personas raised the issue of gender parity in toilet provision.

Smaller numbers of personas mentioned the need to plan for good, unobstructed access to toilet facilities, and some suggested that provision should be made in every town centre for a toilet with an adult changing bench and/or hoist. Others wanted family toilets to be provided in all town centres, adequate signage to the toilet facilities, toilets in safe, well-used locations, and toilets provided as standard at all transport facilities. The issues of unisex facilities and free public toilets were also raised.

Toilet templates

By studying the demand for and use of accessible toilets in city centres by means of street surveys, the toilet audit tool and the creation of personas, the research team was able to pinpoint disabled users' needs. The research identified several common or generic requirements that linked what some might consider quite different disabilities and health conditions. This led us to design templates for a wide range of inclusive and accessible toilets that amplified

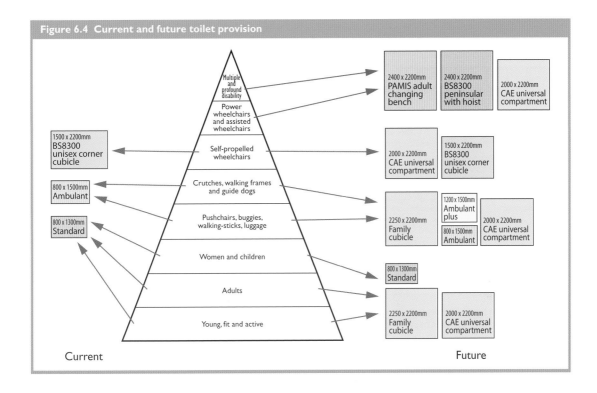

Figure 6.4 Current and future toilet provision

These have been shown, to scale, on the left-hand side of Figure 6.4, which illustrates current and future toilet provision.

The most widely available cubicle designs have been matched with their intended populations in a population pyramid (after Goldsmith, 2000), where the area covered by each layer in the pyramid conveniently indicates the proportion of the population involved. The pyramid can be split notionally into two: a large 'base' of able-bodied individuals, and a top 'cone' of people with disabilities. The bottom (widest) layer of the pyramid represents fit and active people, both male and female, who do not experience any architectural barriers. Row two also represents normal adults who are less active but can still move about freely. Row three represents women of all ages, who are considered to be 'architecturally disabled' owing to the gender inequality that is inherent in current provision, and which has resulted in the need for women to queue.

the recommendations published in BS 6465 (BSI, 2006) *Sanitary Installations*, BS 8300 (2001) *Design of buildings and their approaches to meet the needs of disabled people*, and Approved Document M (2003) *Access to and use of buildings*, as well as drawing on design guidelines produced by the many access groups consulted in connection with the project.

At the time the research was conducted, three preferred designs for an accessible toilet cubicle, all specified in Approved Document M (2003), were widely in circulation.[9] They were:
• ambulant cubicle, provided in larger standard toilet facilities
• unisex corner accessible cubicle
• peninsular accessible cubicle, generally regarded as suitable only for installation in a situation where assisted toileting is required.

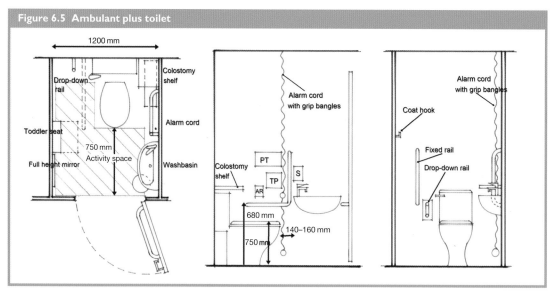

Figure 6.5 Ambulant plus toilet

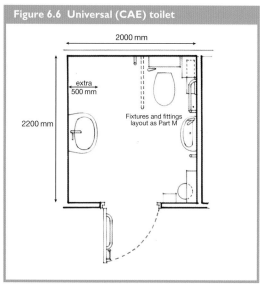

Figure 6.6 Universal (CAE) toilet

This row highlights the needs of women with babies and toddlers, young girls and older women, who are all expected to use standard provision.

Row four represents older people who, although less active generally, do not identify themselves as having a disability, as well as families with young children who require pushchairs. Row five represents ambulant disabled people who need a stick or frame to move about safely but who may feel that, as non-wheelchair users, they also cannot use the accessible toilet. These groups could use an ambulant cubicle in standard provision, if this were provided. Row six represents independent wheelchair users whose toileting needs have been met by the provision of a unisex accessible WC compartment, and rows seven and eight represent users who need assistance to go to the toilet and scooter users, respectively. At present, their needs are not catered for. As Figure 6.4 shows, the vast majority of users are currently forced to rely on the smallest standard toilet cubicle design, large numbers of disabled people rely on the accessible cubicle, and a very small minority of the population, whose needs are more complex, require the largest and most specialised cubicle space for toileting.

However, the VivaCity2020 research has shown that in reality many more people regularly used the accessible toilet cubicle than the population that it had been designed to serve. For example, there were many people whose disability was hidden but who still required certain design features found in the accessible cubicle. In addition, the lack of provision

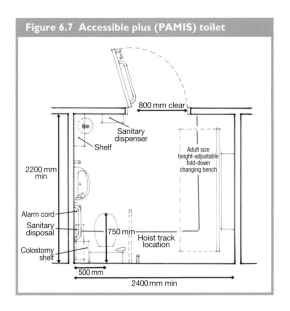

Figure 6.7 Accessible plus (PAMIS) toilet

Figure 6.8 Family toilet

for women resulted in some women choosing to use the accessible facility even though they did not have a disability. The lack of family-friendly toilets resulted in mothers taking sons and fathers taking daughters into the accessible provision. As a consequence, disabled users who must use the accessible cubicle reported that they often have difficulty in finding a vacant toilet due to its use by people whom they perceive to be able-bodied.

Generally speaking, design guidance that was intended to specify the minimum standard for provision has been taken to be the maximum that was required. Moreover, where there was once too little guidance on the design of toilet facilities, now there is an abundance, much of which differs in minor respects from that set out in the British Standards and Building Regulations. With so much information available, it could be argued that designers face great difficulty in determining the most appropriate solution to the design of an inclusive and accessible toilet.

At the same time, the reported experience of many users was that the minimum level of provision in accessible toilets did not adequately cater for their specific needs. Some users needed more space and others less; some users required all the grab rails specified in design guidance while others needed only one or two. There is no optimum solution that suits everyone. People's needs have to be met by providing the right mix to suit local demand.

On the right-hand side of Figure 6.4, the cubicle designs in widespread use have been supplemented by four more, which build on existing provision by offering enhanced space standards that allow access for a wider range of users:
- ambulant plus cubicle (Figure 6.5)
- universal cubicle (CAE) (Figure 6.6)
- accessible plus cubicle (PAMIS) (Figure 6.7)
- family cubicle (Figure 6.8).

This group of templates includes the Centre for Accessible Environment's recommended 'universal cubicle' that meets the basic standards of accessible provision in small premises where only one toilet compartment can be accommodated, and a toilet compartment recommended by PAMIS, a charity that campaigns for adult changing places for people with profound and multiple learning disabilities, who may need the assistance of up to two caregivers. Two more designs have been developed by the research team to cater for people who required more space that was provided in an ambulant cubicle, and for family use.

On the right-hand side of Figure 6.4 the proposition is illustrated that if these additional cubicles were provided in most situations to augment those already in existence, every group would be able to exercise a choice as to which form of provision they preferred to use. Providers, on the other hand, would be able to match the variety of cubicles they installed to their customer base. Providing a greater range of cubicles to cross-cut Goldsmith's population pyramid should help to overcome the problem identified by the VivaCity2020 research that there is insufficient choice in the range of cubicles that is currently provided to meet the demands of all sections of today's diverse society.

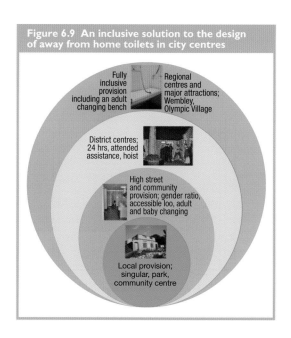

Figure 6.9 An inclusive solution to the design of away from home toilets in city centres

Fully inclusive provision including an adult changing bench — Regional centres and major attractions; Wembley, Olympic Village

District centres; 24 hrs, attended assistance, hoist

High street and community provision; gender ratio, accessible loo, adult and baby changing

Local provision; singular, park, community centre

Recommendations

A hierarchy of accessible toilet provision in the 24-hour city

Inclusive design tries to address the needs of all society's members, so that no one is excluded because of poor design quality based on an inadequate understanding of user needs. However, one of the key criticisms of the inclusive design philosophy is that it is impossible to design a 'one size fits all' solution. However, it is clearly unreasonable to provide each and every type of toilet shown in Figure 6.4 in each and every location. An inclusive solution to the design of away from home toilets in city centres therefore requires four

distinct levels of provision to reflect the different spatial catchments and diverse user profiles of a large, metropolitan authority (see Figure 6.9).

• At the most local level, there is a need for many thousands of small, inclusively designed and accessible 'toilet pods'. To provide choice, these should comprise a mixture of designs that, depending on local circumstances, could be either an ambulant or ambulant plus toilet, a universal cubicle or even a family toilet, located at every local gathering place, park or meeting point. Each might only serve a few hundred people, but collectively the pods would provide a basic safety net across the city so that no one was more than a few hundred metres away from a local community facility if they needed one. Sited in integrated locations, in conjunction with a staffed use, such as a newspaper stand, kiosk or florist that could oversee the facility, the 'pods' would offer a welcome addition to any city's local amenities.

• Where more people congregate, such as on the high street, at a neighbourhood centre or in an 'urban village', basic inclusively designed, gendered facilities are required that include both standard provision, and enlarged cubicles, and which also provide at least one unisex accessible toilet and a baby-changing area to serve thousands of customers. A large city might require many hundreds of these neighbourhood facilities, with the precise mix of templates adopted dependent on an analysis of local needs. They should be placed in integrated locations where needs are concentrated and footfall is greatest, in conjunction with compatible local facilities such as an information point, drop-in centre or café. The facilities would need to be regularly attended during opening hours.

- At the district level, every city should provide substantial 'away from home' facilities to cater for the greater and more diverse footfall that is attracted to concentrations of mixed uses and urban amenities. These should be sited in locations that are well integrated into the urban fabric, and easily accessible on foot and by car to local people and visitors alike. These district-level facilities, which regularly attract hundreds of thousands of people, need to offer a wider range of cubicle choices, including family toilets, and to be attended and open 24 hours. This would meet the apparent shortfall in these essential services, and address the needs of families, older and disabled people that many town centres are hoping to attract to their facilities in the evening and at night.

- Finally, at the small number of strategic and central locations or amenities within the metropolitan region that attract millions of visitors annually (tourist attractions, shopping malls), fully inclusive toilets with the full range of templates to give the greatest possible choice for customers should be provided to serve the metropolitan region, so that the most profoundly disabled people can get out and about within the wider urban region, in the secure knowledge that they will be within reach of an accessible toilet wherever and whenever they need one.

Conclusion

Disabled and older people have much to gain from living in cities, and cities will undoubtedly gain immeasurably from balanced, socially inclusive communities. There is a growing awareness that everyone should be able to carry out their work and leisure activities according to their abilities, at all times of the day and night, and in a manner that is efficient, safe and pleasurable. Yet, despite a wealth of government directives on access, the design of the 24-hour city has lagged behind. Indeed, the urban public realm represents the most concrete example of how people with impairments can be disabled by barriers to access. Within the city centre, public toilets offer a remarkably clear example of how the design of the built environment can exclude individuals and groups from participating fully in civic life.

Well-designed, accessible 'away from home' toilets are the hallmark of a civilised society. Where provision falls short of demand, public health, hygiene and nuisance problems are created by urination in the street and against doorways. This antisocial behaviour is associated with raised levels of aggression, and it poses problems for law enforcement and community policing. The fouling, degradation and physical corrosion of the urban public realm that result from this antisocial behaviour mean that ignoring the problem and simply dealing with the consequences of inadequate provision is not a sustainable long-term option. This VivaCity2020 research has contributed to a better understanding of this complex situation, which falls outside normal planning processes, professional territories and design disciplines. It has shown how high-quality 'away from home' toilets can make cities more sustainable by enhancing the economic vitality of the town centre and by making cities more attractive to visitors, as well as contributing to social equity through ensuring that access is provided for all who require it.

References

Atkins, W.S. (2001) *Older people: Their transport needs and requirements*. London: DTLGR.

Audit Commission (1996) *Protecting the public purse: Ensuring probity in local government*. London: The Audit Commission.

BSI (2001) BS 8300:2001. *Design of buildings and their approaches to meet the needs of disabled people. Code of practice*. London: British Standards Institution.

BSI (2006) BS 6465-3:2006. *Sanitary installations. Code of practice for the selection, installation and maintenance of sanitary appliances*. London: British Standards Institution.

Building Regulations 2000 (2003) *Approved document M: Access to and use of buildings*. Norwich: TSO.

Chisnell, R. (2003) Open letter to the Prime Minister. British Toilet Association press release. Retrieved 3 March 2007 from http://britloos.co.uk/news/dec2003pmletter.html.

Disability Rights Commission (2002) *Code of practice: Rights of access: goods, facilities, services and premises*. Norwich: TSO.

Frye, A. (2003) Transport and inclusion: a government view. Workshop presentation at the Midland Institute of Transport, 10 December 2003.

Goldsmith, S. (1997) *Designing for the disabled: The new paradigm*. Oxford: Architectural Press.

Goldsmith, S. (2000) *Universal design*. Oxford: Architectural Press.

Greed, C. (2003) *Inclusive urban design: Public toilets*. Oxford: Architectural Press.

Kitchin, R. & Law, R. (2001) The socio-spatial construction of (in)accessible public toilets. *Urban Studies*, **38** (2), 287–298.

London Assembly Health and Public Services Committee (2006) *An urgent need: The state of London's public toilets*. London: London Assembly.

Mummery, H. (2005) *Around the clock: Town centres for all*. London: The Civic Trust.

ONS (2002) *Living in Britain: Results from the 2001 General Household Survey*. Norwich: TSO.

Oxley, P.R. (2002) *Inclusive mobility: A guide to best practice on access to pedestrian and transport infrastructure*. London: Department for Transport.

Whitfield, G. (1997) *The Disability Discrimination Act: Analysis of data from the Omnibus Survey*. In-house Report 30. London: The Stationery Office.

Footnotes

1 The terms 'public toilet' and 'away from home' toilet are used interchangeably, to include both toilets provided by local authorities and toilets belonging to private providers for the use of their customers. Note that the facility is frequently referred to in signage, and by some disabled people themselves, as the 'disabled' toilet. Though reference may occasionally be made to other types of toilet cubicle, urinal, automatic public convenience (APC) or grouped toilet provision, the location and design of these facilities are not addressed in detail.

2 A standard key issued to disabled people by the Royal Association for Disability and Rehabilitation (RADAR) that will enable them to access a locked accessible toilet.

3 Disability access auditors give advice about how best to meet the requirements of the Disability Discrimination Act (DDA). They are expert in disability law, building and construction requirements, and customer and provider needs. Access auditors exercise judgement about what it is reasonable for a company to provide and what its customers are entitled to expect.

4 Toilets from the London Borough of Westminster, generally recognised as one of the most responsible of public toilet providers, were also audited.

5 This is the open, unobstructed area adjacent to the WC pan on the side where the drop-down rail is positioned, which allows a wheelchair user to enter, position the wheelchair and transfer from the wheelchair to the WC and back. The size of space required and the transfer technique used vary according to a variety of factors, such as the size and design of the wheelchair, the level of function that the disabled user has, whether transfer is achieved independently or with assistance, and personal preference. The recommended size of the transfer space is 680 mm wide by 750 mm deep.

6 The tool allowed 10 mm flexibility either way in all measurements. For example, if a grab rail of the required length 680 mm measured either 670 mm or 690 mm, it was still considered to have met the guidance.

7 BS 8300 and Part M of the Building Regulations do not specify a particular make of single-sheet toilet paper dispenser, but types of large-roll dispenser in which the loose end of the paper roll may become trapped inside the holder, and stacking single-sheet dispensers that are overfilled, may be equally difficult for disabled people to use.

8 Available free to download at http://eprints.ucl.ac.uk, The Accessible Toilet Resource.

9 As these layouts are widely available they will not be reproduced here.

ENVIRONMENTAL SUSTAINABILITY AND CITY-CENTRE LIVING

While VivaCity2020 research has only touched on a few issues related to environmental sustainability, through its in-depth empirical data collection, the findings from the work in Sheffield, in Manchester, and in Clerkenwell, London, have illustrated some important issues:

- People are critical to understanding the changing dynamics of the environment, urban design and the quality of life in cities. When making design decisions it is important to consider earlier evidence, case studies or experience.

- Subjective input from residents can help to provide and deepen understanding of the effects of environmental pollution in the urban environment.

- Most people who live in a city enjoy the richness of the offering, the nightlife and the culture, but they also experience higher levels of noise and pollution than those living in rural environments. Many people enjoy the buzz of the city, but they need respite, normally found close to nature. The provision of open spaces such as parks and canals provides welcome respite, and is highly valued by residents.

While people do not want these places to be harmed by drugs, drink and illicit sex, cities do need to make provision to accommodate those who engage in such activities. Strong policing will not eradicate these activities. Decision-makers will need to research the options and make informed decisions in conjunction with residents.

To aid in a more inclusive society, public toilets need to be made available in sufficient numbers, and be well designed to be accessible to all.

SECTION 3
URBAN FORM AND SOCIAL SUSTAINABILITY FOR CITY-CENTRE LIVING

The social dimension of sustainability is as diverse as, and probably more opaque and complex than, the environmental dimension. Commentators suggest various qualities: for instance, socially sustainable development means developing a social system that enables education standards to rise, a nation's health to improve, and the overall standard of living to improve (Pearce et al., 1989). The standard of living can be measured in terms of increased food, real income, educational services, health care, sanitation and water supply, and emergency stocks of food and money (Barbier, 1987). In addition to the improvement of the general standard of living, a sustainable society must exist within a framework of cultural diversity (Munasinghe & Shearer, 1995) and it must also be a society based on social justice, as disparities of privilege and wealth will lead to disharmony (Pearce, 1988; Hossain, 1995; Marcuse, 1998).

This section explores two issues upon which to focus questions about the sustainable city: housing and crime. Both of these issues are key to understanding how to design cities that are more sustainable, particularly as more people move to urban areas and densities increase. With a glut of individuals living, working and recreating in city centres, how do we create spaces and places that foster a mix of different tenures and cultures, yet are also safe and secure? Decision-makers involved in the design of housing need to consider form and scale more carefully (from the building to the neighbourhood) as well as the needs of different groups of people moving into neighbourhoods. Crime and perceptions of crime also play an important role in the design of housing and neighbourhoods, and should be integrated into the urban design decision-making process. This section addresses these issues, and provides recommendations about what to consider during urban design decision-making and how to consider it.

References

Barbier, E. (1987) The concept of sustainable economic development. *Environmental Conservation*, **14** (2), 101–110.

Hossain, K. (1995) Evolving principles of sustainable development and good governance. In K. Ginther, E. Denters & P.J.I.M. de Waart (eds), *Sustainable development and good governance*, pp. 15–22. Dordrecht, Netherlands: Martinus Nijhoff.

Marcuse, P. (1998) Sustainability is not enough. *Environment & Urbanization*, **10** (2), 103–111.

Munasinghe, M. & Shearer, W. (1995). *Defining and measuring sustainability: The biogeophysical foundations*. Washington, DC: World Bank.

Pearce, D. (1988) Economics, equity and sustainable development. *Futures*, **20** (6), 598–605.

Pearce, D., Markandya, A. & Barbier, E. (1989) *Blueprint for a green economy*. London: Earthscan.

CHAPTER 7

HOUSING IN THE TWENTIETH-CENTURY CITY

Reem Zako and Julienne Hanson

local environment. The findings have highlighted the emergence of a 'developer's' model of a mixed-use urban block as a new residential type that, along with a twenty-first century model of streets and squares, has come to represent a culturally specific response to the perceived need to reintroduce housing into the inner city.

Background

An important constituent of any city is its residential districts. For most of urban history, housing has been the dominant land use and the most important ingredient in giving a distinctive shape, form, appearance and character to cities throughout the world (Schoenauer, 1981; Oliver, 1987, 2003; Edwards, 2006). In common with many advanced economies, the UK has seen a huge amount of architectural experimentation in housing during the past two centuries that has been crystallised in the built form and fabric of the urban heritage, which now provides a 'living laboratory' in which to study the relationship between the design of housing and the experience of living in local communities.

The evolution of traditional historic towns has long received scholarly attention (Conzen, 1960; Carter, 1983; Moughtin, 1999), and our understanding of the growth and form of suburbs has also improved in recent years (Fishman, 1987; Moudon, 1992; Whitehand & Larkham, 1992; Harris & Larkham, 1999). By comparison, the built form and space organisation of the modern, inner-city residential district has been under-researched. As a consequence, most urban housing types are derived from geometric principles that rely on a visual inspection of the figure/ground representation of the estate layout (Sherwood, 1978; Scoffham, 1984; Panerai et al., 2004; Zhou, 2005). The objective of the research undertaken as part of VivaCity2020 and discussed here has been to develop more rigorous qualitative and quantitative descriptions of housing type that can inform enquiries into the experience of urban living.

Introduction

This chapter addresses the changing residential culture within UK city centres during the last 150 years. It is based on research in the three major cities in the UK studied by the VivaCity2020 team: the historic London neighbourhood of Clerkenwell, central Manchester, and Sheffield city centre. Thirty residential areas were selected from these three locations, to serve as case studies of the various types of housing that have been built in the UK between the 1820s and the present day. The starting point has been to understand these case studies as examples of different housing types, by considering the architectural elements and morphological arrangements that are characteristic of each example. This has led to an investigation of the ways in which built form and housing layout might contribute to the creation of sustainable housing environments and thriving local communities.

The approach has been to combine conventional analytical measures used by architects and town planners, such as building density, housing density, land use characteristics and road hierarchy, with the more specialised tools of space syntax. These modes of analysis have been supplemented by detailed photographic surveys of the housing and open spaces within each residential development, to record the condition of the properties and any evidence of antisocial behaviour. An attitudinal postal survey was also distributed to all the residents in each housing development, to obtain their views about the 'liveability' of their home and its immediate

In many parts of the world, housing and neighbourhood developments of the late twentieth century have been shaped by the belief that it is important to create communal open spaces that can provide a physical focus for local communities. This has given rise to a range of modern housing types that are based on an ethos of building or creating 'community through design', using concepts such as enclosure, repetition and hierarchy to shape the public open space of the development (Hillier, 1996). This, in turn, gives rise to different degrees of community co-presence and mutual awareness, which might vary from 'living in a goldfish bowl' – a state of mutual surveillance where neighbours are very conscious of one another all of the time – to 'living in perpetual night' – where people feel very cut off and isolated from one another in their homes, and have no way of relating spatially to other people who live nearby, or even of knowing their neighbours. The impact of these ideas on the legacy of inner-city housing will be evaluated in the account that follows.

The UK is currently experiencing a massive housing shortage at a time when house building is at an all-time low. Projections of households for England published by the then Office of the Deputy Prime Minister (ODPM, 2006a), for example, estimate that 4.8 million new households will form between 2003 and 2026, as a combined result of immigration, a rise in the number of adults as the age structure of the population changes, the formation of more single-person households, and the growth in pensioner households. Housing types is once more under the microscope as both the public sector and the private sector struggle to meet this rising demand

for more homes by reinterpreting traditional and modern housing types and inventing new ones that are more appropriate to life in the twenty-first century. An important constituent of the debate is that the new communities formed by residential development should not repeat the mistakes of the past but should be socially as well as economically and environmentally sustainable. The primary research on which this chapter is based aims to make a contribution to this debate.

Cities

The three cities where the research was carried out have very different origins and place histories. Within London, the focus of the research was Clerkenwell, which is a mixed-use 'urban village' close to the heart of the City, London's financial centre. It dates back to the twelfth century and has evolved in a piecemeal, organic and unplanned way. It has experienced a series of transformations throughout its history, and is currently undergoing major redevelopment and regeneration programmes.

Clerkenwell was associated with several of the monastic orders in the twelfth century. It was also known as a resort, famous for its spas and theatres, including the still active Sadler's Wells Theatre. After the dissolution of the monasteries the land was given to the aristocracy, and new occupations of farming and animal husbandry flourished in the area, including a thriving meat market at Smithfield where Clerkenwell abuts the City of London.

During the Industrial Revolution the area once more changed its character through the introduction of light industry, including craft workshops, breweries, distillers and printing. Another change of character that took place in the area was the transformation of its housing: the former houses of the aristocracy deteriorated and fell into disrepair, and mass housing in the form of terraced houses and blocks of walk-up flats increased in the area, eventually became associated with poor-quality housing and general social decline.

It was not until the period immediately post World War II and the following decades that Clerkenwell experienced gentrification, and it has lately become very desirable, both as a residential area and also to small businesses because of its vibrant urban locality. In its current guise, the area has managed to retain elements that reflect every era of its colourful history, all of which contribute to its rich and diverse urban mix. Today, it is the epitome of a natural, organic, mixed-use urban neighbourhood that planners hope to re-create through urban design.

Hulme is a nineteenth-century, working class industrial suburb close to the centre of Manchester, which grew up rapidly in the heyday of the cotton industry as a mixed industrial district of large factories and warehouses intermingled with small terraced houses. It has since been redeveloped twice, during the 1960s and the 1990s. Hulme's original Victorian gridiron street pattern had a distinctive urban character, and the area supported a diverse local community with a strong sense of neighbourhood, which was nonetheless physically and socially integrated with the rest of the city of Manchester.

The first redevelopment, which was initiated during the 1930s but not implemented until the 1960s, aimed to sweep away the close-packed, high-density terraces when, in 1934, Hulme was declared a clearance area and its housing unfit for human habitation. The community was moved out to new cottage estates on the edge of Manchester. As a result of this decline in population, industry began to move out and shops to close down. Stretford Road, Hulme's old high street, was closed and plans were drawn up for comprehensive redevelopment. However, these plans were delayed by and not realised until after World War II.

Warner House, Clerkenwell, London

Wholesale slum clearance in the 1960s was followed by a comprehensive redevelopment of the area in the 1970s. At this point Hulme boasted Britain's largest system-built housing estate, which provided over 1000 homes in four eight-storey-high concrete, crescent-shaped blocks linked together by deck access. Together with 13 new tower blocks, 12 000 people were rehoused, but this figure represented a fraction of the original population of 130 000. The new Crescent blocks soon began to suffer from a cocktail of problems that included inadequate heating, pests, child safety problems and poor health. Families moved out, and the homes were let to young single adults, which skewed the demographic profile towards a population that was transient and unemployed.

By the mid-1980s it had become clear that this Modernist reconstruction of Hulme was unsustainable, and after much debate the area became a City Challenge project during the 1990s, with a plan to clear and rebuild the Crescents in order to provide 3000 new homes, together with new roads, shops, offices and community facilities. This time, a clear urban framework guided the development, which was intended to result in a high-density, mixed-use neighbourhood of streets and squares with a busy feel and a strong sense of local community, which supported a diversity of tenures and retained the ability to accommodate change.

Table 7.1 Composition of the sample of 30 residential developments, by city and by EHCS time band

Location	Time band			
	Traditional (pre-1890)	Early Modern (1891–1944)	High Modern (1945–1980)	Post Modern (post-1980)
Clerkenwell	Lloyd Baker Estate, 1819–1820 Myddleton Square, 1824–1827 Cavendish Mansions, 1882	The Bourne Estate, 1901–1903 Charles Rowan House, 1928 Claremont Close, 1920 Margery Street Estate, 1930–33 Trinity Court, 1934	Spa Green Estate, 1948–1950 Bevin Court, 1954 Langdon House, 1963 Finsbury Estate, 1966–68 Weston Rise, 1964–69 The Triangle, 1972 New Calthorpe Estate, 1978	Catherine Griffiths, 1981 Warner House, built as a factory 1930s Refurbished as housing in 1995 Clerkenwell Central, 1998 Brewhouse Yard, 2001–2003 Dallington Street, 2001–2003
Manchester	Traditional Terraces, 1880		Bentley House Estate, 1947–1949 Royce Court, 1968	Homes for Change, 1996 Rolls Crescent, 1997
Sheffield		Edward St. Flats, mid-1930s	Exeter Drive, 1968	Westfield Terrace, 1985 Broomhall, 1990 West One, 2003–2004
	4	6	10	10

Chapter 8 will describe the character of modern Hulme in more detail, reporting specifically on crime.

The Devonshire Quarter of Sheffield is a modern invention of Sheffield's City Council and its development agencies. Historically, the area to the west of the old town centre might have been referred to as 'Broomhall', or by the location of the Royal Hospital (1895) on Westfield Terrace. As a suburban development of early nineteenth-century Sheffield, Broomhall rapidly became part of the metals and cutlery industry, characterised by a mixture of workshops and small factories, some of which still remain today. Further to the west, the area retained a more suburban character, though it was densely populated with many back-to-backs, shops, pubs, chapels and other communal facilities.

Broomhall was subject to a programme of slum clearance from 1920 to 1970, as well as suffering from bombing during World War II. The area now defined by the low-rise Broomhall housing estate was originally part of the large Broomhall Flats social housing scheme that was built in the 1960s while Lewis Wormersley was City Architect.[1] The Broomhall Flats were on a large scale and poorly built, and were demolished in 1988. The Royal Hospital was demolished in 1981, and subsequently most of the site was used as a car park, apart from Devonshire Green itself, which was created as a new focus for the area where local factory workers could find a lunchtime retreat and children living in the nearby Broomhall Flats could play. The whole area has recently taken on a new lease of life as a new 'urban village', with residential and mixed uses based on specialist shopping, leisure and entertainment facilities.

Clerkenwell, Hulme and the Devonshire Quarter are each located on the city-centre fringe of their respective cities, in the area that lies between the high-density historic urban core and the low-density suburbs, where run-down property and relatively

Figure 7.1 A photographic survey of the 30 residential developments from London, Manchester and Sheffield

Traditional era pre-1890

Lloyd Baker Estate   Myddleton Square   Cavendish Mansions   Manchester Terraces

Early modern era 1891–1944

Bourne St. Estate   Charles Rowan House   Claremont Close   Margery St. Estate   Trinity Court   Edward Street Flats

High modern era 1944–1980

Spa Green Estate   Bevin Court   Langdon House   Finsbury Estate   Weston Rise Estate   The Triangle   New Calthorpe Estate

Bentley House   Royce Court   Exeter Drive

Post-modern era post-1980

Catherine Griffiths Ct   Warner House   Rolls Crescent   Westfield Crescent   Broomhall

Street-type layouts

Clerkenwell Central   Brewhouse Yard   Dallington St   Homes for Change   West One

Mixed-use urban blocks

low rents offer a climate that nurtures residential development and business enterprise. However, these hinterlands have different characteristics that result from their location with respect to the wider metropolitan areas of London, Manchester and Sheffield respectively. London is a world city covering 1579 km² that accommodates a population of 7.2 million at a density of 46 people per hectare. Greater Manchester covers an area of about 1276 km² and has a population of about 2.5 million at a density of 20 people per hectare. Sheffield metropolitan district occupies a mere 368 km² and has a population of

0.5 million at a far lower density of 14 people per hectare (Census, 2001). These 'vital statistics' have a direct impact on urban morphology, which has to be taken into account when drawing comparisons.

Twenty housing developments from Clerkenwell have been included in the research, while Hulme and Sheffield have each contributed five schemes (see Table 7.1 and Figure 7.1). The selected case studies are typical of the housing stock found in each city, but they vary in terms of their morphological

Table 7.2 Quantitative data for the 30 residential developments, by EHCS time band						

Variable	Traditional (pre-1890)	Early modern (1891–1944)	High modern (1945–1980)	Post modern (post-1980)	Post-modern 'streets'	Mixed-use urban blocks	Sample average
Figure/ground ratio	3.541:1	3.859:1	3.929:1	1.910:1	2.857:1	1.166:1	2.870:1
Average building footprint, ground floor only, m²	5095.108	2685.288	4362.567	3108.809	3161.913	3034.464	3669.486
Average building area, all floors area, m²	16522.900	18196.815	27201.264	18558.093	11806.994	28009.632	20936.945
Residential area, all floors m²	12982.663	12725.293	18547.400	13785.323	9632.217	19599.672	14974.384
Non-residential area, all floors m²	1319.965	1899.047	2096.007	3792.338	1130.221	7519.300	2598.196
Ratio residential/non-residential development	28.088	6.000	166.600	11.362	21.604	5.216	60.742
Examples that are 100% residential	0	4	4	2	2	0	10
Household density/ha.	188.82	177.94	119.61	153.63	65.10	277.57	151.96
Mean floor area/unit	123.55	69.33	84.28	134.18	138.77	127.74	105.10
Paths as % ground	41.231	47.413	37.932	49.375	37.63	67.22	44.413
Green as % ground	25.039	31.922	34.039	3.208	2.47	4.24	20.956
Gardens as % ground	31.399	15.621	12.308	23.556	36.01	6.12	19.534
Surface parking (%)	1.5	3.257	6.853	6.916	9.44	3.39	5.533
Primary boundaries (%)	52.8	60.83	56.53	64.56	51.27	83.16	59.88
Doors and windows (%)	53.87	28.68	30.48	33.97	47.23	15.42	34.38
Blank walls (%)	14.15	12.14	25.18	21.44	16.86	27.86	19.95
Windows only (%)	16.11	32.23	13.79	15.29	20.43	8.09	18.1
Upper-level visibility (%)	13.77	22.17	16.7	14.17	9.72	20.39	16.41
Active frontages (%)	1.67	2.42	5.18	12.09	4.21	23.11	6.81
Doors only (%)	0.43	2.36	8.67	3.05	1.55	5.14	4.35
Secondary boundaries (%)	47.2	39.17	43.47	35.44	48.73	16.84	40.12
Low fences (%)	35.4	27.61	19.91	55.11	63.31	40.75	36.42
High see-through fences (%)	26.33	22.21	32.58	21.96	8.11	46.2	25.78
High opaque fences (%)	31.39	16.67	30.36	20.63	27.79	8.09	24.19
Very low fences (%)	6.88	33.51	17.15	2.3	0.78	4.95	13.61
Integration r = n	1.400	1.238	1.178	1.159	1.129	1.200	1.210
Mean axial lines/scheme	9	23	38	12	12	11	22
Mean site area (m²)	19226.90	10705.79	19979.07	11500.34	14947.92	6673.72	14966.78
Mean site area (km²)	0.02	0.01	0.02	0.01	0.01	0.01	0.01
Mean estate axial density (per km²)	1125.81	2195.98	2155.52	1825.00	1020.80	2950.89	1910.45

characteristics, age and type of housing, tenure and the social diversity of their residents. Four time bands based on those adopted by the English House Condition Survey (ODPM, 2003), an agency that provides official government statistics for all housing in England, have been utilised to further explore the evolution of housing over the last 150 years. The EHCS type differentiates the major construction cycles that have occurred in the English housing stock during the last 200 years. Each major cycle is associated with different building materials, construction methods and preferred built forms, and also with different types of tenure. These cycles were produced by global phenomena that included two world wars and a worldwide economic depression, as well as a decline in the UK's industrial base in favour of a service economy and the rise of consumerism and the information society.

The housing types represented by the pre-1890 examples include two traditional streets and squares morphologies, some terraced housing, and an early walk-up block of mansion flats. From the early modern period, the case studies include a block of closed-court walk-up flats, three examples of balcony access slab block flats, a group of detached council house flats set round a green space, and an early example of a tower block.

Among the examples from the high modern period are four examples of 'mixed development', the form of English social housing that was most typical of this era and comprised a mix of either tower or slab blocks and low-rise blocks of maisonettes, as well as two purely slab block estates, a high-rise tower block, two labyrinthine 'casbah' style developments (Oxman et al., 2002) and an estate of walk-up flats. The post-modern case studies comprise five examples of low-rise, new urban village 'street'-type layouts, that attempt through their built form to replicate the urban fabric of the traditional pre-1890 era, and five examples of contemporary developers' mixed-use urban blocks[2] (MUUBs), a type that its protagonists claim is a sustainable way of combining residential with non-residential uses (Rogers, 1999; Rudlin & Falk, 1999). The sample is biased to the period after World War II, as this is the time when the greatest amount of architectural experimentation and innovation took place in house form in the UK. As there is a particular need to understand the emerging trends in respect of the current house-building boom in the inner city as well as the development processes of the recent past, the sample includes three residential developments that were completed since the year 2000.

A multilayered approach to understanding housing

Primary data have been gathered for each case study on building and housing density, the types of land uses designated for planning purposes, the metric areas of all types of building and hard and soft landscaping, the metric length and type of all building boundaries and street frontages, and the layout and type of all roads and paths. Data collection and analysis were governed by strict protocols. The survey work, which took place in the spring and autumn of 2005, was supported by a detailed photographic record of each development and a search of local historical and archival sources to unearth the history and evolution of each scheme; a note was made of the precise location of any obvious antisocial activity such as fly-tipping, vandalism or graffiti. The data produced were then assembled into a statistical database that allowed morphological and configurational information to be compared with relevant demographic and socio-economic data available on public domain databases, such as census data, measures of social deprivation, crime data and the like (see Table 7.2). At this stage, metric measurements were converted to proportions, to allow comparisons to be drawn between residential developments of different sizes.

Quantitative data have been calculated for all 30 schemes, to facilitate the comparison of average data for the whole sample with that for each construction phase. The account that follows will begin from a figure/ground analysis of the buildings and open spaces, and will move on to consider the character of the open spaces, the proportions of primary (building) and secondary (open space) boundaries, and how these relate to the axial organisation.

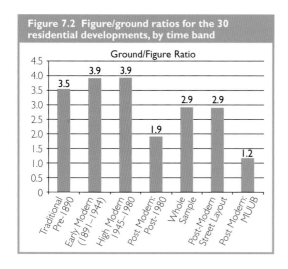

Figure 7.2 Figure/ground ratios for the 30 residential developments, by time band

Ground/Figure Ratio

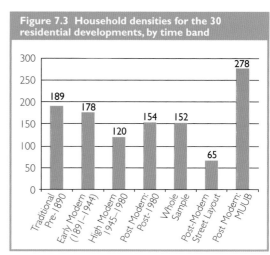

Figure 7.3 Household densities for the 30 residential developments, by time band

Understanding the layout of buildings and open spaces

The foundation representation in space syntax,[3] on which all other representations and measures are based, depicts the figure/ground map for each housing scheme in the form of a plan or Nolli map[4] that contrasts the buildings, shown in solid black, with the open spaces, shown in white. This way of representing urban space has been popularised by Rowe & Koetter (1978) in their book *Collage City*, as well as by Hillier & Hanson (1984).

From the figure/ground map it is possible to measure the total area of the building footprint for each urban block, and compare it with the amount of unbuilt space that is left over. The lower this ratio, the more built-up the block; the higher the ratio, the more open space there is left around the buildings. Given what has been said already about the transformations that have occurred in the urban tissue over the last 100 years, it is to be expected that housing from different historical periods will have different figure/ground ratios that reflect the prevailing architectural philosophies of the day.

The mean figure/ground ratios (or more accurately the ground/figure ratios, since the former is usually greater than the latter) were calculated for the

whole sample and for the four time bands (see Figure 7.2). This shows that the average ratio for the whole sample is 2.9 : 1 ground to figure,[5] meaning that there is nearly three times as much unbuilt space as there is building footprint, but this overall mean disguises important time-related differences between the various schemes in the sample. For the traditional (pre-1890) urban blocks the mean ratio is 3.5 : 1, while the early modern estates (1891–1944) and high modern (1945–1980) housing schemes share the slightly higher mean ratio (more unbuilt space) of 3.9 : 1. Despite its higher ground coverage, the traditional streets and squares morphology is not significantly more built up than the early and high modern housing estates, but for the post-modern (post-1980) period the mean figure/ground ratio is a much lower figure (more built space) of 1.9 : 1. A closer examination of the ten post-modern schemes reveals that they fall into two distinct subtypes: half are post-modern 'streets', and the rest are innovative, inner-city MUUBs that correspond to the type of developers' mixed-use urban block described earlier. The two subtypes have

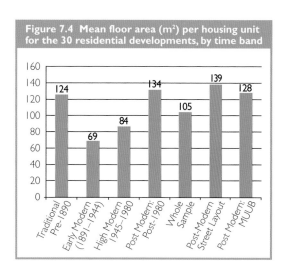

Figure 7.4 Mean floor area (m²) per housing unit for the 30 residential developments, by time band

very different figure/ground ratios: 2.9 : 1 for the 'streets', which is close to the mean for the whole sample, and 1.2 : 1 for the MUUBs.

Figure/ground ratios may provide a useful first indication of the density of building development but, for various reasons, they do not give a direct reflection of the density of residential development. First, ever since Martin & March's (1972) seminal land use and built form studies, it has been known that a site of the same area can house very different residential densities, depending on the built form adopted. Conversely, they demonstrated that it is possible to achieve the same density by adopting very different built forms. Building footprint gives few clues about the composition of the built form, as it does not take account of the number of storeys. Second, despite the fact that it seems to be a simple concept, density is quite difficult to pin down or measure accurately. Housing density can be measured in various ways: as the development density, in terms of the gross or net residential density, in terms of floor space per acre/hectare, the number of habitable rooms or bed spaces per acre/hectare, or by counting the number of dwellings or households per acre/hectare. The development and the residential density draw attention to the mix of uses accommodated in a housing development, which may not be exclusively residential. For the sample of 30 schemes, ten are exclusively housing, while the most diverse mix has eight different land uses in addition to residential use.

For this research, household density – the number of houses or flats on a piece of land of a given size, and therefore the most accessible way to measure residential density – was adopted.[6] Average

household densities were calculated for the whole sample and for the four time bands (see Figure 7.3). The results show that the average density for the whole sample is 152 housing units per hectare across all time bands, but this average disguises important time-related differences between the various schemes in the sample. For the traditional (pre-1890) urban blocks the average housing density was the highest of all four time bands, at 189 housing units per hectare, followed by 178 housing units per hectare for the early modern estates (1891–1944). The high modern era (1945–1980) was characterised by a relatively low housing density for inner-city areas of 120 housing units per hectare, which later increased to 154 housing units per hectare for the post-modern (post-1980) period. A close examination of the ten post-modern schemes reveals that their two subtypes have extreme housing densities: the post-modern 'streets' have exceptionally low densities at 65 housing units per hectare, while the MUUBs have exceedingly high densities at 278 housing units per hectare.

The mean floor area per housing unit, calculated by taking the total area of residential use and dividing this by the number of housing units accommodated,[7] also varied widely (see Figure 7.4). The least generous provision coincided with the early modern

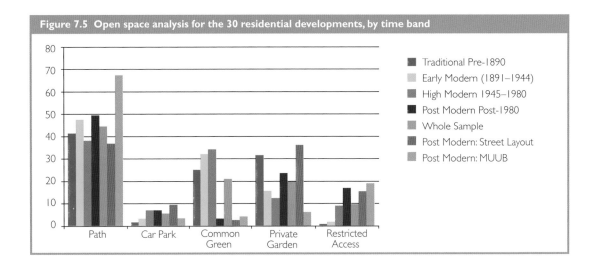

Figure 7.5 Open space analysis for the 30 residential developments, by time band

pre-World War II era at 69 m² of floor area per unit, but this figure rose during the post-war high modern era to 84 m² per unit to coincide with the state housing programme, when minimum standards applied to all public-sector housing (Parker Morris, 1961). Still, these figures were lower than the traditional (pre-1890) era, which showed an average mean floor area of 124 m² per housing unit for the residential developments studied. Although the developments of the post-modern era have acquired a reputation for accommodating small, one- and two-person households, the average floor area per housing unit for these developments was the highest of all at 134 m² per unit, with the post-modern 'streets' having the highest mean area per housing unit at 139 m², followed by the MUUBs at 128 m² per housing unit, just slightly higher than the traditional terraces of the previous century.

Understanding open spaces

The next representation classifies all of the 'ground': that is, all the unbuilt open spaces within the urban blocks on which the buildings stand, in order to identify the use and 'ownership' of those spaces (see Figure 7.5). Unclear ownership of spaces in the public domain has been identified with social malaise (Coleman, 1990). The type differentiates between

pedestrian paths and other hard landscaped areas, areas for car parking, common green areas, private yards and gardens, and areas of restricted access that no one can use. The proportions as well as the areas of each type of space in each estate or residential development have been calculated in order to eliminate the effects of developments of different metric areas.

Unsurprisingly, the most common space type is a path. On average, paths occupy 44% of the ground, but the proportion of open space devoted to public circulation varies from as little 38% in the high modern era to as much as 49% in the post-modern period. If the post-modern examples are split into the 'streets' and the MUUBs, then the average amount of space devoted to paths in the 'street' layouts is 37%, less than the mean for the sample as a whole, but the comparable figure for the MUUBs is nearly twice this at 67%.

A common theme across all the historical periods represented by the 30 case studies is that of creating shared, open green spaces for the local community to use. Common green spaces are the

Devonshire Green, Sheffield

next most prevalent space type, occupying on average 21% of all the unbuilt space in the sample. A quarter of the unbuilt space is dedicated to this use in the traditional era, and it is greatest in the high modern estates (34%), but this use has almost disappeared in the post-modern period, where only 3% of all unbuilt space is dedicated to common green areas. If the post-modern schemes are separated into the 'streets' and the MUUBs, as before, this confirms that shared green space has almost disappeared as a phenomenon associated with contemporary housing, whether this be of a 'streets' (2%) or MUUB (4%) type.

Private gardens occupy, on average, another 20% of all the unbuilt space. These are most prevalent in traditional housing layouts, occupying, on average, 31% of unbuilt space, and in the post-modern period (24%), while gardens are least numerous in the early and high modern periods (16% and 12% respectively). Thus, generally speaking, the proportion of the ground dedicated to public and private green space is in an inverse ratio. A third of the schemes from across all time periods have few or no private gardens. However, if the post-modern case studies are separated into the 'streets' and the MUUB types, then a profound difference emerges in respect of private green space, with 36% of open space in post-modern 'streets' given to this function, representing an even higher proportion of the 'ground' than in the traditional layouts, whereas just 6% on average is dedicated to this function in the MUUBs.

Perry (1929/1998) was one of the first to observe that the car was one of the most significant drivers of change in housing morphology, and this has been reiterated many times since (McCluskey, 1992; Jenks et al., 1996, Panerai et al., 2004). The average proportion of unbuilt space dedicated to car parking across the sample is 6%, but this masks a profound split between the two pre World War II eras, which dedicated 2% and 3% respectively of the ground to car parking space, and the two post-war eras, each of which had 7% of the ground for car parking. If the post-modern part of the sample is split as before, then the post-modern 'streets' are unlike their traditional counterparts in that a quite generous 9% of the unbuilt space is dedicated to car parking, while the comparable figure for surface parking in the MUUBs is 3%, the same level as before the last world war when cars were still a novelty. This can be partly explained by the fact that most MUUBs are served by underground car parking but, even allowing for this, very little parking provision was made for visitors in the examples studied. Finally, the amount of the site where access is restricted, so that only the maintenance staff and facilities managers can effect entry, has increased dramatically between the pre- and post- World War II periods, and has become most marked in the MUUBs.

Understanding boundaries

The main way that the open spaces of the urban landscape are laid out on the ground and shaped architecturally is by the combined placement of primary and secondary boundaries. Primary or

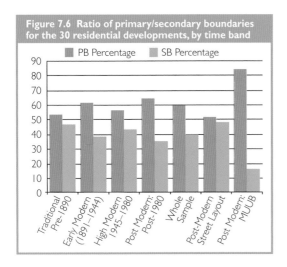

Figure 7.6 Ratio of primary/secondary boundaries for the 30 residential developments, by time band

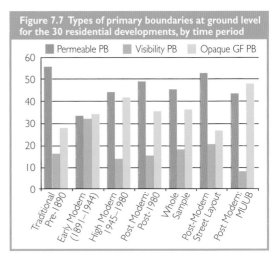

Figure 7.7 Types of primary boundaries at ground level for the 30 residential developments, by time period

building boundaries are materially formed from the perimeter of the 'figure' or building footprint that outlines the building's shape and the position of its facades. Secondary or open space boundaries are the walls, fences and the like that divide the 'ground' or unbuilt spaces on which the buildings are placed.

The definition of the buildings and open spaces of the 30 housing schemes by boundaries of various kinds has been further broken down to examine the proportion of primary boundaries to secondary boundaries. Primary boundaries comprise 'active' frontages constituted by retail or commercial premises, houses or flats with doors and windows at ground level, homes with just doors or just windows at ground level, buildings with blank walls at ground level and upper-level visibility, and buildings with totally blank walls. Secondary boundaries have been subdivided to identify which boundaries are high opaque walls/fences, high see-through walls/fences, low walls/fences or very low walls/fences that can easily be stepped over.

The primary boundaries comprise different proportions of the total boundaries that define the open space of residential developments built at different time periods (see Figure 7.6). Some developments have few secondary boundaries while others have elaborate landscaped and bounded external spaces that shape, define and add complexity to the layout of the public space of the residential area. For the whole sample, the proportion of primary to secondary boundaries is 3:2, or 60% primary boundary to 40% secondary boundary but, as before, this relationship differs for different time periods.

For the traditional developments, the ratio is close to that for the whole sample: 53% primary to 47% secondary boundaries. In the early modern period this rises to 61% primary and 39% secondary boundaries, suggesting that the figure/ground relationship of estates built before World War II was simple, with relatively undifferentiated external space. In the high modern period the ratio returns to 57% and 43% respectively, and in the post-modern era it climbs again to 65% primary and 35% secondary boundaries. Looking separately at the post-modern 'streets' and MUUBs, the relevant percentages for the post-modern 'streets' are 51% primary to 49% secondary boundaries, almost the same as for traditional streets, but for the MUUBs it is 83% primary and 17% secondary boundaries, showing that for this particular residential type the

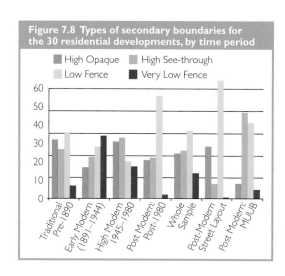

Figure 7.8 Types of secondary boundaries for the 30 residential developments, by time period

space is overwhelmingly shaped by buildings and not nearly so much by landscaping, with its attendant hedges, walls and fences.

The mean figures for the whole sample reveal that the primary boundary with the greatest proportion of metric length is constituted by doors and windows (34%), followed by blank walls (20%), windows only (18%), and upper-level visibility (16%). The other two categories, active frontages (7%) and doors only (4%), are only weakly represented in the sample schemes. These relationships can be further simplified to differentiate the proportion of the boundaries at ground level that are permeable (active frontages, doors and windows, doors), as opposed to just permitting visibility at ground level (windows) or that are opaque and impermeable at the ground level (upper-level visibility, blank walls). For the sample as a whole, just under half of all primary boundaries are permeable (46%), just over a third are opaque and impermeable (36%), and just over a fifth permit a visual link (18%). However, the distribution of these different boundary conditions is very different in each of the four time periods under consideration (see Figure 7.7).

The traditional street layouts of the pre-1890s era have the highest percentage of permeable primary boundaries (56%), followed by the post-modern examples (49%), but a closer examination of the two subsets within the post-modern era highlights once more the difference between the 'streets' type, which has a much higher percentage of permeable boundaries similar to that of the traditional street layouts (53%), and the MUUBs (43%). This similarity between the traditional street layouts and their contemporary equivalents is also evident in the percentages of their opaque and impermeable boundaries at 28% and 27% respectively and the boundaries that only offer a visual link, 16% and 20%. On the other hand, the post-modern MUUBs appear to have followed on from the developments of the high modern era in respect of the percentage of primary boundaries that are permeable, within the region of 44%, yet at the same time the post-modern MUUBs have a much higher percentage of opaque boundaries at 48% than the developments of the high modern period, where just 42% of the building facades are opaque. The early modernist era seems to be unique in that the percentages of the different main types of primary boundary (permeable, visual and opaque) are about a third each.

Looking in more detail at the composition of secondary boundaries (see Figure 7.8), the rank order for the whole sample is as follows: low fences are the most numerous (36%), followed by high see-through fences (26%) and high opaque fences (24%) and finally very low fences (14%). The greatest proportion of secondary boundaries across the sample therefore maintain physical as opposed to

Table 7.3 Axial data for the three cities and for the three study areas

Variable	London	Manchester	Sheffield
Area of city in km²	1579	1276	368
Population of each city (millions)	7.2	2.5	0.5
Density of people (per ha)	46	20	14
	Clerkenwell	Hulme	Devonshire
Radius of axial map (km)	3	4	7
Area of axial map (km²)	32.54	50.14	142.65
Total number of lines	5103	10341	11625
Axial line density (per km²)	157	206	81
Mean global integration	1.274	0.897	0.517
Total axial lines of all developments	288	76	125
Mean integration minus housing	1.272	0.895	0.513

symbolic distinctions within the public realm. For the post-modern 'streets', however, there are twice as many low fences (63%) as high opaque ones (28%), with few high see-through and almost no low fences at all. The use of these to symbolise the front (low, surveillance) and back (high opaque, target-hardened) of the dwellings is far more clear-cut than in the traditional neighbourhoods. For the set of MUUBs, half of the boundaries that do exist are low or very low, but the dominant type of boundary is a high see-through fence.

Understanding axiality

Because urban space is for the most part linear, space syntax normally represents a street network as a matrix of axial lines. The theory proposes that the axial structure of the urban grid shapes movement, which then attracts land uses that require footfall to some locations and those that do not (such as housing) to others. Uses that depend on the passing trade then act as attractors, creating multiplier effects on movement, which then attract yet other and different land uses to the axial line. This 'city-creating process' seems to be set in

motion by the axial structure of the urban grid itself. In this respect, streets are not just inert channels for movement that link buildings and urban areas together, but a dynamic system that is more often than not a record of the historical process by which the city has evolved. The external residential environment that has been previously described therefore constitutes both a network of routes through the unbuilt space that connects each residential development with the wider urban context, and also an interface that permits both residential and non-residential uses to flourish, by providing an appropriate degree of busyness or quietness on the adjacent streets and footpaths. Likewise, the axial structure of the urban grid may encourage or inhibit co-presence among inhabitants and between those resident locally and passers-by.

Various integration values for the 'walkable' axial map of each site plan, in isolation and embedded within a larger urban hinterland, were therefore calculated for each example to explore the axial structure of urban space created by the various residential developments. The axial maps of the 30 residential areas in Clerkenwell, Hulme and the Devonshire Quarter were drawn, checked on site for accuracy, and inserted into a hinterland of 3 km radius in order to eliminate any 'edge effects'. All the well-tried and -tested axial measures were calculated for the residential developments considered both in isolation and embedded in their respective hinterlands, but in the account that follows the global integration of each development within its hinterland has been selected as the most useful representation for comparative purposes.

It has already been established that though the location of all three case study areas is at the urban fringe of each city centre, the cities themselves are very different in size, population and density and hence in urban built form characteristics. This is reflected in the axial maps of the urban hinterlands for the three study areas (see Table 7.3). The residential developments from Clerkenwell are embedded in an axial map that is just over 3 km in radius and covers an area of just under 33 km². Cut from a pre-existing axial map of Greater London, it reaches the villages of Highgate and Hampstead to the north, eastwards as far as Bow and Tower Hamlets, down to the Elephant and Castle in the south, and to the Edgware Road in west London. The map contains just over 5000 axial lines, resulting in an axial line density of 157 lines/km².

As Sheffield is a much smaller and more discrete entity than London, it made no sense to artificially limit the boundary of the axial map of Sheffield, and so the developments from the Devonshire Quarter have been embedded in a larger map that extends to the boundaries of the entire city. It was purpose-made for the VivaCity2020 project, and covers a radius of nearly 7 km and a metric area of 142 km². It has the highest number of axial lines of the three

large-scale maps, but the lowest axial line density, 81 lines/km². The map of Manchester's hinterland was based on an existing map of the city centre, which was extended in all directions and re-centred on Hulme. This map stretches out over a 4 km radius and includes 50 km² of urban fabric. With just over 10 000 axial lines, this map has the highest axial density, at 206 lines/km².

The axial map of Clerkenwell's hinterland together with all its residential developments is over twice as integrated (mean integration 1.274) as the Devonshire Quarter's (0.517) and nearly one and a half times as integrated as Hulme's (0.897). The residential developments themselves constitute only a fraction of the axial lines in each map – 288 for London, 125 for Sheffield and 76 for Manchester – and so the local structure of the residential developments has a negligible impact on the mean integration of the large-scale axial maps (1.272, 0.513 and 0.895 respectively). Thus it can be said that the overall structure of the urban grid is very robust, in the sense that it is not greatly transformed by even quite major housing developments.

The mean number of axial lines created by the housing schemes is 22, but this figure varies markedly for different historical periods. The average number of axial lines contributed by the traditional developments is 9, for the early modern it is 23, for the high modern estates this rises to 38, but the recent post-modern developments have on average just 12 axial lines, with almost no difference between the 'streets' (12) and MUUBs (11).

Although the cities have different physiognomies,[8] the architecture of modernism is generic, such that all three cities contain housing schemes that are similar to one another and typical of their period. The estate morphologies of modernism, whether

these are early modern walk-up flats or high modern mixed developments, tend to be 'small-scale, separate, inward facing, unconstituted and hierarchical' (Hanson, 2000), to the point where Hillier (1996) has coined the term 'disurbanism' to refer to the complex and segregated morphologies that mark out modern housing estates within axial maps of cities. Described as 'the urban renaissance' (Urban Task Force, 1999), post-modern urban design and town planning have sought to achieve urban integration, through making direct connections between the buildings and the streets and public spaces of the city. The UK's post-modern schemes appear to have reversed the process of disurbanism by stitching themselves into the city, an effect that may even be directly attributable to the impact of the use of space syntax (Urban Task Force, 1999).

The housing estates of the high modern era are characterised by having, on average, the largest sites of all four eras, with a mean area of just below 20 000 m², and also the highest mean number of axial lines per development, at 38. On the other hand, the residential developments of the early modern era are the smallest in terms of site area, with a mean area for the examples studied of just over 10 000 m², but nonetheless these developments have the second highest mean number of axial lines per development, at 23. They also have the highest estate axial line density (see Table 7.3). The traditional pre-1890 examples are the second largest in their site area, yet have the lowest mean number of axial lines, averaging only 8.5 per scheme, and also the lowest axial line density. The post-modern examples taken together are consistently ranked third in terms of their mean site area, mean number of axial lines and mean axial density, yet splitting the examples from this era into

Great Northern Warehouse and Hilton Tower, Manchester

two subsets, as before, provides the most interesting and extreme results. The mean number of axial lines of the examples within the two sets are within the 11–12 range, yet they vary dramatically in their site area, with the MUUBs' mean area (6700 m^2) being less than half that of the street-based systems (15 000 m^2). This results in the MUUBs having the highest axial line density while the post-modern 'streets' have the lowest axial line density of all.

This trend can be further examined by considering how the various examples that have been studied here are integrated within their localities. The mean global integration of all the residential developments embedded within their hinterlands is 1.210, and the mean global integration values for each time period suggest a gradual decrease in mean integration with the passage of time, from 1.400 in the traditional streets to 1.238 in the early modern period, 1.178 in high modernism and 1.159 in the post-modern period.

However, this is an illusion. If the mean integration values of the developments are plotted separately against time for each of the three cities, only London shows a negative trend (greater segregation from 1820 to early 2000s), and this so weakly as to have occurred by chance, while there is a strong and positive association between time and mean integration in Sheffield (the more modern, the more integrated) and a weaker and positive association in Manchester. At the city level, the mean integration of all the residential developments within their surroundings is slightly higher than the mean for the city as a whole, but in all three cities the values for the two periods of modernism are below the mean integration for all time periods, and are balanced by the values for the traditional and post-modern schemes, which are above mean integration. This suggests that the traditional and post-modern

schemes in this sample are located on sites with urban characteristics while the residential developments of early and high modernism are located on sites that are more suburban in character.

Understanding liveability

During the summer of 2006, a questionnaire-based postal survey was distributed to all the households living in 29 out of the 30 housing developments in the sample.[9] The questionnaire was based on the British government's 'liveability agenda', which has been developed in recent years (ODPM, 2006b) to capture the residential satisfaction of an area. It comprised 16 questions, broadly divided in three themes: upkeep, management or misuse of the private and public space and buildings; road traffic and transport-related issues; and abandonment or non-residential use of domestic property. A further eight questions were incorporated, relating to antisocial behaviour.

A total of 4886 surveys was distributed, of which 502 were received back. Eight of these were excluded from the analysis, resulting in an overall response rate of 10.11%. Householders were asked to score each issue on a scale ranging from 1 (indicating no problems) to 5 (indicating major problems). The housing areas could then be rank-ordered from the most liveable (lowest score) to the least liveable (highest score), and the most serious issues (scoring higher than 3) affecting each residential neighbourhood could be identified. A map was provided, so that householders could indicate the location of any liveability issues that were causing problems on or close to the development.

Variable	Traditional (pre-1890)	Early modern (1891–1944)	High modern (1945–1980)	Post modern (post-1980)	Post-modern 'streets'	MUUBs	Sample average
Upkeep (adjusted)	8.7	9.1	10	7.7	7.7	7.7	8.7
Road traffic noise, etc.	8.7	7.9	8.8	8.0	8.5	7.4	8.3
Void/non-residential use of dwellings	6.2	6.3	6.1	6.1	5.8	6.4	6.1
Unadjusted mean liveability, ODPM	32	32	35	29	30	29	32
Antisocial behaviour ASB (adjusted)	8.1	8.9	9.9	8.5	8.6	8.2	8.9
Unadjusted total score including ASB	49	50	54	46	47	46	50

Table 7.4 Unadjusted scores (shaded) and adjusted scores for the 30 residential developments, by EHCS time band

The highest possible combined score for all 24 items named in the questionnaire was 120, but the 'least liveable' estate in the sample, which had the most reported problems of all kinds, had a raw, unadjusted mean score of 63,[10] while the 'most liveable' development of all scored 38, and the average for the sample was 50. Most estates therefore suffered from relatively few problems. Within the sample as a whole, the average score for the post-modern developments (46) was lower (more liveable) than that for the traditional areas (49), while the early modern estates (50) were generally more liveable than the high modern estates (54). See Table 7.4. Simple correlations between syntactic variables and mean liveability scores failed to identify any significant relationships, but a close visual inspection of the sites where problems were reported to have arisen revealed that each was associated with a clutch of spatial factors that could be conducive to poor liveability and especially to antisocial behaviour.

Looking in more detail at the survey results for the different components of liveability, however, it was observed that when these were adjusted to take account of the higher number of variables regarding upkeep and antisocial behaviour, residential developments from the different time periods displayed different profiles of liveability problems. Traditional street layouts appeared to be equally troubled by poor upkeep and road traffic problems, and were less affected by unsuitable uses and antisocial behaviour. Estates from the early modern and high modern eras reported the most problems with upkeep, followed by antisocial behaviour and then by transport-related issues and finally non-conforming uses. Post-modern developments, on the other hand, recorded the highest scores for antisocial behaviour, followed by traffic, upkeep and finally unsuitable uses. Across all four time bands, the fewest problems of all related to abandoned or non-residential use of domestic property. The residential developments of the high modern period were particularly marked out as having the highest scores across all time bands for poor upkeep, traffic problems and antisocial behaviour. The MUUBs scored highest out of all time periods in respect of problems relating to vacant sites and buildings, whereas post-modern 'streets' appeared least affected by this phenomenon.

Out of the eight upkeep issues considered, litter and rubbish consistently scored the highest across all time bands and types of development, and so this can be considered a generic problem that detracts from the liveability of inner urban residential developments. On the other hand, the lowest mean score was for graffiti, though admittedly this was more pronounced in the high modern housing schemes than elsewhere.

In addition to litter and rubbish, the high modern housing estates also reported the most problems with scruffy buildings, poor-condition housing, vandalism and dog excrement, while the MUUBs suffered most from street parking nuisance. Poor-condition housing was not perceived to be a problem among the occupants of post-modern housing, especially the MUUBs.

Poor air quality consistently scored highest amongst the four transport-related issues, while railway and aircraft noise were the least troublesome and scored lowest within this set. There were no consistently high scores amongst the four elements relating to the abandonment or non-residential use of domestic property. Prostitution was the least reported form of antisocial behaviour, except within the early modern examples, while gatherings of young people and drunken behaviour were forms of antisocial behaviour that were reported across all time bands but especially in the MUUBs, which also had a relatively high score for problems relating to begging and homelessness. Car theft and car vandalism scored highest in the post-World War II estates and on post-modern 'streets', which also returned the highest reported scores for property-related crime. Crimes against the person, drug dealing, gatherings of young people and drunken behaviour were particularly associated with high modern estates.

Discussion: post-modern housing types

In the post-war era, the UK underwent an extensive social housing programme, and this chapter has shown that in many respects the new housing types that were constructed as part of the apparatus of the modern welfare state, and which are regarded as characteristic of high modernism, had their origins in early experiments in social housing by philanthropic and charitable organisations as well as by the embryonic welfare state. By contrast, the closing decades of the last century and the first years of the new millennium have been characterised by large-scale, private high-density 'street' and MUUB types that have been fostered within a more entrepreneurial, free market economy and designed mainly for owner-occupation.

The origins of the MUUB model for development can be traced back to the report of the Urban Task Force (Urban Task Force, 1999) referred to earlier. Drawing on a discussion about the relationship between built form and urban density that was first aired by Martin & March (1972) in the early 1970s, the report discussed the relative merits of three stereotypical built forms built to the same density of 75 dwellings per hectare, but displaying very different architectural characteristics.

The first example illustrates a typical high-rise tower block standing on a large, open site where 'there are no private gardens or amenities … no direct relationship between the building and the surrounding streets'. The open green space surrounding the block requires a high level of investment and maintenance if it is to be attractive to the residents. The second example is a typical traditional low-rise, high-density street system of houses with front and back gardens, where 'public space is defined by continuous street frontages (and) the streets form a clear pattern of public space'. Here, there is little shared green space because of the low-rise, high-density solution. The third example 'shows how the same ingredients can be harnessed to create a strong urban focus to a residential community'. Here the buildings, which vary in height and appearance, hug the perimeter of the site to enclose a communal open space that contains

Thorpe Street, Hulme, Manchester

community facilities. Commercial uses address the surrounding streets to take advantage of the 'passing trade', with flats and maisonettes located on the floors above.

The report does not explicitly make the link, but at first sight the proposed model seems not dissimilar to that of the traditional urban blocks that lie at the heart of historic Clerkenwell, where what were once large Georgian or Victorian terraced houses were remodelled into flats in the late nineteenth and early twentieth centuries, and commercial uses began to occupy the ground floors and street frontages of those premises that were located on well-integrated and therefore busy streets. It also stops short of recommending this particular form of development above others, but it does strongly advocate mixed use, whether this is in a neighbourhood, street, urban block or building, as a more sustainable and desirable way of living in the inner city. However, the built forms that have emerged since this report was written bear little or no resemblance to the piecemeal and organically grown mixed-use urban blocks that characterise not only Clerkenwell but also the historic cores of traditional towns and cities throughout the UK. In just about every respect, the most recent examples studied exhibit distinctive and unique characteristics when compared with the housing developments of earlier periods.

Compared with their historic counterparts, the post-modern 'streets' in this study have a few more axial lines and a slightly lower axial density, suggesting that the 'urban grain' of the two types is comparable, but the new streets exhibit a lower ground/figure ratio, indicating that the contemporary house plots are more tightly packed than those of the large, predominantly middle-class traditional terraced houses. However, the household density of the post-modern street is nearly three times lower than that of the traditional streets, reflecting the predominance of the single-family house as opposed to one subdivided into flats. The mean floor area of a house on a post-modern street is the most generous in the sample, and compares favourably with that of a typical converted flat in a traditional house. The proportions of the site given over to different types of open space show some changes from the traditional to the new street type: paths and private gardens occupy about the same proportion of the site, but there is more parking space and far less green space in a typical post-modern street block. A greater proportion of the site has restricted access. The ratios of primary to secondary boundaries are similar, and so are the proportions of the permeable, overlooking and opaque building boundaries. Externally, post-modern streets have a far greater proportion of low fences and fewer high or very low fences than traditional streets. Even so, the new clearly relates to the old, both geometrically, in terms of the preferred built forms, and architecturally, in terms of the appearance and detailing of the building facades.

However, the same cannot be said of post-modern MUUBs. This type has by far the highest axial line density and also by far the greatest amount of building footprint relative to plot size. Its mean

Warner Street, London

household density approaches twice that of the sample average. The open space left over after building is dominated by hard landscape. This new type also has the highest proportion of open space with restricted access, and almost no shared green space or private gardens. It follows from the above that the ratio of primary to secondary boundaries is also extreme: more of the building facade is blank walled and less is made up of windows than for any other type, so that there is less natural surveillance from the buildings to the surrounding streets, yet the dominant secondary boundary is high opaque fences. Morphologically speaking, contemporary MUUBs bear little or no relation to residential developments from previous eras, let alone adapted historic mixed-use urban blocks, but are a genuinely new type. Redeveloped on 'brownfield' land, often on waterside sites where former industrial uses have been abandoned, the popularity and acceptability of the MUUB as a new city-centre housing type seems to suggest that a new set of cultural values is emerging within contemporary society. The trend, which originated in large urban centres such as London, Manchester and Sheffield, is now influencing the redevelopment of many smaller towns and cities throughout the UK.

The new MUUB morphology also seems vulnerable to new forms of 'liveability' issues: that of vacant sites in the vicinity could well disappear with time, as the run-down neighbourhoods at the city-centre fringe where these developments tend to be located gradually regenerate and consolidate, but parking problems are unlikely to go away as so little has been provided at street level. Reported antisocial behaviour – drunkenness, youths hanging about, begging, homelessness – may be difficult to eradicate as the interface between the buildings and the hard landscaped public realm is immediate, small scale and in many places 'unpoliced' by doors or windows. Developments that encourage the public into the heart of the urban block to enjoy ground-level commercial activities such as cafés and bars merely add to the underlying tension between residents and visitors over the 'ownership' of public space.

The long term success or failure of these new developments is particularly pertinent to the 24-hour city because, to date, for many local authorities in the UK the 24-hour economy has meant little more than a growth in the numbers of convenience supermarkets and eating and drinking establishments such as bars, pubs and restaurants, fast-food takeaways and nightclubs (Mummery, 2005). The monopoly that youth-orientated, alcohol-related entertainment holds over the 24-hour city does not sit well with the accompanying residential uses that have been encouraged back into the city centre by MUUBs. Fear of crime and disorder, perceived as a major barrier to greater participation in the night-time economy, is equally a major issue for the residents living alongside these non-residential uses in the new post-modern MUUBs. However, post-modern streets are not without their problems, such as vandalism and car and property crimes.

The MUUB embodies a particular spatial and social manifestation of mixed use in respect of the combination of ground-level retail, commercial and office uses with residential use above. It also represents a particular view of mixed use in terms of the mixed tenure that is achieved in most schemes by combining a large number of luxury private apartments intended for sale to well-educated, affluent, childless professionals, with a social housing element provided as planning gain.[11] Many of these new residential developments are promoted as a new type of chic, bourgeois inner-city lifestyle that claims to reproduce something of the mystique of 'loft living', now that older industrial properties suitable for remodelling into residential lofts are in short supply. The lifestyle that is on offer seems to combine an antidote to suburbia with a stylish, minimalist approach to contemporary urban living, an attractive combination of sentiments that can then be exploited for their commercial possibilities. Meanwhile, the social housing is usually relegated to a separate, less attractive part of the site. Though it can appear quite extensive on the site plan, affordable housing may be only a small proportion of the overall value of the development. These factors are changing the social geography as well as the morphology of new social housing provision. The MUUB is a new residential type that is providing an infrastructure for the post-industrial service economy, but only time will tell whether it is a sustainable solution to the perceived need to revive the residential culture of the inner city.

Recommendations

When creating policy or making urban design decisions in respect of sustainable housing for the 24-hour city, the following issues need to be carefully considered in respect of the strategic design of the public realm.

Building footprint and residential density

The relationship between the building footprint (figure) and the space left over after planning (ground) is of fundamental importance for the overall design quality and lived experience of a successful mixed-use, inner-city housing development. It is not appropriate to spell out a specific ratio that should be adhered to, as this will depend on the context, residential density and local design constraints. The figure/ground ratio is largely independent of the residential or building density of the scheme, but overdevelopment or 'site cramming' should be avoided, as it reduces the amenity and character of the project.

Open spaces

For a mixed-use residential development to be successful in a 24-hour city-centre context, it is essential to make the best possible use of all the ground-level space around and between buildings. Within the public realm good space is well-used space, so the relationship between the public realm and the adjacent buildings needs to be carefully considered to ensure that all the surrounding spaces are attractive, well designed, accessible and usable. The proportion of the open space dedicated to public as opposed to private uses, and especially the amount of space given over to private gardens, needs to be carefully considered in the light of the intended population of the residential development and any commercial uses such as a café, which may benefit from access to external space. Developments that contain family dwellings should ensure that these have adequate access to private or communal gardens. The proportion of private gardens to communal grounds is a matter for detailed design, but it should be borne in mind that while private gardens may encourage a clear sense of ownership, some shared external space may be desirable for recreational purposes and to encourage the development of community activities.

Primary boundaries

Constitutedness is the key to any successful mixed-use development. Wherever practicable, blank-walled spaces should be avoided, as these may become magnets for petty crime and antisocial behaviour. All the open spaces within the public realm of a development should therefore be at least overlooked by, and at best fronted by doorways that give access to, the adjacent buildings. There is a benefit to having significant amounts of housing fronting onto integrated streets, as this provides a good mix of 'eyes onto the street' (residents) and 'eyes from the street' (passers-by). Space that is naturally well policed benefits from both kinds of informal surveillance, but residential uses need to be present in sufficient numbers to establish a residential culture in the area. The benefits to residents of such a culture are more significant in streets than in culs-de-sac, and especially in integrated locations.[12] Commercial uses that require a high footfall should not be sited in segregated locations. A problem with many ground-level 'active' frontages in mixed developments is that they are effective only during the daytime and early evening, and operate as if they were unconstituted blank walls at night. Wherever possible, the ground-level frontages of non-residential uses within a mixed development need to be, or appear to be, active throughout the 24-hour cycle. Likewise, the relationship between the entrances to the housing from the public realm should be simple, direct and legible.

Secondary boundaries

In respect of secondary boundaries, it is preferable to restrict these to the minimum and to keep their design simple. The materials, strength, transparency or opacity and heights of any secondary boundaries should be appropriate for the types of uses they are intended to delineate and contain, but the overarching need to preserve the constitutedness of and surveillance over the public realm should be borne in mind when specifying the hard and soft landscaping of a mixed-use urban development. Avoid narrow indents and cul-de-sac areas with high walls or dense foliage, which may heighten the apprehensions of passers-by that public open spaces are unsafe or afford a hiding place where criminals may lurk. Housing developments should avoid creating local vulnerability by providing back or side alleyways that expose private yards or gardens to unauthorised access over unsupervised walls or fences. Corner locations are especially vulnerable in this respect. On the other hand, people may utilise well-designed and strategically located low walls, steps and grassy slopes as informal seating, thus animating and informally policing the public realm.

Axiality

The scale and grain of the street grid of a mixed-use housing scheme should respect, take advantage of and enhance the surrounding context for development. The route structure should be simple and intelligible, and should fit into pre-existing patterns of local and long-distance movement within and through the neighbourhood. The uses of the various faces of the urban blocks that constitute the development should be appropriate to the degree of integration of the adjacent roads, streets or pedestrian paths. Commercial uses that require a

Roseberry Avenue, London

high visibility or 'footfall' should normally be located in strategic, well-integrated locations; residential development may benefit from a less integrated and therefore quieter location, but segregation, particularly of large 'clumps' of adjacent streets and spaces, should be avoided. Over-elaborate or labyrinthine layouts are generally undesirable, as are large numbers of dead end, cul-de-sac spaces.

Liveability

A clear, accessible and well-defined public realm designed according to these principles should benefit from good natural surveillance and avoid many of the liveability issues such as loitering and antisocial behaviour, petty crime, vandalism, littering and graffiti that have been identified in the residential developments studied by the VivaCity2020 consortium.

References

Carter, H. (1983) *An introduction to urban historical geography.* London: Edward Arnold.

Census (2001) *Census 2001: The most comprehensive record of the British population.* London: Office of National Statistics. Retrieved from http://www.statistics.gov.uk/census2001/census2001.asp.

Coleman, A. (1990) *Utopia on trial: Vision and reality in planned housing* (2nd edn). London: Shipman.

Conzen, M.R.G. (1960). *Alnwick, Northumberland: A study in town-plan analysis.* London: George Philip.

Edwards, B. (ed.) (2006) *Courtyard housing: Past, present and future.* Abingdon: Taylor & Francis.

Fishman, R. (1987) *Bourgeois utopias: The rise and fall of suburbia.* New York: Basic Books.

Hanson, J. (2000) Urban transformations: a history of design ideas. *Urban Design International,* 5, 97–122.

Harris, R. & Larkham, P.J. (1999) *Changing suburbs: Foundation, form, and function.* London: E & FN Spon.

Hillier, B. (1996). *Space is the machine: A configurational theory of architecture.* New York: Cambridge University Press.

Hillier, B. & Hanson, J. (1984) *The social logic of space.* Cambridge: Cambridge University Press.

Jenks, M., Burton, E. & Williams, K. (eds) (1996) *The compact city: A sustainable urban form?* London: E & FN Spon.

Martin, L. & March, L. (eds) (1972) *Urban space and structures.* Cambridge: Cambridge University Press.

McCluskey, J. (1992) *Road form and townscape* (2nd edn). Boston: Butterworth Architecture.

Moudon, A.V. (1992) The evolution of twentieth-century residential forms: an American case study. In J.W.R. Whitehand & P.J. Larkham (eds), *Urban landscapes: International perspectives,* pp. 170–206. London: Routledge.

Moughtin, C. (1999) *Urban design: Street and square* (2nd edn). Oxford: Architectural Press.

Mummery, H. (2005) *Around the clock: Town centres for all.* London: The Civic Trust.

ODPM (2003) *English house condition survey 2001.* London: ODPM.

ODPM (2006a) New projections of households for England and the regions to 2026. Retrieved from http://nds.coi.gov.uk/content/detail.asp?NewsAreaID=2&ReleaseID=191108.

ODPM (2006b) *English house condition survey 2003 Annual Report: Decent homes and decent places.* London: ODPM.

Oliver, P. (1987) *Dwellings: The house across the world.* Oxford: Phaidon.

Oliver, P. (2003) *Dwellings: The vernacular house world wide.* London: Phaidon.

Oxman, R., Shadar, H. & Belferman, E. (2002) Casbah: A brief history of a design concept. *ARQ,* **6** (4), 321–336.

Panerai, P., Castex, J. & Depaule, J.-C. (2004). *Urban forms: The death and life of the urban block* (trans. O.V. Samuels). Oxford: Architectural Press.

Parker Morris (1961) *Homes for today and tomorrow. Report of the Parker Morris Committee.* London: HMSO.

Perry, C.A. (1929/1998). *A regional survey of New York and its environs.* Reprinted in R. LeGates & F. Stout (eds), *Early urban planning.* London: Routledge/Thoemmes Press.

Rogers, R. (1999) Towards an urban renaissance: report of the urban task force, Department of the Environment, Transport and the Regions. London: Spon.

Rowe, C. & Koetter, F. (1978) Collage city. Cambridge, MA: MIT Press.

Rudlin, D. & Falk, N. (1999) Building the 21st century home: The sustainable urban neighbourhood. Oxford: Architectural Press.

Schoenauer, N. (1981) 6,000 years of housing (3 vols). New York: Garland STPM.

Scoffham, E.R. (1984) The shape of British housing. London: Godwin.

Sherwood, R. (1978) Modern housing prototypes. Cambridge, MA: Harvard University Press.

Urban Task Force (1999) Towards an urban renaissance: Final report of the Urban Task Force. London: Spon.

Whitehand, J.W.R. & Larkham, P.J. (eds) (1992) Urban landscapes: International perspectives. London: Routledge.

Zhou, J. (2005) Urban housing forms. Oxford: Elsevier.

Footnotes

1   J. Lewis Wormersley, who was the City Architect of Sheffield from 1953 to 1964, was also a partner in the architectural practice Hugh Wilson and Lewis Wormersley, which designed both Park Hill, Sheffield (1955–1961) and the Crescents at Hulme.

2   Like its historic counterpart, a contemporary mixed-use urban block (MUUB) comprises both residential and non-residential uses. In the historic urban block a wide range of different small-scale retail, office and light industrial uses have colonised the ground-level street frontages, the upper levels of premises that overlooked the street or the ground-level backland areas of the block, with the precise location dependent on whether or not the particular use depended on 'passing trade'. In contemporary MUUBs the different uses are invariably stratified vertically, with commercial or retail uses occupying the ground-level street frontages. Offices may be located on lower floors above ground level that overlook the street, and residential uses occupy the upper storeys of buildings that possess a street frontage and those that front onto private, internal courtyards.

3   For an explanation of the space syntax methodology refer to the Appendix.

4   After the black-and-white ichnographic plan map of Rome drawn by surveyor Giambattista Nolli in 1748 (ca 1692–1756) The map, the first since antiquity to be drawn in plan as opposed to a bird's eye perspective, records the streets, squares and public urban spaces of Rome, and all its buildings are accurately recorded, hundreds of which show the detailed plans of the interior.

5   All figures reported in this paper have been calculated to three decimal places and are shown in full in the relevant tables, but for convenience they have been rounded in the text, as we are concerned more with identifying large rather than pinpointing minute numerical differences between individual residential developments.

6   Note that the figures for the developments in our sample are high, compared with most previously published figures. This is because all our examples have been standardised at the level of the urban block: that is, each example occupies one complete urban block, and it is the urban block that is the 'ground' in the figure/ground ratios. This is unlike most density calculations, which are carried out at the neighbourhood scale, and thus include roads, local amenities related to residential development, and additional public open space. However, the household densities for the examples can safely be compared with one another, as they have all been computed in the same way.

7   This is not the same as the average flat size, as it includes common circulation. Mean floor area was adopted for this research, as it obviated the need to carry out detailed surveys of individual flats, a procedure that was not possible, given the wide range of flat types in each development and the fact that all the flats were occupied.

8   Literally meaning the art of judging a person's character from facial expression, the concept that each city has an unique physiognomy that reveals its essential characteristics has been employed to good effect, particularly by contemporary geographers and social historians.

9   We were not permitted to distribute the survey in one estate in Sheffield.

10 Because 'upkeep' and 'antisocial behaviour' each had eight items while 'traffic' and 'non-residential uses' had just four, it was necessary to adjust the average scores for 'upkeep' and 'liveability' reported in Table 7.4 by dividing them by two, in order to compare directly the relative impact of each group of items on the overall liveability of the area.

11 Under Section 106 of the 1990 Town and Country Planning Act, which sets out a mechanism for achieving more affordable housing through the workings of the UK planning system.

12 For further guidance on how the numbers of entrances may statistically affect vulnerability to crime, see Chapter 9.

CHAPTER 8

DESIGNING SAFE
RESIDENTIAL AREAS

Introduction

Community safety and crime reduction are now prime concerns for central and local government (ODPM, 2003), with crime and 'fear of crime' key performance indicators of sustainable development (DEFRA, 2008). Local authorities are also under increasing pressure to ensure that new developments are both secure and good for the environment. This means designing safe, interconnected (i.e. permeable) streets that encourage people to walk, cycle or take public transport, rather than take the car. However, design solutions seeking to embody the concept of permeability may undermine security, a point fiercely debated by some police architectural liaison officers wedded to Crime Prevention Through Environmental Design (CPTED) and architects and planners seeking to promote New Urbanism. This chapter asks how sustainable urban environments can be achieved without incurring actual or perceived increases in crime.

Background and context

Local authorities are expected to ensure that residents are not vulnerable to crime and antisocial behaviour, and that they feel safe at home and in their local environment. The Crime and Disorder Act made it a statutory requirement for local authorities, the police and other key stakeholders to consider the reduction of crime and disorder in all aspects of their work.

Local authorities are therefore expected to consider crime prevention through the design and planning process (see Planning Policy Statement 1 and Planning Policy Guidance Note 3, Housing; ODPM, 2000, 2005). Where crime prevention is a material consideration in the determination of planning permission, applicants have to demonstrate how crime prevention measures have been taken into account. Developments judged vulnerable to crime may be denied planning permission. Ideally, developers, designers and other stakeholders seeking planning permission will consult with police architectural liaison officers and crime prevention officers during the pre-planning stage, thus ensuring that the detailed plans meet criteria for crime prevention. Where the issue of crime is material to the proposed development, local planning authorities may want to set security measures as a planning condition. A *planning condition* must be necessary, relevant to planning, permitted, precise, reasonable and enforceable, as outlined in DoE Circular 11/95. Under these circumstances, the architect/developer must contact the architectural liaison officer or crime prevention officer once the development is complete, and gain written confirmation that the condition has been discharged (ODPM, 2004).

Architects and developers may be encouraged – or required – to apply for Secured By Design accreditation for a building development. Secured By Design is a police initiative to encourage the UK building industry to adopt crime prevention measures within the design of the built environment. Secured By Design status may be awarded to developments that meet the necessary design and security criteria. However, the architect or developer must submit a form explaining how the criteria have been met in order for the development to be approved (see the website, www.securedbydesign.com, for more information). Dwellings that have been awarded the accreditation have been shown to be less vulnerable to burglary (Armitage, 2000).

The research into the relationship between crime and the urban environment, conducted as part of the VivaCity2020 project, aims to help planners, designers and developers address a number of questions in relation to residential and mixed-use areas. In this chapter the following question is considered through case study research:

> 'How can open and permeable residential environments required for sustainability be achieved without incurring actual or perceived increases in crime?'

This research also attempts to contribute constructively to the discussion regarding the compatibility of New Urbanism and CPTED (Knowles, n.d..; Schneider & Kitchen, 2002, 2007; Armitage, 2005; Kitchen, 2005; Town & O'Toole, 2005), moving beyond the simple 'culs-de-sac versus through roads' debate (Fairs, 1998).

We begin by reviewing the literature on New Urbanism, highlighting the similarities to and differences from CPTED. The question of how to achieve permeable and safe urban environments is then explored using qualitative methods involving case studies to understand whether developments have addressed crime, and fear of crime, within the design and planning process.

Review of New Urbanism and CPTED

New Urbanist principles were developed by American architects and urban theorists such as Andrés Duany, Peter Calthorpe, Michael Corbett, Elizabeth Moule, Elizabeth Plater-Zyberk and Stefanos Polyzoides. In 1991 they authored a document that advocated the development of buildings and neighbourhoods that protect the environment and promote quality of life (CNU, n.d.), called the *Ahwahnee Principles for Resource Efficient Communities*. The aim was to encourage the creation of compact, mixed-use, walkable, transit-oriented developments within local communities. The authors hoped that creating vital urban centres would 'break the cycle of urban sprawl' and address problems such as air pollution, dependence on the automobile, and the loss of sense of community (Katz et al., 1991). They believed that well-designed public places and integrated communities should be full of people:

> 'Public spaces should be designed to encourage the attention and presence of people at all hours of the day and night.' (Katz et al., 1991).

Design had a key role to play in promoting vitality, and facilitating walking and cycling:

> 'Streets, pedestrian paths and bike paths should contribute to a system of fully connected and interesting routes to all destinations. Their design should encourage pedestrian and bicycle use by being small and spatially defined by buildings, trees and lighting; and by discouraging high speed traffic.' (Katz et al., 1991).

In 1993 the Congress for the New Urbanism (CNU) was founded to guide public policy, development practice, urban planning and design. The CNU comprised public- and private-sector leaders, community activists and multidisciplinary professionals (see the CNU website), and was led by Peter Katz — one of the editors of the Ahwahnee Principles. These principles are promoted via the

Gell Street Park, Sheffield

Charter of the New Urbanism (n.d.), which maintains that compact neighbourhoods should be created that provide affordable housing and easy access to jobs and local amenities:

> *'Many activities of daily living should occur within walking distance, allowing independence to those who do not drive, especially the elderly and the young. Interconnected networks of streets should be designed to encourage walking, reduce the number and length of automobile trips, and conserve energy ...*
>
> *'Schools should be sized and located to enable children to walk or bicycle to them.'* (Charter of the New Urbanism n.d.)

New Urbanism stresses the importance of restoring urban centres and towns, creating real communities, and preserving the built and natural environment (Schneider & Kitchen, 2002, 2007).

Neighbourhoods planned on New Urbanism principles have a visible centre, perhaps a public square or green park, and are surrounded by streets that are connected in a grid-like fashion – meaning no dead ends or culs-de-sac (Kelly, 2006). It is believed that the cul-de-sac undermines willingness to walk or cycle, because of the increased distances that have to be travelled (DETR, 2000). There are a variety of building and house types, as well as local

amenities. The houses and amenities should be densely situated in the centre, and located further apart in outer areas to preserve surrounding green space. The idea is that 'From proximity, community will respond and develop' (Kelly, 2006: 3).

The design features advocated within New Urbanism include the following (Schneider & Kitchen, 2002, 2007):

- *Increased pedestrian friendliness:* The creation of bounded, 'walkable' neighbourhoods, including introducing rear alleyways, narrowing streets to reduce the speed of cars, widening pavements, lighting pavements rather than roads, planting trees and encouraging houses to have porches and large windows that facilitate surveillance of the street.
- *Prioritisation of public transport and less dependence on the car.* The development and use of public transport and the reduction of car use by, for example, reducing provision of car parking spaces. Garages exist off the streets and behind buildings in a network of alleys (Kelly, 2006).
- *Reduced monoculture:* Mixed-use policies, including diversified house types and businesses, local shopping areas and corner shops.
- *Increased permeability:* Streets, squares and courtyards that are connected to each other to form a network.

In contrast to the Ahwahnee Principles, the importance of safety and security is emphasised within the Charter of the New Urbanism. The assumption is that people on the street will reduce vulnerability to crime:

> *'Streets and squares should be safe, comfortable, and interesting to the pedestrian. Properly configured, they encourage walking and enable neighbours to know each other and protect their communities.'* (Charter of the New Urbanism, n.d.).

However, accessibility and permeability remain the priority within New Urbanism (Kitchen, 2005):

> 'The revitalization of urban places depends on safety and security. The design of streets and buildings should reinforce safe environments, but not at the expense of accessibility and openness.' (Charter of the New Urbanism, n.d.).

CPTED was developed by an American criminologist, C. Ray Jeffrey (1971). Dissatisfied with the effectiveness of the criminal justice system, Jeffrey aimed to develop a new theory of crime prevention based on an understanding of the relationship between humans and their environment. Basically an academic approach, CPTED drew on a range of psychological theories, including behaviourism and learning theory. Whereas previous criminological approaches had focused attention on the subjective state and social environment surrounding criminals – conditions that are difficult to alter – CPTED examines the impact of the physical environment on crimes such as burglary, street robbery, vandalism and vehicle crime, and fear of crime in public places. It seeks to persuade policy-makers, planners and architects to take practical steps to address crime issues through the design of the physical environment (Schneider & Kitchen, 2002).

CPTED was introduced to the UK by Alice Coleman in the 1980s (Colquhoun, 2004). In Europe, CPTED is referred to as 'the reduction of crime and fear of crime by urban planning and architectural design' – or Designing Out Crime (van Soomeren, 1996). CPTED comprises a number of design principles:

- *Division of public and private space (defensible space):* It should be clear to residents and non-residents – including intruders – when an individual moves from public to private space, as this reinforces notions of ownership amongst residents (Town et al., 2003). In this way, CPTED has much in common with the concept of 'defensible space' (Newman, 1973).
- *Increased surveillance*: Residents should be able to see what is happening in and around the building. This may be achieved by choosing housing layouts that allow neighbours to see other properties easily, and by placing windows and doors in locations that allow users – and potential intruders – to be observed (Town et al., 2003; Colquhoun, 2004).
- *Increased access control:* Houses and cars are potential targets for offenders, and access therefore needs to be controlled. Barriers and boundaries may physically impede access (e.g. doors, fences and gates) or psychologically deter intruders from entering an area (e.g. symbolic gateposts, and changes in road surface texture or colour) (Town et al., 2003), creating a sense of risk amongst potential offenders. In addition, access control may be used to concentrate pedestrian movement on particular routes – busy routes can improve surveillance and reduce fear of crime (ODPM, 2004).

- *Increased perception of territoriality*: Residents should feel a sense of ownership in relation to their property and their neighbourhood. This can be achieved with the use of physical and symbolic barriers, and by subdividing residential environments into zones. Communal areas should be accessible to a relatively small number of residents (Schneider & Kitchen, 2002; Colquhoun, 2004).
- *Good management and maintenance*: Residential areas should look well maintained to prevent residents from feeling stigmatised, to encourage care for the environment, and to reduce crime and antisocial behaviour. The importance of building image was recognised following the publication of the 'broken windows theory'. The image of 'broken windows' is used to explain how neighbourhoods descend into incivility, disorder and criminality when insufficient attention is paid to maintenance (McLoughlin, 1999).

Armitage (2005) argues that, although the number of evaluations of Secured By Design remains small, there are many studies showing the crime reduction benefits of the individual principles – in particular, minimising access, maximising surveillance, increasing physical security and increasing territoriality.

CPTED principles and checklists are used by police architectural liaison officers to help designers, developers, planners and clients 'design out' crime. They are also embodied within the accreditation scheme Secured by Design.

Comparison of New Urbanism and CPTED

New Urbanism tends to be optimistic, and assumes that human activity is inherently desirable because it encourages a sense of stewardship and community (Schneider & Kitchen, 2002). CPTED practitioners argue that the movement of people through residential areas increases the risk of burglary. In addition, some activities, such as young people 'hanging around', generate nuisance, opportunities for crime and antisocial behaviour, and fear of crime amongst residents – especially older people (Hampshire & Wilkinson, 2002).

The major areas of contention centre on the New Urbanist requirement for permeability in relation to residential areas. Crime prevention experts attempt to prevent crime by controlling access to properties and developing a design that enables residents to 'police' the area. CPTED practitioners recommend an 'island layout', with dwellings surrounded by roads, and gardens lying within the interior, as this prevents access to the back of dwellings – the most common entry point for burglars. While other layouts are acceptable, designs that are perceived to facilitate illegitimate access to buildings are not supported. CPTED practitioners also argue that the cul-de-sac is a safe urban form, and that street closures are sometimes necessary. Footpaths are allowed, but should be limited in number, and carefully designed to prevent increasing crime in residential areas. In particular, footpaths should be wide, well maintained, and overlooked by dwellings. CPTED practitioners are opposed to footpaths and alleyways running along the backs of properties, and to unmaintained vegetation – factors associated with crime in the UK (Town et al., 2003).

While New Urbanists seek to minimise car use, and to hide cars out of sight, CPTED practitioners accept that cars are part of modern living, and recommend

Table 8.1 Comparison of design features promoted by New Urbanism and CPTED

	New Urbanism	CPTED
Founded by	American architects, urban planners and urban theorists	American criminologist
Primary objective	To create vibrant city centres and neighbourhoods that encourage walking, cycling, use of public transport, and use of local amenities	To ensure safety and security
Principles relating to the movement of people	Permeable and interconnected streets are desirable because they encourage people to use the streets. Culs-de-sac and other streets with dead ends encourage car use	The use of the street by residents is desirable, encouraging 'eyes on the street'. Access control and territoriality should be used to limit the movement of non-residents through an area
Preferred street layout	Deformed grid	Cul-de-sac, island layout
Approach to car parking	Minimise car use; hide cars away in courtyards	In-curtilage parking (i.e. within the area, usually enclosed, immediately surrounding a home)
Approach to footpaths etc.	Use footpaths and cycles routes to increase movement, and reduce car use	Minimise the number of footpaths. Carefully design footpaths and cycle routes to ensure the safety of users
Housing density	Promotes higher densities, using low-rise flats	N/A
Land use	Promotes mixed use, where shops and other local amenities are provided in residential areas	N/A
House types/occupancy	Diversity of house types to reduce monoculture	Diversity in terms of occupants

measures to ensure their security. They prefer cars to be parked at the front of dwellings, where they can be seen. Ideally, cars should be parked in a garage at home or within the dwelling boundary – in-curtilage – as this is safer than the alternatives (Town *et al.*, 2003). CPTED practitioners tend to believe that practical crime prevention should take precedence over concerns about aesthetics and clear sight lines (Schneider & Kitchen, 2002, 2007).

New Urbanism also encourages a mix of land uses within a development to ensure that residents have access to local amenities, such as shops (cf. Chapter 10). The term 'mixed-use' is used within CPTED, but actually relates to the occupancy of the dwellings (i.e., a temporal and social mix). Ideally, developments should include families and older people, not just young, working couples, who are likely to be away at work during the day – leaving the home unoccupied and at risk of burglary, and with low natural surveillance.

New Urbanism does, however, share some similarities with CPTED (see Table 8.1). Both recognise the potential impact of physical design on behaviour, citizenship and feelings of security. Like CPTED, New Urbanism encourages designs that enable 'eyes on the street' (e.g., large front windows, and dwellings set back a minimal distance from the street). CPTED and New Urbanism also agree that smaller-scale developments and/or clear boundaries can promote positive stewardship (Schneider & Kitchen, 2002).

To help planners, developers and designers consider crime prevention, in 2004 the Office of the Deputy Prime Minister (ODPM) published *Safer places: The planning system and crime prevention*. This guidance was developed by consultants and a steering group comprising government departments, the

Commission for Architecture and the Built Environment (CABE), the Planning Officers Society, and the Association of Chief Police Officers' Crime Prevention Initiatives organisation (ACPO CPI Ltd). Consultation was also undertaken with a range of experts in the fields of design, planning and crime prevention. At the time when *Safer places* was being developed, arguments were taking place between some planners and designers committed to New Urbanism and some police architectural liaison and crime prevention officers committed to the principles of CPTED. Optimistic about the future of city living, New Urbanists believed that their plans regarding the creation of vibrant, interconnected or 'permeable' streets that allow through movement would transform city living for the better. Furthermore, they offered to achieve a range of objectives compatible with the government's sustainability agenda (Schneider & Kitchen, 2002). Police architectural liaison officers were more sceptical – some outright hostile – fearing that the principles of New Urbanism, and permeability in particular, would generate opportunities for crime that would be exploited by potential offenders, and undermine their efforts to address crime prevention through the design and planning process (Schneider & Kitchen, 2007).

Safer places successfully trod a middle ground between the competing approaches, stating that sustainable communities require 'places with well-defined routes, spaces and entrances that provide for convenient movement without comprising security' (ODPM, 2004: 13). It recommended 'a good movement network of primary routes to concentrate pedestrians on safe routes; footpaths and cycle routes running alongside roads; and good signage'. It defined permeability as being:

> *the degree to which an area has a variety of pleasant, convenient and safe routes through it'.* (ODPM, 2004: 104).

However, designers and planners need to know how factors such as permeability impact on crime and fear of crime, and how to integrate crime prevention within the design and planning process for all developments, including those following the principles of New Urbanism. As Kitchen (2005) notes, the guide does not really help with this, and simply states that: 'Too few connections can undermine vitality, too many – and especially too many underused or poorly thought out connections – can increase opportunities to commit crime' (ODPM, 2004: 16).

The potential for environments to be both safe and permeable was explored in our research, with the focus on residential areas.

A qualitative approach using case studies on crime

In analysing the relationship between crime, urban design and housing development, a qualitative methodology can explore the ability of design and development teams to address vulnerability to crime, and reconcile potential trade-offs between security and other design issues, such as permeability. Case studies have been used extensively to investigate how products, environments and communications may be designed against crime (Davey *et al.*, 2002a). As part of our research, three aspects of city living connected with the 24-hour city and crime were investigated in detail using literature reviews and case studies: retail services, the late-night economy, and residential areas in or near city centres. This chapter focuses on residential areas, examining how crime prevention was considered within Hulme, near to Manchester city centre. Following this, Chapter 9 discusses the findings from an assessment of crime and the built environment in the London borough of Brent.

Hulme and its regeneration were chosen as a case study because the area is held up as a best-practice exemplar for New Urbanism – along with Poundbury in Dorchester (Schneider & Kitchen, 2002). Hulme is also of interest because, before its redevelopment in the 1990s, it comprised award-winning buildings of the 1960s – 'The Crescents' – and was distinctive for its multi-storey deck-access dwellings and tower blocks. Unfortunately, by the 1980s and early 1990s problems included poor heating, pest infestation, child safety issues, high crime, and poor mental health amongst the residents (Manchester City Council, 1992; Hulme Regeneration Limited, 1994).

Data on Hulme were collected from the following sources:

- crime statistics from Greater Manchester Police
- two site visits – one at the beginning of 2004 with a team of police architectural liaison officers, planners and architects, and another in 2005 with a team of researchers
- nine in-depth interviews with residents, community centre employees, three local authority officers and a police officer
- a review of websites and e-groups set up by local residents (e.g. www.hulme-residentsmanchester.co.uk)

- a review of published literature – strategy and consultation documents on Hulme and its development (Hulme Regeneration Limited, 1994, 1996; North British Housing Association Hulme Team, 1994; Symes, 1998; McLoughlin, 1999; Manchester City Council, 2002, 2003, 2004;); local newspapers – *Manchester Evening News*; community newsletters – e.g. *Hulme Matters* and *Moss Side and Hulme News* (Moss Side and Hulme Partnership and Manchester City Council, 1998); free newsletters produced by the local residents; and reviews and evaluations of Hulme (Ramwell and Saltburn, 1998; SURF, 1999, 2002).

Integrating crime prevention into design activities: Hulme regeneration

To help examine the ways in which crime prevention should be integrated within design and development activities, the authors draw on the Design Against Crime evaluation framework developed by Wootton & Davey (2005). This identifies four main phases of activity within which crime and antisocial behaviour may be addressed:

- project set-up
- project development
- use and performance
- learning and business strategy.

The ways in which crime and antisocial behaviour were addressed in the regeneration of Hulme are described below.

Project objectives

The prevention of crime was not one of the explicit objectives of the Hulme regeneration project, despite a history of high crime and fear of crime dating back to the 1980s (Manchester City Council, 1992, 1993; Hulme Regeneration Limited, 1994). The strategic objectives were to strengthen the local economy, provide access to employment for local people, improve housing stock, improve the quality of the physical environment, and sustain and develop the social fabric (Manchester City Council, 1993). While it might be argued that the objective to 'improve the quality of the physical environment' could be construed as including the reduction of crime and fear of crime, this was never made explicit. Furthermore, the development team did not consult with police about crime issues affecting the proposed development.

Project set-up

Project structure and process
Funds were obtained from a variety of sources, including central government City Challenge funding 1992–1997 (£37.5 million), public-sector resources in Hulme and Moss Side (£24 million), and Capital Challenge 1997–2000 (£11.2 million), as well as money from the European Union Regional Development Fund and the URBAN community initiative programme. The funding was short term

and specific, having to be spent within extremely tight deadlines: any underspend during the early years risked being 'clawed back' (Ramwell & Saltburn, 1998: 18). Consequently, insufficient time and resources were allocated to address relevant crime issues, especially during the early stages of the project.

Guidance and support materials were provided in the form of 'design codes' (e.g. Hulme Regeneration Limited, 1994), but some of the ideas contained in these documents contradicted Manchester City Council's own standards relating to crime prevention, parking, density and distances between buildings (Ramwell & Saltburn, 1998). The principles were supported by planners and architects with a background in design; however, crime prevention experts were not part of the development team.

Project development

Briefing and response to the brief
It is argued that Hulme adhered to the principles of New Urbanism and the work of the Urban Villages Group (Symes, 1998). The idea was 'to create a new neighbourhood with the "feel" of a more traditional urban community' (Hulme Regeneration Limited, 1994: Section 3), in which main streets would have a mix of uses so as to be busy at 'most times of day and night', public spaces would be self-supervised areas of public contact and interaction, and walking and cycling would be promoted rather than the car (Hulme Regeneration Limited, 1994: Section 3). The 'natural supervision' of streets meant not having blank, windowless walls facing streets, or excessive distances between footpaths and windows. There was also an attempt to 'reinvent the terrace', according to Ramwell & Saltburn (1998: 75).

Seeking to overcome the isolation and artificial separation of communities, 'permeability' was a key concept in the design guide. The principle of permeability was: 'If you can't get to a place, you can't use it' (Ramwell & Saltburn, 1998: 76). Thus streets were to be designed to encourage through movement. The cul-de-sac was seen as anti-urban, reducing permeability and free movement. In-curtilage parking was to be avoided: parking was to be provided either on street or behind buildings.

West One, Devonshire Quarter, Sheffield

These principles were summarised in the *Urban Design Code for Hulme* (North British Housing Association Hulme Team, 1994), and were as follows:
- different building types in close proximity
- a variety of streets servicing equitably the needs of people, bikes and vehicles
- streets to terminate at other streets
- clearly defined public and private spaces, squares and parks
- well-placed civic buildings becoming landmarks to express community identity
- buildings at street corners, consolidating the corners
- buildings forming a hard edge to the street, and to front the street
- street edges to be unbroken by car parking, and on-street parking to be encouraged.

The importance of crime prevention was emphasised, although it was not one of the formally stated project objectives, notes Symes (1998). *A Guide to Development for Hulme* stated that 'particular attention needed to be paid to designing secure and "self-policing" developments, where neighbourliness is encouraged'. In subsequent briefing documents, sustainability issues were implicit rather than explicit, and references to crime prevention were omitted.

Although the original objectives conform to New Urbanist principles, the term 'New Urbanism' was used only in later discussions about Hulme (McLoughlin, 1999). It is unclear how the perspective of New Urbanism came to dominate the design brief in Hulme, and further research would be required to trace the influences and considerations in the decision-making processes. The case study revealed that a team of planning consultants and an architect strongly endorsed New Urbanism – and their response to the brief may have reflected these views.

Research and consultation
According to Ramwell & Saltburn (1998), the police Architectural Liaison Unit was opposed to the reinvention of the terrace, with the disputed issue of back access. They also questioned the appropriateness of applying New Urbanism to a high-crime context such as Manchester, and challenged some design decisions that were made – for example, the inclusion of courtyard parking, and alleyways allowing access to the backs of properties. The police appear to have been excluded from the consultation process, and crime prevention-related planning and design standards/guidance (e.g. *Secured By Design*, design codes, etc.) were ignored. The principles contained in the brief also seemed to override tenants' views

obtained through an extensive consultation process. For example, crime and fear of crime issues were raised by tenants in the consultation exercise (L4a, 1991; *Hulme Public Information Gazette*, 1992). However, there appear to have been no outcomes relating to crime documented from discussions.

Concept generation and design
The aspects of New Urbanism that conflicted with CPTED principles were:
- increasing permeability
- minimising the effects of the car, with parking either on street or behind buildings
- providing access to the back of properties via 'ginnels' – narrow passages between dwellings.

Good surveillance and 'eyes on the street' were relied upon to overcome any security issues that arose.

Detailed design, implementation and handover
Problems have emerged in Hulme, including concerns about build quality within private housing, and incidences of crime. Unfortunately, the detailed design, implementation and handover activities are poorly understood, and developers and housing management organisations are in dispute about where fault and responsibility lie. It should be noted, however, that the privately owned dwellings suffered more quality problems than the housing association properties, as the latter were more heavily regulated, and it is suggested that they are of a higher quality (Perry & Harding, 2003).

Use and performance
Ongoing evaluation
The regeneration of Hulme was evaluated against the City Challenge Criteria in 1999 and 2002 by the Centre for Sustainable Urban and Regional Futures (SURF), based at the University of Salford. The evaluation conducted in 2002 demonstrated mixed results, concluding that:
- The development successfully introduced a mix of housing, comprising 42% public sector, 22% housing association and 36% private.
- The number of Hulme residents seeking to move out of the area dropped by 63%, compared with a reduction of only 8% in the city as a whole.
- Rising house prices priced some Hulme residents out of the market (Perry & Harding, 2003), and purchasers of properties in Hulme tended to be professionals (Breheny, 1999).
- While the housing association developments are of a high quality, this is not the case with the private developments.
- Unemployment had dropped from 31.2% (Manchester City Council, 1993: 29) to 16.6%, although there was an 8% drop in unemployment throughout the UK, and the Hulme figure remained higher than for the rest of Manchester, which was 7.9% (Ottewell, 2003).
- There was a growth in the range and volume of businesses operating out of Hulme. However, some business premises remained empty (Lashley, 2004), and architectural liaison officers reported ongoing problems with crime and fear of crime for owners and staff.

Crime prevention was not part of the second evaluation (SURF, 2002), and none of the 25 interviewees was a member of the police force. The report does, however, note that: 'crime in Hulme has risen, both overall and in all but one of the major

Table 8.2 Burglaries and vehicle crime in Hulme Regeneration Area		
Crime Type	April 2002 – March 2003	April 2003 – March 2004
Burglary dwelling/ aggravated burglary dwelling	215 (70.24)	208 (67.95)
Theft of motor vehicle	45	60
Theft from motor vehicle	153	228

Source: Figures provided by Greater Manchester Police. Requested by Lesley Mackay, University of Salford, 2003/2004

Table 8.3 National burglary averages per thousand households		
Burglary dwelling	2002/3	2003/4
National rate	20	19.7
Greater Manchester Police area	39.5	n/a
Hulme Regeneration Area	70	68

Source: Figures provided by Greater Manchester Police. Requested by Lesley Mackay, University of Salford, 2003/2004

crime categories – theft of a vehicle – in recent years' (SURF, 2002: 33). Similarly, 'residents' experiences of crime – and equally important, their fear of crime – rank high on the list of issues that are most likely to cause them to consider whether they wish to remain in Hulme' (SURF, 2002: 34). The authors point out that crime and fear of crime in Hulme 'result in the underuse of some of the assets the regeneration programme has helped develop' (SURF, 2002: 34). Initial evaluations of Hulme in the late 1990s found that crime had gone down, with the police reporting a 40% reduction across the board in key crimes, and 43% reduction for robberies (Ramwell & Saltburn, 1998).

Crime and antisocial behaviour and its relationship to design were explored in more detail (Hulme-residents-Manchester e-group, January 2003, 2004; Moss Side and Hulme Partnership and Manchester City Council, 2002–2004; Ramwell & Saltburn, 1998). Based on figures supplied by Greater Manchester Police, it appears that in 2002 there were 215 recorded burglaries in domestic dwellings, and in 2003 there were 208 burglaries (see Table 8.2). The italicised figures in parentheses represent recorded burglary rates per 1000 dwellings. This is based on a calculation that takes the number of domestic addresses within the Hulme Regeneration Area as 3061.

The national reported rate of burglary was 20 per 1000 households in 2003 (Dodd *et al.*, 2004). It would therefore appear from the above information that burglary rates within the Hulme Regeneration Area are significantly more than three times the national average. They are also higher than for the Greater Manchester area in general (see Table 8.3).

The site visits conducted by police architectural liaison officers and researchers suggested that crime, antisocial behaviour and fear of crime may be linked to the design, construction, management and maintenance of properties, as follows.

Design
- Balconies with supporting struts (i.e. not cantilevered) permit offenders to gain access to first and second floors of flats.
- Ginnels/alleys between houses provide potential offenders with access to the back of properties.
- Courtyard parking increases vulnerability to theft of, or from, a vehicle.
- Courtyard parking provides potential offenders with access to the back of properties.
- Outward-facing properties surround the courtyards, and parked cars are relatively poorly surveyed by residents.
- Dwellings have one level access directly to the road, which improves disabled access but means that passers by – including potential offenders – can easily look through the ground floor windows. This enables potential offenders to ascertain easily whether the property is occupied and/or contains valuables.

Problems with the design have been noted by residents:

> '... it takes the kids seconds to climb up to one of these balconies. And the flats have struts all the way up to the top, so that they can just climb all the way up – no problems. If there weren't legs, they couldn't have done it. So there's an obvious error that the builders for some reason decided to include, whereas in other places you haven't got them.' (Resident)

Construction

- The use of ordinary rather than laminated glass in windows and patio doors facilitates access for potential offenders.
- The poor quality of the locks on patio/balcony doors has resulted in their being circumvented, and burglars gaining access to dwellings.
- Poor design of the locks can lead to patio doors being accidentally left open by residents.
- Poor lighting in courtyards contributes to the poor surveillance of parked cars by residents.
- The gates providing entry to the back gardens from the courtyards are often unlocked. Since the fencing between gardens is relatively low, once potential offenders have gained access to one garden, they can gain access to a whole row of dwellings.
- The front doors used for flats are unable to withstand a concerted attack from a potential offender, owing to weak construction and/or poor locking devices.

These problems have been discussed by residents groups:

> '... the weak front doors of the apartments' communal entrances. During the summer of 2003 these doors were kicked in roughly every three nights (I am not exaggerating, it was a horrible

Saffron Club, Glossop Road, Sheffield

period), and the weak locks and glass panels beside the doors made this extremely easy. I would estimate no fewer than 20 separate occasions when this happened, some nights to 5 blocks of flats, one after the other.' (Hulme-residents-Manchester e-group, January 2003, 2004)

Maintenance and management issues
- Faults reported by residents have not been dealt with adequately during the defects liability period and ongoing maintenance of properties. The failure to repair doors, locks and gates promptly may undermine security.
- Flat numbers are used to indicate parking slots, and the absence of a car may indicate visually to potential offenders that a property is unoccupied.
- Wheelie bins have been introduced, and are used by potential offenders to scale security gates and fences surrounding the properties and courtyard parking.
- While the original fencing allowed some surveillance of surrounding properties and cars, some residents have put wooden boards along the fence to increase privacy. This reduces surveillance of the courtyard area.

These factors have led to dissatisfaction amongst some residents, which in turn has impacted negatively on the reputation of some of the developers and housing management organisations. However, several crime issues have been recognised, and steps have been taken to address these. In particular:
- Organisations and residents' groups have been established to address building quality, maintenance and crime issues.

- Gates have been installed to limit access to the courtyard car parks. However, these electronic, key-fob-operated gates frequently break down, which undermines security and causes inconvenience for residents. In addition, the gates initially fitted to some courtyard parking areas could be easily forced open.
- Laminated glass is being fitted to properties that have been subject to burglary.

Learning and business strategy

It is still unclear whether lessons have been learned from the Hulme regeneration, or whether the experiences have informed the business strategies of the various professionals and consultants who were involved.

Discussion

Our research revealed aspects of the physical environment that could decrease vulnerability to burglary – including some that have not previously been identified. Elsewhere it has been found that risk of burglary falls with increasing numbers of dwellings on the street segment (cf. Chapter 9), with higher residential density at ground level associated with lower rates of both burglary and robbery. One conclusion is that planners and designers should create residential areas with higher dwelling densities at ground floor level and larger block sizes, as this reduces the risk of burglary and makes it possible to ensure the presence of sufficient people to create a residential culture. The UK government is committed to achieving higher-density housing, and to reusing existing urban land (e.g., brownfield, infill), as outlined in its Urban Policy White Paper (DETR, 2000). This goal should support crime prevention efforts.

It should be noted, however, that residents may attempt to increase privacy in dwellings situated in close proximity to each other by boarding up visually permeable garden fences, closing curtains, etc. – factors that reduce the possibilities for surveillance of streets and car parking areas. Higher densities may also encourage courtyard parking rather than in-curtilage, and thus increase vulnerability to car crime. *Safer places* advises that courtyards should be smaller, well surveyed and gated. But the Hulme case study suggests that efforts to promote surveillance may not be successful. Residents are perhaps deterred from using balconies or gardens that overlook car parking facilities, because of the unattractive view. Gates to courtyards frequently break, and can be circumvented by climbing or tailgating.

The primary aim of our research was to understand how residential areas could be made both safe and permeable.

Designers and planners clearly have to tread a middle ground in relation to permeability. Poorly used access is a hazard, because it provides opportunity without surveillance, and is often used for antisocial activity (Hillier, 1996). The provision of permeability for its own sake risks decreasing street segment size and providing access to the back of properties. Permeability needs only to sustain adequate movement and co-presence – 'good space is used space' (Hillier & Sahbaz, 2005). The findings

suggest that designers should encourage local residents to use the street and discourage global movement through residential areas. Global movement might be concentrated on main routes, as stated in *Safer places* (ODPM, 2004). Local residents may be encouraged to use the streets through the availability of play areas for children, and the creation of home zone areas (Biddulph, 2001; Davey et al., 2002a, 2002b).

CPTED practitioners argue that the cul-de-sac is safe. The Hulme case study suggests, however, that insisting on the cul-de-sac can lead to conflict between architectural liaison officers and architects/planners. The authors suggest that the cul-de-sac should not become a bone of contention, as it represents only a small component of any development. Because design solutions need to be adapted to different approaches and contexts, architectural liaison officers and urban designers must work together to ensure that connectivity is implemented appropriately (i.e. without increasing vulnerability to crime). The ODPM (2004) also recommends keeping an open mind regarding the cul-de-sac, stating that it may be appropriate in some circumstances, and that a cul-de-sac should be short and straight, and integrated into the grid network.

Unfortunately, differences in approach between New Urbanists and architectural liaison officers were not resolved during the regeneration of Hulme, where arguments about permeability in general, and the cul-de-sac in particular, appear to have undermined efforts to address crime prevention.

Opportunities for incorporating crime prevention measures into the design, construction and maintenance of Hulme were certainly missed, resulting in patio doors, front doors and balconies that were insufficiently resistant to burglars. Burglars could also access the back of some properties via ginnels and courtyard car parks.

Conflict between CPTED practitioners and New Urbanists possibly stems from their different backgrounds. Architectural liaison officers are generally serving police officers, who receive training in CPTED. Police officers understandably prioritise crime over other objectives, and perhaps feel that any attempt at compromise would represent a failure to ensure the achievement of this important goal. Daily contact with offenders probably encourages a more pessimistic view of human nature, heightening awareness of opportunities within environments for crime and antisocial behaviour. They appear to favour 'planning for the worst', rather than risk the development being vulnerable to crime owing to lack of security. In addition, few architectural liaison officers have a background in the design or planning disciplines, or experience of working with the development industry. Consequently, police architectural liaison officers perhaps feel more comfortable applying standard principles and checklists, rather than adapting solutions to different design approaches or contexts (Schneider & Kitchen, 2002).

Design professionals, on the other hand, seek to achieve a range of objectives related to commercial success, aesthetics and convenience, making trade-offs where appropriate. They are trained in a discipline that values creativity, and are often opposed to the application of standard principles, which are seen as overly constraining. Designers also tend to be optimistic about human nature and the potential for design to improve society, as evidenced by their commitment to social issues (Whiteley, 1993; Davey et al., 2005).

While opportunities to address crime and antisocial behaviour were missed in Hulme, there are still examples of good practice. For example, careful attention was paid to issues of crime, antisocial behaviour and fear of crime in the design of Hulme Park (Davey et al., 2002a). In addition, crime prevention is now better integrated into the design and planning process, thanks to changes to the Architectural Liaison Unit in Manchester. Architectural liaison officers working for Greater Manchester Police have a background in the development industry, and are therefore better able to engage with architects and developers, and to tailor design advice to the particular contexts. Architects and developers consult with architectural liaison officers earlier during the design and planning process, thus making it easier to incorporate security measures into their designs. In addition, architects and developers are more likely to listen to advice, as this increases their chances of being granted planning permission (Armitage et al., 2007a, 2007b).

The creation of a 24-hour culture promotes the building of residential dwellings in the city centre, thus avoiding streets being deserted once the shops have closed and the bars and clubs are yet to open. Mixed-use developments in cities can work, but only with a sufficiently high ratio of residential dwellings to business premises, and a diversity of business and social uses (cf. Chapter 10). It is important to get this mix right, because crime and fear of crime may deter businesses from locating or remaining in the area, generate fear amongst staff, and deter residents from walking to local amenities.

Table 8.4 The government agenda and crime prevention issues

Government objective	Research findings from VivaCity2020 project
Objectives that may increase vulnerability to crime	
To promote the benefits of city-centre living	Dwellings in town centres are more vulnerable to crime. Affluent residential areas located near to town centres are also vulnerable. Additional security measures are required for properties in such areas.
To increase permeability	Local movement appropriate to the area should be facilitated – not global or unnecessary movement. The ODPM (2004) suggests that pedestrians and bicycles be concentrated on main routes, and this would appear appropriate.
To reduce car parking and therefore discourage car use	In-curtilage is the most secure form of parking, but this is not always possible with higher densities. According to the ODPM (2004), courtyards should be small, gated and well surveyed. However, the VivaCity2020 project found that cars in courtyards were vulnerable to crime, and that security measures (e.g. gates and natural surveillance) often failed.
To encourage the provision of footpaths and cycle routes	Footpaths should not provide access to the back of properties.
To encourage mixed-use developments (i.e. shops, etc. in residential areas)	Mixed use increases vulnerability to burglary. There should be sufficient dwellings to create a residential culture. Additional security measures may also be required.
Objectives that may reduce vulnerability to crime	
To promote the development of higher housing densities	Increased housing density at ground level reduces vulnerability to crime.
To help create a sense of community	Large block sizes and sufficient numbers of dwellings on streets reduce risk of burglary and should help generate a residential culture – an important factor in security

Our research suggests that the government agenda affects vulnerability to crime. Objectives that risk increasing crime include: permeability in relation to global movement through residential areas; the provision of footpaths and cycle routes; and mixed-use developments when the numbers of residential dwellings are low. In some cases, *Safer places* provides guidance on how to minimise any potential risk, but this is not always possible, or may not work in practice. An objective that potentially decreases vulnerability is higher-density housing developments. The Hulme case study showed that community/residents groups have an important role to play in ensuring that crime issues are addressed – thus 'a sense of community' may also help reduce crime (see Table 8.4).

The VivaCity2020 project has highlighted a range of difficulties when residential areas and local amenities coexist, including noise, rubbish and disturbance. In addition, some crime prevention issues arise from attempts to meet other sustainability criteria.

Dwellings at street level ensure accessibility for disabled people in Hulme. However, when such dwellings front onto the street, residents find that their privacy is undermined, and potential offenders can easily look in through their windows. This may encourage residents to close their curtains or blinds, thus reducing surveillance of the street. Innovative solutions to this problem are required.

Conclusion and recommendations

The literature review confirms that New Urbanism conflicts with CPTED advice regarding access, parking and street layout – particularly the cul-de-sac. *Safer places* (ODPM, 2004), treads a middle ground between these competing approaches, stating that: *'Too few connections can undermine vitality, too many – and especially too many underused or poorly thought out connections – can increase opportunities to commit crime'* (ODPM, 2004: 16).

Space syntax analysis (see Chapter 9) suggests that street layout should facilitate local movement – but not global movement. It also found that the risk of burglary is decreased when there are more dwellings along a street and within higher-density developments at ground level. These factors increase 'eyes on the street', and mean there is a lower risk of any one house being burgled when an area is targeted by offenders.

Attempts should therefore be made to ensure sufficient numbers of residential dwellings on street segments, and to control the global movement of people. However, this may be difficult in relation to city centres, and to dwellings located near to local amenities. Additional security measures are required for dwellings judged to be at risk.

The cul-de-sac is found to be safe under certain circumstances. However, the case study of Hulme shows that arguments about permeability and the cul-de-sac have undermined efforts to address crime prevention. We are nevertheless optimistic that policies adopted by the local authority and the police Architectural Liaison Unit in Greater Manchester will enable conflicts to be better resolved in the future.

Based on our findings, it is also recommended that crime prevention issues should be incorporated within the urban design and planning process, following the guidance contained in the *Design Against Crime Evaluation Framework* (Wootton & Davey, 2005). In particular:

Stage 1: Creating teams, appraising the situation and forming goals

Appraising the situation and forming goals

The crime risks need to be identified at this early stage. This involves:

- consulting with crime prevention experts
- considering the extent to which national and local factors increase or decrease the crime problems
- considering the users and the 'mis-users'
- consulting appropriate guidance (e.g. European Standard on Designing Out Crime, *Secured by design*, and publications such as *Safer places* (ODPM, 2004)). Detailed guidance on residential areas is provided by Town *et al.* (2003)
- examining examples of good practice (e.g. social housing in Northmoor, and housing by Royds Community Association; www.designagainstcrime.org)
- where the risks of crime are high, specifically incorporating crime prevention in the project's objectives.

NB: The identification of crime issues and their incorporation into the project's objectives may be undermined by ideological conflicts between planning/design approaches, such as New Urbanism, and crime prevention schemes. This problem may be exacerbated by crime prevention schemes that are wedded to particular design solutions or one-size-fits-all interventions, rather than being focused on the criteria for success – which may be met in other, more innovative ways.

Creating teams

- The project team should include individuals skilled in design, crime prevention, and the understanding and interpreting of requirements.

NB: Individuals skilled in crime prevention may be excluded from the team owing to personal or professional biases or ideological conflict.

Project timetable and budget
- Adequate time and resources need to be dedicated to addressing crime issues, especially at the front end of the project development process. Embedding the prevention of crime, antisocial behaviour and fear of crime within the project at the outset will help reduce the impact and cost of remedial interventions at a later stage.

NB: Efforts to consider crime issues may be undermined by tight deadlines or funding problems. However, it may be an expensive mistake to 'leave it until later' and 'retrofit'.

Stage 2: Designing and developing
Developing project brief
- The brief should contain crime-related requirements.
- Crime-related issues should be discussed by the designers/planners and client during the briefing activities.

NB: Crime issues are sometimes played down in the brief, or are even omitted from later versions of the brief, owing to conflict between crime prevention experts, or concerns about other issues (e.g. funding constraints, the perception that crime is too 'negative', for PR reasons, and timescale pressures).

Research and involvement of stakeholders
All the relevant stakeholders and information sources should be identified and prioritised, including:
- clients/customers
- users – especially vulnerable groups
- potential misusers
- crime experts (e.g. local police)
- design-led crime prevention experts.

NB: Information about requirements and constraints needs to be gathered and analysed, and the findings used to generate the specification.

Conflict between crime prevention experts and crime prevention approaches may lead to their being excluded from the research and consultation process. Users may be consulted, but the results of this may not be incorporated into subsequent design decisions. Consultation with potential misusers may not even be considered. Failure to incorporate crime prevention in the design specification can lead to decisions that compromise security, leave users dissatisfied, and impact negatively on users' quality of life.

Identifying crime prevention options
- The potential effect of crime scenarios and risk factors on different design solutions should be considered, and innovative thinking used to address crime issues creatively.

NB: Crime prevention may be treated as a constraint to be resisted by the development team, rather than as an opportunity to use innovative thinking to address an important issue in a novel way.

Stage 3: Evaluating, selecting and creating a plan
- Crime scenarios should be reviewed, and integrated into the final design.
- The final design solution(s) should be tested with relevant stakeholders and against existing standards and guidance. The guidance developed by Wootton & Davey (2003) may be helpful in this respect.

NB: Clearly, it is difficult to incorporate crime prevention during the detailed design stage, if crime has not been addressed to some extent in the preceding activities. Failure to do this can result in the inclusion of core design features that increase vulnerability to crime (e.g. courtyard parking, easy access to the back of properties, or balconies accessible to potential offenders). Unfortunately, the security measures required to lessen the impact of such embedded 'crime-friendliness' in a design may ultimately thwart the original inspiration of the planners to create a quality design environment.

Stage 4: Implementing, monitoring and following up
Production/implementation
- The production/implementation function should be involved in the project at an early stage in the design process, and should be made aware of the importance of the project addressing crime issues effectively – preferably through a clear design specification.

NB: Materials and components used during the construction phase may undermine security. For example, weak doors/gates, inappropriate glass and cheap locking mechanisms can all increase vulnerability to crime.

Taking over the project on completion
- Crime prevention elements within the design should be clearly communicated to clients, maintenance staff and users.

NB: Poor maintenance procedures and ill-informed user behaviour may undermine the security of dwellings by enabling illegitimate use and hindering surveillance (e.g. leaving gates/doors open, boarding up visually permeable fences, and leaving wheelie bins near gates and fences, where they can be used as stepladders).

- Management and maintenance activities should be planned and implemented to ensure the ongoing security of the development.

NB: Failure to undertake repairs quickly may allow access to private areas (e.g. shared hallways and stairwells, and car parks). Management and maintenance issues may be poorly handled owing to conflict at the handover stage and during the defects liability period, and consequent confusion over responsibility for repairs.

Revisit and review progress
- New developments should be subjected to ongoing evaluation to determine their performance, cost-benefits, and user experience.

NB: Development projects are usually evaluated against project objectives. Consequently, projects that fail to incorporate crime prevention in their objectives are likely to exclude crime prevention from the evaluation process.

Communicate with stakeholders
- The ability to address crime issues effectively can form the basis for strong relationships with clients and users.

NB: The failure to address crime issues can lead to resentment amongst users and generate negative publicity for the developer, through pressure campaigns, website discussion groups (Bellway Home Buyers Survival Site, 2003) and articles in the press.

References

Armitage, R. (2000) *An evaluation of secured by design housing within West Yorkshire*. London: Home Office, Policing and Reducing Crime Unit.

Armitage, R. (2005) Sustainability versus safety: confusion, conflict and contradiction. In G. Farrell, K. Bowers, S. Johnson and M. Townsley (eds), *Imagination for crime prevention: Essays in honour of Ken Pease, Vol. 21: Crime prevention series*, pp. 81–110. New York: Criminal Justice Press.

Armitage, R., Monchuk, L. & Wootton, A.B. (2007a) *Greater Manchester Police Architectural Liaison Service Evaluation. Work package 1 report. Service providers*. Salford: Design Against Crime Solution Centre, University of Salford.

Armitage, R., Monchuk, L. & Wootton, A.B. (2007b) *Greater Manchester Police Architectural Liaison Service Evaluation. Work package 2 report. Service users*. Salford: Design Against Crime Solution Centre, University of Salford.

Bellway Home Buyers Survival Site (2003) Retrieved from http://www.buggers.org.

Biddulph, M. (2001) *Home zones: A planning and design handbook*. Bristol: Policy Press.

Breheny, M. (1999) Jobs as well as homes are crucial to urban renaissance. *Urban Environment Today*, 23 December, 86.

CNU (n.d.) *Charter of the New Urbanism*. Retrieved 1 August 2008 from http://architecture.about.com/library/bl-urbanism-charter.htm.

Colquhoun, I. (2004) *Design out crime: Creating safe and sustainable communities*. Oxford: Architectural Press.

Davey, C., Cooper, R. & Press, M. (2002a). *Design against crime: Case study exemplars*. Salford: University of Salford.

Davey, C.L., Cooper, R., Press, M., Wootton, A.B. & Olson, E. (2002b) *Design against crime: Design leadership in the development of emotional values*. Paper presented at the 11th International Conference of the Design Management Institute, Boston, United States. Available from www.sociallyresponsibledesign.org/resources.htm.

Davey, C.L., Wootton, A.B., Thomas, A., Cooper, R. & Press, M. (2005) Design for the surreal world? A new model of socially responsible design. Paper presented at the European Academy of Design, Bremen, Germany. Available from www.sociallyresponsibledesign.org/resources.htm.

DEFRA (2008) *Sustainable development indicators in your pocket 2008*. London: Department for Environment, Food and Rural Affairs.

DETR (2000). *Building a better quality of life: A strategy for more sustainable construction*. London: Department of Environment, Transport and the Regions.

Dodd, T., Nicholas, S., Povey, D. & Walker, A. (2004) Crime in England and Wales 2003/4. *Home Office Statistical Bulletin*, 10/04.

DOE Circular 5/94. Planning Out Crime. London: HMSO.

Fairs, M. (1998) End of the road for the cul-de-sac. *Building Design*, 1373, 1.

Charles Rowan House, Clerkenwell, London

Hampshire, R. & Wilkinson, M. (2002). *Youth shelters and sports systems: A good practice guide*, 2nd edn. Kidlington, Oxfordshire: Thames Valley Police.

Hillier, B. (1996) Cities as movement economies. *Urban Design International*, 1 (1), 49–60.

Hillier, B. & Sahbaz, O. (2005) High resolution analysis of crime patterns in urban street networks: an initial statistical sketch from an ongoing study of a London borough. *Proceedings of the Fifth International Space Syntax Symposium*, Delft, The Netherlands, Vol. 1, pp. 451–478.

Hulme Public Information Gazette (1992) *Little extra tabloid*. Manchester: Manchester City Council.

Hulme Regeneration Limited (1994) *Rebuilding the city: A guide to development in Hulme*. Manchester: Hulme Regeneration Limited.

Hulme Regeneration Limited (1996) *The new Hulme: An update from Hulme Regeneration Limited*. Manchester: Hulme Regeneration Limited.

Hulme-residents-Manchester (2003) Hulme-residents-Manchester. Retrieved from http://www.hulme-residents-manchester.co.uk/ and http://groups.yahoo.com/group/Hulme-residents Manchester/database?method=reportRows&tbl=4&sortBy=1& SortDir=dpwn&startAt=&prntRpt=1

Jeffrey, C.R. (1971) *Crime prevention through environmental design*. Beverley Hills, CA: Sage.

Katz, P., Corbett, J. & Weissman, S. (eds) (1991) *The Ahwahnee principles for resource efficient communities*. Sacramento, CA: Local Government Commission.

Kelly, J.M.W. (2006) Can we afford New Urbanism? *Pine Magazine*. Retrieved 14 January 2008 from http://pine-magazine.com/content.php?id=103.

Kitchen, T. (2005) New Urbanism and CPTED in the British planning system: some critical reflections. *Journal of Architecture and Planning Research*, **22** (4), 342–357.

Knowles, P. (n.d.) *Designing out crime: The cost of policing New Urbanism*. Available from http://americandreamcoalition.org/safety/policingnu/policingnu.html.

L4a (1991) *Not just bricks and mortar: Bringing the dignity back to Hulme. Report from two residents' workshops in Hulme area*. Hulme, Manchester: L4a.

Lashley, B. (2004) Jobs pledge gets a stamp of approval. *Manchester Evening News*, 16 January. Available for download from: www.manchestereveningnews.co.uk/news/s/78/78394_jobs_pledge_gets_a_stamp_of_approval.html.

Manchester City Council (1992) *City Challenge: Hulme Action Plan 1992/97*. Manchester: Manchester City Council.

Manchester City Council (1993) *The Hulme baseline study: A portrait of Hulme before Hulme City Challenge*. Manchester: Manchester City Council.

Manchester City Council (2002) *Ward performance plan 2002–2003, Hulme matters*. Manchester: Manchester City Council.

Manchester City Council (2003) *Ward performance plan 2003–2004, Hulme matters*. Manchester: Manchester City Council.

Manchester City Council (2004) *Hulme matters*. Manchester: Manchester City Council.

McLoughlin, B. (1999) A guide to development in Hulme, Manchester. Paper presented at the Conference on the Inclusive City, Lyon, France, 6–10 May.

Moss Side, Hulme Partnership and Manchester City Council (1998) *Moss Side and Hulme News*, Issue 2.

Newman, O. (1973) *Creating defensible space*. Washington, DC: US Department of Housing and Urban Development Office of Policy Development and Research.

North British Housing Association Hulme Team (1994) *Urban design code for Hulme: Main points of the guide to development in Hulme, Manchester*. Manchester: Manchester City Council.

ODPM (2000) *Planning Policy Guidance 3: Housing*. London: Office of the Deputy Prime Minister.

ODPM (2003) *Sustainable communities: Building for the future*. London: Office of the Deputy Prime Minister.

ODPM (2004) *Safer places: The planning system and crime prevention*. London: Thomas Telford.

ODPM (2005) *Planning Policy Statement 1: Delivering sustainable development*. London: Office of the Deputy Prime Minister.

Ottewell, D. (2003) Jobs slump dims Games afterglow. *Manchester Evening News*, 13 October. Available for download from: www.manchestereveningnews.co.uk/news/s/69/69856_jobs_slump_dims_games_afterglow.html.

Perry, B. & Harding, A. (2003). Off the critical list. *New Start*, 24 January, 14.

Ramwell, R. & Saltburn, H. (1998) *Trick or treat? City Challenge and the regeneration of Hulme*. Manchester: High Wycombe, North British Housing Association, Preston and The Guinness Trust.

Schneider, R.H. & Kitchen, T. (2002) *Planning for crime prevention: A transatlantic perspective*. London: Routledge.

Schneider, R. H. & Kitchen, T. (2007) *Crime prevention and the built environment*. Abingdon: Routledge.

Soomeren, P. van (1996). Safe and secure cities. The physical urban environment and reduction of urban insecurity: a general introduction. Paper presented at the Conference on the Reduction of Urban Insecurity, Barcelona, Spain, 1987 (revised edition issued by van Soomeren and Partners).

SURF (1999). *Hulme City Challenge: Did it work?* Manchester: Centre for Sustainable Urban and Regional Futures, University of Salford.

SURF (2002). *Hulme: Ten years on*. Draft Final Report to Manchester City Council. Manchester: Centre for Sustainable Urban and Regional Futures, University of Salford.

Symes, M. (1998). *Hulme design guide: Sustainability section*. Manchester: Manchester City Council.

Town, S. & O'Toole, R. (2005). Crime-friendly neighbourhoods: how 'New Urbanist' planners sacrifice safety in the name of 'openness' and 'accessibility'. *Reason*, **36** (9), 30–36.

Town, S., Davey, C.L. & Wootton, A.B. (2003). *Secure urban environments by design: Guidance for the design of residential areas*. Salford: University of Salford.

Whiteley, N. (1993) *Design for society*. London: Reaktion Books.

Wootton, A.B. & Davey, C.L. (2003) *Crime life-cycle: Guidance for generating design against crime ideas*. Salford: Design Against Crime Solution Centre, University of Salford.

Wootton, A.B. & Davey, C.L. (2005) *DAC Evaluation Framework: A framework to support and evaluate the integration of design against crime within development projects*. Salford: Design Against Crime Solution Centre, University of Salford.

Statutes

Crime and Disorder Act 1998. Chapter 37. London: HMSO.

Websites

Congress for the New Urbanism (CNU) website. Retrieved 9 January 2008 from www.cnu.org.

Secured by Design website. Retrieved 9 January 2008 from www.securedbydesign.com.

CHAPTER 9
CRIME AND URBAN DESIGN: AN EVIDENCE-BASED APPROACH

Bill Hillier and Ozlem Sahbaz

Design and crime: the open and closed solutions

It is generally agreed that a key priority in the design of cities is, insofar as it is possible, to make life difficult for the criminal. But is that really possible? Different crimes, after all, are facilitated by very different kinds of spaces: picking pockets is easier in crowded high streets, street robbery is easier when victims come one at a time, burglary is helped by secluded access, and so on. In inhibiting one crime, it seems, we might be in danger of facilitating another.

Even so, the sense that some environments are safe and others dangerous is persistent, and inspection of crime maps will, as often as not, confirm that people's fears are not misplaced. So is it possible to make environments generally safer? Strangely, although it is now widely believed that it is, there are two quite different schools of thought about how it should be done. The first is traceable to Jane Jacobs's book *The death and life of great American cities* in 1961, and advocates open and permeable mixed-use environments, in which strangers passing through spaces, as well as inhabitants occupying them, form part of an 'eyes on the street' natural policing mechanism that inhibits crime. The second, traceable to Oscar Newman's book *Defensible space* in 1973, argues that having too many people in spaces creates exactly the anonymity that criminals need to access their victims, and so dilutes the ability of residents to police their own environment. Crime can then be expected to be less in low-density, single-use environments with restricted access to strangers, where inhabitants can recognise strangers as intruders and challenge them.

We could call these the 'open' and 'closed' solutions, and note that each in its way seems to be based on one kind of common-sense intuition, and

each proposes a quite precise mechanism for maximising the social control of crime through design. Yet the two solutions seem to imply design and planning solutions that are in many ways the opposite of each other. The problem is further complicated by sustainability. To minimise energy consumption, we are said to need denser environments, which are easier to move about in under personal power, and with more mixing of uses to make facilities more easily accessible. This implies permeable environments in which you can easily go in any direction without too long a detour. From this point of view, the way we expanded towns in the later part of the twentieth century, with large areas of hierarchically ordered culs-de-sac in relatively closed-off areas, made trips longer and so more car dependent. So if it were criminogenically neutral, the open solution would be preferable. But its critics say it is not. The open solution, they argue, will facilitate crime and so create a new dimension of unsustainability.

So what does the evidence say? The fact is that on the major strategic design and planning questions it says precious little. The points at issue were recently summarised by Stephen Town and Randall O'Toole (Town & O'Toole, 2005) in a table of six points where the 'open' position, which they say is preferred by Zelinka & Brennan (2001) in their New Urbanist book *SafeScape*, is contrasted with the closed 'defensible space' position, which has dominated most thinking until quite recently (see Table 9.1).

Table 9.1 SafeScape versus defensible space

	SafeScape	Defensible space
Public versus private	Maximise commons to promote interaction and a sense of community	Maximise private areas to create defensible space; create a sense of community through smaller developments with fewer strangers
Uses	Mix uses to provide activity and increase eyes on the street	Mixed used reduces residential control and therefore increases crime
Streets and footpaths	Encourage walking and cycling; increase surveillance through a grid street pattern	Limit access and escape opportunities to provide more privacy and increase residential control
Alleys	Face buildings towards alleys to provide eyes on the alley	Eliminate or gate alleys, as they increase burglary and are dangerous for pedestrians
Automobiles	Build homes close to the street, forcing parking to be on the street or in rear courtyards	Automobiles are safest in garages or visible in front of the house; rear courtyards facilitate burglary
Density	High density to promote activity, sustain public transit, and reduce sprawl	Density creates vulnerability when it increases common areas or unsafe parking

Source: Town & O'Toole (2005)

On some of the more detailed issues in the table, for example, the dangers of rear or courtyard parking, or the risks introduced by footpaths and alleys, there is ample evidence that the advocates of 'defensible space' are right (e.g., Hillier & Shu, 2000; Hillier, 2004). But on the 'big' issues of grid versus tree-like layouts, public versus private space, developmental scale, permeability, mixed-use and residential density, hard evidence is sporadic and inconclusive (for a fairly recent review, see Shu, 2002).

The open question then is: Can the open, permeable, dense, mixed-use environments that would seem to be preferable for sustainability be constructed in such a way as to also make them safe? Or are such environments by their nature criminogenic? The aim of the VivaCity2020 research on crime was to try to provide a methodology and a body of evidence to address this question. Is one view right and the other wrong? Or is it possible, as will be argued here through a very large body of evidence, that both are right about some things and wrong about others, and that both sets of common-sense intuitions need to be seen as part of a more complex model that incorporates the underlying ideas and mechanisms of both?

The research questions

A first step in the research was to break down the two models into a number of key questions that should be answerable by evidence, but so far have not been, or not decisively:

- Are some kinds of dwelling safer than others?
- Is density good or bad for crime?
- Is movement in your street good or bad?
- Are culs-de-sac safe or unsafe?
- Does it matter how we group dwellings?
- Is mixed use beneficial or not?
- Should residential areas be permeable or impermeable?

While looking at these questions we shall also bear in mind another major unresolved question that may underlie all the others: Do social factors interact with spatial and physical factors?

The existing evidence base

Some of these questions have been addressed before through research, but in terms of compelling, empirically based studies the evidence base is astonishingly poor, and mixed with anecdote and prejudice. For example, Oscar Newman's work on social housing projects in New York in the 1960s gave flats a bad name (Newman, 1973), but Tracey Budd's multivariate analysis of the British Crime

Clerkenwell Road, London

Survey data in 1999 (Budd, 1999) suggested that once social and economic factors were taken into account, flats were the safest dwelling type, followed by terraced houses, semi-detached houses and finally detached houses, though the more often quoted raw data said the inverse. Subsequent evidence (Hillier & Shu, 2002) suggested that the multivariate order of safety, with flats safest and detached houses least safe, might sometimes be the case even without taking other factors into account.

Similarly, density has always been assumed to increase crime. Again, Newman's (1973) work was interpreted as inculpating density, although what Newman actually said was that is was not density per se that facilitated crime, but the building form (double loaded corridors) that was necessary to achieve that density. A series of recent studies has also failed to find any association between higher densities and crime (Haughey, 2005; Harries, 2006; Li & Rainwater, 2006), though none has so far shown it to be unambiguously beneficial.

On movement, closeness to main roads is widely thought to increase vulnerability to burglary, but recent studies (reviewed in Hillier, 2004) have suggested that it may also be the case that away from the main roads and within residential areas roads with more movement potential are actually safer, unless other dwelling-related vulnerability factors, such as basement entrances or back alleys, are in play. The related issue of the safety of culs-de-sac again is a core belief in the 'defensible space' view, but it is difficult to find hard evidence one way or the other. Before the turn of the century, the British Crime Survey reported lower burglary rates on culs-de-sac than side roads, and less burglary on side roads than main roads, but there are no reports that these raw figures were tested by multivariate analysis, as they would need to be to take out possible bias due to social variables. The clearest evidence on culs-de-sac in fact comes from space syntax studies (Hillier, 2004), where it is suggested that simple linear culs-de-sac with good intervisibility of dwellings, set into a through-street pattern, can be very safe, but hierarchies of interlinked culs-de-sac can be highly vulnerable, especially if connected by poorly used footpaths.

On grouping dwellings, again we find belief ascendant over evidence in the form of a widely held view that small numbers of dwellings facing each other around a space will promote community and so inhibit crime (for a critique of this concept see Hillier, 1989), but compelling evidence that this is so is hard to find. The same is the case with mixed use, permeability and social factors. Passionately held beliefs abound, but little evidence can be located that would enable a reasoned judgement to be made. It must be said also that the polemic positioning that currently marks this debate is often characterised by claims that an evidence base exists when closer examination shows that it does not. Newman (1973), for example, whose Defensible Space is often referred to by the supporters of culs-de-sac, provided no evidence about culs-de-sac in that research, and indeed expressed the view that well-used 'streets provide security in the form of prominent paths for concentrated pedestrian and vehicular movement' (p. 25), adding that 'the street pattern, with its constant flow of vehicular and pedestrian traffic, does provide an element of safety for every dwelling unit' (p. 103).

Methodology

Why then, after all this time and interest, is the evidence base so sparse? One reason is certainly methodological. To examine the spatial distribution of crime in an urban environment systematically, it would be necessary to have a rigorous, consistent and precise way of describing the differences between one urban environment and another, and between the different locations that make up that environment where crimes may or may not occur. The number of variables involved makes this formidably difficult, and the emphasis in computer packages for 'crime analysis' on 'hot spots' independent of the precise spatial and physical features of locations has perhaps distracted attention from this core problem.

It is here that the space syntax techniques of spatial analysis can play a role. Space syntax is a set of techniques for representing and analysing the street networks of cities in such a way as to bring to light underlying patterns and structures that influence patterns of activity in space, most notably movement and land use. The model works at the level of the 'street segment' between intersections, and research has shown that there are ways of analysing the network that allow potential movement rates along each street segment to be approximated from the spatial analysis alone, and through the relation between the street network and movement, to identify the ways in which centres and subcentres form in the network. As a consequence of this research, space syntax sees the city as being made up of a foreground network of high-activity linked centres at all scales (conventionally coloured red, orange and yellow in a space syntax analysis of the network) set into a background network of lower-activity residential space (conventionally coloured green and blue). The model is explained more fully in Appendix 2.

Because movement, land use and high- and low-activity patterns are all thought to be linked in some way to crime, space syntax might offer not only a way to describe and compare urban environments from the point of view of crime distributions, but

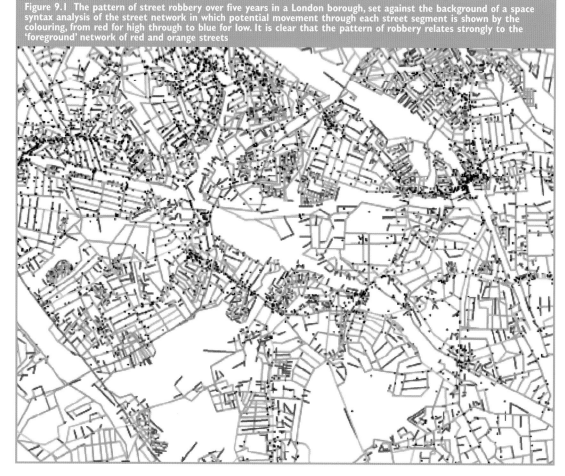

Figure 9.1 The pattern of street robbery over five years in a London borough, set against the background of a space syntax analysis of the street network in which potential movement through each street segment is shown by the colouring, from red for high through to blue for low. It is clear that the pattern of robbery relates strongly to the 'foreground' network of red and orange streets

also a means to link crime to the patterns of urban life in that environment. Evidence that this is so can be seen in Figures 9.1 and 9.2.

Figure 9.1 shows that the pattern of street robbery over five years in a London borough clearly relates to the redder lines of the foreground network, while Figure 9.2 shows that the much more diffused pattern of residential burglary does not follow anything like the same logic. But more importantly, because the colours stand for numerical values describing each street segment in the network, statistical comparisons can be made with other numbers representing located crimes. In fact, space syntax can do more than this. Because it provides a method to numerically index a large number of

properties of the locations and areas that make up the urban environment, it can be used as a basic spatial description to which social, economic, demographic and other kinds of information can be added. In this way spatial factors can be brought into the statistical analysis of crime patterns on a common numerical basis.

The database for this study is made up of five years' worth of police crime data in a London borough with a population of 263 000, 101 849 dwellings in 65 459 residential buildings, 536 km of road, made up of 7 102 street segments, and many centres and subcentres at different scales. The crime database covers five years

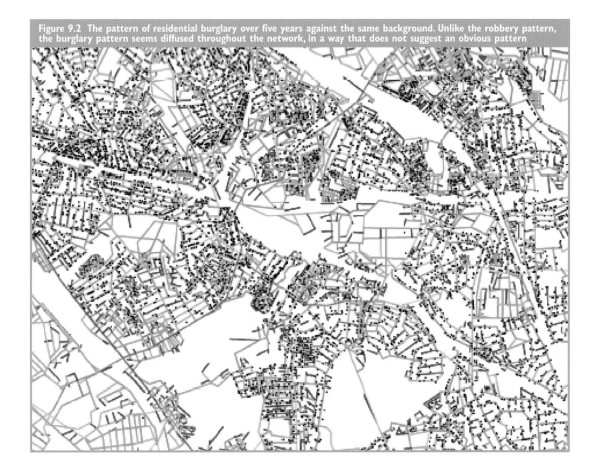

Figure 9.2 The pattern of residential burglary over five years against the same background. Unlike the robbery pattern, the burglary pattern seems diffused throughout the network, in a way that does not suggest an obvious pattern

and has over 13 000 burglaries and over 6000 street robberies, all spatially located, to which can be added social and demographic data from the 2001 Census, and local authority data on the building stock, brought in wherever possible, as well as spatial data from the syntax analysis. But because different kinds of data are available only at different scales, data tables have been created at four levels:

- 21 wards (around 12 000 people) that make up the borough. At this level, spatial data are numerically accurate, but reflect only broad spatial characteristics of areas. Social data from the 2001 Census are available, but at this level patterns are broad and scene-setting at best.
- 800 output areas (around 125 dwellings) from the 2001 Census. At this level, social data are rich, and include full demographic, occupation, social

deprivation, unemployment, population and housing densities, and ethnic mix, as well as house types and forms of tenure, but unfortunately spatial data are fairly meaningless at this level owing to the arbitrary shape of output areas.
- 7102 street segments (between intersections) that make up the borough. Here we have optimal spatial data, good physical data, and 'council tax band' data indicating property values, which can act as a surrogate for social data.
- 65 459 individual residential buildings, comprising 101 849 dwellings. Here spatial values are taken from the associated segment. Here we have good spatial and physical data, but no social data, though council tax band can be used as a surrogate.

So the richest demographic and socio-economic data do not quite overlap with the richest spatial data, but the usefulness of creating data tables at different levels with different contents will become clear below as we switch between levels to seek answers to questions.

With this methodology and database we can now address our research questions. But we must first offer a health warning. Although the database is very large, it is confined to one London borough, and the findings would need to be reproduced in other studies for us to be sure that they have any generality, even in one country. Having said this, the area is highly differentiated in terms of social composition and urban type, from inner city to suburban, and this will allow any overall patterns and correlations to be tested by subdividing the data, for example into the 21 wards to see whether the findings hold for each area taken separately. We can do the same with dwelling types or council tax bands (a UK local tax based on property values) to see whether patterns hold for each subdivision separately.

Some general patterns

The research questions will be addressed largely through the high-resolution (segments and buildings) data tables, but before we begin it is worth looking at some broad patterns identified through multivariate analysis of the low-resolution data tables (wards and output areas). Multivariate analysis is a set of statistical techniques in which the effects of different factors on an outcome (in this case crime)

can be considered simultaneously and so allow it to be shown that an apparent relationship between variables disappears when the influence of another factor is taken into account (as in Budd's study of dwelling types in the British Crime Survey above).

For example, at the ward level, we find that higher residential burglary rates are, on the face of it, associated with social factors such as smaller household size and lower rates of owner-occupation, but we also find that physical factors are strongly represented, including a higher proportion of converted flats, lower proportions of residents at ground level, and even a high incidence of basements. These factors are already linked together in the different living patterns and lifestyles to be found in different parts of the borough, so care must be taken not to mistake associations for causes. Great care must also be taken in interpreting figures at all at this scale, since there will often be a double effect, in that a high proportion of crimes will be carried out by criminals who also live in the ward, so crime figures may index the local availability of criminals as much as the vulnerability of victims. At most, ward-level patterns suggest an interactive process involving the physical and social circumstances under which different social groups find themselves living, rather than simply a social or spatial process.

The interweaving of social and spatial factors is also suggested by a multivariate analysis of the 800 output areas, where the double effect we noted will be less marked. Social deprivation factors are associated with the incidence of residential burglary, though interestingly, it is employment deprivation rather than income deprivation that is strongest, but even stronger are physical variables such as housing type, with purpose-built flats and terrace houses beneficial and converted flats and flats in commercial buildings vulnerable. More unexpectedly, there is a decrease in residential burglary with increased housing density (and the same with population

Table 9.2 Burglary rates for dwelling types

Band		A	B	C	D	E	F	G	H	Mean
Type 1	Sample			590						
	Burglary rate (5 yrs)			0.084						0.084
Type 2	Sample			228						
	Burglary rate (5 yrs)			0.046						0.046
Type 3	Sample	732	588	1098	1031	431	87	23		
	Burglary rate (5 yrs)	0.086	0.193	0.118	0.111	0.105	0.093	0.087		0.109
Type 4	Sample	1018	2198	5673	1136	256				
	Burglary rate (5 yrs)	0.096	0.081	0.08	0.065	0.142				0.084
Type 5	Sample		133	594	1296	358	24			
	Burglary rate (5 yrs)		0.132	0.098	0.093	0.159	0.391			0.111
Type 6	Sample	66	1176	5013	4201	2070	847	175		
	Burglary rate (5 yrs)	0.18	0.111	0.116	0.107	0.117	0.165	0.231		0.120
Type 7	Sample	175	444	1070	1403	296	53	41		
	Burglary rate (5 yrs)	0.137	0.136	0.129	0.059	0.062	0.019	0.073		0.078
Type 8	Sample		237	599	446	37	–	75		
	Burglary rate (5 yrs)		0.063	0.13	0.213	0.159	–	0.393		0.193
Type 9	Sample		859	2349	8076	2570	153			
	Burglary rate (5 yrs)		0.177	0.102	0.113	0.138	0.149			0.117
Type 10	Sample		493	3268	4268	10819	2529	507		
	Burglary rate (5 yrs)		0.249	0.097	0.12	0.145	0.148	0.152		0.138
Type 11	Sample		307	1581	1322	969	606	489		
	Burglary rate (5 yrs)		0.268	0.169	0.153	0.21	0.211	0.26		0.199
Type 12	Sample	5	73	433	276	363	896	1367	17	
	Burglary rate (5 yrs)		0.151	0.113	0.120	0.209	0.169	0.169	0.235	0.166
Type 13	Sample	15	89	436	440	512	67	378	151	
	Burglary rate (5 yrs)		0.112	0.169	0.136	0.125	0.179	0.304	0.450	0.200
Mean	Sample	2253	9613	27 265	27 706	20 578	5836	3218	217	101 849
	Burglary rate (5 yrs)	0.101	0.109	0.102	0.109	0.140	0.157	0.208	0.530	0.123

Key:
Type 1: very tall blocks, point block slabs, 0.084
Type 2: tall flats, 6–15 storeys, 0.046
Type 3: medium-height flats, 5–6 storeys, 0.109
Type 4: lower 3–4 storey and smaller flats, 0.084
Type 5: low terraces with small T extension 0.111

Type 6: low terraces with large T extension 0.120
Type 7: linked and step-linked, 2–3 storeys and mixed, 0.078
Type 8: tall terraces, 3–4 storeys, 0.193
Type 9: semis in multiples of 4, 6, 8, 0.117

Type 10: standard-sized semis, 0.138
Type 11: large property semis, 0.199
Type 12: small detached, 0.166
Type 13: large detached, 0.200

density, but housing is stronger, though the two correlate closely). Against this background, then, we can then pursue our specific questions through the high-resolution tables with some expectation that there may be answers to be found.

Are some dwelling types safer than others?

Table 9.2 summarises the interrelations between residential burglary rates and dwelling types, aggregated from the database of 65 450 residential buildings. The types are arranged on the horizontal axis roughly in order of the number of sides on which the dwelling is exposed to outside space: that

is, not at all in higher-rise flats, and on all four sides for detached houses. The vertical axis shows council tax bands from A, the lowest, to H, the highest. Since council tax bands are based on property values, they can be assumed to give some indication of relative household affluence. The residential burglary rates are for the full five-year period.

The most notable thing about the overall figures is a more or less consistent rise in average rates, from higher flats with the lowest rates through to detached houses with the highest. There could of course be a problem with the high-rise flats. All are local authority provision, and it could be that the

| Table 9.3 The effect of building-centred density on burglary risk by ward, based on the 65 459 buildings data table ||||||||
| | Single Dwellings ||| Multiple Dwellings |||
Ward	Number of dwellings	% risk change Ground+upper	% risk change Ground only	Number of dwellings	% risk change Ground+upper	% risk change Ground only
1	2548	-41.7 (.0001**)	-46.2 (.0001**)	541	+26.1 (.0295**)	+2.4 (.8308)
2	2887	-46.3 (.0001**)	-51.2 (.0001**)	507	+13.7 (.1758)	+11.3 (.3859)
3	1574	-25.3 (.0141**)	-44.9 (.0001**)	703	+15.7 (.0446*)	-31.2 (.0005**)
4	2702	-55.9 (.0001**)	-61.8 (.0001**)	367	-.098 (.3059)	-24.1 (.0217**)
5	2734	-42.4 (.0001**)	-49.7 (.0001**)	829	-25.7 (.0002**)	-32.8 (.0001**)
6	2711	-32.6 (.0315**)	-35.6 (.0001**)	580	+4.2 (.7254)	-25.9 (.0049**)
7	1363	-27.6 (.0073**)	-45.3 (.0001**)	1699	-19.9 (.0010**)	-34.3 (.0001**)
8	1762	-30.7 (.0001**)	-34.6 (.0001**)	1544	-30.6 (.0001**)	-35.8 (.0001**)
9	3072	-13.0 (.3102)	-17.1 (.2586)	314	+3.4 (.8245)	-.4.9 (.7575)
10	789	-14.3 (.3308)	-46.4 (.0011**)	1343	+15.6 (.0033**)	-29.8 (.0001**)
11	1295	-28.7 (.0029**)	-59.6 (.0001**)	1305	+7.8 (.2471)	-20.0 (.0071**)
12	2785	-25.2 (.0452**)	-23.2 (.0884*)	334	-30.9 (.0049**)	-30.2 (.0094**)
13	3026	-38.7 (.0003**)	-41.1 (.0002**)	439	-11.7 (.2455)	-14.6 (.1381)
14	1945	-19.5 (.0790*)	-38.4 (.0031**)	1524	-1.5 (.8559)	-24.5 (.0007**)
15	3445	-3.7 (.8003)	-.02 (.9925)	332	+9.4 (.4907)	-7.2 (.5820)
16	2228	-45.3 (.0001**)	-55.3 (.0001**)	688	+2.2 (.7090)	-35.9 (.0001**)
17	2578	-53.9 (.0001**)	-57.8 (.0001**)	609	+22.8 (.0391**)	-1.8 (.8657)
18	2784	-24.9 (.0739*)	-43.3 (.0013**)	434	+1.2 (.3545)	-7.6 (.4878)
19	2758	-28.0 (.0062**)	-24.7 (.0247**)	787	+1.6 (.8666)	-11.4 (.2932)
20	2208	-24.4 (.0234**)	-46.4 (.0001**)	648	+8.1 (.4437)	+3.6 (.6886)
21	1155	-27.0 (.0161**)	-33.2 (.0050**)	1547	-21.8 (.0002**)	-23.0 (.0001)
ALL	48350	-27.7 (.0001**)	-38.9 (.0001**)	17103	+ 2.2 .1784	-16.0 .0001

lower rates result from non-reporting rather than actual incidence. However, examination of the rates per tax band will suggest this is unlikely to be strongly the case. In the two highest-rise groups, all dwellings are in the second lowest tax band, B, so we can compare these with the Bs in other dwelling types to see how far they fit into a broader pattern.

Examining the overall pattern of rates, what we find is that, for most kinds of flat, rates are lower than for houses and tend to fall with increasing tax band – that is, with greater social advantage – while the rates for houses are higher than those for flats, and tend to be U-shaped, with the higher rates for the least and most socially advantaged. This suggests not only that dwelling type is a critical factor in vulnerability to residential burglary, but also that two factors are involved in the shifting pattern of risk: the simple physical fact of degree of exposure (i.e., on

how many sides is your dwelling protected by being contiguous with others?) and social advantage, with the poor and the rich at higher risk. But, overall, houses are more at risk than flats, the more so as they become more detached, and the better off you are the more you are at risk in a house and safer in a flat. It should also be noted that although within most dwellings types the pattern of vulnerability with tax band is U-shaped, with the least and most well off most vulnerable, if we look at the overall rates per tax band, the bias of lower tax bands towards flats means that there is a simple linear increase in vulnerability with increasing tax band.

Although these results are consistent with the multivariate results from the British Crime Survey, they invert the raw results. Is this a problem? We think not. The BCS covers the whole of the country, and represents the whole range of spatial and social circumstances; in many cases dwelling types such as detached houses will be in historically low-crime areas, and the converse for flats. Here our data are for a single continuous urban area where the distribution of all kinds of target is much more compressed. What is taken out of the raw BCS pattern by the multivariate analysis is the influence of very different area and social types, and the degree of separation of these is much less in an urban environment. So it seems likely that both sets of figures are correct, but also of course that the underlying reality is that flats really are safer than houses.

Is density good or bad?

We have already seen that the low-resolution data suggested that higher densities may be associated with lower rates of residential burglary. But the arbitrariness of the shape of output areas may mean that factors such as parks, other open spaces and non-residential uses may be playing a role. To test this, we developed a measure of what we call building-centred density in which we take the centre of each residential building and calculate how many dwellings are, wholly or in part, within a radius of 30 metres. We distinguish between buildings that are single houses as opposed to some kind of multiple, and also between ground-level and off-the-ground dwellings within the 30 m radius. The measure in effect indicates density around each building separately, and so is not subject to the problems of

area-based density measures. With this technique we can use another multivariate technique called logistic regression, to measure how far this, or any other variable, increases or decreases the risk of each building having at least one burglary.

The results are summarised in Table 9.3 for the overall area and broken down by wards. The left half of the table deals with single houses, the right with buildings with multiple dwellings. In each half of the table the first column shows the number of buildings in the sample, and the second column the average increase (+ sign) or decrease (− sign) in burglary risk with increased density. The values in parentheses are the statistical significance of each figure, with ** meaning highly significant, and * significant. The first risk column measures the risk change with ground- and upper-level density, and the second for ground-level density only. The table shows that for single dwellings all wards show decreased risk with increased density, with an average 27.2% reduction for ground- and upper-level density together and 38.9% for ground level only.

For multiple dwellings, great care must be taken in interpreting the figures, as the logistic regression technique means that all we can look at is whether or not a burglary occurs in the building, without regard for the number of dwellings in the building. A factor affecting the analysis will then be that the greater the number of dwellings in the building, including on upper floors, the higher the density is likely to be. The fact, then, that the first column shows a more or less neutral result can be taken to mean that increasing numbers of dwellings in the building does not increase risk to the building, and that means that the risk to individual dwellings will be less in buildings with more dwellings. This can be tested by adding the number of dwellings in the building into the equation. We find that in 16 of the 21 wards risk is decreased with increasing on- and

Table 9.4 Logistic model coefficients table for Burgled L

Split by: LU and RU=1 then 1 else 0

Cell: 1.000	Coeff.	Std error	Coeff./SE	Chi-square	p-value	Exp. (coeff.)	95% lower	95% upper
I: constant	-1.140	0.175	-6.522	42.539	<0.0001	0.320	0.227	0.450
TOmovCITYscale	0.171	0.020	8.402	70.596	<0.0001	1.187	1.140	1.235
THRUmovCITYscale	0.097	0.013	7.237	52.379	<0.0001	1.102	1.073	1.131
TOmov300m	0.003	0.001	2.716	7.376	0.0066	1.003	1.001	1.005
THRUmov300m	-0.166	0.045	-3.681	13.552	0.0002	0.847	0.775	0.925
Cell: 0.000								
I: constant	-1.139	0.233	-4.898	23.990	<0.0001	0.320	0.203	0.505
TOmovCITYscale	0.061	0.028	2.192	4.805	0.0284	1.063	1.006	1.122
THRUmovCITYscale	0.039	0.018	2.222	4.937	0.0263	1.040	1.005	1.076
TOmov300m	0.010	0.001	8.276	68.486	<0.0001	1.010	1.007	1.012
THRUmov300m	-0.129	0.055	-2.347	5.510	0.0189	0.879	0.790	0.979

off-the-ground density, although the simple number of dwellings is of course associated with higher risk because there are more targets. As shown in the final column of the table, however, when only ground-level density is taken into account, even without adding the effects of numbers of dwellings, in 18 of the 21 wards there is a marked decrease in risk with ground-level density for multiple occupancy buildings, with an average of 16%.

These are quite remarkable results, and the fact that they are so consistent across the great range of social, spatial and physical circumstances found across the borough suggests they might be found elsewhere. How are they to be explained? It could be a surveillance effect: that having many other dwellings close to you inhibits the burglar. But it also might be a statistical effect, though none the less real for that. It could be that burglars do not go to the same target zone too often within a certain time frame, as people might be on their guard, and this could have the effect that having more dwellings in a potential target zone, however defined, would mean that the number of burglaries in the same zone would be a smaller proportion of the number of targets. In the case of the negative effects of off-

the-ground density, it could of course simply be that residents were more vulnerable because they were 'close to the flats'. But it could also be a statistical effect, in that having more upper-level dwellings, which are less vulnerable to burglary, presumably because they are harder to burgle, will often mean that there are smaller numbers of more easily burgled houses on the ground, so the ones that are there are more likely to be selected as targets within that zone. Whatever the mechanism, there is little doubt that in this urban area ground-level density is a benefit, and upper-level density probably so, though the degree to which it is a benefit remains unclear.

Is movement in your street good or bad?

Multivariate analysis on the most high-resolution data table also allows us to approach the 'movement good or bad?' question in a new way. Space syntax allows us to distinguish between two aspects of movement: the accessibility of each street segment as a potential destination from others; and the degree to which movement is likely to pass through each segment on trips between other segments. We can call the first the 'to-movement' potential of a segment, i.e. how easy is it to get to, and the second the 'through-movement' potential, i.e., how much movement is likely to pass through. We can also limit each measure to whatever radius from each segment we like, meaning that we can ask what the to- and through-movement potential of a segment is within a radius of, say, 400 or 800 metres. In effect, we can use space syntax to measure movement potential either at a localised scale or at the level of the whole city, or anything in between. These are movement potentials, of course, not actual movement rates, but in general there is about a 60–80% correlation between the potentials and observed movement rates.

So we again take the highest-resolution (buildings) data table, but this time assign to each building values indicating the two types of movement potential at different radii. We then use the same technique as before, multivariate logistic regression, to find out which, if any, potential movement factors increase or decrease the risk of burglary. The background to this is, as indicated before, that some studies have found that there is more burglary close to main roads, explaining this through dwellings being on the natural search paths of would-be burglars, while others have shown that within residential areas the more important streets have less burglary, rather than more, and this has been assigned to a greater surveillance effect from movement.

In fact, with the space syntax analysis, we find a neat reconciliation of these two points of view, and one that makes intuitive sense. In Table 9.4 the upper table deals, as before, with single houses, and the lower one with multiple-dwelling buildings. The key figures are under 'Exp. (coeff.)': above 1.0 indicates a percentage increase in risk, below 1.0 a percentage decrease. The figures to the immediate left indicate statistical significance, which should be below 0.05 if the Exp. (coeff.) value is to be taken seriously. As we see, the figures are higher for houses than flats, which is a good start, since we would expect houses exposed to the public realm to be more affected by movement than more remote flats.

So, for houses we find an 18.7% increase in risk from to-movement and a 10.2% increase from through-movement from being on a main city-scale route. This would seem to confirm the 'search path' hypothesis. But for local movement using a 300 m radius, we find that to-movement is more or less neutral while through-movement reduces risk by 15.3%. The pattern is the same for multiple dwellings, though all values are smaller and less significant. These results then suggest that both the 'search path' and 'surveillance' hypotheses may be right in different circumstances. Being on an important global route does increase risk, but being on an important local route decreases it.

Culs-de-sac versus grids?

The study area has relatively few culs-de-sac, and most follow the formula identified in previous studies as safe (Hillier & Shu, 2002; Hillier, 2004): that is, simple and linear, and attached directly to the through movement network. There are no hierarchical cul-de-sac complexes of the kind built in the second half of the twentieth century, largely because the area was more or less fully built by World War II. The small size and relatively undifferentiated typology of the culs-de-sac should be borne in mind in what follows.

There is also a methodological problem. For a large dataset the spatial analysis must be carried out automatically, and it is not a straightforward matter to identify what is and is not a cul-de-sac algorithmically, though of course it is easy enough by eye. For

Table 9.5 Logistic model coefficients table for Burgled L

	Coeff.	Std error	Coeff./SE	Chi-Square	p-value	Exp. (coeff.)	95% lower	95% upper
1: constant	-0.392	0.144	-2.722	7.410	0.0065	0.676	0.509	0.896
TOmovCITYscale	0.225	0.016	13.980	195.442	<0.0001	1.253	1.214	1.293
TOmov300m	0.009	0.001	10.556	111.427	<0.0001	1.009	1.007	1.010
THRUmovCITYscale	0.062	0.011	5.824	33.913	<0.0001	1.064	1.042	1.087
THRUmov300m	-0.149	0.036	-4.157	17.278	<0.0001	0.862	0.804	0.925
SEGMENTlinks	-0.037	0.014	-2.607	6.797	0.0091	0.963	0.937	0.991

Figure 9.3 Segment connectedness

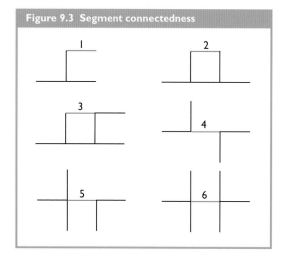

example, if we use the number of connections that a segment has, as in Figure 9.3, a one-connected segment can only be the end of a cul-de-sac, since a cul-de-sac connected to a route from which you can turn in two directions will be two-connected (to one in each direction), as will the deepest space in a crescent. In some circumstances, even a three-connected segment can be a cul-de-sac, namely one that is connected to a through road but with another connection on the other side of the road. At the other end of the spectrum, a six-connected segment (to all intents and purposes the maximum in most types of urban system) will usually be part of a grid-like layout, but again this will not necessarily be so.

Even so, provided we bear these caveats in mind, it still turns out to be useful to proceed by examining segment connectivity in relation to residential burglary. If we aggregate the one- and two-

connected segments, and assume that they will cover most culs-de-sac, we find that on average they have a burglary rate nearly a third lower at 0.088 compared with an average of 0.123, and in general higher connectivity is associated with higher burglary rates, though the peak is at five-connected, with a fall at six-connected. However, this seemingly clear pattern becomes much more complex when we take into account other variables. First, when we add segment connectedness to the logistic regression analysis we showed in Table 9.4, we find that in the presence of other movement-related spatial variables, higher segment connectivity is marginally beneficial (see Table 9.5). Low segment connectedness should not then be taken in itself as automatically positive.

More importantly, segment connectedness is dramatically affected by two other variables. The first is council tax band, which we have previously used as a proxy for social affluence. Figure 9.4 shows the burglary rates for one to two up to six connections for single-occupancy houses in tax bands B–H (A has too few cases). This shows there is great variation in the direction of shift, in that while rates for the D and G bands rise with segment connectedness, the B, C and H bands tend to fall, though with fluctuations, while the E and F bands both rise and fall. Even more striking is the variation of rates by tax band, which is greater than the variation by connectedness. Most striking of all are the very high rates for the top H band, and the fact

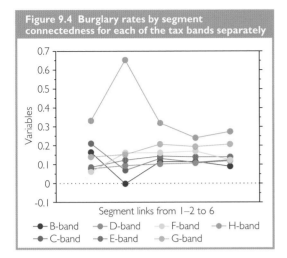

Figure 9.4 Burglary rates by segment connectedness for each of the tax bands separately

that the highest of all are in the low-connectedness bands. We have already seen in our analysis of dwelling types that increasing affluence increases the vulnerability of houses. Now we see that this is particularly focused on houses lying on street segments with few local connections.

The second factor that strongly affects segment connectedness is the number of dwellings on the segment. One- and two-connected segments with no more than ten dwellings, for example, have a burglary rate of 0.209, or nearly twice the average, while six-connected (grid-like) segments with more than 100 dwellings (which account for over 3000 dwellings) have a rate of 0.086, very substantially below the average. In general, we find that for both low- and high-connected segments, the greater the number of dwellings on the segment, the lower the burglary rate. Most at risk are small groups of affluent houses in poorly connected locations. We might conjecture that the more attractive the target, the more the isolation of the cul-de-sac, or near cul-de-sac, benefits the burglar, while for less attractive, perhaps more opportunistic targets, culs-de-sac tend to be off the search path, and hence their lower rates. So again we can say that culs-de-sac, or near culs-de-sac, are not safe in themselves, but they become safe with larger, not smaller, numbers of neighbours, and with less affluent occupants.

Does it then matter how we group dwellings?

What implications might this then have for how we group dwellings? For most of urban history the commonest way to group buildings has been in linear streets, with buildings opening onto the street on both sides, and recent years have seen a return to this formula and a move away from the late twentieth century preference for small-scale enclosure around green spaces or piazzas (Hillier, 1989). But how big should each segment be: that is, how frequent should intersections be, and what should be the overall block size? The recent fashion to increase permeability has led to smaller block sizes and to fewer dwellings on each segment. Does this matter? Or are there perhaps scale effects with street networks in general, as there are with culs-de-sac?

It turns out that there are indeed scale effects, and understanding them is one of the keys to designing safe open environments. For example, if we take the 328 segments in our sample with only one dwelling on them, we find that a total of 197 residential burglaries have occurred over five years in the 328 dwellings, a rate over 60%, or 12% per year. But if we take the 34 segments with more than 90 dwellings per segment we find a total of 3708 dwellings and 419 burglaries over five years, a five-year rate of 11.3%, or 2.26% a year.

To explore this further, we divide all 4439 segments with at least one dwelling into bands according to their number of dwellings. This gives an average of 94 segments per band, and so a total street length per band of 9.3 km with an average of 1600 dwellings.[1] We then calculate the rates for each band, and plot them on a line chart with dwellings per segment on the horizontal axis and the burglary rate on the

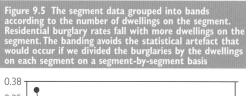

Figure 9.5 The segment data grouped into bands according to the number of dwellings on the segment. Residential burglary rates fall with more dwellings on the segment. The banding avoids the statistical artefact that would occur if we divided the burglaries by the dwellings on each segment on a segment-by-segment basis

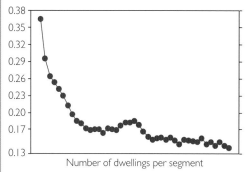

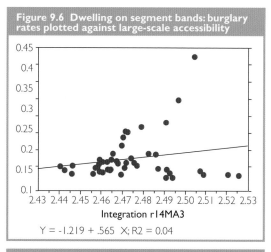

Figure 9.6 Dwelling on segment bands: burglary rates plotted against large-scale accessibility

Y = -1.219 + .565 X; R2 = 0.04

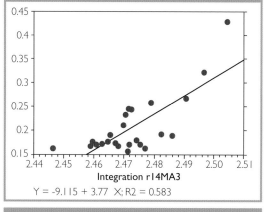

Figure 9.7 Dwelling on segment bands: burglary rates plotted against large-scale accessibility, with the primary risk band split about halfway into those with less than 25 dwellings per segment

Y = -9.115 + 3.77 X; R2 = 0.583

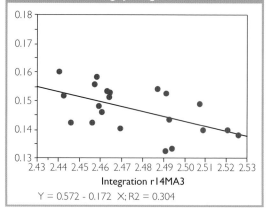

Figure 9.8 Dwelling on segment bands: burglary rates plotted against large-scale accessibility, with the primary risk band split about halfway into those with more than 25 dwellings per segment

Y = 0.572 - 0.172 X; R2 = 0.304

vertical (in fact taking the log of each). We see in Figure 9.5 that the risk of burglary decreases steadily with increasing numbers of neighbours on the street segment. This is a remarkable effect, but not unexpected to anyone familiar with the history of cities, as in general we find that residential areas have larger block sizes, and so more buildings per street segment, than high-activity central areas. It is not a surprise that this makes sense in terms of security. This does of course argue that the current emphasis on as much permeability as possible can easily be overdone. This result, as with density, could be explained by increased surveillance, but it could also be explained statistically by the 'safety in numbers' argument we conjectured for density.

The central importance of block scaling in residential areas can be shown by another remarkable result. We noted earlier that higher accessibility for to-movement at the larger scale of movement was associated with higher risk of residential burglary. By bringing the safety in numbers factor into the equation, we can show that it is not so simple. If we take our dwelling on segment bands and plot the burglary rates against large-scale accessibility, we find a bifurcation in the data, with one arm rising and the

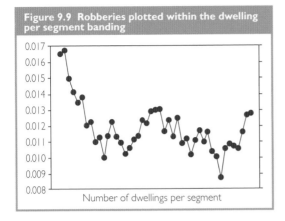

Figure 9.9 Robberies plotted within the dwelling per segment banding

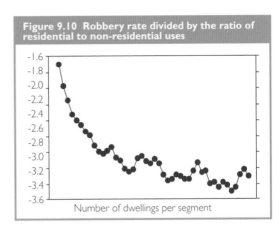

Figure 9.10 Robbery rate divided by the ratio of residential to non-residential uses

other seemingly falling with integration (see Figure 9.6). If we then split the primary risk band about half way into those with fewer than 25 dwellings per segment on the left (see Figure 9.7) and those with more on the right (see Figure 9.8), then it seems that the negative effect of large-scale accessibility on crime is eliminated and becomes favourable with increase in the amount of residence. More residences, it seems, balance out the negative effect of being close to large-scale movement, and makes it positive. Eyes from the street and eyes on the street conspire to create greater safety. This result also helps to explain the apparently divergent findings in earlier research discussed above.

Is mixed use beneficial or not?

As we are using the street-segment-level data for the above analysis, we can also test the effects on street robbery. We must again take care because, on such a large database as this, if street robberies happen randomly, then longer segments will have more robberies purely as an effect of chance, and longer segments are likely to have more dwellings on them. We can overcome this, as before, by the banding technique: that is, by aggregating all the segments into bands of a certain length, then calculating the robbery rate as the total robberies over the total length within the band. Again, the length of the segment is not involved in the calculation of the rate, so we have a measure that is independent of this.

By plotting this measure within the dwelling per segment banding we find not, as with burglary, a simple fall, but fluctuations within an overall fall (see Figure 9.9). These fluctuations are due to the presence of non-residential uses. This can be shown by dividing the robbery rate by the ratio of residential to non-residential uses (see Figure 9.10). The linearity of the relation now shows not only that street robbery is strongly affected by the presence of non-residential uses on the street, which is well known, but also a new phenomenon: that fluctuations in the pattern due to the presence of non-residential uses are overcome to the degree to which there is a high ratio of residential to those non-residential uses. In other words, as with burglary, residential numbers seem to be the key to a safer environment.

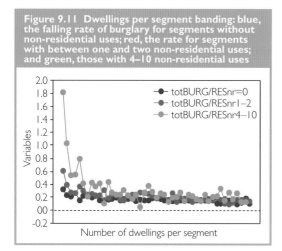

Figure 9.11 Dwellings per segment banding: blue, the falling rate of burglary for segments without non-residential uses; red, the rate for segments with between one and two non-residential uses; and green, those with 4–10 non-residential uses

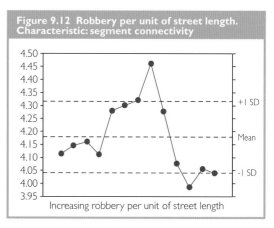

Figure 9.12 Robbery per unit of street length. Characteristic: segment connectivity

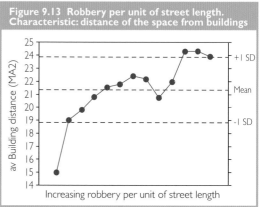

Figure 9.13 Robbery per unit of street length. Characteristic: distance of the space from buildings

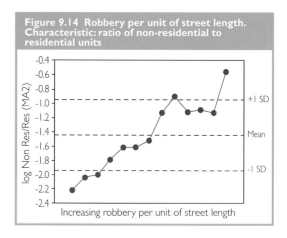

Figure 9.14 Robbery per unit of street length. Characteristic: ratio of non-residential to residential units

We can use a similar technique to see whether a similar pattern is found for burglary. In Figure 9.11 we use the dwellings per segment banding to plot first, in blue, the falling rate of burglary for segments without non-residential uses, then in red the rate for segments with between one and two non-residential uses, and then in green those with four to ten non-residential uses. On the vertical axis is the burglary rate for the band. We see on the left of the figure, when the numbers of dwellings per segment is low, that the burglary rate with four to ten non-residential uses is six times that for the bands without non-residential, and for one to two it is twice as high. So when residence is sparse, there is indeed a penalty for mixed use. But as we move right and increase the numbers of dwellings per segment, all the rates not only fall but also converge, so that when we reach about 15 dwellings per segment the penalty for four to ten non-residential uses has become very small, and for one to two it has vanished. The implications of this are very significant. It means that mixed use works, in security terms, when residential numbers are high, but not when they are low.

But what about robbery in and around the network of linked mixed-use centres where we saw in Figure 9.1 it tended to be concentrated? There are relatively few residents in these areas, so what are the characteristics of the space where it does occur? We can take the first step towards an answer by using the banding technique again, but this time banding all the segments according to their rate of density of robbery (robbery per unit of street length), and asking

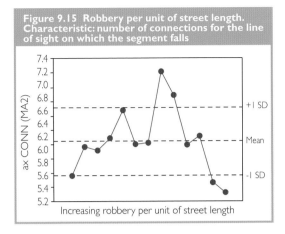

Figure 9.15 Robbery per unit of street length. Characteristic: number of connections for the line of sight on which the segment falls

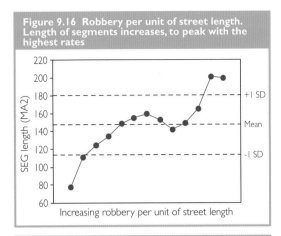

Figure 9.16 Robbery per unit of street length. Length of segments increases, to peak with the highest rates

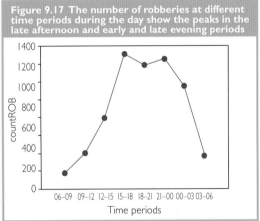

Figure 9.17 The number of robberies at different time periods during the day show the peaks in the late afternoon and early and late evening periods

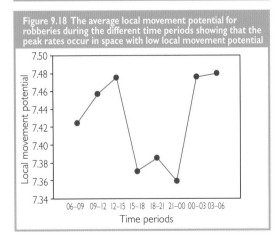

Figure 9.18 The average local movement potential for robberies during the different time periods showing that the peak rates occur in space with low local movement potential

whether the bands with high densities of robbery have different characteristics from those with low rates. We can begin with the simplest spatial variable, segment connectivity. Starting with the lowest rates on the left, Figure 9.12 shows first a rise with increasing rates, but with the three highest-rate bands there is a very sharp fall to less connected segments. Using the same technique, we see that robbery rates increase with the distance of the space from buildings (see Figure 9.13), with the ratio on non-residential to residential units (see Figure 9.14), and the number of connections for the line of sight on which the segment falls lowest for the highest robbery rates (see Figure 9.15), but the length of segments increases to peak with the highest rates (see Figure 9.16). In this way, we build a profile of high robbery street segments as being long (in spite of the fact that segments in mixed-use areas tend to be shorter) and poorly connected, on poorly connected lines and with very low ratios of residence to non-residence.

We find equally informative patterns by dividing the data into time periods. Figure 9.17 plots the number of street robbery through eight three-hour periods making up the day, starting on the left with 6–9 am. Figure 9.18 then plots the average movement potential in the segments in which they occur. Once again we see that the high rates occur in more isolated spaces. This shows that it is not the high

street where the danger lies, but in much less significant segments close to the high street. However, the situation changes after midnight. As Figure 9.17 shows, high rates are associated with lower movement potential segments and low rates with higher, but with an important exception. In the post-midnight period high rates of street robbery return to the high-movement-potential spaces. The maxim would seem to be: Don't go on the high street after midnight, but don't leave it before midnight.

The final question about mixed-use areas is what we might call Newman's question: Is the high street safer or less safe? That is, is the increase in robbery rates in and around mixed-use areas less than or greater than the increase in pedestrians? It will be this that governs the risk to potential victims. We cannot of course observe pedestrian flows in all the relevant segments, but we can make use of our extensive London database on all-day pedestrian (and vehicular) flows on over 367 street segments in five London areas to ascertain the average difference in pedestrian flows on segments with and without retail.

Mean pedestrian movement on all 367 segments is 224.176 per hour. For segments without retail the rate is 158.476 for 317 segments, and for those with any retail (without distinguishing how much) it is 640.714 for 50 segments. This means that the movement rate on segments with retail is 4.042 times that on segments without. The average robbery on segments without non-residential uses, as previously shown, is 0.0074, while the rate for segments with non-residential uses is 0.0176, or 2.4 times as high. The rate of increase in robbery is then substantially less than the increase in movement rates, and dividing one into the other, 2.4/4.042, we get 1.68, so that we can say in terms of people risk you

are 68% safer on busier street segments with non-residential uses than on those without. This of course is a very provisional figure, but it is probably a conservative one. The conclusion is that the apparently higher rates of street robbery in and around high-activity centres are not a reason to avoid them. You are actually at lower risk in the high-activity centres, in spite of the apparent concentration in these areas.

How permeable should residential areas be?

We cannot answer this question directly with this database, as we do not have a level of resolution in the data that reflects plausible area structures below the level of the ward. However, certain results we have already presented are directly relevant to this. First the high integration – and so more movement potential – segments with more than 25 residential units per segment, that were shown in Figures 9.6, 9.7 and 9.8 to associate higher integration with lower burglary rates, will in most cases be the dominant strategic alignments in residential areas. This reinforced earlier findings that the main alignments that structure movement in residential areas tend to be safe. Since integration reflects all-round permeability, it is safe to infer that well-structured areas with enough permeability to link them in all directions can indeed be relatively safe – though other factors will also be involved here.

The findings in Tables 9.4 and 9.5 also have a direct bearing on this, since they show that local movement up to a certain radius is beneficial. This implies that residential areas should be structured so as to achieve a good integration with local movement, though care should also be taken to ensure that lines that were likely to feature in more global movement patterns were also well above the threshold of 25 residential units per segment that would make them safer. Again, this shows that areas can safely be structured for enough permeability to facilitate movement in all directions, provided the rules about the numbers of dwellings per segment are also in play.

In fact, although the wards of the borough were well above the scale of anything we might call 'natural areas', it is instructive to examine them from the point of view of the 'potential movement' variables. At first sight it seems that there is a weak but consistent positive association between various scales of integration and burglary rates. However, the pattern of integration reflects the order in which the borough was built: from the more urban, and so more integrated, areas closer to the city centre that were built from the early nineteenth century on, through to the more suburban areas constructed for the most part in the decades between the two world wars. It is this that produces the apparent association between the movement potential variables and higher burglary rates, and in fact under multivariate analysis with physical and social variables the association disappears, and the only variables that are linked to burglary rate are the proportion of converted flats, which are exceptionally vulnerable, and the proportion of houses with basements. At this level it seems that we find simple physical variables in the driving seat, and we need only bring in a fuller social account to explain the historical process that accounts for the higher number of houses divided into flats and the greater frequency of basements in areas built at a certain time.

The answers to the questions

On the evidence of this study we can then suggest the following answers to the questions.

- Which dwelling types? In this area, the relative safety of different types of dwelling is affected by two simple interacting factors: the number of sides on which the dwelling is exposed to the public realm – so flats have least risk and detached houses most – and the social class of the inhabitants. All classes tend to be safer in flats, but with increasing wealth the advantage of living in a flat rather than a house increases, as does the disadvantage of living in a house – in spite of the extra investment that better-off people are believed to make in security alarms. At the same time, purpose-built flats are much safer than converted flats. The overall advantage of flats is in spite of the high vulnerability of converted flats.

- Density high or low? Higher ambient ground-level densities of both dwellings and people reduce risk, though the influence of off-the-ground density is less clear. But, taking both together, overall density is beneficial.

- Movement or not? Local movement is beneficial, larger-scale movement not so – but where there is large-scale movement, spatially integrated street segments (more movement potential) have lower risk to the degree that they are lined with high numbers of dwellings per segment, and higher risk where numbers of dwellings on the segment are low.

- Culs-de-sac or grids? The principle that larger numbers of dwellings on the street segment reduce the risk of burglary applies both to culs-de-sac and to grid-like layouts. Small numbers of dwellings in a cul-de-sac are vulnerable, especially if the dwellings are affluent. Relative affluence and the number of neighbours have a greater effect than either being in a cul-de-sac or being on a through-street. The earlier finding that simple linear culs-de-sac with good numbers of dwellings set into a network of through-streets tend to be safe is confirmed by this study.

- Can mixing uses be safe? Mixed-use street segments are relatively safe with good numbers of residents, and vulnerable with few residents. Increased residential population neutralises the risk that is found with sparse residence on mixed-use segments.
- How should we group dwellings? Dwellings should be arranged linearly on two sides of the street. Residential blocks should be larger rather than smaller.
- How permeable should residential areas be? Local movement reduces risk, so residential areas should be designed to structure local through-movement, while exercising care about larger-scale movement. Where there is larger-scale movement, safer dwelling types should be used to balance eyes on the street with eyes from the street. Residential areas should be permeable enough to allow movement in all directions but no more. The overprovision of poorly used permeability is a crime hazard.
- Do social factors interact with physical and spatial factors? Social factors interact with physical and social factors in several ways: for example, burglary risk is U-shaped, with the least and most well-off most vulnerable, while robbery risk increases in less well-off areas; the advantage of living in a flat is great for better-off people, though still present for the less well-off; and the well-off are particularly at risk in small culs-de-sac.

So do we need to change the paradigm?

So where does this leave the debate between the 'closed' and 'open' solutions? In one sense both sides are right about some things and wrong about others, and each side could, if it wished, claim some selective

vindication from the results we have shown. That would misrepresent the situation. At the very best, the evidence presented here suggests that certain principles in each argument form part of a larger and more complex picture, and that each side needs to rethink its principles in terms of this more complex picture. The advocates of the closed solution seem to have been too conservative in overstating and oversimplifying the case for culs-de-sac and closed areas, in insisting on small rather than larger groupings of residents, and in underestimating the potential for, and the importance of, life outside the cul-de-sac and the closed-off area. The advocates of the open solution have been too optimistic about exposing the dwelling to the public realm, in not linking permeability to a realistic understanding of movement patterns, and perhaps in not appreciating the interdependence between residential numbers and the safety of mixed-use areas.

But who is right and who is wrong may not be the most important debate. Throughout the analysis we have presented evidence that calls into question some of the most deeply held assumptions that have been made on all sides about the relation between spatial design and security. The most important of these is perhaps the 'safety in numbers' argument that reappears again and again in our evidence. This challenges long-held beliefs that small is somehow beautiful in designing for well-working, low-risk communities. On the basis of the evidence we have presented, the contrary may be the case. The benefits of a residential culture become more apparent with larger rather than smaller numbers. Bigger may be stronger.

A no less challenging implication of this body of evidence is that the relation between crime and spatial design may not pass through the intervening variable of community formation. Again and again, the evidence suggests that the simple fact of human co-presence in space, coupled to simple physical features of buildings or spaces, is enough to explain differences in victimisation rates in different types of location and area, albeit with variations due to social factors. It is not clear from our evidence where we would need to look for further clarification through such variables as community formation. There is a plausible alternative argument here: that simple human co-presence, coupled to such features as the presence of entrances opening on to space, is enough to create the sense that space is civilised and safe. The idea that community formation is the intervening variable between spatial design and urban security may be an unnecessary hypothesis.

Other features of the evidence also suggest modifications to current paradigms. One is that features of environments that relate to crime risk rarely work on their own but interdepend with other features, social as well as spatial and physical. We cannot introduce one feature at a time and expect good results. Good design must reflect the interdependence of features as we have outlined them. Similarly, local areas rarely work on their own. Every area, closed or open, interdepends with its context, and both design and research must reflect this.

Most important of all perhaps is the need to recognise that the urban environment is a continuous whole. It is not a set of discrete areas that are somehow joined together to form a whole, but a continuous structure in which the connecting tissue between recognisable areas is as critical as the areas themselves. This is perhaps where space syntax can make its most significant contribution. It tells us that the whole pattern of urban space is involved in the sense of civilised and safe existence, which it is the aim of all urban design to create. This most elementary of urban facts should be reflected in future research as well as in spatial design and planning.

References

Budd, T. (1999) *British Crime Survey: The 2001 British Crime Survey.* London: Home Office Statistical Bulletin.

Harries, K. (2006) Property crimes and violence in United States: an analysis of the influence of population density. *International Journal of Criminal Justice Sciences*, 1 (2), 24–33.

Haughey, R.M. (2005) *Higher-density development: Myth and fact.* Washington, DC: Urban Land Institute.

Hillier, B. (1989) Against enclosure. In T. Markus, T. Wooley & N. Teymur (eds), *Rehumanising Housing*, pp. 63-85. London: Butterworth.

Hillier, B. (2004) Can streets be made safe? *Urban Design International*, 9 (1), 31–45.

Hillier, B. & Shu, S. (2000) Crime and urban layout: the need for evidence. In S. Ballintyne, K. Pease & V. McLaren (eds), *Secure foundations: Key issues in crime prevention, crime reduction and community safety*, pp. 224–248. London: Institute for Public Policy Research.

Jacobs, J. (1961) *The death and life of great American cities.* New York: Random House.

Li, J. & Rainwater, J. (2006). The real picture of land use density and crime: a GIS application. Retrieved 14 May 2007 from http://gis.esri.com/library/userconf/proc00/professional/papers/PA P508/p508.htm.

Newman, O. (1973) *Defensible space: Crime prevention through urban design.* New York: Macmillan.

Shu, S. (2002) *Crime and urban layout.* PhD Thesis, Bartlett School of Graduate Studies, University College London, University of London.

Town, S. & O'Toole, R. (2005) Crime-friendly neighbourhoods: how 'New Urbanist' planners sacrifice safety in the name of 'openness' and 'accessibility'. *Reason*, 36 (9), 30–36.

Zelinka, A. & Brennan, D. (2001). *SafeScape: Creating safer, more livable communities through planning and design.* Chicago: APA Planners Press.

Footnotes

1   The banding is necessary, since if we calculate rates of burglary on a segment-by-segment basis, then a random burglary on a segment with more dwellings will appear as a lower rate than one occurring on a segment with fewer dwelling. The rates would then be 'artefacts' of the way we have made the calculation. With banding we avoid this problem, since the number of dwellings on each segment is not involved in each band calculation, and is only an extraneous condition for the band.

URBAN FORM AND SOCIAL SUSTAINABILITY FOR CITY-CENTRE LIVING

This section has focused on two social sustainability issues: housing and crime.

Chapter 7 looked at housing in cities and city fringes. The VivaCity2020 team undertook an extensive survey of different types of housing form. Differences occur in density, boundaries, axiality and perceptions of quality of life by the residents between block types and ages. One clear finding that emerges is that the modern urban block is a new urban form that may relate to the change in Western demographics, lifestyles and culture (i.e., more single homes, city-centre living and fewer family households). Yet we have still to see whether this is just a short-term trend or a sustainable housing form. What we can say is that 'mixed use' is central to this type of urban living, and along with it come aspects of 'liveability'. The research found that 'doorstep' issues such as rubbish, waste and antisocial behaviour figured as a nuisance, and annoyed residents of all urban blocks. Also, crime was a significant factor that affected all building types.

Chapters 8 and 9 looked at crime and focused on residential crime, its relationship to urban form and the design and construction of that form. It has not explored the relationship between crime and other forms of urban sustainability, primarily because we are only too aware that crime is a major factor in our perception of quality of life in cities. We know that a vibrant economy and a crime-free environment make cities more pleasant and desirable places to live. Reducing the fear of crime and crime itself by the way we design the residential aspects of our cities is one great step towards making them liveable for this, and future, generations.

The research and recommendations presented in this section have focused on the social aspects of sustainability that relate to a core aspect of human experience: our homes, their form in relation to city space, how that has changed, how residents perceive their quality of life in cities, and their relationship to crime.

The results suggest that while urban planners and designers are often concerned with economic vibrancy and developing 'character' and culture in our cities, we must not forget the importance of the homes people live in, their connectivity and safety. Also, while they may concentrate on building in an environmentally sustainable way, they must remember societal trends and behavioural factors. Will use of the car ever decline? Do people need private outdoor space? What type of mixed use is appropriate? What are the best ways to design out crime and fear of crime? Answers to these questions are, of course, often related to demographic trends and the economic strategy for a city, so before making design decisions it is critical that the context is understood and alternative futures considered. Section 4 will go on to look in more detail at these interdependent factors and dimensions of mixed use and diversity at varying scales of the urban environment.

SECTION 4
DIVERSITY AND MIXED-USE FOR CITY-CENTRE LIVING

Throughout the previous chapters we have been discussing various dimensions of sustainability, how people live with and respond to changes in their environment, how the built environment is created and its impact on our quality of life. We have also looked at who makes the important influencing decisions in the urban design and development process. This section considers how 'practice' interprets and responds to 'policy', and vice versa, and how this is manifested in urban form and quality of life. A particular focus of our investigation has been the processes of densification (i.e. dwellings, public/private space, 'compact city') and intensification (e.g. 24-hour city).

In both policy and practical terms these are conflated in the physical/land use, as well as in the social and economic sense, through the related phenomena of 'diversity' and 'mixed-use'.

Underneath these concepts, which have gained renewed popularity in the post-industrial urban era, are particular interrelationships that are traditionally separate in disciplinary discourses, in design and building approaches, and also in urban policy and land use planning. The social, economic, environmental and temporal dimensions have therefore been considered in this research as they are negotiated through governance and market systems – and governance, it is claimed, is now the 'fourth pillar of sustainability' (Hawkes, 2001). Because we have been assessing everyday lives, and how quality of life is experienced by residents, 'agents' and other occupants of higher-density, diverse, mixed-use areas, there is also a cultural dimension to governance and to human behaviour. Together these influence how the social, economic and environmental mix impacts in practice. This is therefore a case of 'sustainable development' (and 'communities'; ODPM, 2003) empirically tested in depth from a behavioural perspective. This includes the political economy and market behaviour (development and design industry) and the implications of their decision-making, as well as local stakeholders in their respective neighbourhoods. Triangulation of all of these aspects has been undertaken through three VivaCity2020 city-centre/fringe case studies, from the perspective of local planning authorities, police, property developers and agents and, critically, local householders and businesses. The notions of diversity and scale feature both in the research questions and in the emerging findings of this section, in an effort to move on from the unhelpful (and arguably unsustainable) concepts of mixed-use and density as policy and design panaceas for city growth and regeneration.

Chapter 10 provides the urban policy and planning context, explored through comparative surveys of mixed-use city areas with varying degrees of diversity. Chapter 11 further explores the notion of diversity. This takes as its starting point a biological and ecological analogy, which is applied through agent-based modelling using simulations, as well as land use and pedestrian movement observations undertaken in the demonstration case study area of Clerkenwell and other areas in London. The spatial structures, social (usage and behavioural) and informational aspects of the built environment and space are found to interact, to both define and 'produce' (Lefebvre, 1974) areas of genetic and sustainable diversity.

References
Lefebvre, H. (1974) *The production of space* (trans. D. Nicholson-Smith). Oxford: Blackwell.
ODPM (2003) *Sustainable communities: Building for the future*. London: Office of the Deputy Prime Minister.
Hawkes, J. (2001). The fourth pillar of stability: Culture's essential role in public planning. Melbourne: Cultural Development Network.

CHAPTER 10

URBAN SUSTAINABILITY: MIXED-USE OR MIXED MESSAGES?

Graeme Evans, Rosita Aiesha and Jo Foord

Introduction

'The mixing of urban uses – of living, moving, working – is possible and, increasingly, necessary. This new concept takes as its model the old, traditional life of the European city, stressing density, multiple use, social and cultural diversity.' (CEC, 1990: 43)

This chapter interrogates the resurgent concept of mixed-use in the post-industrial setting. The notion and practice of mixed-use development, as manifested through planning, guidance and strategic policy initiatives (e.g., *Sustainable communities*; ODPM, 2003), can be traced back to several models of urban development with similar perceived advantages. These are closely associated with movements promoting the compact city, urban village and New Urbanism, primarily emanating from the USA, as well as continental European approaches (CEU, 2004). These approaches incorporate aspects of accessible, legible/permeable and liveable cities, notably the 'exemplar' compact city, Barcelona, but also high-density cities such as Amsterdam, Berlin and Stockholm.

Mixed-use concept: back to the future

This is not of course a new concept or lived experience. As Zeidler (1985: 11) observes:

'Before the industrial revolution, describing buildings as multi-use would have seemed irrelevant. Such buildings existed as a matter of course and were integrated into the fabric of European towns and cities. They have been built and used by and for centuries.'

Historically, therefore, mixed and multi-use buildings and architecture were the norm prior to industrial society and the gradual separation of land use, reaching its peak with the modern(ist) movement (*Athens Charter*; CIAM, 1942), which drove the rationale for much of twentieth-century town planning (e.g., *Greater London Plan*: Abercrombie, 1944). This rigidity, particularly in the era after World War II, which was accelerated by the decline in traditional industries and post-Fordist relocation of production from urban heartlands, required a more flexible approach. For example, Charles Jencks saw this failure of modern town planning where:

'masterplans were drawn up with the city parts neatly split up into functional categories marked working, living, recreation, circulation … inevitably these mechanistic models did not work; their separation of functions was too coarse and their geometry too crude to aid the fine-grained growth and decline of urban tissue. The pulsations of a living city could not be captured by the machine model.' (Jencks, 1996: 26)

The so-called urban renaissance that has been used as a political and symbolic saviour to late-industrial decline also draws on the vitality and benefits that a combination and proximity of uses can bring to urban living and working. Thus: 'the long argued distinctions between activity and movement, between land use and transport, between production and consumption have begun to dissolve' (Solesbury, 1998). This looked perhaps nostalgically to Jane Jacobs's (1961) observations on what creates vitality and 'exuberant diversity' in city street life – in particular, variety in the primary functions of an area; short street blocks; diversity in building types and morphology; and density of occupation and of usage. Secondary uses therefore grow in response to the primary uses, and generate a mix of usage and people flow development, but on the other hand, short-sighted not to recognise the new opportunities which it presents' (Gruen, 1973); and, as Zeidler (1985: 9) noted:

> 'Multi-use buildings are not a placebo for urban problems. There are no guarantees that in certain situations a multi-use project would serve any better than single-use ... too many massive multi-use complexes have been built with the same sweeping urban renewal intent witnessed in the 1950s ... only now that they are intended for the consumer. Too often they have swallowed up the varied uses and activities along the street and sealed them into a monotonous indoor environment.'

(Montgomery, 1998). The corollary to this is large buildings closing themselves off from the street, combining functions internally and hidden, but which reflect the modern building type, from office block, supermarket and institutional building, with little variation in temporal use. Much of the adaptation and more contemporary building styles have sought to make entrances and facades more open to the street, and encourage mixed temporal use (activities, user groups, e.g., street markets, co-location, dual-use community facilities) – in short, the relationship to the street and public realm and greater 'transactional diversity', not just in consumption and social interaction (e.g., cafés and restaurants), but also in production. Examples here include shared/managed workspaces, studio/workshops on the ground floor combining retail and showcasing, and small/micro enterprises with informal production/supply chain links ('cluster effects').

While British planning policy and sustainable development strategies have focused on mixed-use over the past ten years, the promotion and critique of multi-use design have their origins in the USA of the 1970s (Witherspoon et al., 1976), where its resurgence was positive but conditional: 'it would be foolish to under-estimate the task of mixed-use

Mixed-use can therefore be seen as a practical application and interpretation of these urban planning ideals and design concepts, in a post-industrial context. However, it needs to be borne in mind that many of these concepts, including design and building types, have been imported and adapted to the British situation (e.g., the shopping mall, multiplex, waterfront/festival marketplace), as well as generated through the 'vernacular' configuration of building/land use. The extent to which these 'models' (if they indeed amount to such) can and have been transferred successfully therefore needs consideration, and in particular, the conditions that apply in the UK which may limit their successful adoption – for example, large, so-called mixed-use commercial developments, whose 'design and management mean they offer few of the benefits associated with traditional mixed-use areas' (Rowley, 1996b: 85). Notable factors include the liberal/flexible land use planning and development control system (and professional fragmentation) in the UK – versus the Napoleonic 'code', the Germanic and dirigiste US systems – the differing urban densities and morphologies (particularly in contrast to the USA, France and the Netherlands), and social and cultural factors, such as the night-time economy and licensing, household formation (houses versus apartment living, single persons versus extended families) and cultural diversity ('lifestyles'). Economic structures also differ between, for example retailing – – the balance between large/chain and small/independent shops – and employment – with a large number of small and micro firms, a small number of large firms and public institutions with large workforces – and the consequent employment premises and travel to work distributions.

However, 'mixed-use' is now a widely used term, which has become a shorthand for an urban design and building type, but one that conflates what are more complex, even conflictual configurations, uses and scales of development – from single buildings to blocks, complexes, streets and urban districts and quarters. Development and design paradigms and practice are increasingly global, and replicate architectural design styles and 'solutions'. The adoption of mixed-use policies has found favour in the UK with both left- and right-wing governments, commencing with the return to a more plan-led system (ten-year Unitary Development Plans) in the early 1990s and the Conservative government's U-turn on the expansionist out-of-town/edge city drift and a re-prioritisation of existing town centre revitalisation:

> 'Mixed-use development should increasingly become the norm rather than the exception … We will be expecting developers to think imaginatively in future as to how proposals can incorporate mixed land uses, to produce lively and successful developments over both the short and long term, and provide a positive contribution to the quality of our towns and cities.' (Gummer, 1995)

The benefits of mixed-use development are seen in terms of vitality, safety and sustainability (see Figure 10.1), extended here to include the economic dimension often overlooked in policy statements.

Figure 10.1 Advantages of mixed-use

Concentration and diversity of activities		
Vitality	Less need to travel	Local economy & clusters
A more secure environment	Less reliance on car	Production chain; innovation spillovers
More attractive and better quality town centres	More use of and opportunity for public transport	More local employment and services
Economic, social and environmental benefits		

Source: Adapted by the authors from DoE (1995)

The new Labour government reinforced this preference, initially with revised Planning Policy Guidance (PPG):

> 'Within town centres, but also elsewhere, mixed-use development can create vitality and diversity and reduce the need to travel. It can be more sustainable than development consisting of a single use. Local planning authorities should include policies in their development plans to promote and retain mixed uses, particularly in town centres, in other areas highly accessible by means of transport other than the private car and in areas of major new development.' (DoE PPG1, 1997)

This was reaffirmed a year later by John Prescott:

> 'Promoting mixed-use development is essential to our planning approach: it brings new life back into our towns and cities, enhances our quality of life and character of place, and creates patterns of development that we can sustain in the long run.' (English Partnerships, 1998)

Most recently, sustainable communities were to be

> 'well designed and built – including appropriate size, scale, density, design and layout, including mixed-use development, high-quality mixed-use durable, flexible and adaptable buildings, with accessibility of jobs, key services and facilities by public transport, walking and cycling, and strong business community with links to the wider economy.' (ODPM, 2005).

Diversity in terms of mixed-use and mixed communities (social, tenure) also extends to the temporal use of space, both built and open: e.g., markets, parks/squares, festivals, public art/animation, through the evening economy, 'leisure shopping' and 'mixed-use streets' (Jones *et al.*, 2007).

Scale and distinctions

The scale at which 'mixed-use' operates and has evolved – until recently 'organically' rather than plan- or design-led – ranges from the micro to the meso level, and at larger and smaller physical scales. Rowley (1996a) identifies the following key variables in mixed-use, suggesting that the practice is not homogeneous and that local/specific conditions need to be taken into account:

- *Location types, uses and activities*: Nature of users, occupiers, comings and goings, mix and balance of primary and other uses, compatibility, synergy
- *Intensity/density; grain of development; permeability*: Street layout – ease of movement, footfall along routes; grain (fine, coarse, sharp, blurred)
- *Character of surrounding development*: Age of area and buildings – capacity to respond and accommodate to change; range of design considerations, within and between buildings/public spaces – vertically and horizontally, size of units, visibility and legibility of uses
- *Market*: local/regional property and development economics; organisational flexibility
- *Social-cultural mix*: history, settlement; lifestyle trends/demands, tenure
- *Planning and urban policy*: e.g., regeneration, design guidance, licensing.

Measuring mixed-use

These variables, and their uneven distribution in urban settlements, have meant that in practice the planning and development system (and building and urban design) has had difficulty in dealing with mixed-use in a consistent and equitable manner. The concept is both ambiguous and defined differently according to the perspectives, priorities and imperatives at play, and the underlying land use planning and development regimes. For instance, in the USA 'mixed-use' is normally residential mixed with commercial: two commercial uses, e.g., shops and offices, would not meet this test. In the UK mixed-use is commonly dual use, with retail (A1) or food and drink (A3) on the ground floor and residential (or less commonly, offices, B1) above. For example, in London, where there is only one non-residential use, 50% is usually retail (including banks but rarely offices). When two or more non-residential uses combine, over three-quarters are retail and/or offices, but seldom industrial (B2–8), hotel (C1) or leisure uses (Craine *et al.*, 2007). In the USA, the Urban Land Institute requires three or more revenue-producing uses, integrated in terms of pedestrian access and layout (Marsh, 1996), which are normally achieved only in planned, rather than retrofitted, schemes. British land use classes have been developed deliberately to distinguish and separate, not to combine. So a mix of uses goes against the land use development control system, requiring specific policies and precedents that vary widely between planning authorities. In London these range from 0% to 82% (average 40%) of development as 'mixed-use', across the 33 boroughs in 2006/2007. To undermine the land use (and economic industry use) classification even further, the uses of land have also broken down and are no longer rigid or controllable, given the liberalisation of licensing and trading hours, lifestyle and working practices (e.g., live–work) and the consequent uses of the built environment and space.

Attempts to develop a generic definition of mixed or multifunctional land use have relied on an exclusive list of land use elements (Rodenburg & Nijkamp, 2007) – residential, work and business, infrastructure, recreation and culture and so on – although these do not necessarily map onto administrative land use classes as used by town planners. Multifunctional land use has also been defined in terms of intensification (efficiency, intensity of usage), interweaving (mixed-use of same area/building), and several usages over a time period (temporal mix) (Lagendijk & Wisserhof, 1999), where one or more of these conditions implies mixed-use. In practice the temporal and geographic (scale) aspects need to be specified to determine the extent of mixed-use, while diversity of the built form and appearance (whether by an extension, or intensification and reorganisation of the existing space usage), and the synergy of economic and spatial functions (see Jacobs, 1961) need explicit consideration (Rodenburg & Nijkamp, 2007). This multifunctionality indicator has been taken further by measuring the level of diversity of a given area/site, taking the actual number (frequency) of different land use functions, divided by the maximum number (in the UK these could be use classes, as above) with a maximum of one. Another measure is dispersion, which takes the degree to which each of these functions is present by land area (m²) as a

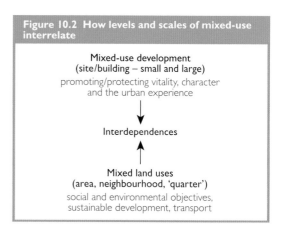

Figure 10.2 How levels and scales of mixed-use interrelate

Mixed-use development
(site/building – small and large)
promoting/protecting vitality, character
and the urban experience

↓

Interdependences

↑

Mixed land uses
(area, neighbourhood, 'quarter')
social and environmental objectives,
sustainable development, transport

proportion of the whole area. These measures indicate the equal or unequal distribution of diversity within an area or development. The dual-use or low-diversity examples of mixed-use would score low on both of these measures, while a diverse mixed-use area or street would score highly with a broad range of usage and distribution, not dominated by single or large-area uses (e.g., residential, offices, retail, i.e., supermarket, mall).

How these levels and scales of mix operate and, importantly, are experienced, we have sought to interrogate through the VivaCity2020 project (Evans & Foord, 2007) – in particular, how the physical (including 'design'), economic (production, consumption, location) and social interrelate in mixed urban environments and at differing scales. This includes where synergies and advantages are realised, but also where conflicts of 'use' arise. The delineation of the scale at which mixed-use evolves and operates successfully has been a particular focus, given its importance in defining both genuine and more sustainable mixed-use, including the relationships between these levels and between mono-use and mixed-use buildings and areas (see Figure 10.2).

Twin-speed cities

The adoption and promotion of mixed-use, compact city development zones is now a common phenomenon in post-industrial cities worldwide. In

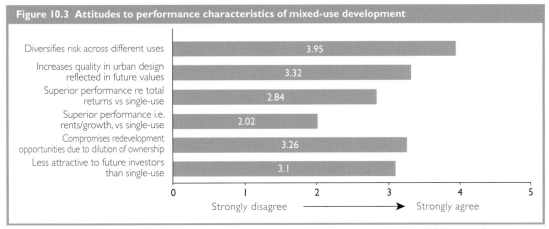

Figure 10.3 Attitudes to performance characteristics of mixed-use development

Source: Jones Lang LaSalle in BCO (2005, p. 4). Reproduced with permission of the British Council of Offices.

the UK, cities undergoing public-sector-led regeneration have used this development formula to rejuvenate waterfront (docks, canals), former industrial and city-centre retail and older office sites. The development industry has embraced this style, despite difficulties in investment finance and markets that are traditionally exclusive (i.e., residential, offices, leisure, retail) (Savills, 2003). From the perspective of the development sector, diversifying risk and future values attaching to better-quality mixed-use schemes in part offsets higher risk in terms of returns and the complications of ownership and variable lease terms within a mixed-use development (see Figure 10.3).

Two commercial development models of mixed-use have emerged: the self-contained 'box' combining ground-floor retail, restaurants and leisure with upper-floor office and – latterly – apartments; and the 'dual-use' housing-led development with ground-floor retail, community or leisure facilities (e.g., gym, crèche). The former is celebrated in terms of central city or waterfront (docks, canals) regeneration locations such as Brindleyplace, Birmingham: dual-use/housing is less high profile but more numerous in terms of both developments and geographic distribution, driven

by the demand for both private and affordable housing. Neither model presents successful examples of mixed-use, as the focus is on the 'block'/site, rather than on neighbourhood (or even street), despite claims and community benefits usually promoted at the development stage (see West One, Sheffield, below). They tend to revert to dual use, and despite the proclaimed design quality (e.g., Brindleyplace, Birmingham: CABE, 2001) fail to integrate over time with the urban fabric or economy of the area, or to produce sustainable mixed-use in terms of economic and amenity diversity or quality (Ricketts & Field, 2007). At worst, infill developments of this kind in already intense land use areas 'crowd out' existing residents and pedestrian access, block views/light, and further strain already fragile infrastructure and resources (e.g., transport, or social amenities such as GPs).

The apartment-based developments now commonly seen in city-centre, fringe and suburban locations (e.g., conversion of former department stores) struggle to find a use and market for the ground-floor. This is critical for mixed-use to work, and for the animation and surveillance benefits that can be generated by compact, mixed-use development. In London for example, with acute excess and latent housing demand, developments granted planning

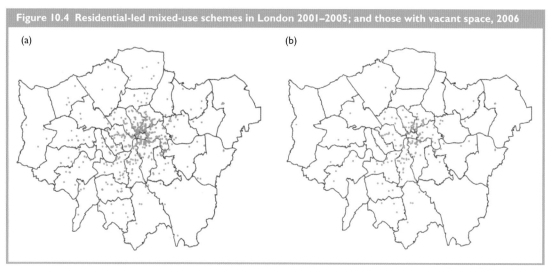

Figure 10.4 Residential-led mixed-use schemes in London 2001–2005; and those with vacant space, 2006

(a)

(b)

Source: Craine (2006: 18)

permission for 'mixed-use' housing schemes report vacancies of over 25% of the ground-floor space usage, several years after occupation of the accommodation spaces above (see Figure 10.4). A respondent in our survey commented:

> 'If you're in the market for different products in a building it's more difficult to market. Typical around here is commercial on the ground floors, and residential on upper floors. Equally typical is all the residential selling out and commercial spaces vacant for a long time.' (local estate agent, Clerkenwell)

This unused ground floor is a common sight in these flat-fronted, often characterless building types here and in other towns and cities e.g. Sheffield (see Figure 10.5).

The levels of dwelling density being achieved across urban areas are also highly variable, with key factors of connectivity/transport, economic diversity and growth (endogenous and inward investment, tourism), determining the rate of property development and success of mixed-use schemes and areas. This design and development model does not appear to be successful where these primarily economic factors are weak (and where urban design/build quality is poor). Variations in housing

Figure 10.5 Residential building with ground floor vacant, Sheffield

density in our three case study cities over a five-year period reveal this contrast (see Table 10.1). This measures not the misleading 'dwelling density' – the official government indicator – but the overall density of land use ('ambient density') taking into account outdoor/public realm space, which provides a more realistic measure of urban space intensification and quality. A high-density housing block may overlook another block, or an open space – quite different levels of amenity and 'density', and 'liveability'.

Densification in some inner urban schemes is often offset by reduced densities in other urban areas or

Table 10.1 Change in ambient density 2000–2004: largest 60 urban areas							
	Stock 2000	Total area (ha)	Populated area 2004 (ha)	Density pop. 2004	Overall density 2004	Change in density 2000–4	Rank 1–60
Islington, N. London	76 300	1500	1300	58.5	51.5	2.8	1
Manchester, N. West	194 900	10 300	5600	34.7	19.0	0.5	19
Sheffield, North	192 300	11 100	5300	36.3	17.3	0.1	49

(Source: Bibby, 2006)

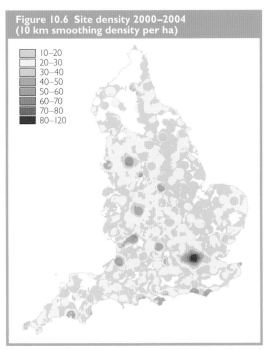

Figure 10.6 Site density 2000–2004 (10 km smoothing density per ha)

10–20
20–30
30–40
40–50
50–60
60–70
70–80
80–120

Source: Bibby (2006)

Figure 10.7 Types of urban locale

Villa suburb
Low-density suburb
Low-density edge suburb
Medium–high density suburb
City living
Other

Source: Bibby (2006)

even in the same neighbourhood (demolition/new build), such as in Liverpool and Salford (north-west) and also in Sheffield, where vacant land (including redundant industrial, mining areas) is prevalent, in contrast to London and other regions.

Over the recent period of housing growth, densities have increased, but at uneven rates across the country and within cities. Figure 10.6 indicates the concentration of site densities (dwellings per hectare) in the UK, with inner London and Manchester exhibiting the highest density levels in development between 2000 and 2004. Figure 10.7 analyses development over this period in terms of housing

type. This confirms the prevalence of city-centre living in these cities, but also the fact that most brownfield development has taken place in suburban and city fringe areas, but with few of the amenity, diversity or connectivity advantages of compact city locations.

While mixed-use, higher-density development and compact city hierarchies now underpin sustainable communities (ODPM, 2003) and housing growth plans, these basic concepts are reflected neither in planning legislation nor in guidance, which can inform the design, location and impact assessment of mixed-use. For example, there is no planning use class for mixed-use, nor an institutional property investment category (separate residential, retail, commercial sectors), and thus no detailed standards on what constitutes a sustainable mix, at what scale, or which combination of activity (Evans, 2005a, 2005b). Conversely, building regulations can restrict and limit the flexible use of space (i.e., means of escape/shared stairways, work and living space use). In short, it is a policy panacea without a sound evidence base or detailed design guidance – 'nostalgia and propaganda overtaking research and analysis' (Rowley, 1996b: 85). Commonly requested guidance from our consultations throughout this study have included: the proportional mix of uses in building design (architects); measures of 'urban carrying capacity', e.g., retail, evening economy and transport (town planning and licensing officers); and housing mix in terms of tenure, amenities and densities (housing associations and developers).

Methodological approach

Our response to the conceptual and qualitative question surrounding mixed-use in its various guises has been, first, the development of a comprehensive data architecture to capture and interrogate the social, economic, land use and related aspects that make up the compact city in practice. This entailed drawing on and analysing data, policy and indicators that previously had not been considered or viewed together, let alone synthesised. A range of local area geocoded data included the following:

- socio-economic: Census (community, demography, travel to work)
- index of multiple deprivation (IMD): areas ranked by factors of need/risk

- economic activity and 'health': industry activity and classification, employment (scale), start-ups/closures, clusters/location quotients
- crime: recorded crime data (e.g., burglary, 'street', vehicle)
- land use: classifications, floor space and valuation (non-domestic premises)
- pollution: noise complaints, air quality, and commercial traffic flow
- points of interest: commercial, retail, visitor attractions, amenities and transport.

National administrative data, supplemented with locally generated data (e.g., crime), exist at various levels of local geography representing output areas (OAs: lower, middle, upper) below the level of ward (electoral area), as well as point and postcode data (e.g., businesses, recorded crime). Premises data, key to modelling mixed-use, is, however, divided between non-domestic and housing, while the vertical mix and activity classifications required to understand the economic and social interrelationships and flows require a more detailed analysis, which was undertaken in this case through local area surveys. This entailed land use surveys based on observation, photographic recording, and the creation of a classification database that expanded normal land use categories, recording aspects such as opening and closing times and street-level (ground floor) activity during day- and night-times. Pedestrian activity was also monitored through timed counts at key nodes (Aiesha & Perdikogianni, 2005).

Test-bed

A test-bed area in which to pilot the methodology and tool kit was selected – Clerkenwell, in London's City fringe – based on a historic and contemporary mixed-use 'urban village' (Aldous, 1992). This area has both established and growing residential ('loft living') uses, large and small offices/studios, evening

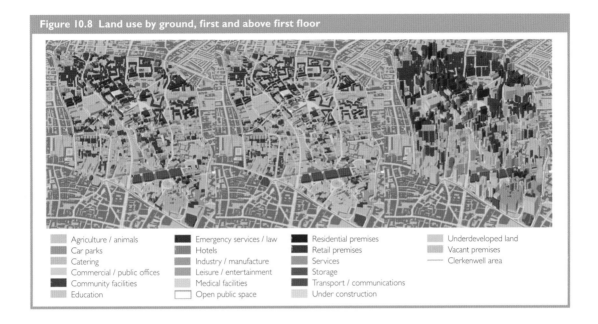

Figure 10.8 Land use by ground, first and above first floor

Agriculture / animals	Emergency services / law	Residential premises	Underdeveloped land
Car parks	Hotels	Retail premises	Vacant premises
Catering	Industry / manufacture	Services	—— Clerkenwell area
Commercial / public offices	Leisure / entertainment	Storage	
Community facilities	Medical facilities	Transport / communications	
Education	Open public space	Under construction	

entertainment and 'new economic' activity, and straddles three local authorities. This pilot was followed by test-bed areas in the city centre of Sheffield, which has been undergoing boosterist redevelopment, including new build and conversions of mixed-use accommodation.

A key issue in the mixed-use, high-density debate is quality of life. The research questions included: How is mixed-use defined and experienced? Is it sustainable? What mix works and does not, and at what scale: building, block, street, neighbourhood? The compact city model also suggests that vibrant local economies can be supported without significant inward travel (commuting), and that business location choices and markets reflect this reality. In order to test this aspect, questionnaire-based interviews were conducted with residents and businesses, as well as semi-structured interviews with policy and development industry representatives, to gauge their respective views and approach to mixed-use in practice. A more detailed analysis of the methodology and techniques is available in Aiesha & Perdikogianni (2005), Aiesha & Evans (2006, Clerkenwell), and Evans & Foord (2006, Sheffield; 2007, Clerkenwell).

Correlating land use and economic activity with social and other environmental factors has for the first time enabled concepts and questions of mixed-use scale and impacts to be assessed, supported by empirical evidence drawn from local and regional stakeholders (below). Figure 10.8 shows the results of the vertical land use analysis by floor, and in terms of land use types. Five zones within the area were selected for detailed observation (delineated below in Figure 10.18), based on analysis of building types/morphology, road/pedestrian networks (space syntax) and land use mix (see Chapter 11, pp227-9). This clearly shows the north–south separation between residential and more commercial/mixed-use zones, but also the residential use above first floor, as the darker, shaded blocks expand upwards with high-rise dwellings, and encroach into the more mixed land use area.

Table 10.2 Household surveys – summary of respondent profile

Respondents	Clerkenwell %	Sheffield %	Manchester %
Housing type:			
House	27	28	14
Flat	70	69	86
Gender:			n/a
Male	36	56	
Female	64	44	
Work:			
Full-time	39	55	49
Retired/student	21	12	51
Age:			n/a
26–35	23	22	
36–45	19	29	
56–65	29	9	
Tenure:			
Rent	53	57	73
Own	44	43	27
Landlord:			
Local authority	32	21	} 36
Housing association	8	12	}
Private	17	21	64
Ethnicity: White	61	73	80

Respondents	Clerkenwell %	Sheffield %	Manchester %
Access to/own car	34	44	50
'Lost sleep' (Noise, 'antisocial')	32	32	n/a
Secure at home after dark	92	83	n/a
Transport to work:			n/a
Walk	18	24	
Bus	10	10	
Train/tube/tram	6	3	
Car	6	22	
New residents:			n/a
Change mode	43	40	
Decrease car use	16	5	
Increase public transport	33	12	
Increase walking	33	14	
Disabled	13	14	n/a

N = 186 (80 Clerkenwell, 76 Sheffield, 30 Manchester)

Figure 10.9 Household survey: elements that are most valued in the home environment

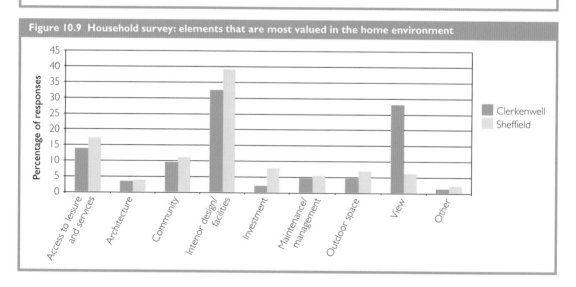

Household survey

Surveys of households in mixed-use case study areas were undertaken using structured questionnaires, administered both face to face and by self-completion through local 'gatekeepers' (residents/tenants). Over 150 completed questionnaires have been analysed.

Focus group interviews conducted in Manchester are based on a survey undertaken by the IPPR on city-centre living (Nathan & Urwin, 2006), targeting three groups: students, young professionals, and lower income groups (30 interviews in all).

The profile of respondents is summarised in Table 10.2. Key distinguishing characteristics include higher car ownership and usage in Sheffield (although a

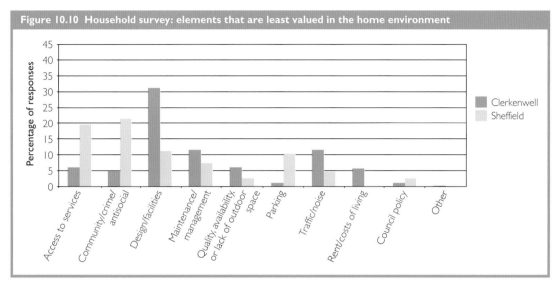

Figure 10.10 Household survey: elements that are least valued in the home environment

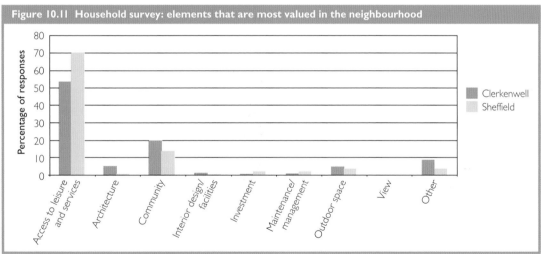

Figure 10.11 Household survey: elements that are most valued in the neighbourhood

higher percentage also walked to work) and Manchester, lower employment and higher retired and older age groups in Clerkenwell, and also a higher female respondent number compared with Sheffield. Other factors were similar, including basic housing type and tenure in London and Sheffield (Manchester is biased towards renting by students and lower-income groups). The benefits of connectivity and compact city living for new residents were most evident in Clerkenwell in terms

of transport usage, with switching from car to public transport/walking, unlike Sheffield, where reduction in car usage was less pronounced.

Quality of life: values

The values – positive and negative – ascribed to various features in the home and in the neighbourhood are summarised in Figures 10.9– 10.11, comparing two city case study areas: Clerkenwell (London), and central Sheffield. The design of interiors and access to leisure services

rated highly, with 'views' particularly important in Clerkenwell, but less so in Sheffield. Clerkenwell is located in a borough (Islington) with one of the lowest areas of open/green space per capita in England; Sheffield, by contrast, is surrounded by hills and is in close proximity to the Peak District National Park. Density levels are also higher in inner London, as already noted.

Negative aspects showed more divergence between cities, with an almost equal proportion in Clerkenwell not valuing the design of facilities, and also maintenance, traffic noise and cost of premises in comparison with Sheffield. Here access to services, community/crime, parking and council policy ranked as the least valued.

Neighbourhood factors provide a similar but subtly different perspective in higher-density urban environments. Here, access to leisure services scored most positively, also community, but less so other

OXO Tower, Southwark, London

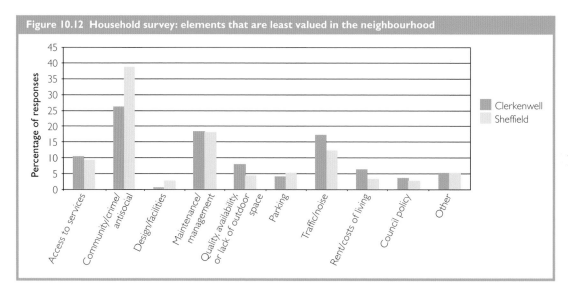

Figure 10.12 Household survey: elements that are least valued in the neighbourhood

factors, including outdoor space. Negative values included crime/antisocial behaviour (very high in Sheffield) in both areas, as well as maintenance/street management and traffic/noise (see Figure 10.12).

In the Manchester focus group study, simpler 'impressionistic' questions were asked of the three city dweller groups with a younger profile (students, young professionals). Here particular satisfaction was felt by students with their area and neighbourhood, but slightly less so their actual accommodation; likewise young professionals. This was in contrast to lower-income groups, who not surprisingly were less satisfied with their immediate environment and (rented) property, although social group D also rated the city's leisure and retail amenities highly, but less so group E (with the least disposable income) (see Figure 10.13).

Of the three city groups, Manchester participants had the highest car ownership, including students (often parked out of the city centre) and the lowest ethnic group proportion. Access to a car, even if not used daily for travelling to work, represents a key division between car users and non-car users, who rely on public transport and taxis for social, leisure and larger shopping trips outside the neighbourhood. These

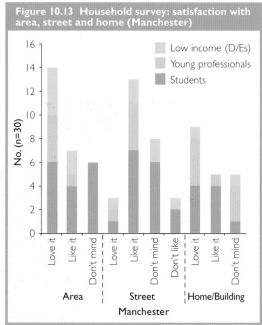

Figure 10.13 Household survey: satisfaction with area, street and home (Manchester)

trips increase as local amenities, notably food shops, health, school and entertainment facilities are located further away from residents and workers.

Business survey

One of the aspects introduced in our study has been the under-researched relationship between the local economy, employment and premises, and

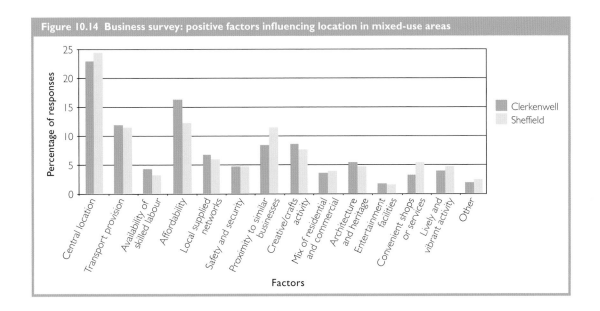

Figure 10.14 Business survey: positive factors influencing location in mixed-use areas

residential, travel and consumption activity. Despite the predictions of firm dispersal to lower-cost and accessible locations (transport, traffic, parking), clustering of certain economic functions, including those servicing the inner urban area itself, persists in certain urban areas (but not in others). The importance of a robust and critical mass of economic activity has been identified in maintaining more sustainable communities – at neighbourhood, borough and subregional levels. The profile of our case study economies provides a summary in terms of the main industry sectors measured by employment. These will be supplemented with significant self-employed, freelance and informal economic activity not captured in firm data in the Annual Business Inquiry (ABI).

The proportion of employment by sector shows the highest element in various business services, including real estate/property, particularly in Clerkenwell (containing a high proportion of all architecture firms in England), followed by education

(highest in Sheffield, with two universities located in the central area), public administration (Sheffield City Hall), financial services, wholesale and retail (low in Clerkenwell, with few large stores) and 'manufacturing' – higher in Clerkenwell, including long-established printing, jewellery and metal crafts trades (with specialist steel finishing in Sheffield). Total 'registered' employment totalled 37 000 in Clerkenwell and 45 744 in central Sheffield. Manchester, like Sheffield, has seen post-industrial structural change in employment, with less than 25% employed in manufacturing, transport and communication in 2001 (compared with over 50% in 1961) and approximately 70% in the service sector, but this is still less than those employed in these sectors in 1961, indicating a fall in total employment in the city over this period. These cities all present legacies from their industrial pasts: Sheffield (steel), Manchester (cotton) and Clerkenwell (printing and metal/jewellery).

A survey of businesses was conducted in order to gauge the experience and location factors affecting firms in these mixed-use areas (see Figure 10.14). Over 160 questionnaires were returned and analysed in Clerkenwell and Sheffield. Data on the local economy in both authorities were poor, however, signifying not only churn (dynamic change and declining economic sectors) and premises change of use, but also poor intelligence-gathering by local agencies, despite the level of public-sector activity promoting economic development. This self-completed questionnaire survey assessed the 'quality of business life' from the perspective of owners/managers, their staff and customers. In Clerkenwell, for instance, a range local shops and restaurants/cafés was valued by both residents and businesses. Local services such as banks, bars and pubs were appreciated more by firms rather than by residents, who favoured health services, and parks and play facilities.

In both areas the key location factors were centrality, affordability, transport access and proximity to similar firms (especially in Sheffield). Production chain effects may explain this in both traditional firms (manufacturing, legal services) and new economic sectors (e.g., creative industries): both areas supported creative industry quarters. Problems were prosaic, with parking/delivery access, litter/rubbish collection, crime/antisocial behaviour, as well as building, noise and air pollution. 'Neighbour activity' (i.e., relationships, cohesion) was not a factor in these mixed-use areas (see Figure 10.15).

A feature of a successful compact city and local economy is economic diversity and activity. The extent to which local firms inter-trade and support one another through supply and production chains is a key measure of diversity and tacit knowledge transfer ('innovation spillovers'). Another is the availability of a range of services and amenities to residents and workers (see Figure 10.16). In both areas, local shops and banking facilities, as well as hospitality and eating places, were used frequently and valued by businesses. Restaurants and cafés/pubs were valued more in Clerkenwell, a reflection of supply (limited in Sheffield) and a more established and reputable evening economy (in proximity to the City of London), which Sheffield has yet to develop more fully, alongside its retail, creative industry and educational facilities.

Night-time economy

The residential quality-of-life factor most associated with mixed temporal use relates to night-time activity, particularly pubs/bars, dance and music clubs, and related antisocial behaviour on the streets as well as from 'neighbours'. The liberalisation of licensing hours and Sunday trading from the 1990s has fuelled an explosion of alcohol-based activity in city-centre sites. In Manchester city centre, the number of licensed premises increased from 225 in 1995 to 430 in 1998 and to over 540 by 2002, with 166 venues holding public entertainment licences with a total capacity of over 110 000 persons (Hobbs et al., 2003) – predominantly non-restaurant and non-nightclub 'bars'. Friday- and Saturday-night young visitors trebled from an estimated 30 000 in 1992 to 100 000 a decade later. The domination of one user group creating a monocultural night-time scene has not only raised the level of street violence, antisocial behaviour and a flourishing control and security class (Hobbs et al., 2003), but has also crowded out a wider range of activities and users, particularly older people and families. This scenario is now played out in British city and town centres from Leeds to Swansea (Thomas & Bromley, 2000). In our Clerkenwell case study area, however, while licensed clubs and drinking venues serve a late-night consumer, a wider range of eating

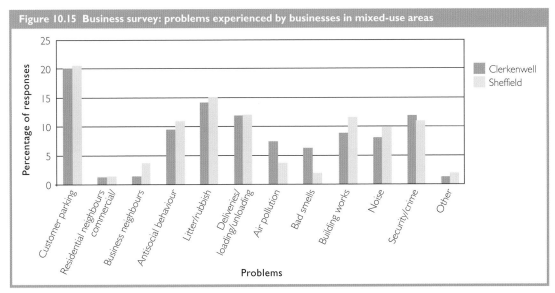

Figure 10.15 Business survey: problems experienced by businesses in mixed-use areas

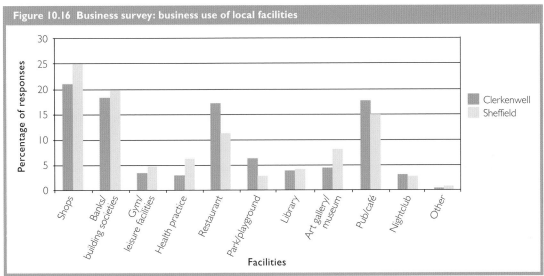

Figure 10.16 Business survey: business use of local facilities

establishments also serve a weekday office and residential market, so that one use/user group does not dominate, and the groups occupy the area at different, complementary times of the day and night. This city fringe location suffers less from the city-centre night-time crush and conflicts experienced elsewhere (including London's West End and Soho), maintaining both production and consumption activity in smaller-scale (and more upmarket) venues. Most

residential accommodation is sufficiently far removed from this activity and flow of people. Where they combine, conflicts can arise, but these are often very isolated cases of street disturbances (see below).

Data from noise complaints in Clerkenwell confirm the prime source of nuisance. Of over 2200 complaints in the period 2003/2004, 50% were from

Figure 10.17 Exmouth Market: left, graffiti and rubbish (alleyway); right, street use

'music', of which 88% occurred during the night-time. (In central Sheffield the source of complaints was also concentrated around clubs/nightlife areas: two-thirds were 'noise' from commercial/leisure activities.) The highest daytime noise complaints were from construction and machinery, as well as loud music. Six nightclubs with late-night music licences are located in the central area, including the first 24-hour licensed club in London. Late nights tend to run from Thursday through to Sunday, with 20 000 clubbers attending over this period. The local police maintain a close relationship with club management, mainly over drug use and parking. They sweep local streets to deter parking in or near residential areas to prevent noise after closing, and in fact few of the residents' complaints relate to late-night club activity: several owners and staff live locally, and have a detailed knowledge of the area and the community. More problematic noise pollution emanates from smaller bars and restaurants, which are located on the ground floors of residential blocks (Figure 10.17). Environmental issues, including litter, antisocial behaviour and street crime (e.g., bike theft) represent the prime challenge for mixed-use involving visitor activity, while gentrification effects impact on the character and amenity for residents, and ultimately threaten the mix itself:

> 'There's Exmouth Market. 25 years ago it was a market, you had food stores and utility stores, somewhere to get your boots sorted or your clothes and there was a Woolworth's at the end of the road. There has been a change from traditionally working class things – you had a pie and mash shop down there. Now, you have wine bars and flash restaurants.' (Local resident, 2004)
>
> 'For me the problem is the litter … it stinks. There are two problems with rubbish, there are no bins in most places so they drop things along the street. The other is the problem on the street. A lot of people put their rubbish out when they feel like it – maybe three days before the collection. It's not pleasant in the summer, especially when the cats get to it. In Exmouth Market they put the rubbish by the trees – you get one rubbish bag – 2 hours later you've got 10. Every tree has a mountain of rubbish bags.' (Local resident)

More serious impacts are evident in Figure 10.18, which overlays recorded crime densities ('hot spots') for commercial burglary, mapped against office/services premises. This indicates the concentration of break-ins in the commercial zone, which are less prevalent in the more mixed-use area, but more frequent in the fringe of the area that reverts to mono-use. Domestic burglary (not shown) mapped against residential property, not surprisingly ('supply-led') also shows a higher concentration in the housing-only area, but is less evident in the mixed properties ('living above the shop'). This contradicts the received wisdom that mixed-use areas are more vulnerable and mono-use safer; the reverse seems to be the case here. Resident surveys confirmed a low level of 'fear of crime', but greater concern about antisocial behaviour, particularly environmental (litter/rubbish, noise). On the other hand, robbery ('street crime') mapped against evening activity such as bars, clubs and restaurants highlights key crime hot spots, in this case focused on specific 'café culture' streets, where pickpocketing, snatch theft and vehicle crime (bike theft, car break-ins) are very high. These

Figure 10.18 Proximity of commercial burglary and offices (left), and 'street' crime and evening economy (right)

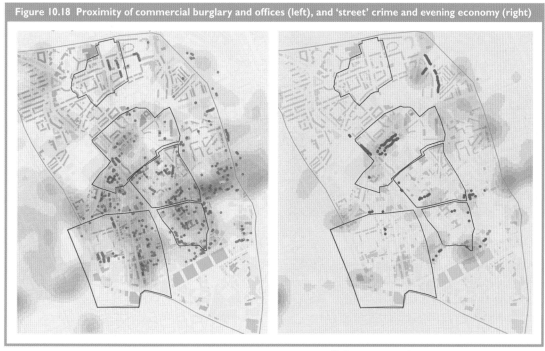

© Crown copyright. Ordnance Survey. All rights reserved

few partially permeable streets present too many open access points for pedestrians and bikes, and have poor surveillance (a conclusion shared by the local police), despite high levels of pedestrian flow and street activity.

Governance: gentrification and resistance

'Pity that the Council doesn't really listen to public opinion. Too much has been predetermined on political and economic grounds, making consultation a mockery, e.g., on the 32-storey tower.' (Sheffield City Masterplan, EDAW, 2007).

The trade-offs and the mediation of conflicts of usage (economic, spatial, temporal) arising from our investigation of diversity and density in these inner urban areas reveal key quality-of-life factors and tipping points that can maintain or destroy sustainability for residents and other occupiers. The mix we have captured and attempted to codify includes social uses as well a range of property, space, economy and temporal uses. The image often

portrayed of inner-city living and regeneration (Nathan & Urwin, 2006) is that of a younger, childless and transient resident and visitor (student, worker, tourist). However, it is clear that incumbent and long-established communities also inhabit these areas, in both social rented flats and owner-occupied houses and flats. Over 20% of (former) council blocks had been purchased under buy-to-let legislation, and there was evidence of subletting by council tenants to benefit from higher rental income. In Sheffield (e.g., the Devonshire Quarter Figure 10.19), buying new apartments 'off plan' by external (including overseas) investors for rental (e.g., students) was common, even in some cases leaving properties empty/pristine for future capital gain. 'Who' the community is at any point is therefore dynamic, and not reliant upon census and other official data profiles: 'If you don't mind never knowing your neighbours then it's OK. In the city people move all the time' (student, Manchester). Churn (turnover of residents) is high in the regenerating area of

Rolls Crescent, Hulme, Manchester

Clerkenwell, London (15–25% a year versus 10% for a more residential borough); however, there is also continuity in local communities who wish to remain in the area in which they were brought up and work. What is self-fulfilling in this market-led system is that rising property values squeeze out incumbent lower-income residents, with first-time buyers and young couples unable to afford family accommodation:

> 'Where are the sons and daughters of today's council tenants going to live in 20 years' time? They are never going to be able to get council accommodation, and it's very unlikely that many of them will be able to buy or rent in this area.' (Islington housing officer).

This is exacerbated by restriction on the adaptation and conversion of rented/council properties – for example lateral extensions – unlike for owner-occupiers. Usage of local amenities and school rolls consequently fall and these therefore decline, closing off the opportunity for both retention and inward settlement of families:

> 'You move to the city for a lifestyle – so you can go out easily and so on. But when you have children, you can't go out anyway, so what is the point?' (Young professional, Manchester)

> 'To be honest, it's a bit selfish of the parents to bring their children up in a city centre.' (Student, Manchester)

In this city, these young people saw city living as a phase ideal for singles but unsuitable for family living. Children were seen to lack space both in and around the home and in parks and streets that were noisy and chaotic, with constant risk of crime, unstable communities, poor schools, etc. However, there was optimism expressed by those who had spent time in Barcelona and New York (Nathan & Urwin, 2006), and in our Sheffield case study the benefit of maintaining families was also expressed during the recent masterplanning consultation exercise:

> 'Don't just pay lip service to family accommodation in the city centre. People are more committed to an area if they are bringing up a family there. We already have a lot of people who look upon the centre as simply a place to work and sleep.' (Sheffield City Masterplan, EDAW, 2007)

This highlights a problem of amenity and infrastructure planning for new and expanding communities that now underpins (and constrains) the delivery of the massive house-building plans under government sustainable communities and housing growth area plans (i.e., 3 million new 'homes'). The planning horizons of social and utility providers (i.e., local and regional authorities, private operators – transport, electricity, gas, water, etc.) are too short for the medium- to longer-term planning required to provide for new schools, health, recreation and other services. As housing population and density levels increase in both brownfield/infill and new housing 'estate' developments, this highlights the absence of a robust 'carrying capacity' measurement and scenario model that can be integrated into the land use, facility and economic (including 'planning gain'/roof tariff) feasibility and funding arrangements.

Developers (including design and construction intermediaries) are short-term stakeholders, passing on responsibilities to housing and other landlords and authorities, post occupation (or even earlier, at sale, often 'off plan', i.e., before residents actually exist and their current and future needs are identified). Such amenity, 'quality of life' aspects therefore need to be factored in at this front-end stage, or not at all. In all of our case study sites the issues of schools, facilities for young people, local shops, access/transport to work/leisure, and the safe and clean environment within which genuine higher-density, mixed-uses can coexist are universal concerns and prerequisites for sustainable urban communities.

In all the case study areas and cities local and regional governance systems had been inadequate in limiting and controlling the deleterious effects of property and amenity gentrification, high-density development and vagaries of the housing market. Reaction, if not resistance, has come from several sources – academics, local residents and artists. From academics, see for example Ward's (2005) 'Re-imaging Manchester' and Bolchover and Basar's (2005) 'Demolition Hulme', both in Oswalt (2005), and Peck and Ward (2002: 5), who maintained that:

> 'Many of the city's underlying social and economic problems have been displaced rather than solved ... for all the manifest progress which has been made in turning around the city centre ... the effect of this activity on the socio-economic "fundamentals" has been extremely modest.'

Manchester city dwellers' attitudes towards the new regeneration and housing market renewal areas in the region reveal strong prejudices: neighbouring Salford was seen as a very unattractive place to live, owing to crime and low environmental quality; likewise Hulme. Only new development zones such as New Islington and Ancoats (situated north of the centre) were seen to be acceptable, owing to their close proximity to the city centre. Salford's regeneration has been a tale of two halves, with Salford Quays receiving substantial European and national regeneration funding to develop flagship cultural facilities such as the Lowry, Imperial War Museum, Calatrava bridge, and latterly, new housing. Salford town centre, on the other hand, not benefiting from a Metro transport connection to Manchester or the Quays, is undergoing masterplanning through an urban development corporation (see Chapter 2), with key partners the University of Salford and Salford City Council. Community reaction to redevelopment and regeneration programmes that some see as divisive is also evident.

Sheffield, which has been emulating the more successful inner-city renewals, such as Birmingham, Manchester and its regional neighbour Leeds, has pursued a belated boosterist city planning regime. But emulation has its critics: 'Don't just clone Leeds/Manchester! Be original ...' (EDAW, 2007). Seeking to attract Grade A office developments to compete with these core cities, city masterplanning and 'quarters' have been used to focus the development of retail, market, transport and housing schemes, but less so employment, despite the support of one of the first cultural industry quarters (and compare Manchester's northern 'creative industries' quarter). Diversifying these residual and new creative economy production areas has, however, failed to gain hold in terms of mixed-use, evening economy or public realm improvements (Moss, 2002) – until the city-centre makeovers and a further masterplan exercise currently under way (EDAW, 2007). The examples of mixed-use higher-density development and renewed cultural renaissance have yet to produce the buzz associated with the more organic diversity seen in Clerkenwell, where the compact city is more embedded economically, culturally and – despite gentrification effects – socially. Sheffield has been dominated by a few landowner/developers (universities, city) and a liberal development regime attracting hotel and apartment developers (including student accommodation). Unlike the situation in London and also Manchester, younger professionals and middle classes have not returned to the city, with consequent high car usage and commuting, and poorer-quality housing developments and urban amenities, notably schools (Evans & Foord, 2006). This is neither 'community' nor 'sustainable' development.

The role of artists in interpreting and intervening in the development change process is evident here also (see below). In Manchester, however, the creative and subsequent 'knowledge/science' city movements have been associated both with universities, individual academics and creatives, who identify with the city's resurgence, its competitive (including with London), vibrant ('Madchester', 'Gaychester': Hobbs et al., 2003) and enterprising image (Williams, 2003), and with flagship regeneration schemes such as the URBIS Centre, Bridgewater Hall, the 47-storey Hilton Tower, the 2002 Commonwealth Games, renovation of the main station interchange (Piccadilly) and East Manchester – and the redevelopment of the city-centre retail area following the IRA bomb in 1996.

In Sheffield, the large footprint offices that Manchester has been able to create – generating high commercial rents and utilising large-scale industrial buildings such as in Castlefield, ripe for loft and apartment conversions (Urban Splash) in close proximity to the centre – were not available. Sheffield's legacy of small workshops, institutional towers (universities, Department of Employment at Moorfoot, council buildings), low-quality markets, a hilly topography and post-war housing estates such as Park Hill[1] has limited the city-centre developments and flagships seen in other northern cities. Its late-1990s cultural regeneration project, the National Centre for Popular Music, funded by National Lottery and European (ERDF) capital, failed within a few years of opening, and now serves as a student facility for Sheffield Hallam University (Evans & Foord, 2006).

Here artists have been directly engaged in the process of redevelopment of the city, in the Devonshire Quarter, one of the areas that have been the focus of our survey. Andy Hewitt and Gail Jordan are 'site-based installation' artists with a studio overlooking Devonshire Green near Sheffield city centre (below). Two projects were commissioned

Figure 10.19 Devonshire Green and West One Plaza

and undertaken by this team, both focused on the Devonshire Quarter (branded 'DQ') area: Outside Artspace (2001–2002) and I Fail to Agree (2003), 'which highlight the contradictory relationship between public or democratic concerns and the interests of private property developers' (Hewitt & Jordan, 2003: 24). In Outside Artspace the artists worked with the city planning department to help develop a vision, and 'to reinforce the identity of the area and improve land use, transport, urban design, the local economy, housing mix, sustainable living, quality of the environment and community safety' (Hewitt & Jordan, 2003: 26). This area has been associated with youth activity and small businesses serving this market (skateboarding, record shops, cafés, etc.) and a growing university student body, owing to the development of new halls of residence. During this process West One, a large-scale eight-storey apartment development was under construction overlooking the Green (see Figure 10.19), the only large green space in the city centre. The artists visited the West One showroom to discuss their vision for the development. They said the council planned to build a bandstand, create a pleasant safe area, with CCTV – an image directed at the 'exclusive' apartment market, with the Green as a 'front garden' feature for new residents, rather than

a community, social and public space. The artists' proposals arising from community consultations included a venue for art projects, exhibitions, film, performance, music events – as part of an annual programme – and youth facilities, including a skateboard park. These proposals were received by the Council and contact with them then stopped – the recommendations were not taken up. Five years later in the masterplanning consultation [sic] exercise, 'Concern was expressed that the Green skate park was not shown on the (new) plans, and they had heard that it was being got rid of' (EDAW, 2007).

The second artists' intervention went even more directly to the development process. In 2003, Showflat re-created a mock apartment overlooking DQ from the artists' own studio premises, using the interior design and finishes familiar to these developments (white walls, wood laminate floors, minimal décor, contemporary door furniture, etc.). Marketed on similar terms, with an external estate agents' sign, 'a unique opportunity for a new adventure in urban living', prospective buyers viewed the studio. Offers in excess of £80 000 were received (for two unfitted rooms with no running water!): 'How long we operate within this changing environment is in question: any significant rise in rent would certainly prompt us to move' (Hewitt & Jordan, 2003: 28) Here, as in countless central and fringe locations in post-industrial cities, established small firms, opportunities for start-up enterprises and artists ('stormtroopers of gentrification') are displaced by the ostensible pursuit of mixed-use, diverse 'communities' and developments: 'the increase in real estate values in the area [has] begun to push the eclectic mix of light industry and cultural activity out of (Devonshire) Quarter' (ibid.). Likewise in Manchester: 'increasing property rents are forcing out creative industries' (in Evans, 2004: 90).

As these inner-city/fringe neighbourhoods experience population growth again (although nowhere near the peak of their industrial heydays), and also structural changes in their community, economy and physical landscape, frustration with local governance and planning processes has led some to challenge them politically, as well as through cultural and community action. In Clerkenwell, locals despairing of what they see as both council and market failures have contested local ward seats – in this case coming second to the incumbent Liberal Democrats (the elected party), but displacing Labour.

This public polarisation may become more prevalent where the high density, mixed-use development formula creates a 'Pareto loss' in local sustainability and political terms.[2] Evidence from households surveyed in both Clerkenwell and Sheffield points

to differences between incumbents and newcomers in terms of everyday actions such as putting out the rubbish, as well as noise, parking and the social use of space. New residents not used to living in denser, mixed areas can be seduced by estate agent's urban living images and rhetoric, but the reality is somewhat different:

> 'One of the problems is with some of the incomers: new residents don't quite understand that it's a mixed-use area, so they don't like a nightclub, for example, they don't like people wandering down the street at two o'clock in the morning making noise ... classic environmental health cases, when new residents moved in and within a few weeks they've filed a formal complaint to environmental health against office air-conditioning in firms who've been there for 25 years.' (Islington development control planner)

Conclusion

The grounded, multi-criteria methodological approach adopted in this research suggests that, by generating new knowledge of the range of interactions that take place in mixed-use neighbourhoods, the concerns that different stakeholders express can be addressed and contextualised spatially and socially. The household and business surveys reveal evidence of the negative and positive externalities that influence both resident and business occupiers' experiences of dense/diverse land use areas.

The risks of social (and economic, housing) polarisation are emerging, questioning the wisdom of higher-density policy promotion without concomitant attention to amenity, environmental management and more active governance systems. The analysis has enabled us to conclude that the

Hodgson Street, Sheffield

notion of a successful diverse urban environment seems to bear witness to a dynamic relation between spatial, occupational patterns and individual/group behaviour and aspirations. The spatial data analysis highlights the scale – from the micro to macro – at which the city and 'urban village' operate.

This suggests that one key to understanding and ultimately achieving a sustainable city is to explore the dialectic relation between the different scales within which the mixing of uses occurs. It could also be argued that the perceived risks, expressed both by residents and by decision-makers, regarding a diverse and dense city could be mitigated if the approach to development, change-of-use and amenity/infrastructure planning incorporates this understanding, and measures incremental and cumulative change more intelligently and inclusively.

Promoting mixed-use as a sustainable development and design form therefore requires a more comprehensive consideration and understanding of the mix and the scales at which this can operate mutually. As we and others have found, the mixed-use block and large-scale commercial schemes, where space is dominated (whether technically 'mixed' or not) by homogeneous user groups, are producing less successful and less sustainable environments. They are also proving to be economically inefficient (e.g., ground floor vacancies) and will be further exposed as the development market tightens under recessionary pressures (for

example in central Manchester). The design and planning of areas where uses (of buildings and space) are separate, but in close proximity, is, however, feasible at the urban village scale, provided environmental management and local governance are robust.

The unifying model that urban design, planning and development practitioners demand, and the test of sustainability from the perspective of residents and occupants, is that of 'carrying capacity'. This elusive measure requires further research to determine the factors and their weighting that contribute to a well-planned and well-lived urban scale. Simple land and building use classifications, plot ratios, employment categories and housing tenure distinctions do not meet this goal, because they are largely binary/exclusive and, critically, make no allowance for the interrelationships between each of these dimensions and their impacts, which together go to make up urban living in practice. An urban carrying capacity model is likely to require a more comprehensive and sensitive assessment of a neighbourhood's and area's capacity for growth, as part of the planning/development control, design and infrastructure processes. This will need to encompass – as our investigation and analytical tools have sought to apply – social, economic, environment/design, and cultural aspects of urban living and working.

The local development framework ('borough plan'), sustainable community strategies,[3] and quality-of-life performance measurement, which planning authorities are having to undertake, will be further challenged as the development density and housing growth pressures intensify. Lessons learned therefore need to be disseminated at all levels of decision-making – public and commercial – and the distinctions between sustainable and less sustainable higher density, mixed-use, more clearly understood.

In policy and guidance terms, the planning and development industry now demands better integration and decision-making tools that can link these aspects to support development, investment, design and environmental impact assessments. These need to include: detailed design and planning guidance on the implications of and options for mixed use; the densification/intensification of land and building use; and more responsive environmental management and governance over what gets built and amenity provision that will be required over time – not limited to the developer contributions negotiated under current planning gain (S.106) agreements. It should be remembered that developers and designers are short-term actors, rather than ongoing stakeholders in the urban environment.

References

Abercrombie, P. (1944) *The Greater London Development Plan*. London: HMSO.

Aiesha, R. & Evans, G.L. (2006) VivaCity: Mixed-use and urban tourism. In M. Smith (ed.), *Tourism, culture and regeneration*, pp. 35–48. Wallingford: CAB International.

Aiesha, R. & Perdikogianni, I. (2005) Decoding urban diversity in 'mixed-use' neighbourhoods. *Proceedings of Sustainable Environments: Vision into Action*, University of Birmingham, March.

Aldous, T. (1992) *Urban villages: A concept for creating mixed-use urban developments on a sustainable scale*. London: Urban Villages Group.

BCO (2005) Mixed-use development and investment. London: British Council of offices.

Bibby, P. (2006) *Measures of density: A note*. Sheffield: Sheffield University.

Bolchover, J. & Basar, S. (2005) Demolition Hulme. In O. Oswalt (ed.), *Shrinking cities*, Vol. 1, pp. 608–617. Ostfildern-Ruit: Hatje Cantz Verlag.

CABE (2001) *The value of urban design*. London: Commission for Architecture and the Built Environment/Department of the Environment, Transport and the Regions.

CEC (1990) *Green paper on the urban environment*. Luxembourg: Commission of the European Communities.

CEU (2004) *General agreement on mixed use for cities*. Council for European Urbanism. www.ceunet.org/mixeduse.htm.

CIAM (1933) *Athens Charter*. Paris: Congrès International d'Architecture Moderne.

Craine, T. (2006) *Mixed-use performance in residential-led developments in London*. London: London Development Research.

Craine, T., Christensen, T. & Giddings, E. (2007) *Planning comparables: Comparable residential s.106 obligations & precedents in London*. London: London Development Research with London Metropolitan University.

DoE (1995) PPG13: A guide to better practice. London: HMSO.

DoE (1997) *Planning Policy Guidance PPG1 revised: General policy and principles*. London: Department of the Environment.

EDAW (2007) *Report of city-centre masterplan 2007. Review and roll forward*. Comments from public exhibition: 29 November–2 December 2006. Sheffield: Sheffield City Council.

English Partnerships (1998) *Making places: A guide to good practice in undertaking mixed-use development schemes*. London: English Partnerships/Urban Villages Forum.

Evans, G.L. (2004) Cultural industry quarters: from pre-industrial to post-industrial production. In D. Bell & M. Jayne (eds), *City of quarters: Urban villages in the contemporary city*, pp. 71–92. Aldershot: Ashgate Press.

Evans, G.L. (2005a) Urban sustainability and mixed-use design. *Planning in London*, **52**, 43–46.

Evans, G.L. (2005b) Mixed use or mixed messages? Planning in London, **54**, 26–29.

Evans, G.L. & Foord, J. (2006) Small cities for a small country: sustaining the cultural renaissance. In M. Jayne & T. Bell (eds), *Small cities: Urban experience beyond the metropolis*, pp. 151–168. London: Routledge.

Evans, G.L. & Foord, J. (2007) The generation of diversity: mixed use and urban sustainability. In S. Porta, K. Thwaites, O. Romice & M. Greaves (eds), *Urban sustainability through environmental design: Approaches to time-people-place responsive urban spaces*, pp. 95–101. London: Routledge.

Gruen, V. (1973) *Centers for the urban environment*. New York: Van Nostrand Reinhold.

Gummer, J. (1995) *More quality in town and country*. Environment news release. London: Department of the Environment.

Hewitt, A. & Jordan, M. (2003) *I fail to agree*. Sheffield: Site Gallery.

Hobbs, D., Hadfield, P., Lister, S. & Winlow, S. (2003) *Bouncers: Violence and governance in the night-time economy*. Oxford: Oxford University Press.

Jacobs, J. (1961) *The death and life of great American cities*. Harmondsworth: Penguin.

Jencks, C. (1996) The city that never sleeps. *New Statesman*, **28** (June), 26–28.

Jones, P., Roberts, P. & Morris, L. (2007) *Rediscovering mixed-use streets. The contribution of local high streets to sustainable communities*. York: Joseph Rowntree Foundation.

Lagendijk, A. & Wisserhof, J. (1999) Geef ruimte de kennis, geef kennis de ruimte, deel 1: Verkenning van de kennisinfrastructuur voor meervoudig ruimtegebruik (Give knowledge to space, give space to knowledge, part 1: Exploration of knowledge infrastructure for multifunctional land use). *Rapport aan de Raad*, RMNO-nummer 136.

Marsh, C. (1996) *Mixed-use – a mixed blessing? The cutting edge*. London: RICS Research.

Montgomery, J. (1998) Making a city: urbanity, vitality and urban design. *Journal of Urban Design*, 3 (1), 93–116.

Moss, L. (2002) Sheffield's cultural industries quarter 20 years on: what can be learned from a pioneering example? *International Journal of Cultural Policy*, 8 (2), 211–219.

Nathan, M. & Urwin, C. (2006) *City people: City-centre living in the UK*. London: IPPR Centre for Cities.

ODPM (2003) *Sustainable communities: Building for the future*. London: Office of the Deputy Prime Minister.

ODPM (2005) *What is a sustainable community?* London: Office of the Deputy Prime Minister.

Oswalt, O. (ed.) (2005). *Shrinking cities*. Ostfildern-Ruit: Hatje Cantz Verlag.

Peck, J. & Ward, K. (eds) (2002) *City of revolution: Restructuring Manchester*. Manchester: Manchester University Press.

Ricketts, S. & Field, D. (2007) Large-scale mixed-use development and the UK planning system: does it fit, and will the Planning White Paper assist? *Journal of Urban Regeneration and Renewal*, 1 (3), 240-250.

Rodenburg, C. & Nijkamp, P. (2007) The assessment of multifunctional land use. In M. Deakin, G. Mitchell, P. Nijkamp & R. Vreeker (eds), *Sustainable urban development, Vol. 2: The environmental assessment methods*, pp. 285–305. London: Routledge.

Rowley, A. (1996a) *Mixed-use development: Concept and realities*. London: RICS.

Rowley, A. (1996b) Mixed-use development: ambiguous concept, simplistic analysis and wishful thinking? *Planning Practice and Research*, 11 (1), 87–99.

Savills FPD (2003) *Investment in mixed use*. London: Savills FPD.

Solesbury, W. (1998) *Good connections: Helping people to communicate in cities*. Working Paper No. 9. Stroud: Comedia/Demos.

Thomas, C.J. & Bromley, D.F. (2000) City centre revitalisation: problems of fragmentation and fear in the evening and night-time city. *Urban Studies*, **37** (8), 1403–1429.

Ward, K. (2005) Re-imaging Manchester. In O. Oswalt (ed.), *Shrinking cities*, Vol. 1, pp. 596–607. Ostfildern-Ruit: Hatje Cantz Verlag.

Williams, G. (2003) *The enterprising city centre: Manchester's development challenge*. London: Spon Press.

Witherspoon, R.E., Gladstone, R.M. & Abbett, J.P. (1976) *Mixed-use developments*. Washington, DC : Urban Land Institute.

Zeidler, E.H. (1985) *Multi-use architecture in the urban context*. New York: Van Nostrand Reinhold.

Footnotes

1 Park Hill (Grade II listed post-war estate) is now under redevelopment by Urban Splash requiring the decanting of council tenants, for a mixed-use 'makeover'.

2 The idea of Pareto efficiency is used in modern welfare economics, and is named after Vilfredo Pareto, whose *Manual D'Economie Politique* was published in 1909. An allocation or land use is Pareto-efficient for a given set of consumer tastes, impacts, benefits or resources if it is impossible to move to another that would make some people better off and nobody worse off. Winners and losers arising from a development would therefore be inefficient, and a Pareto loss.

3 The main aim of the Sustainable Communities Act 2007 is to give local people more control over improving their community, by allowing a community panel to suggest ways in which local spending could be better used to improve local services and improve quality of life. The Act has a broad remit to improve local sustainability, with local services understood as anything from the post office and public house to open spaces and social housing.

CHAPTER 11

THE GENERATION OF DIVERSITY

Alan Penn, Irini Perdikogianni and Chiron Motram

There are two predominant forms of sustainability. To use a biological analogy, sustainability can be achieved either through an excellent match between an ecological niche and an organism, or through flexibility and resilience – the propensity to adapt to a changing ecological niche. The shark has changed little in a hundred million years because it is so well suited to its (relatively stable) environment – by any measure it is sustainable. Humans have changed and evolved considerably over just the last million years, to survive in possibly the widest range of environmental conditions of any organism, and to change those environments to suit their needs. By any measure they are resilient.

To pursue the biological analogy one step further; there is a current orthodoxy that the basis of resilience of an ecosystem lies in its diversity (Wilson, 1992). This idea has been adopted in the field of urban planning and design, and has been highly influential, both in policy formation and in design culture. It is perhaps the most important principle behind post-modern planning, linking it to contemporary design. However, despite its apparent obviousness, diversity as applied to urban systems remains poorly defined. Like the elephant ('it's large and its grey and I know one when I see one'), diversity's best definitions appeal to exemplars.

This chapter explores the role played by diversity in urban social and economic systems, and its relationship to resilience and sustainability. It starts by developing a working definition of diversity as this applies to urban areas, building upon geographic and economic theories of the city, before moving on to examine the relationship between land use patterns, spatial configuration and the economic dimensions of urban systems. It argues that a definition of diversity must include not only the physical material and spatial properties of urban form, but also the socio-economic and cultural properties of the communities that inhabit and use the city as their behaviours affect sensory perceptions in urban space. In this it must appeal both to static morphology and to those dynamic and time-bound aspects of history and individual experience through which diversity arises and is perceived. The last requires an understanding of the cognitive dimension through which diversity becomes meaningful in informing our individual actions.

The principal methodology used in this examination is agent-based simulation. Building on this develops the argument that diversity allows the maintenance of different structures – social, economic, physical, etc. – that may become critical to survival in an indeterminate future. However, the maintenance of diversity has associated costs. Often for a well-specified situation there is a defined efficient strategy, and so long as that situation persists other strategies present in a diverse environment will perform less well. Over the long term, in the face of environmental stability, less efficient strategies tend to die out and diversity reduces. Diversity takes on particular importance, however, when the environment is subject to rapid change. In this situation a different strategy already present in a

Hodgson Street, Sheffield

diverse pool may become more efficient than its predecessor, last for some period as the strategy of choice, only to be replaced in turn as the environment changes. The maintenance of diversity can thus be seen as a cost associated with maintaining the efficiency of a population as a whole in a rapidly changing and unpredictable environment.

Jane Jacobs described the outcome of this process in her comparison of the 'company town' of Manchester and the 'craftsman's town' of Birmingham (Jacobs, 1961). Here she demonstrated how a city dependent upon just one major trade – cotton – and composed of a few large companies, although it gained efficiencies of scale, was at the mercy of changes in the global economy and technology. Once the cotton trade began to decline there was nothing to replace it with, and the local economy collapsed. In contrast, the more diverse industrial base in a range of trades and skills allowed Birmingham, confronted with equally disruptive changes in the economy, to innovate and to survive. In spite of its comparative lack of central coordination and organisation, Birmingham proved to be the more resilient.

The importance of the functional aspects of economic, social and cultural diversity seems clear; however, there is another sense in which the word

has been used recently that, although it seems to be related, is less than clear. This is the sense of a diverse experiential urban environment. At its simplest level, 'experiential diversity' seems to encompass diversity in the whole range of physical, spatial and material properties of the built environment. Buildings of different heights, streets of different widths and lengths, buildings of different materials and construction details, all of these would seem to contribute to experiential diversity and have become enshrined in local design guides. And yet there is a very real sense in which this seems inadequate. First, there are many examples of high degrees of experiential diversity in relatively homogeneous physical environments (consider Berlin). Then again, there are many examples of extreme differentiation of these factors that seem not to have resulted in experiential diversity at all. Consider, for example the Essex Design Guide housing estates that have grown around many of the UK's county towns, or the more sophisticated Poundbury, a model of New Urbanist design on the edge of Dorchester.

It seems important, then, to include a full set of social, economic and behavioural factors in the consideration of diversity. Land uses and the effects that these have upon the physical detail of the buildings; human occupation densities, movement patterns and behaviours; the economic life of land parcels, and the relation of these to development density and human occupancy – all these seem to be key factors in our experience of urban diversity. In other words, a diverse physical or architectural fabric alone seems inadequate to account for what we think of as a diverse urban environment: in order to be experientially diverse an urban area must support a diverse social and economic life as well, with all the outward manifestations of that which are open to the sensory experiences of sound, sight and smell.

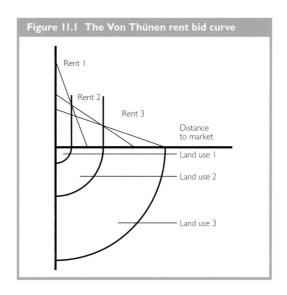

Figure 11.1 The Von Thünen rent bid curve

Lastly, there is a question: is diversity equivalent to 'mixing' – mixing of uses, mixing of cultures, mixing of economies? Here again our experience of recently planned 'mixed-use' development suggests not. There seems to be more structure to diverse urban areas than would be implied by a mere random mixing of uses or forms. Here, to pursue the biological analogy, it is useful to invoke the concept of ecology. An ecological system comprises more than just a mixing of flora and fauna; it is composed of a structured system or network of interrelated organisms and habitats in which each is dependent to a greater or lesser degree on the others in the system. Loss of a particular species has systematic knock-on effects on others, while importing an alien species can also cause severe disruption. Here, then, the suspicion is that diverse urban areas are far from random mixtures, but are formed of highly structured sets of related systems – social, cultural, economic – as well as the physical/spatial environments which support these, and their basis in temporal cycles, through patterned effects on human socio-economic behaviour and individual experience. The sociological interpretation, after Durkheim, is that diversity is a property of an organic social form, and comprises the set of interrelations between diverse systems needed to maintain and generate divisions of labour, along with the efficiencies derived from these.

This sets the goal for this chapter: to develop an explication of the relations between some of the key dimensions of urban systems that could be considered to constitute diversity, and their effects on social and economic life. First, however, we must briefly review the predominant theories of how urban physical and spatial patterns relate to social and economic systems. The twentieth-century schools of economic geography have given us a very well-developed set of theories in this area. Von Thünen's theory of central places, as developed by William Alonso, brings together spatial pattern and the urban economy (Alonso, 1964; Hall, 1966). The concept is simple: land rent and transportation costs to a market centre are related, since any landowner must trade one off against the other in deciding where to locate and what kind of productive activity to pursue in that location. The canonical illustration for this theory in terms of rent bid curves is shown in Figure 11.1.

The product is a pattern of land use centred on the central business district of a city, and consisting of a set of concentric rings of reducing rent producing land uses. As transportation costs increase, the steepness of the rent bid curves increases, and land uses concentrate towards the centre. This gives a theoretical account of the often observed concentric pattern of urban land use and density; however, it does little to explain the finer-scale patterns of land use aggregation that we observe in urban areas when we consider land uses at the level of streets and individual properties.

The classical explanation of patterns of land use aggregation at this scale in the geographic literature is given by Hotelling, whose memorable illustration of the logic for two ice cream sellers on a beach both to locate at its centre accounts for aggregation on the basis of rational self-interested agents acting to secure maximum market share (Hotelling, 1929). The illustration shows that the market catchment of a central location will always outweigh the disbenefit of competition if the consumer has an unlimited capacity to travel. Of course, limitations on travel occur in reality. For example, if the beach in question were to take half an hour to walk from end to end, and if bathers were evenly distributed and only willing to walk for ten minutes to get an ice cream, then the central location would no longer be optimal for both vendors. In fact they would be best off located one-third and two-thirds along the beach respectively. This illustrates the scale-dependent nature of aggregation with respect to markets, and helps explain why it is that local outlets such as pubs or convenience stores are dispersed across the landscape – settling as far from competitors as possible and obtaining a near-monopoly within a local travel-constrained market (this being the meaning of 'convenience') – while those selling more specialised goods will often aggregate together with their competitors in a location accessible to a larger catchment. In this case the advantages of aggregation must outweigh the disadvantages of competition from one's immediate neighbours in a number of

ways: through the access to the large market that the location affords; through the benefits of flows of insider information, experienced staff and other advantages from one's immediate neighbours, in spite of the fact that these may be competitors in one's market; and through the advantage to the buying public offered by a critical mass of differentiated outlets in approximately the same location. This last factor allows the shopper for a particular kind of goods to compare those goods on price, design, quality and service amongst a number of competing retailers while searching in a confined geographic area. We know, for example, in London that if we walk the length of Tottenham Court Road we shall be able to find whatever kind of electronic goods we might want, and that we shall be able to compare price and specification between a number of suppliers.

This argument appears to account for aggregations of similar retail outlets in geographic clusters, and the dispersion of convenience stores across the urban landscape; however, more recent analysis by Yang demonstrates the important role that multi-purpose trips have in generating aggregation economies for dissimilar goods and services (Yang, 2001). It was established by Christaller, for example, that the range of service functions found in a settlement depends in a systematic way upon the population of that settlement (Christaller, 1966); however, he gave no satisfactory behavioural account for why these apparently logical processes should arise. Yang argues that if one assumes that all shopping trips are single purpose, there is a significant cost associated with travel (Yang, 2001). This cost can be reduced by making the same trip work for multiple purposes, accounting in turn for the diversity of goods and services found in the urban centre. Aggregations of dissimilar goods and service outlets cater to the shopper's aim to reduce the travel costs associated with fulfilling their needs, and this is done through the multi-purpose trip.

There appear then to be at least three competing forces at work in the distribution of kinds of function in the urban landscape: first, a process driving towards aggregation of similar kinds of activity to support comparison; second, a process driving towards aggregation of different kinds of activity to support multi-purpose trips; and third, a process driving dispersion amongst similar activities in order to offer convenience by minimising travel distance to local catchments. An important constraint on these processes is provided by those imposed by the cognitive capacities of people to search for what they are interested in, and it seems clear that purely randomised mixing of different kinds of land use does not afford the level of intelligible structure required to allow people to search for what they need. However, it is also clear that a strict zoning of similar functions supports neither experiential diversity nor the multi-purpose trip, nor indeed the dispersion of activities needed for convenience. What we understand as diverse and thriving urban areas seem to display a much more complex kind of mixing – a kind of semi-structured mixing of uses that supports comparison and multi-purpose trips at one and the same time, and in which the searcher is neither lost, nor at a loss as to where to find what they are looking for. This places intelligibility of urban structure and human cognition as central components in the definition of urban diversity.

The concept of intelligibility is well defined in the space syntax literature (Hillier et al., 1987), and there is a growing literature on the interaction of urban morphology and cognition (Penn, 2003; Hillier & Iida,

2005). The predominant discussion in these works has focused on spatial morphology and the definition of intelligibility in terms of the correlation between local and global measures of the spatial network. However, here we must generalise the concept of intelligibility considerably. Intelligibility can be defined as the systematic relationship between those aspects of an individual's immediate perceptual environment and those affordances of the environment outside their immediate perception. In an intelligible environment, correlations between the local (immediately perceptible) and global (outside immediate perception) allow an environment to be learned in such a way that perception of the local can usefully inform one's choices of action to take advantage of global affordances. In an unintelligible environment, no such correlation exists, and so there is little useful to be learned from exploration that would assist one to find things in areas that are as yet unvisited. This does not mean that one cannot operate in an unintelligible environment, but it does mean that the way one operates is different: one is forced to think consciously and remember the map, rather than to allow more intuitive learning to guide behaviour subconsciously.

In terms of the specific issue considered here – of affording access to different kinds of land use, goods and services – the more generalised concept of intelligibility is important, since it is this that allows a link to be made between functional and experiential diversity. It seems likely that intelligibility is based not only upon correlations between spatial properties of the street network that can be learned as one moves from space to space around an urban area, but also upon correlations between a full range of other aspects of perceptual experience: changes in information perceived by sight, sound, smell and touch all play an active role, and these perceptual experiences depend upon the functional distributions in space of economic, social and cultural life. However, it is not just the diversity of these perceptual inputs that makes for intelligibility, but their systematic correlation – a noisier street will be more trafficked, may smell more polluted, will carry different types of land use, and will vary in spatial extent, height of buildings and length of views from the quieter street around the corner where the smell may be of ethnic food shops, and the population's dress code may differ along with their language and the decoration of shop fronts. All aspects of experience change as one moves, and it is the way that these change in consort with each other that is 'learnable' and gives us a good guide to what to expect if we take one route or another at any specific decision point on our way around the city.

It is the systematic variation of information of different kinds, one with another, as we move through the urban realm that transforms random noise into something meaningful. It is the different forms of systematic variation that distinguish one neighbourhood of London from another, and different cities and cultures from each other. If there is no system to the variations we experience, we are left only with noise and informational overload. Consider being lost in the woods: there is a lot of information – every individual tree is different from the next – but little that gives you usable knowledge about where to go next. Equally, if nothing changes as you move through an environment – think of being on a snowfield in a whiteout – then you have the opposite of informational overload, but to little better effect. It is worth considering the ways in which this can happen if we want to understand how intelligibility is achieved. First, it is clear that there should be variation in more than one kind of information: for any meaningful correlation to appear, at least two dimensions must both show variation. If either remains constant then nothing can be said. Equally, if

Off Wardour Street, Soho, London

either varies purely randomly then little can be said. In this sense, random mixing or 'pepperpotting' and monofunctional zoning are both equivalent in their reduction of intelligibility and meaningfulness.

Next, it is necessary for changes to be correlated in our experience through time: when one factor changes then so too should the other, as it is this correlation that makes the variations 'learnable' and meaningful. This requires not only that there be a relation between deformation of the spatial structure of an area that defines the different extents of the local and immediately perceptible environment, and changes in other perceptual characteristics, but also that there be a relationship between their rates of change over time. A sudden change in the extent of the visual field would be expected to relate to a sudden change in other factors, while a continuous smooth change in the one would be expected to relate to more continuous changes in the others. These seem to provide the ground rules for constructing diversity as something intelligible and socially meaningful, which can be taken advantage of intentionally by the citizen in planning their actions. The alternatives of more or less haphazard mixing or of monofunctional zoning are similar in the way that they deprive the citizen of autonomy in their use of the city.

This last point merits more detailed consideration. What exactly is involved in smooth or sudden change in the extent of a visual field? Let us consider someone moving along a street at a steady pace. As they move, their view is constrained by the buildings on either side, but if the street is straight they can see off into the distance. As they move forward, the nature of their visual field remains more or less constant. If the street is relatively long, then although, as they move, the buildings immediately to either side fall behind them and out of view, the majority of what they can see ahead of them remains unchanged. Now let us imagine that they are approaching an intersection with another street. From some distance they can see that there is an intersection ahead, but they gain little information as to where it might go or what opportunities it might offer until they are actually at the intersection. All of a sudden, as they pass the corner, they can see off into the distance not only ahead of them along the continuation of the path they have been following up until now, but also along the new street that intersects theirs. The morphology of space suddenly affords them significant new information as well as a choice of route. Now it is possible that the two streets look similar, in which case the real choice may seem arbitrary; however, it is also possible that the character of each of these streets is remarkably different. In this situation a sudden change in the extent of the visual field is correlated with a change in the nature of other perceptual factors.

Linearity and angular deviation of routes in urban space are thus integral not only to providing route choice, but also to the rate of change of locally perceptible information in the urban environment. As one moves along a linear segment of street, the information afforded by the local environment remains relatively constant. As one reaches a corner one gains a great deal of new information very quickly. In order for factors in the experiential environment to be correlated with each other as people move through space and over time it seems necessary that the rate of change in each factor will also need to be correlated with linearity and angular deviation of the space structure. This accounts theoretically for the empirical phenomenon Bill Hillier and Alan Penn noted as 'marginal separation by linear integration', in which urban land use, building scale and character, and pedestrian and vehicular traffic flows change only slowly as one moves along a street, but may change radically when one turns a corner (Hillier & Penn, 1992).

This observation suggests an account of the semi-structured nature of mixing of functions we recognise in diverse urban neighbourhoods. It also throws some light on the way in which urban design can sidestep the apparent need for a trade-off between the requirements of comparison activities (the aggregation of similar functions) and multi-purpose trips (the aggregation of dissimilar functions). Here it seems that the concept of a 'trade-off' may itself be erroneous. It implies a causal relation between two factors such that an increase in one involves a decrease in the other. If both factors are desirable a trade-off must therefore be made between the two: one is forced to decide how much of one 'good' one wishes to achieve at the cost of the other. However, although a correlation between two factors can give the impression that one is dealing with a trade-off, this may not in fact be the case, since the correlation can be a result of their individual relations to a third variable. Urban function offers a case in point where, all too often, different factors bear independent relations to urban morphology, and so give rise to the impression one is dealing with a trade-off. However, in this situation it may be possible to discover strategic design solutions that reduce or eliminate the apparent effect of one factor on the other, making it possible to 'have your cake and eat it'. Marginal separation by linear integration seems to offer one such strategy – aggregations affording comparison between similar functions are arranged along linear street segments, while different functions are just around the corner, minimising the cost of multi-purpose trips. At the level of the urban neighbourhood this delivers intelligible and searchable diversity while offering the benefits that come from aggregation.

Amongst the benefits of aggregation are those involved in affording efficient search by the shopper for goods or services. Search efficiency can be thought of in two ways. First, in terms of knowing where to find something. Thus, where there is an aggregation of similar kinds of goods or services, the sheer mass of these makes it easier for people to know about and to associate the location with a specific kind of requirement: geographic aggregation of functional specialisation makes for a simpler cognitive landscape. Second, in terms of supporting multi-purpose trips. Here an aggregation of similar goods and services supports comparison, while finding a series of different goods or services within a small geographic area requires diversity. In previous research Turner and Penn used software agents with forward-facing vision moving in a series of experimental virtual environments to establish the relationship between time taken to discover a given number of shops, the degree and pattern of aggregation or dispersion of those shops, and the degree to which the spatial structure of the environment was globalised (in the form of a regular grid with long lines of sight) or localised by randomly jiggling the blocks of the grid to break street alignments and restrict visual fields (Penn & Turner, 2004). The results were simple. If one wants to visit just one shop on a trip, dispersed shop locations afford the fastest search on the part of the shopper. However as soon as a shopper is required to visit multiple shops on the same trip, whether for the purpose of comparison or to satisfy a diverse shopping list, clustering affords greater efficiency. In the regular grid a single central aggregation of shops offers greatest efficiency for any multi-purpose trip. Disruption of the grid to create a more localised spatial structure results generally in reduction of search efficiency (time taken to visit a given number of shops), but it also leads to linear aggregations of shops along street alignments and multiple smaller clusters of shops, affording greater efficiency than a single central cluster, at least up to a threshold number of shops visited, above which the single central cluster again affords the most efficient search. There appears to be, in effect, a relationship between spatial scale, aggregation cluster size and the number of different outlets that a shopper can visit efficiently.

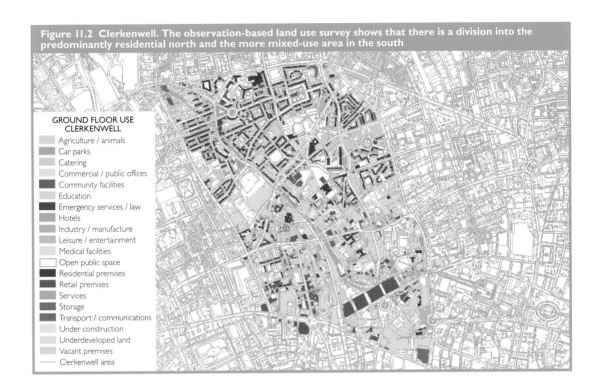

Figure 11.2 Clerkenwell. The observation-based land use survey shows that there is a division into the predominantly residential north and the more mixed-use area in the south

GROUND FLOOR USE
CLERKENWELL

Agriculture / animals
Car parks
Catering
Commercial / public offices
Community facilities
Education
Emergency services / law
Hotels
Industry / manufacture
Leisure / entertainment
Medical facilities
Open public space
Residential premises
Retail premises
Services
Storage
Transport / communications
Under construction
Underdeveloped land
Vacant premises
Clerkenwell area

VivaCity2020

The VivaCity2020 project developed both empirical observation and computer simulation approaches to test this theoretical formulation of diversity. The objective of the former was to understand the ways in which the spatial structure of urban areas is related to the spatial distribution of property uses at the micro level, the ways in which these are related to patterns of pedestrian and vehicular accessibility, and the motivations on the part of local residents and businesses to locate there. The objective of the latter was to test 'in silico' the interactions between some of the key dimensions of the theoretical model, and to see what effects manipulations of these had upon emergent morphology and distributions of land uses.

A study was carried out in London's Clerkenwell, on the western edge of the City of London, and a recognisably diverse area. Amongst the key findings of the VivaCity2020 research were that for both residents and businesses the main attraction of the Clerkenwell area was its accessibility in the larger scale. Residents valued the access it afforded for employment, leisure and shopping to the much larger area of central London, the City and the West End, as well as to Islington immediately to the north. Business networks were also substantially outward facing. Networks of employees, clients and suppliers were all drawn from the larger London area, and Clerkenwell's central location and accessibility in the large scale was seen as a major benefit to trade. In contrast, the main perceived problems of the location for both business and residents were related to the immediate local environment: noise, litter and lack of parking, for example, figured in responses to questionnaire surveys (Aiesha & Perdikogianni, 2005). A detailed land use survey was carried out of all 3618 premises in the area (Figure 11.2). This shows a predominant division between a residential north and a more commercial south, with two clusters of diverse retail activity in Exmouth Market (top centre) and Hatton Garden (lower left), and a smaller pocket near Clerkenwell Green to the north side of Smithfield Market. There is evidence of an almost direct relation between land use distribution (and consequently, the diversity of land uses) and the urban grid configuration. At the local scale of a neighbourhood, retail streets are part of areas with a denser and more intensified local grid (Zhang, 2005).

Observations of pedestrian movement in the area also showed a high degree of fragmentation. The area appears not to function as a single pedestrian system, but as a number of smaller more localised systems, each bearing a different relationship between pedestrian movement rates and spatial accessibility in the street grid as this is quantified using space syntax measures of integration. This analysis of spatial structure suggests that Clerkenwell is a marginal area in the larger processes of development and change identified in central London. It suggests that the degree of spatial fragmentation of its structure may have prevented the area from being redeveloped, and this long and complex history is itself one factor accounting for its diversity today (Perdikogianni & Penn, 2005). The degree of fragmentation of the area itself appears to be a product of a long historical/structural process during which different factors such as pre-existing land ownership patterns and transport interventions played an important role in the formation of today's spatial, and thus functional, patterns. In particular, Clerkenwell originates in low-lying land traversed by the River Fleet outside the walls of the City of London, used for the major cattle market for the City, and broken up by a series of larger monastic properties at the beginning of the twelfth century and later by large mansions separated from each other by high walls during the sixteenth century. This structure has then been affected by nineteenth-century road improvements. Farringdon Road and Clerkenwell Road, for example, were constructed to take people and traffic through the area on larger-scale trips, and are poorly related to the neighbourhood itself, acting effectively as inner-city 'bypasses'. The effect of this specific history in shaping the morphology of the area seems to have had a persistent effect in encouraging a high level of social and land use diversity in the face of significant potential development pressures that might otherwise have agglomerated land parcels and led to wholesale redevelopment, as has taken place in the adjacent City of London. The research suggests that one component in the stability over time shown in this area lies in the maintenance of a relatively complex and difficult-to-understand whole composed of relatively easy-to-understand parts. It seems to be the complex history and geography of the area, including apparent accidents of land ownership, plot boundaries and topography, which have dictated the linear structures of space and angular deviation as well as their larger-scale global location with respect to the City of London and the West End, that are responsible. In this way, knowledge, cognition and intelligibility, informed as these are by spatial morphology, seem to be of direct relevance to the generation and maintenance of diversity in urban development processes.

The simulation of diversity

In order to investigate these issues further we developed a series of agent-based simulations of urban growth, based on elementary economic and space-use behaviour models. In these experiments highly simplified processes are constructed that allow one to focus on a series of quite specific higher-level interactions: what are the relations, for example, between visual information and spatial morphology under different taxation regimes or costs of movement? What are the effects on emergent land use distributions of giving agents knowledge of the global orientation in which specific goods lie? While there can be no implication that these simulations in any sense approximate to the real world in all its complexity, they do allow one to investigate the interactions between different issues in a complex and dynamic environment. An agent-based simulation was constructed in which mobile agents inhabit a two-dimensional environment. Agents have forward-facing vision and are able to move forwards at a uniform speed. They can also change direction. Agents have a list of 'needs', which they can fulfil by visiting an appropriate shop. If an agent cannot find the goods required to fulfil a particular need, after a sufficiently long time it may set up shop selling those goods. A shop is a static,

square patch, larger than the agent, with a defined front face. A shop has the effect of interrupting agent vision and movement, and so as shops are built, the initially open visual landscape of the environment becomes increasingly constrained. Shops survive according to the trade they do, and that is dependent on how accessible they are to the population of moving agents. Agents visit shops that they can see that fulfil a current 'need', but otherwise they move according to the open space they can see ahead of them. Goods sold in shops vary between cheap and expensive; agents generally have a greater need for cheap goods than for expensive. If a shop goes bankrupt it is demolished and the agent becomes mobile again. The site of the shop becomes available for building a new shop.

In a typical simulation experiment, after an initial construction phase, there follows a phase of consolidation when the morphology of the settlement changes relatively slowly, but when patterns of shop type (cheap to expensive) change. The main experimental set-up involved applying variations in tax regime, or in agent knowledge of location of desired goods, and observing the differences in the emergent morphology, movement behaviours and location of shop types in the long run. We chose to use the efficiency of the shopper's search (the mean number of steps between shops visited) as a measure of the system's degree of optimisation. It soon became clear that an income tax had little effect on the system, since it applied uniformly across space with no negative effect on lack of trade, while a property tax or business rate had the effect of forcing marginal shops to go bankrupt more quickly, and so speeded up the evolution of the system. Finally, we developed a tax on shoppers entering the shop from the rear. This 'thief tax' had the effect of encouraging shops to

Figure 11.3 Experiments in effects of taxation on emergence of morphology supporting search efficiency by agents with vision

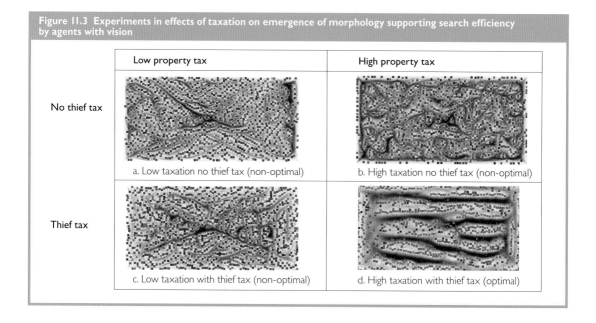

	Low property tax	High property tax
No thief tax	a. Low taxation no thief tax (non-optimal)	b. High taxation no thief tax (non-optimal)
Thief tax	c. Low taxation with thief tax (non-optimal)	d. High taxation with thief tax (optimal)

cluster next to each other and to maintain a more continuous frontage onto the emergent 'street'. Only when these two critical factors were combined with 'reasonable' parameters did optimisation occur. Optimisation was high in that an increase in tax could be almost completely offset by an increase in the number of purchases achieved in a more optimal morphology. The 'reasonable' parameters were found by letting the tax levels float, dependent on the proportion of shops to shoppers, and on various parameters of the economic health of the system.

Figure 11.3 shows the result of a series of experiments. Very clear morphological differences emerge under the different taxation regimes, which point towards increasing coordination as taxation becomes more onerous. Ultimately, under the highest taxation regime with a thief tax (bottom right), almost complete coordination emerges into a simple street grid with back-to-back properties. Main street alignments run along the long axis of the simulation space, and property uses favour those selling more expensive goods.

These simulations used shoppers who only had local (immediately visual) knowledge of where shops were, but had no knowledge at all of anything that could not be directly seen. They were like tourists who had never visited the town before. The next experiment was to take shoppers in the high taxation with thief tax regime and give them additional global knowledge in the form of the direction and distance they had to go to get the next item on their shopping list. This is much like asking the shopkeeper of your current shop where to go to buy something that her shop doesn't stock. Here the information is given once, but if the target shop goes bankrupt and disappears while the shopper is in transit, the shopper wanders as they did before without knowledge. Since the shoppers now have detailed information on how far away an item is, we

Figure 11.4 Experiments on the effects of shopper knowledge and cost of movement on emergence of stable shop aggregations

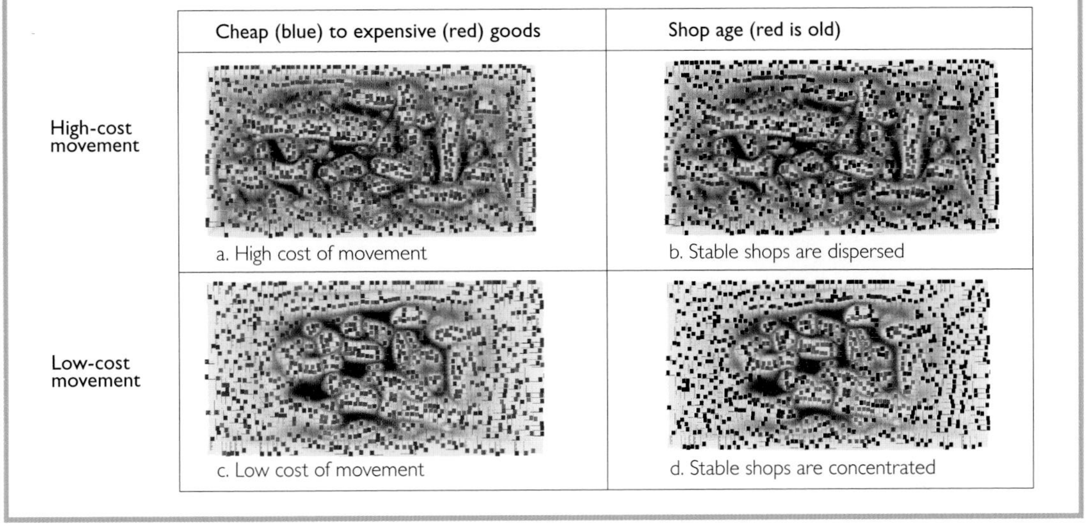

	Cheap (blue) to expensive (red) goods	Shop age (red is old)
High-cost movement	a. High cost of movement	b. Stable shops are dispersed
Low-cost movement	c. Low cost of movement	d. Stable shops are concentrated

introduced an associated estimation of effort required to fulfil their needs. Figure 11.4 compares low and high 'cost of distance' against the closeness of fit of the desired goods to those on offer.

Two effects are very clear. Given global knowledge of shop location, a low cost of movement leads to a centralised agglomeration of high-value shops and an associated higher density of shoppers (bottom left). Conversely, a high cost of movement results in dispersion of shops and of shoppers (top right). The second effect is on the stability of the shop. Shops survive longer if located in the central core of the low 'cost of distance' settlement, while in the periphery shops have difficulty attracting sufficient trade to survive. In the high 'cost to distance' settlement longer-life shops are also more dispersed (right). In both cases the stable core of the agglomeration involves the development of back-to-back blocks of shops that protect each other from entry from the rear and so save 'thief tax'. The

arrangement of these blocks leads to the development of a rudimentary grid of streets and squares that structure the main agent movement patterns in the area.

Having developed reasonable parameters for the shops and shoppers, the next stage of research involved putting the shoppers back into a real street plan of the West End of London to see where the clusters of shops developed, given a realistic urban morphology. Here we used a map of the area to create the virtual landscape within which agents could see and move. Again agents could set up shop, and their primary objective was to acquire goods. Experiments were carried out under different regimes as before, but here we focus on just one

Figure 11.5 Part of London. Agents with global knowledge of shop location: clusters emerge in the Angel, bottom end of Gray's Inn Road and Berkeley Square

© Crown copyright. All rights reserved

result. Figure 11.5 shows the effect of agents with good global knowledge of shop location. It can be seen that in this larger and more structured space, in which agent movement is constrained by the existing street pattern of the city, a sizeable aggregation of shops emerges at the southern end of the Gray's Inn Road. There are smaller clusters at the Angel, Islington, and in the west around Berkeley Square. It is notable in the first two cases, at least, that clusters appear to build out in all directions from a route intersection node forming a relatively convex aggregation.

If we now contrast this with Figure 11.6, which shows the result of the same experiment, but in which agents have no prior knowledge of shop location, the results are strikingly different. There is a much larger number of smaller clusters of shops around road intersection nodes, but the major aggregations emerge as linear structures, for example along Victoria Street in the east and Marylebone Road in the west. The distinction is clear

Figure 11.6 Agents without global knowledge of shop location: linear structures emerge

© Crown copyright. All rights reserved

between convex aggregation in the cases where shoppers have knowledge and linear aggregation where they do not.

Conclusion

The argument developed in this chapter is threefold. First, diversity is far from equivalent to 'mixed use': it implies a higher degree of structure, as this is experienced as we move through urban space over time, than is achieved by random mixing or 'pepperpotting' on the one hand, or by functional zoning on the other. Second, in order to understand diversity we must include the cognitive dimension of intelligibility through which our local and instantaneous experience is made meaningful. We argue that this allows us to act in an intentional and autonomous way. Third, the production of diversity is time bound, both at the experiential scale of seconds, minutes, daily, weekly and seasonal cycles, which affect what we experience and perceive as we move through urban areas, and at the historical scale of years and centuries over which urban forms, spatial structures and land use dispositions, resident population demography and economic cycles in urban areas evolve and change.

The quaintness and unpredictability that seem to be defining characteristics of diversity in our cities look, from our studies, to be the historical summation of many influences. The boom and bust of the economy, coupled with the resultant expansion and contraction of the commercial sector, the changes in government and the subsequent changes in social policy and planning – all contribute to the richness and diversity of city life. We argue that this happens in a very specific way. In this there is a primacy to the distribution of land use functions in relation to the open space structure of cities that seems to emerge to support both the economics of agglomeration on the part of resident businesses, and the efficiency of search of those looking to find those goods and services. However, central to our definition of diversity is the notion of a meaningful relation between the rates of change of visual information as one moves, the shape of local space, and the rates of change of other aspects of the urban environment – in particular land uses and development densities – and the perceivable outcomes of these resident uses. We define this correlation in space, and its experience by the moving observer over time, as a generalised form of

Smithfield Market, London

the space syntax concept of 'intelligibility', and this offers a strong constraint on spatial patterning. It means that there must be a 'learnable' association between different factors in the environment, and that these change slowly or rapidly in association with one another and with respect to the local geometry of space as that is experienced by the moving observer.

The analysis of Clerkenwell suggests, however, that the survival of diverse urban areas over time depends, partially at least, on a relative lack of intelligibility. It is the fragmentation of the area coupled with its marginal economic status that seems to be at the heart of its survival in the face of schemes for wholesale redevelopment. A more intelligible and economically successful morphology in this location would have been likely to be subject to redevelopment, and history suggests this would have reduced diversity. Here perhaps is the underlying dynamic: the role of urban diversity lies in resilience more than in efficiency for a single outcome. Wholesale redevelopment will (in general

terms) always be driven by a restricted set of economic or social motivations at some particular point in time. It may well deliver a highly efficient solution to that set of goals, but in doing so will tend to reduce the diversity of the social, cultural and economic base. In this it may reduce resilience by removing the capacity for new and different goals to be served by the urban fabric.

There is, however, another sense in which the ecological analogy used at the start of this chapter is pertinent. Humans, more than perhaps any other organism, owe their resilience to two propensities: the first is to come together into collaborative social cultures; the second is to intervene in their environment and to adapt it to their purposes. Amongst the innovations of the former are: the invention of money to support transaction; the emergence of the economic life of markets; and the invention of institutional, administrative and juridical systems, of politics and social structure. All of these ultimately depend upon the transmission of meaningful information through language and behaviour, and its use to coordinate the social whole. The key suggestion of this chapter, however, is that our interventions in the built environment are equally about the representation and transmission of meaningful information. The distinction here is that information transmission is not spoken in language, but is behaved and perceived through our movement in the city. The diverse urban neighbourhood is no less than an environment rich in meaningful information, and the meanings carried are those needed to generate and reproduce social and economic behaviours through which collaborative culture takes place.

Diversity in urban terms can thus be thought of in terms of three distinct forms. First, it comprises diverse spatial structures in the urban network in which multiple different local centres come together in close proximity. These kinds of fragmented networks remain well structured and intelligible at a local scale, while they may remain relatively unintelligible and detached from each other at a global scale. A network in this form acts as the equivalent of a diversity of ecologies, offering different opportunities for social, cultural and economic forms. Second, it comprises a diversity of 'species' of social, cultural and economic uses and behaviours, each occupying different niches within the spatial network. Third, it is informationally diverse, where information is of the kind that is perceived and retrieved from our experience of the environment, and of which we learn correlations that form the basis for intelligibility and our meaningful, autonomous actions. This last form of diversity is tremendously important. It offers the mode through which divisions of labour are brought together into a coherent social and economic organism, through which these divisions of labour are constructed and reproduced over time. Ultimately it is through information transmission of this kind that social and cultural life maintains a stable form over durations longer than the lifetime of the individuals of which it is composed, at the same time as affording rapid change in response to changes in the environment. Diversity of this kind is effectively a form of 'genetic diversity' in the descriptors of socio-economic forms.

References

Aiesha, R. & Perdikogianni, I. (2005). Decoding urban diversity in 'mixed-use' neighbourhoods. *Proceedings of Sustainable Environments: Vision into Action*, University of Birmingham, March.

Alonso, W. (1964) *Location and land use*. Cambridge, MA: Harvard University Press.

Christaller, W. (1966) *Die zentralen Orte in Suddeutschland* (C. W. Baskin, trans.) Jena: Gustav Fischer (original work published 1933).

Hall, P. (1966) *Von Thünen's isolated state* (C. M. Wartenberg, trans.). New York: Pergamon Press.

Hillier, B. & Iida, S. (2005) Network and psychological effects in urban movement. In A.G. Cohn & D.M. Mark (eds), *COSIT 2005: Lecture notes in computer science 3693*, pp. 475–490. Berlin: Springer-Verlag.

Hillier, B. & Penn, A. (1992) Dense civilizations: the shape of cities in the 21st century. *Applied Energy*, **43** (1–3), 41–66.

Hillier, B., Burdett, R., Peponis, J. & Penn, A. (1987) Creating life: or, does architecture determine anything? *Architecture & Behaviour*, **3** (3), 233–250.

Hotelling, H. (1929) Stability in competition. *The Economic Journal*, **39**, 41–57.

Jacobs, J. (1961) *The economy of cities*. New York: Vintage.

Penn, A. (2003) Space syntax and spatial cognition, or why the axial line? *Environment and Behavior*, **35** (1), 30–65.

Penn, A. & Turner, A. (2004) Movement-generated land use agglomeration: simulation experiments on the drivers of fine-scale land use patterning. *Urban Design International*, **9** (2), 81–96.

Perdikogianni, I. & Penn, A., (2005) Measuring diversity: a multivariate analysis of land use and temporal patterning in Clerkenwell, **2**, 742-761, proceedings of the 5th International Space Syntax Symposium, Akkelies van Nes (ed.), TU Delft, 2005, ISBN 90-8594-002-8.

Wilson, E.O. (1992) *The diversity of life*. Cambridge, MA: Harvard University Press.

Yang, X. (2001) *Economics: New classical versus neoclassical frameworks*. Oxford: Blackwell.

Zhang, J. (2005) *Shaping the pattern: a historical perspective on the interaction between space and function in Clerkenwell*, **2**, 635-653, proceedings of the 5th international space syntax symposium, Akkelies van Nes (ed.), TU Delft, 2005, ISBN 90-8594-002-8.

DIVERSITY AND MIXED USE FOR CITY-CENTRE LIVING

Defining and capturing the 'mix' of urban society in relation to the built environment is a 'tricky problem' – likewise urban policy that seeks to direct and influence decision-making towards a more sustainable urban form and set of interrelated functions. What has become clear from the investigations outlined in these chapters is that time and space matter. An historic perspective on the evolution of city life and spaces helps us understand the present and future trajectories in terms of the cyclical and incremental nature of development and behaviour – of markets, households and communities. Defining and capturing the 'mix' of urban society in relation to the built environment is a 'tricky problem' – as is developing urban policy that seeks to direct and influence decision-making towards a more sustainable urban form and set of interrelated functions.

Spatial separation and combination of 'uses' also persist, organically and organised, and are required at both the block/street and the urban village scales. But this is no longer consonant with, or enabled by, the land use planning, building regulation, development and industry classifications (Standard Industrial Classification). This is a clear challenge to now outdated land use classes, property investment vehicles and economic development strategies. Higher density and intensification, not just of housing and retail but also of public space, circulation (transport) and informational flows, is a reality – as is population growth, although not evenly distributed within and across urban areas and regions. But this reality suffers from being reduced to measures of dwelling densities, zoning, plot ratios and licensing (e.g., health and safety) controls. It is also clear that, for day-to-day existence, environmental management and 'cohesion' are required (see Section 2), in order to maintain liveability and avoid conflicts of use both within (residents) and between (user group) stakeholders.

Evidence emerging in these chapters of lower burglary and street crime in successful mixed-use areas (adding to the conclusions on residential burglary in Chapter 8) confirms the animation/surveillance advantages. Where intensification strays too close (proximity, temporally) to residential areas, street crime and conflicts can arise – so 'partial permeability' of street and building layout and usage at different times of the day is not a good model. This can be rectified by those responsible for urban design, street/traffic engineering, environmental waste (collections, cleaning), planning/zoning and licensing, joining up their thinking and operations. This is one of many examples of where joined-up thinking would ensure sustainable living in practice.

At neighbourhood level, trade-offs are negotiated implicitly, and the value of amenities (e.g., local shops, schools, health services, parks) and connectivity – the relationship of highly diverse/dense areas to other areas of the city – is an important finding. Getting this combination right can offset living and personal space needs (e.g. gardens, car parking), and maintain economic vitality, while losing such an amenity mix and breaching the carrying capacity of an area starts the breakdown of sustainable living and local economies, from which it can be very hard to recover. Examples of areas that have been the subject of successive regeneration and neighbourhood renewal programmes over many years attest to this. Diversity is therefore a concept and practice that should be better understood and applied in development planning and urban design, as well as in planning and economic policy – not just in established communities or in inner urban areas, but in suburbs, new towns and extensions – not least since a lack of diversity and over-reliance on the car still typifies such settlements in the UK.

The economic dimension to diversity and sustainable mixed use is the least-considered element in planning and design, but, as demonstrated, it is the key driver in location and consumption decisions, and in achieving and maintaining quality of life. The notion of 'mixed economy' is therefore important in practice, and this needs articulation in planning and urban design processes. This is manifested not just in the public policy / political economy sense, but in social (tenure, demographic, amenity), enterprise (public and private, medium and micro) and built forms and flexible/adaptable space, as well as through a mixed economy in property/premises size and rental. So affordable business premises (including the relaxation of barriers to legitimate 'live–work') may be as important as affordable housing (and government housing growth projections are accompanied by substantial employment targets, with little appreciation of the spatial implications and sustainability impacts that will arise).

In contrast, large-scale mixed-use blocks, and 'wholesale redevelopment' (Chapter 11) of 'new urban' villages, whether residential, business or retail park, fail the diversity test and produce mono- or, at best, limited dual use in building and socio-economic uses. Over time (sometimes short, e.g., ground-floor vacancies; Chapter 10) any claim to sustainability is compromised, and areas become exposed to economic and social change and shocks. Paradoxically, such developments and design forms receive much attention in design, property and investor reviews, and in design quality awards, and as a result are widely replicated. Combined with continued brownfield and infill development – the predominant types of urban (re)development – as a response to housing and economic growth imperatives, this is concerning.

Finally, the research used as the basis of these chapters has sought to develop novel analytical and visualisation methods by which multivariate data, knowledge and local experience can be captured and synthesised. This is moving towards a more sophisticated model and tools by which the urban environment in its social, economic and physical dimensions can be better understood over time and space. The findings are also contributing to a more useful set of measures of diversity and mixed use, to support policy and planning at the urban, 'quarter' and building design scale.

This work has required access to and the creation of a wider range of data and modelling than is normally available or applied in practice, or used in traditional disciplinary research approaches. The next section therefore explores the potential for IT-based database design that seeks to integrate these geospatially, in a systematic and integrated way.

SECTION 5
SUPPORTING URBAN DESIGN
DECISION-MAKING: ICT

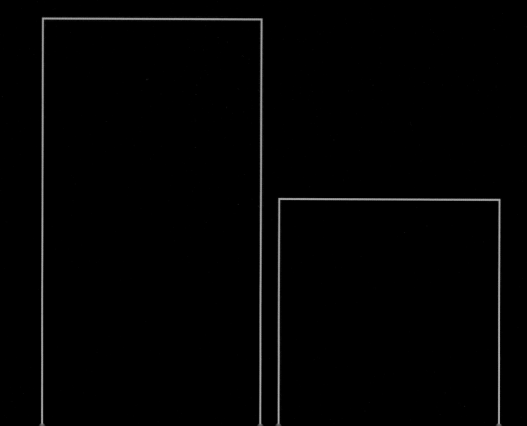

While we can pinpoint current trends and issues related to creating sustainable environments, we also recognise that for decision-makers to have any impact on the endeavour to make the urban environment more sustainable we need tools and techniques to help them understand the context, develop 'what if' scenarios, and provide the evidence for making choices.

This section describes an approach taken by the ICT specialists in the VivaCity2020 team to creating and integrating databases to aid analysis of the urban landscape and its potential to be sustainable.

CHAPTER 12

IT INFRASTRUCTURE FOR SUPPORTING MULTIDISCIPLINARY URBAN PLANNING

Terrence Fernando, Ghassan Aquad, Charlie Fu and Jialiang Yao

Introduction

Urban planning is a complex and multidisciplinary decision-making process, which is concerned with the complex management of change within the built and natural environment: it aims to plan the urban environment in terms of its physical, social, legal, economical, visual and environmental elements. The procedure of planning, in general, is considered to be an iterative process of problem definition, collecting and processing of complex information, exploration of potential designs, and evaluation of these designs according to set objectives, such as sustainability and enhanced quality of life of citizens (Adams, 1994).

In recent years, sustainability of urban environments has been transformed from a rather vague and fuzzy notion of encompassing elements of social, economic and environmental friendliness into a more concrete and measurable theory for development and design evaluation. Various assessment frameworks for urban sustainability have been designed under the auspices of both European and UK legislation, such as the environmental impact assessment, the strategic environment assessment and the sustainability appraisal. Furthermore, a number of tool kits have been developed and enforced to aid in the completion of sustainability assessments, particularly within the UK context. For example, under Section 39(2) of the Planning and Compulsory Purchase Act 2004, sustainability appraisal is mandatory for Regional Spatial Strategy revisions and for new or revised development plan documents and supplementary planning documents. As a result, the contemporary urban sustainability assessments have been shifting from environment-focused assessments (environmental impact assessments) to more systematic and comprehensive assessments with an integrated view of environment, society and economics, such as sustainability appraisal.

In response to these new demands, today there are two key trends in sustainability assessments and analysis in the context of urban planning. The first trend is in the direction of rigorous quantitative assessments of statistical and geospatial data to analyse 'quality of life' indicators, by deploying advanced technologies such as databases and GIS. At present, numerous statistical data are available from many different sources such as national censuses, the the Office for National Statistics, local councils, commercial survey companies, and government departments. These statistical data usually contain rich information about population, the economy, society and the environment within different scopes at the local and national levels. However, such data are based on different geographical boundaries, such as super output areas, electoral wards, statistic wards and postcodes, making them difficult to synthesise within a common geospatial framework. Therefore the first part of this chapter shows how such disjointed datasets can be brought together within a unified information modelling framework to support the assessment of sustainability indicators.

The second trend is in the direction of implementing democratic processes by encouraging wider stakeholder engagement and public participation to ensure that all the environmental, social and economic issues are considered from various viewpoints, leading to sound decisions and consensus. One of the key challenges in supporting greater collaboration between stakeholders is the difficulty in communicating complex ideas or proposals from one discipline to another, or to the citizens in a simple form. Any misinterpretation of ideas could lead to unnecessary debates, bad decisions, suboptimal solutions, or objections from citizens during the subsequent construction. Therefore the second part of this chapter explores how advances in technologies such as GIS, databases, virtual reality and interfaces can be brought together to create a virtual workspace for stakeholders to come together to communicate their ideas, and to reach consensus.

Developing an integrated geospatial and demographic data repository for urban sustainability assessments

This section presents a study of the implementation of information modelling and GIS techniques to enhance the application of statistical data in sustainable urban design. It aims to facilitate quantitative analysis of various sustainability issues, and starts with a review of some typical statistical data resources and data-collection boundaries, including some specifications and formats regarding the National Census 2001, the Index of Multiple Deprivation (IMD), ward boundaries, postcode

boundaries and the Ordnance Survey MasterMap (OSMM). It follows this by developing a conceptual model to clarify the integration of geospatial and non-geospatial data classes, and the links and relations among these classes, which could be involved in sustainability analysis and GIS-based urban information management. Based on the conceptual model, a server-based database is proposed to integrate and encapsulate the statistical data from various sources into one data repository, enabling this information to be shared and accessed by various stakeholders involved in urban sustainability analysis. The database system applied in this study is based on PostGIS (open source), which supports server-based geospatial databases. The advantages and competence of this server-based database in urban sustainability analysis have been demonstrated through the implementation of an open-source GIS package, Quantum GIS, which is compliant to PostGIS. A number of data maps, which illustrate various situations and distributions of social, economic and environmental information in local settings, have been generated in Quantum GIS from the PostGIS database.

Review of demographic and statistical data sources

Although various statistical data resources can potentially be used in urban sustainability analysis, this involves complex and time-consuming procedures. This study picks up only some typical demographic and statistical data regarding social and economic themes. It is well known that in recent years many IT applications, such as databases and GIS, have already been applied in the National Census and national statistics collection. This involves different geographic boundaries within which the statistics and census data are collected or presented. In the sections below, some typical types of statistical and census boundaries are briefly reviewed.

National Census 2001 and census output areas

The latest National Census in the UK was conducted in 2001, and the outputs were released by the UK census authorities in 2003 (ONS, 2003). The output of the census consists of 26 key statistical tables, which include various social variables for 408 local authorities throughout Britain. The National Census 2001 also adopted a new geography called census output area (COA). In this National Census, data were collected within enumeration district geography but released within COAs. Enumeration districts are designed for efficient data collection, whereas COAs are designed to provide the most enduring statistical geography to date (Birmingham University, 2006).

COAs are the clusters of the areas aggregated by similar adjacent postcodes. The purpose of setting COAs is to provide a compact, highly homogeneous area in terms of housing type and tenure. The threshold of the minimum population of a COA is defined as 100 persons or 40 households. Because of these design thresholds, the COAs could only be finalised once the census data had been collated into the relevant databases. A geographic information systems approach was used to iteratively define the census output area boundaries and constrain them to census statistical ward boundaries.

IMD from Office of National Statistics and super output areas (SOA)

The Office of the Deputy Prime Minister, now Communities and Local Government (CLG), uses the Index of Multiple Deprivation (IMD) to map the levels of deprivation across the country. It aims to inform policy better and to help direct resources towards those people living in the most deprived

Farringdon Station, Clerkenwell, London

areas. It is also an important step forward in helping to improve the quality of life of those people most in need. An Index of Multiple Deprivation was published in 2004. It contains seven domains, which relate to income deprivation, employment deprivation, health deprivation and disability, education, skills and training deprivation, barriers to housing and services, living environment deprivation and crime.

In these statistics, the SOA boundaries have been used to replace electoral wards (8 414) for the first time. The main reason for setting SOA boundaries is to enable the statistical data to be more stable and comparable. These SOAs have been defined in three layers:

• A lower layer SOA is the boundary for a minimum population of 1000, with an average of

1500. It is derived from the boundaries of census output areas, and is constrained by the boundaries of the standard table (ST) wards used for Census 2001 outputs.

- A middle layer SOA is the boundary for a minimum population of 5000, with an average of 7200. It is based on groups of lower layer SOAs, and is constrained by the 2003 local authority boundaries used for Census 2001 outputs.
- An upper layer SOA is the boundary for a minimum population of 25 000.

Wards

For many years, before the adoption of more detailed statistical boundaries such as COAs and SOAs, wards have been used as national census and statistical boundaries. There are three types of ward division:

- Electoral wards/divisions are the key building block of UK administrative geography. They are the spatial units used to elect local government councillors in metropolitan and non-metropolitan districts, unitary authorities and the London boroughs in England; unitary authorities in Wales; council areas in Scotland; and district council areas in Northern Ireland. Electoral wards/divisions vary greatly in size, from fewer than 100 residents to more than 30 000. This is not ideal for nationwide comparisons, and it also means that data that can safely be released for larger wards may not be released for smaller wards, owing to disclosure requirements (i.e., the need to protect the confidentiality of individuals). Electoral wards/divisions are subject to regular boundary changes. This creates problems when trying to compare datasets from different time periods. There are 7976 electoral wards in England.

- Statistical wards are the ward boundaries changed and promulgated at the end of each calendar year, which will also be used as the statistical boundaries on 1 April of the following year. This policy aims to minimise the statistical impact of frequent electoral boundary ward changes. The concept of statistical wards applies only to England and Wales, not to Scotland or Northern Ireland.
- Standard table (ST) wards are a kind of statistic geography, and are those for which the 2001 Census standard tables are available. They are an extension of the statistical wards, such as those with fewer than 1000 residents or where 400 households have been merged. This was required to ensure the confidentiality of data in the standard tables. In England and Wales a total of 113 statistical wards have been merged as the standard table set. There are a total of 7932 ST wards in England and 868 in Wales. The types of statistical wards also include census area statistical wards, which are used for 2001 Census output.

Postcode

Royal Mail maintains a UK-wide system of postcodes to identify postal delivery areas. The postcode consists of a hierarchical structure, representing different levels of geographical unit. Postcodes have been used in many statistical and planning activities as the major geographic reference. Data from the National Census 2001 can be searched via postcodes. Many insurance including buildings, roads, tracks, paths, railways, rivers, lakes, ponds, structures and land parcels. Every OS MasterMap feature can be referenced through a unique identifier called a topographic object ID. OSMM also contains many non-topographic features, such as administrative and electoral boundaries, cartographic text, symbols and addresses. Today, OS MasterMap has been widely adopted in geographical analysis and referencing, data association, asset management, route planning and cartographic representation.

Integrated and conceptual data modelling of urban demographic and statistical information

The main reason for developing this conceptual urban information model is to conceptualise the integration and connection of various geographic objects and demographic and statistical data sources that can potentially be used in urban sustainability analysis. As described earlier, various demographic and statistical resources can potentially be used for accurate urban sustainability analysis. However, the analysis of these demographic and statistical data is very time-consuming, owing to their quantity and complexity. Therefore only the adoption of IT applications such as GIS can support this kind of demographic and statistical data-based analysis. As the various demographic and statistical data have been collected with different boundaries, it is crucial to integrate them, and their geo-reference objects, together within one geospatial database, and ensure that it can work with at least one geographic information system (Copp, 2004). To achieve this aim, it is important to clarify the overall data entities and classes of the demographic and statistical resources, and their interrelationships. The Unified Modelling Language has been adopted in this study as a semantically rich common language to present the model.

premium calculations are based on postcodes as the major geo-reference. Postcodes are important information in the Ordnance Survey MasterMap, which is one of the major suppliers of digital map services in the UK. Although postcodes form a compact geographic reference with which the public and businesses are familiar, there are limitations to linking the postcode boundaries to other boundaries. This is because some postcode boundaries straddle a ward boundary. As mentioned earlier, most geographic boundaries adopted national census and statistics derived from ward boundaries, but postcode boundaries are not used in these statistics or the Census. This is because of changes in postcode boundaries owing to changes in address and new developments.

Ordnance Survey MasterMap

Ordnance Survey MasterMap (OSMM) is one of the major GIS-based map systems in Great Britain. It provides a consistent and maintained framework for referencing geographic information of the country. OSMM comprises detailed topographic, cartographic, administrative boundary, postal address, topographic and road network features positioned on a National Grid coordinate system and an imagery layer. OS MasterMap topographic features are representations of real-world objects,

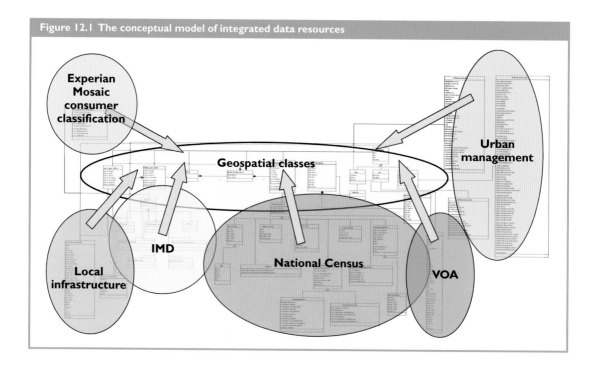

Figure 12.1 The conceptual model of integrated data resources

Figure 12.1 presents the main components of the conceptual data model. They include some typical and major statistical data sources and geographical statistics boundaries, as reviewed in the previous section. At the centre of the model is the core cluster of geospatial classes, which includes Middle Layer Super Output Area (MSOA), Lower Layer Super Output Area (LSOA), COA, local authorities, ST wards, postcode boundaries and postcode sections, and OSMM.

Around the cluster of the geospatial classes, different statistical and demographic data sources are aggregated into the model through connections to at least one type of geospatial class. The crucial part of the model is integration of the spatial classes through their key attributes. The details of this integration will be explained later. The details of the demographic data sources and their connections to the geographic classes are as follows:

• National Census 2001 linked to COA directly. The national census data are connected with COA though the attribute 'COS Code'. It contains 26

key statistics tables covering several variables of demographic distributions. The national census data have been broadly implemented in various analyses of urban studies.

• Index of Multiple Deprivation 2004 linked to LSOA directly. These data can show the deprivation situation from seven different aspects of the overall country. The key attribute to build up this link is LSOA Code.

• Local infrastructure of education and health care, which presents local schools and NHS facilities as points on OSMM. The education facilities include all schools in mainland Britain with detailed variables such as type and size. The medical facilities include all hospitals, primary care centres and GPs, which are also geo-referenced as points. This type of data can be used with other demographic data to analyse the future demands for education and health-care facilities in local areas.

• Data from the Valuation Office Agency (VOA) showing local business information. As provided,

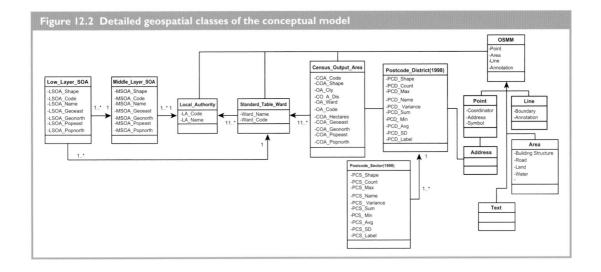

Figure 12.2 Detailed geospatial classes of the conceptual model

these data contain no geo-referenced information other than addresses, but they can be geocoded on OSMM with the correct address information.

- The Mosaic consumer classification for the UK from Experian, which is commercial statistical information reflecting social and economic status. These data are also linked to LSOA as geographic references. Mosaic contains about 400 variables of statistical data based on the electoral roll, Experian lifestyle survey information and consumer credit activity, alongside the Post Office address file, shareholders' register and house price and council tax, covering 46 million adult residents and 23 million householders in the UK. They have been widely used in the analysis of qualitative issues of economic and social diversity.

- Urban management data from local planning authorities, geo-referenced to various geo-objects on OSMM. This information comes with an integrated data structure, which contains information entities covering almost every aspect of the urban environment.

Figure 12.2 represents the central part of the model. To simplify the diagram, it contains only geospatial classes in the conceptual model. These spatial classes cover the geospatial objects applied (geo-referenced)

for most statistics data resources. The model shows the details of class attributes and the connections among these geospatial classes. From the left of this model, it can be seen that a middle layer SOA consists of a group of low layer SOAs. A group of middle level SOA boundaries can be merged into a local authority boundary. Each local authority boundary consists of at least one standard table ward. Every standard table ward can be divided into many census output areas. A group of low layer SOA boundaries can be merged into an entire boundary of a standard table ward. The local authority boundaries are included in OSMM as a type of feature represented as lines. Any geographic objects in OSMM have to be represented as one of the four geometric types point, line, area or text. An address is represented in OSMM as a point, and should be included in a postcode district boundary. Although most of the COS boundaries were derived from postcode districts, postcode district boundaries are not stable boundaries, but have changed from one year to another. Thus the COS boundary can be only approximately connected to postcode district boundaries. The postcode district boundaries can be also detailed down into postcode sector areas.

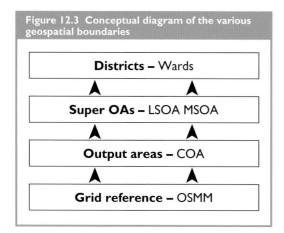

Figure 12.3 Conceptual diagram of the various geospatial boundaries

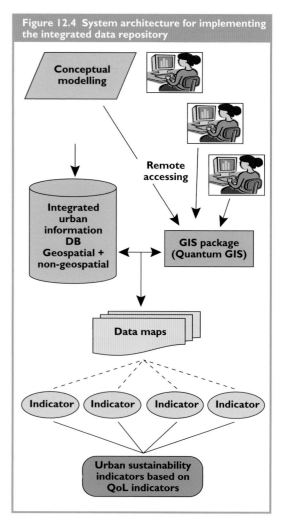

Figure 12.4 System architecture for implementing the integrated data repository

The above model, with its complex classes and relationships, can be simplified into the conceptual diagram in Figure 12.3. This shows the geo-reference areas from detailed coordinates to census output areas, and further to large areas such as wards.

It is impossible to list all types of geographic reference for urban sustainability analysis, but this model covers most different geospatial boundaries and objects that have been used in various statistical resources to collect and represent data geographically. Figure 12.3 shows the different levels of geographic reference for most demographic and national statistics.

Finally, a set of urban management data aggregates is categorised, based on the feature types of their geospatial objects on maps, which are points, lines and areas. These geometrical features are then referred to OSMM. These classes form an integrated data structure to store urban management information, which should be collected and filed by local planning authorities.

System design with integrated data repository

This section describes the system architecture (Figure 12.4) for a sustainability analysis system based on this integrated repository of statistical data. It is intended

to illustrate the concept of implementing this data in the sustainability assessment process and framework. The system architecture starts with conceptual modelling, which conceptualises the various types of geospatial and non-geospatial data entity and their interrelationships. The conceptual model demonstrates the integration of geospatial data entities and the extendibility of non-geospatial entities and data sources.

In this project PostGIS, based on the PostgreSQL database system, has been adopted as a geographic database system. PostGIS is associated with

Figure 12.5 Data map of roadside air pollution in Greater London

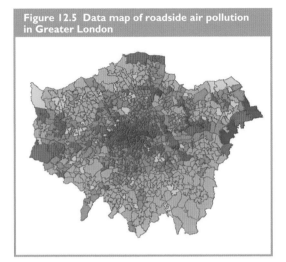

Figure 12.6 Data map of traffic-flow levels in Greater London

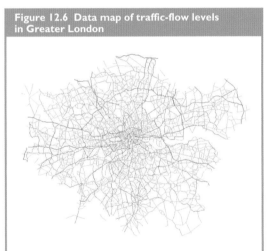

Pilot case studies and evaluation of the integrated database

This integrated database has been evaluated through pilot case studies. First was a study of roadside air pollution and traffic flow in the Greater London area. Figure 12.5 shows the roadside air pollution, of which the air quality was measured on roads, and which was caused mainly by cars (Figure 12.6). In both figures the red colour indicates heavier emissions or busier traffic in comparison with the yellow colour. It can be seen that the levels of air pollution are consistent with the levels of automobile traffic in the same area. This is an example of identifying the interrelationships between different sustainability issues by examining the data. The boundaries used with the air pollution data are the middle layer super output areas (MSOA); the lines in the traffic-flow map are traffic-flow data for the streets in Greater London. The colours of the lines indicate the levels of traffic flow.

Another pilot study generated data maps to target on an analysis of the demand for schools in the regeneration areas of Sheffield city centre. Figure 12.7 shows the locations and types of the existing schools in these areas: nurseries, primary schools, secondary schools and 16-plus schools. Figure 12.8 shows the size of the existing schools, based on the number of pupils. Figure 12.9 shows a comprehensive data map of the school distributions, with location, school type and size on one map. In this figure, the colours represent the various types of school; the sizes of the dots indicate the number of pupils in each school. Figure 12.10 shows the number of children in the various school-age groups (0–5, 6–12, 13–16, and ≤18). The data in Figures 12.9 and 12.10 allow one to work out whether the current school provision can meet the requirements of local children. Such evaluations can be used to assess the future demand for schools, based on predicted demographic information.

Quantum GIS, and is one of the few license-free GIS packages that can support server-based geospatial databases. Quantum GIS, as a user-end GIS tool kit, can enable users to remotely access and handle the PostGIS database like other server-based GIS systems, conduct data queries across different database tables, and produce data maps and other types of data display to target on the analysis and prediction of sustainability issues and breakdown indicators based on quality-of-life indicators.

Figure 12.7 Types of school in Sheffield city centre

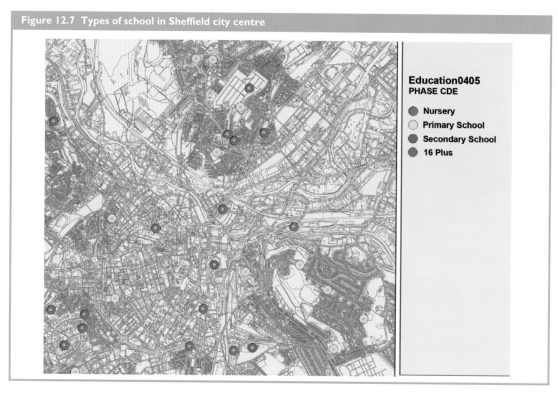

Figure 12.8 Sizes of schools in Sheffield city centre

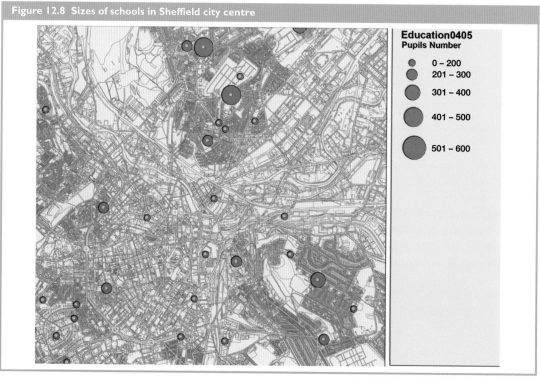

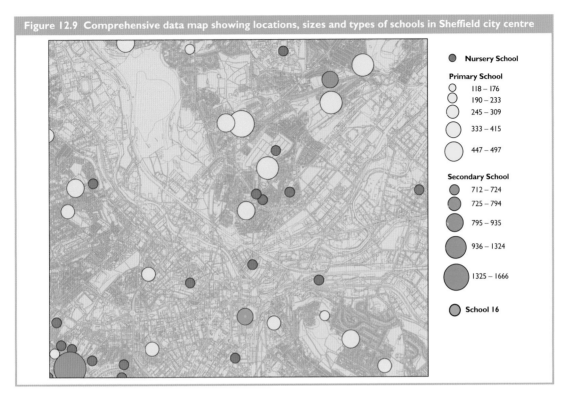

Figure 12.9 Comprehensive data map showing locations, sizes and types of schools in Sheffield city centre

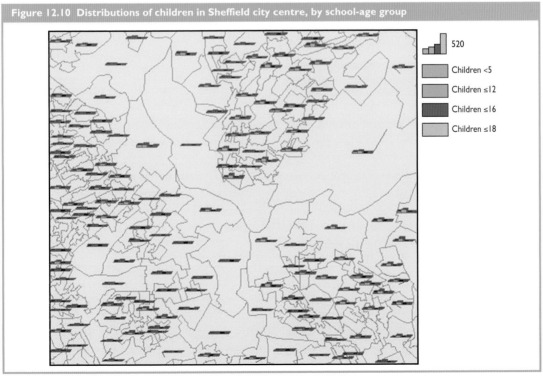

Figure 12.10 Distributions of children in Sheffield city centre, by school-age group

From these pilot case studies, the potential of this integrated database for sustainability assessment is evident. It allows geospatial objects and extendable non-geospatial statistical and demographic objects to be integrated within a single framework. The various stakeholders involved in sustainability assessment can potentially share their information and allow remote access to others via the Internet.

The data maps generated from database information with GIS can give clear distributions, trends and other existing or predicted urban situations in terms of society, economy and the natural environment. GIS systems are powerful IT applications in urban sustainability studies, which can provide users with a comprehensive functional analysis of urban environment issues. In this project we have carried out trials of GIS packages produced by various companies, such as ArcGIS, MapInfo and GeoMedia.

Collaborative consensus - building space for urban planning

Collaboration is an important part of the urban planning decision-making process (Al-Kodmany, 1999; Hudson-Smith & Evans, 2001). Many parties – government officers, urban planners, developers, community groups and environmental groups – are involved in the process, with each stakeholder representing his or her own interest or that of an organisation or community group (Adams, 1994; Greed, 1994; Chan et al., 1998). The importance of collaborative urban planning in urban development and regeneration is now widely recognised (Al-Kodmany, 1999; Hudson-Smith & Evans, 2001). Collaborative participation in environmental decision-making and planning has already become embedded in the planning process (Skeffington, 1969). A major source of complexity in urban

planning is the need to meet different cultural, environmental and business requirements. The collaborative planning process can bring decision-makers into an iterative design loop, to exchange ideas and evolve urban planning solutions.

Stakeholders involved in urban planning activities can be classified into three categories, as shown in Table 12.1 (Mathur et al., 2007): those who affect the project; those who are affected by the project; and others who may be interested.

Complex interaction among them is important in the planning process, since all of them are trying to influence the evolution of the city. The relationship among these stakeholders can be described as follows (Laurini, 2001):

- In cooperation. In this case stakeholders are working together to solve the same sets of problems. They agree on the same solution, share the same action plans, and pool their resources and means.
- In conflict. In this case, stakeholders have divergent interests in solving the problem. The most frequent conflict is one of objectives, as the various stakeholders have different value systems, and may place quite different weights on the various objectives. For example, the government may be focused more on the overall environmental effects and usage of land, whereas the citizens are probably concerned more with their own living conditions.
- In negotiation. In this case the stakeholders know that their best interest is to work together within a limited common objective, and they partially or temporarily agree to share some resources to solve a problem.

As a result, a large amount of translation of ideas between stakeholders is required to solve conflicts and support negotiation and cooperation. One approach presented in this section is the use of an interactive collaborative virtual environment as a tool for presentation, communication, decision-making and consensus building for these stakeholders.

Table 12.1 Generic list of stakeholder categories

Broad category	Subcategory	Types of individuals/groups
Those who affect the project	Those involved in delivery of the project	Developer, client, owner, investor(s), project manager / management team, banks, insurer(s), contractor(s), subcontractor(s) and suppliers, professional consultants (e.g., architectural, engineering and financial)
	Those who determine the context	Local authority – planning department etc. Regional government departments Central government departments Non-departmental public bodies such as Environment Agency, Housing Corporation, etc.
Those who are affected by the project	Directly affected	Users of the buildings, spaces, facilities, etc.
	May be directly or indirectly affected depending on the context	Local/surrounding community members General public Local community groups such as residents' associations, or other community-based groups Specific demographic groups such as those based on race, ethnicity, gender, age, etc.
Others who may be interested		Environmental/social campaigning organisations, researchers/academics, media, potential users / clients for future projects

Source: Mathur et al., 2007

To focus the exploration of this virtual space, the team worked closely with the Black Country Consortium, which is involved in a 30-year regeneration programme for the Black Country region in the UK, involving four city councils (Wolverhampton, Walsall, Dudley and Sandwell).

Black Country case study

In June 2004 the Secretary of State approved the Regional Spatial Strategy for the West Midlands, which sets out an ambitious strategy to guide the future development of the Black Country in the next 30 years. In order to steer the implementation of the strategy, the Black Country Consortium was established by the Regional Planning Body in early 2003, as a strategic partnership between the boroughs of Dudley, Sandwell and Walsall and the city of Wolverhampton. The main challenge for the consortium is to bring together these four boroughs and other public and private stakeholders to implement the 30-year regional development plan to achieve the aim of Black Country 'urban renaissance'.

The goals of this regional development plan are:
- to reverse the trend of people leaving the Black Country
- to raise income levels by ensuring better skills and types of job
- to attract and retain people with higher-level skills (i.e., change the socio-economic mix)
- to protect and enhance the environment, and create a safe, attractive and healthy place in which to live and work.

In implementing the strategy, the Black County regeneration project faces the following challenges:
- selling the vision – a need to communicate, consult, engage, build ownership and understanding of the 30-year vision
- working with a diversity of stakeholders (four local authorities, and other public, private and voluntary agencies; local communities, citizens and businesses)
- creating an environment for the four boroughs to work together using new ways of thinking and working.

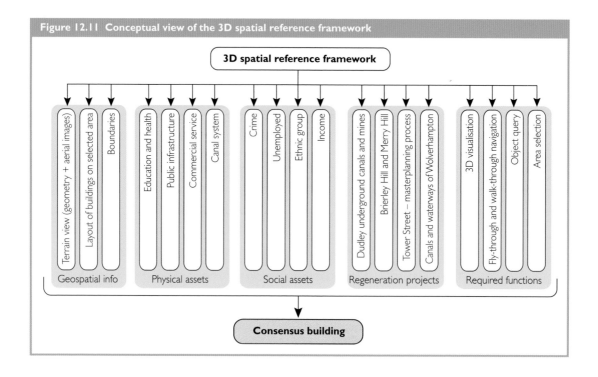

Figure 12.11 Conceptual view of the 3D spatial reference framework

Functional requirements and conceptual view of the collaborative consensus building space

The requirements for creating a collaborative consensus building space for urban planning can be diverse and project-specific. However, in order to ensure that the key functional requirements for such a virtual space were captured thoroughly, several meetings with the key stakeholders involved in the Black Country regeneration were organised around a research prototype to demonstrate the concept. In addition, four strategic regeneration projects were considered in capturing project-specific requirements. The entire IT development work was conducted by establishing a partnership between the University of Salford, the Black Country Consortium and Ordnance Survey.

The key functional requirements identified with the Black Country Consortium and their key stakeholders, for creating the initial collaborative consensus building space, were as follows (Figure 12.11):

- an ability to visualise the entire Black Country landscape with accurate terrain and building forms
- representation of all the regional assets that could be used to build future strategies
- demographic data to provide understanding of the social challenges and diversity in the region
- an ability to incorporate current and future regeneration projects
- visualisation, navigation, and an ability to query objects and other data during meetings.

Figure 12.11 shows a conceptual view of the 3D spatial reference framework that was developed to support the requirements of the Black Country regeneration project. The overall framework comprises categories of data (geospatial, demographic, physical assets and regeneration projects) and a set of interaction functions.

- Geographic information. In this data category, information such as the terrain of the Black Country, high-definition aerial photographs of the terrain, 2.5D representation of the buildings (derived from the MasterMap with height data) and boundaries of the SOA are maintained to superimpose social data. This allows the creation of a virtual representation of the Black Country in order to explore and understand the overall landscape and the building forms in the region.

- Physical assets. This data category captures over 600 types of regional asset, ranging from education and health, public infrastructure, commercial services, canals, hospitals and schools to transport. Interactive exploration of such regional assets could be used in vision building and strategic planning meetings.
- Demographic information. This data category allows users to overlay demographic data such as unemployment, crime and ethnic data to understand the social problems and the diversity in the region.
- Regeneration projects. This data category maintains a VR representation of the proposed regeneration projects to support stakeholder engagement and public participation. Such projects could be loaded into the collaborative consensus building space on demand to support collaborative discussions.
- Interactivity. This category shows the types of visualisation and interaction that are being developed to support communication between the stakeholders. Currently, 3D visualisation of the selected data categories, navigation, area selection and object queries are supported.

System architecture of the collaborative consensus building space

The overall system architecture of the virtual urban planning system is presented in Figure 12.12. It comprises the following three layers:
- database service layer
- visualisation and interaction service layer
- physical display service layer.

The purpose of the database service layer is to maintain a unified urban model that combines data

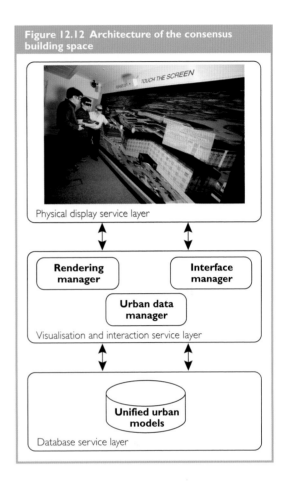

Figure 12.12 Architecture of the consensus building space

from various data sources, such as the Ordnance Survey MasterMap (Yao *et al.*, 2006), demographic data and VR models (Yao & Fernando, 2004). It can also support various analysis services, such as map data querying and spatial analysis functionalities through GIS services. The database services layer has been designed with an open application programming interface to allow integration with third-party applications.

The visualisation and interaction service layer provides rendering and 3D interaction capabilities for the stakeholders to explore the urban information space. This service layer comprises three modules: the rendering manager, the run-time urban data manager and the interface manager.

Figure 12.13 Structure of the unified urban model

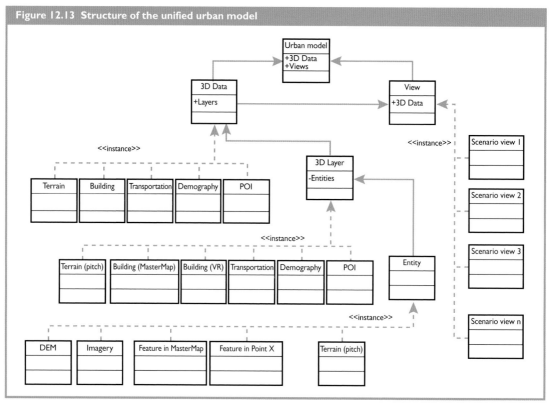

Figure 12.14 Virtual Black Country model

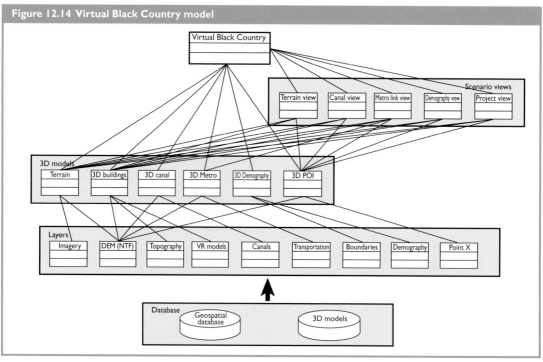

- The rendering manager provides the functionality for visualising information in the virtual environment. It also updates LOD (level of detail) models and manages all visualisation events in real time.
- The run-time urban data manager creates and maintains virtual urban models to support real-time visualisation during meetings. The key functions of this module are: (a) to extract and create a unified urban model from the database service layer; (b) to offer facilities for rendering selected project views; and (c) to provide functions such as information query.
- The interface manager is designed to support multi-user interaction and support functions such as navigation, information query, object selection and other manipulation tasks.

The physical display service layer offers the ability to create different workspace settings to support collaborative urban planning. At present, this layer offers display facilities on a powerwall or on normal workstations. The interaction with the virtual environment can be performed using 3D input devices such as joysticks or optically tracked 3D devices.

Unified urban model for visualisation

As discussed earlier, the data necessary for creating a rich information model are maintained by many different organisations in different formats. Therefore one of the key challenges in creating a practical virtual urban planning environment is to structure and present such information in a meaningful way to participants so that it can be easily understood by them and can support consensus building.

However, the construction of an integrated information model needs to be performed with a particular application in mind. While the integrated

model presented earlier allows statistical and demographic data to be integrated within a common spatial framework, more specific data models would need to be derived from such information models to support real-time applications such as visualisation.

A unified urban model was designed and developed in this work to integrate various kinds of dataset to support information visualisation. This conceptual model is organised into different levels, i.e., urban model, views, models, layers and features, as shown in Figure 12.13.

- In this model, the urban model represents the entire spatial urban model. It is composed of 3D data and views.
- The 3D data comprise different data layers to capture different data types, such as terrain, buildings, transportation and demography.
- Each layer is composed of features. An urban feature is an abstract object of the real world that can be described by geometry and attribute information. Some examples of features used in this work are MasterMap topographic and address data and VR models.
- The concept of views allows the user to pre-program different visualisation views for a specific project scenario. It allows the user to visualise different aspects of the urban information model.

Virtual Black Country

This section summarises how the virtual urban planning environment presented above was deployed in creating a virtual model of the Black Country region to support its regeneration activities.

Based on the conceptual model, the virtual Black Country model was created by populating it with the geographical, demographic and other datasets as shown in Figure 12.14. Furthermore, the model was organised into different views to support various

Figure 12.15 Virtual Black Country model in use

Figure 12.16 Geospatial view of the Black Country

Figure 12.17 Demographic view of crime information for Wolverhampton

project scenarios. The views include overall views of the Black Country (terrain and canal system), demographic views (such as crime, ethnic groups and knowledge workers), and specific regeneration project views (Brierley Hill and Merry Hill regeneration, and Dudley underground canals and mines projects). Each view comprises a set of the data types necessary for visualisation. For example, the visualisation scenario view of the planned metro link includes a terrain model, a metro link model and building models for visualisation. The various data sources are organised into different layers, and every layer is described by some entities. The layers and entities are organised into a back-end database. This database always resides at the back of urban models to support real-time information query.

Result of virtual Black Country

At present, the overall collaborative consensus building space is being used to develop a common vision among the stakeholders of the Black Country regeneration, and this is now being taken up by the developers as a tool for public participation (Figure 12.15).

The following figures show some screenshots generated from this prototype, based on the Black Country scenario: a bird's eye view of the Black Country (Figure 12.16), a demographic view (Figure

Figure 12.18 Physical assets view in the Black Country model. Each T represents a physical asset: clicking on it brings up information on the asset

All images this page
© Crown copyright Ordnance Survey. All rights reserved.
© Crown copyright. All rights reserved (Walsall Council)
(100019529) (2008)

Figure 12.19 Interface views. Left: object query. Right: area selection

© Crown copyright Ordnance Survey. All rights reserved. © Crown copyright. All rights reserved (Walsall Council) (100019529) (2008)

Figure 12.20 Regeneration project views. Left: Brierley Hill and Merry Hill Regeneration Project. Right: Dudley underground canals and mines

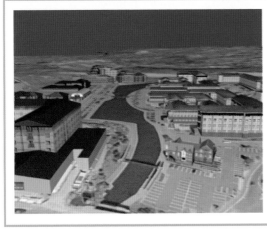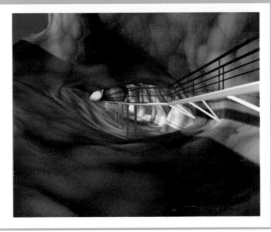

© Crown copyright Ordnance Survey. All rights reserved. © Crown copyright. All rights reserved (Walsall Council) (100019529) (2008)

12.17), a physical assets view (Figure 12.18), interface views (Figure 12.19), and views of proposed development plans (Figure 12.20).

Conclusion

This chapter has explored two potential approaches for enhancing current GIS systems for supporting sustainable urban design and planning. First, it presented a unified information modelling framework that can be used to integrate the various

demographic and statistical data that are captured within different geographical boundaries. By combining this integrated data model with GIS systems, this research showed how correlations between different datasets could be used to make informed decisions on sustainable development strategies. Second, it presented a collaborative consensus building space for different stakeholders to come together to explore urban space and

Langdon House, Clerkenwell, London

project proposals to make sound decisions. The Black Country regeneration project was taken as a case study for creating this innovative collaborative space.

Both research themes focused on improvement of the technology for enhancing the decision-making process for urban design and planning. They adopted typical methods for IT-based research and development, including conceptual modelling, system design and prototype development. These two approaches have been implemented in some case studies to generate various 2D data maps and 3D urban environments at regional and local levels.

Acknowledgements

The research presented in this paper forms part of the VivaCity project supported by EPSRC. The authors would also like to acknowledge the staff from Black Country Consortium, who gave support for assistance and evaluation of the system; the Ordnance Survey, for providing various types of data on the Black Country; and researchers from the Centre for Virtual Environments at the University of Salford, and the University of Wolverhampton, which provided VR models of related Black Country projects.

References

Adams, D. (1994) *Urban planning and the development process.* London: UCL Press.

Al-Kodmany, K. (1999) Using visualization techniques for enhancing public participation in planning and design: process, implementation, and evaluation. *Landscape and Urban Planning,* **45** (1): 37–45.

Birmingham University (2006) Key health data for the West Midlands 2004. http://www.pcpoh.bham.ac.uk/publichealth/publications/key_health_data/2004/ch_01.htm. Accessed September 2006.

Chan, R., Jepson, W. & Friedman, S. (1998) Urban simulation: an innovative tool for interactive planning and consensus building. *Proceedings of the 1998 American Planning Association National Conference,* Boston, MA, USA, pp. 43–50.

Copp, C. (2004) The NBN data model. An internal report produced by the National Biodiversity Network (NBN) on behalf of DEFRA. Reviewed online in September 2007.

Greed, C.H. (1993) *Introducing town planning London.* Longman Scientific & Technical.

Hudson-Smith, A. and Evans, S. (2001) Wired regeneration: GIS in the third dimension. *GIS@development.* December.

Laurini, R. (2001). *Information systems for urban planning: A hypermedia cooperative approach.* London: Taylor & Francis.

Mathur, V.N., Price, A.D.F., Austin, S. & Moobela, C. (2007) Defining, identifying and mapping stakeholders in the assessment of urban sustainability. In M. Horner, C. Hardcastle, A. Price & J. Bebbington (eds), *Proceedings of the SUE–MOT International Conference on Whole Life Urban Sustainability and its Assessment,* Glasgow Caledonian University, June.

ONS (2003) *The Output Prospectus.* Office for National Statistics. http://www.statistics.gov.uk/census2001/op.asp. Accessed 2005).

Skeffington, A. (1969) *People and planning: Report of the Committee on Public Participation in Planning.* London: HMSO.

Yao, J. & Fernando, T. (2004) A unified urban data model based on MasterMap. *Proceedings of the 2004 International Conference on Information and Communication Technologies,* Bangkok, Thailand.

Yao, J., Fernando, T., Tawfik, H., Armitage, R. & Billing, I. (2006) Towards a collaborative urban planning environment. In W. Shen, K.-M. Chao, Z. Lin, J.-P. A. Barthes & A. James (eds), *Computer supported cooperative work in design II,* pp. 554–562. Berlin/Heidelberg: Springer-Verlag.

SECTION 6
VIVACITY2020:
ARTISTS-IN-RESIDENCE

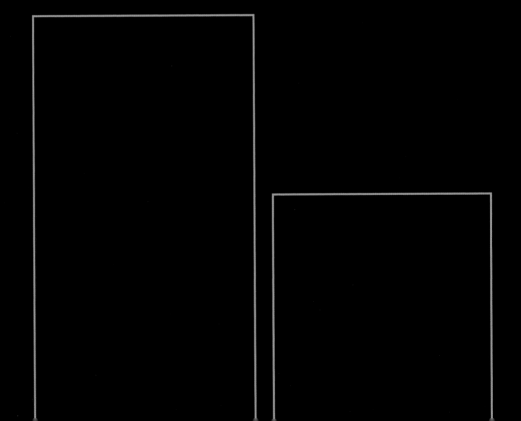

Scientists, social scientist, designers and architects spend a great deal of time researching the dimensions of sustainability. This was done over five years on the VivaCity2020 project. During that period the team recognised from the outset the complexity of the problem and the ways in which different specialisms approach the topic. The VivaCity researchers also knew that what they were researching was intimately related to the users of the city and their need to engage with them to gain their interest and extract their response. The team needed to be challenged to look outside their own scientific and academic silos; they chose to work with two artists to do this.

The following chapters represent the artists' responses to this challenge as they explore the 24-hour city and the issues surrounding the design of sustainable urban environments.

CHAPTER 13
THE ROLE OF ART PRACTICE WITHIN VIVACITY2020

Helen Bendon

Introduction

I am an artist working predominantly in film, video and photography. I make visual narratives involving characters in close relationships or close proximity. Central to my practice is the relationship between the characters' psyche and the physical spaces they occupy. In the work I often play with existing codifications of space, codes that are reinforced in cultural representations and form part of our cultural reading of space. The way in which my practice responds explicitly to types of space led me to consider working with the VivaCity2020 project. In 2005, Jess Thom and I were the selected artists to work alongside the team to make new artworks relating to the research. It was the intention that the inclusion of artists would assist in providing innovative and interactive ways of engaging the public with the research, and would broaden the perspective on issues of change and progressive urban developments. At this stage, the researchers were part way through their work. We were given access to the raw data of the other researchers as well as the evolving papers, presentations and reports.

This chapter details the process of embarking on a creative practice-based investigation into the wider VivaCity2020 project. Taking specific cues from the research being conducted around the needs and experience of those living and working in 'test-bed' areas, I developed a body of work around the city fringe. Initially I explored the fringe as a physical space, and then began to look at the relationship between actual and psychological space. Working in Clerkenwell, one of the test-bed areas, for a concentrated period of time offered an interesting trajectory from my existing practice. By examining an actual space (rather than a generic understanding of a type of environment) I was able to engage in the layered histories present in the architecture itself, and get a sense of how a place is perceived by those living there.

I was aware of the importance of engaging with the space – of mapping experiences and tales to the terrain itself. My first physical encounters with the area involved walking, cycling and riding pillion around Clerkenwell, employing observation as a primary source of research. I was observing the routines, repetitions and rituals performed across the space itself. Although naturalistic observation is an established ethnographic practice (although not prevalent in this particular project), by the very nature of my discipline my approach to the environment (and final dissemination of those materials) is more intimate and subjective than researchers are normally afforded. This decision was very much about my establishing in the wider project the different possibilities that art practice can bring to the discourse. Through this process of being in the environment, I was open to chance encounter, which led to my meeting a huge spectrum of residents who gave an alternative picture of Clerkenwell to the existing research interviews. These included various communities – church groups, volunteer groups, residents, and Smithfield Market traders – with whom I collected further stories and perspectives on the developments of Clerkenwell.

I produced three works for the commission, each one taking a key strand from the wider research project. Working with several fragmented narratives from Clerkenwell residents past and present, *Skirting* (digital video projection, 2006, 14.30 minutes) maps a continuity of experiences and behaviours onto the city fringe spaces.

In contrast, *Flight* (digital video, 2006, 9.00 minutes) is a singular narrative of a lone character attempting to leave her surroundings, and through this failed attempt, is suggestive of a sense of entrapment. The exploration of individual experience is a device to question the inclusiveness of broader notions of progress and change in the 24-hour city raised by the wider VivaCity2020 project.

Lastly, *Cheek by Jowl* (three-screen digital video, 2007, 20.00 minutes) works closely with resident interviews from the VivaCity2020 project. Working from these transcripts, I developed a fragmentary structure of many voices discussing their sensorial relationship to the area in which they live. To some degree the work explores what is revealed in the comfort and safety of home.

In the final realisation of the work, these audio materials are combined with exterior shots of domestic windows to investigate the dynamic of public and private behaviour, and look specifically at the window as the physical and psychological boundary between our homes and the world beyond.

This body of work is the result of creative, practice-led research. Each work has a different focus, form and resolution, but shares a common interest in continuity and resistance in the city fringe. In this chapter, as well as outlining the work produced during my time on the project, I shall also reflect upon the dialogue with the researchers and the relationship with the community in the production and dissemination of the work. By reflecting on these processes I hope to evaluate the role of art practice in terms of what it offers to the wider project. This will involve looking at the original intentions of the commission as well as the shifting questions and issues that arose along the way.

Orientation of Clerkenwell

The VivaCity2020 research was conducted in 'test-bed' areas, one of which was Clerkenwell, an extraordinary corner of London, which has historically been (and arguably still is) on the city fringe. This sense of fringe in Clerkenwell was established by many factors, including the demarcation of the City of London boundary at the River Fleet. The river has played an important part in the area's history. It had once been a shipping route (Pinks, 1865), but from as far back as the thirteenth century there were complaints of 'noxious inhalation arising from the Fleet' (p. 375), and for much of its history thereafter it was a vile, stinking, open sewer. The Fleet ran close to the city's famous Smithfield Market and allegedly ran blood-red at the end of trading. To protect the City of London, there were few crossing places (Pinks, 1865), and expulsion meant that those who could not, or would not, abide by the 'City rules' would be cast out to the wrong side of the Fleet. This consequently meant that oppositional religious movements, sects, artisans and radicals began to establish a presence in Clerkenwell (Ackroyd, 2001). It was a place for the outsider who could not exist within the city's norms and conventions. Perdikogianni, Penn and Mottram (see Chapter 11) suggest that, in stark contrast to the prosperous City of London, the urban fabric of Clerkenwell – the dividing river and the high boundary walls (e.g., of St Mary's Nunnery and the Priory of St John of Jerusalem) – have contributed to Clerkenwell's failure in terms of economic growth (Ackroyd, 2001). In this sense, the built environment itself has resisted certain kinds of change. I was interested in exploring other patterns of continuity and resistance that emerge in this 'failure'.

The demarcation of space between the city – prosperous, socially able, and controlled – and the fringe – poor, lawless and maverick – offers a historical notion of inside and outside, easy to imagine in Clerkenwell's past. We can well envisage the poverty, the stench and despair of living on the fringes, but what of today? Writer and historian Peter Ackroyd (2001: 465) poses the question:

> 'If there is a continuity of life, or experience, is it connected with the actual terrain and topography of the area? Is it too much to suggest that there are certain kinds of activity, or patterns of inheritance, arising from the streets and alleys themselves?'

Ackroyd does not deny the more recent shifts in the area caused by the changing use of spaces and new mixed-use developments, but his research does detail centuries of the same forms of fringe activity: crime, prostitution, suffering, poverty, survival. Much of my existing practice is a visual exploration of the relationship between actual and psychological space, and while Ackroyd's (2001) question is romantic in tone (and context, for his is a playful biography), it has a resonance for my own particular approach to exploring spaces. I shall now go on to expand these considerations in the development of the work for the VivaCity2020 commission.

Methodologies: mapping past and present

Clerkenwell somehow epitomises the changing demographics of London. There are the Dickensian and Gissingian elements of 'olde' London here, sitting alongside rapid urban 'cleansing' developments. Despite our cultural insistence on progress, we also like the aesthetics of this old quarter of London. The past is here in the street names, the architecture and the street design. This palpable evocation of the past led me to look at historical research as well as at the contemporary interviews, data collection and mapping from the research teams to investigate the idea of continuity through the life experiences of the communities in the city fringe areas, finding connections between some of the characters past and present. So my strategy in collecting stories from Clerkenwell, both historical and via contemporary interviews with current residents, was to find as a basis for my work a narrative driven by the intimacy of personal tale and experience. As an artist-film-maker, this is very much what I envisaged bringing to the project.

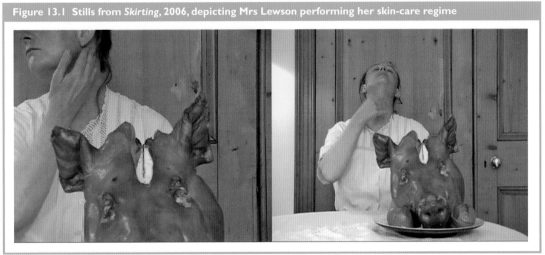

Figure 13.1 **Stills from *Skirting*, 2006, depicting Mrs Lewson performing her skin-care regime**

Copyright Helen Bendon

One such character (who features in *Skirting*: see Figure 13.1) is Mrs Lewson (b. 1700) of Cold Bath Square. In 1865 the historian W.P. Pinks wrote in *The History of Clerkenwell*:

> *'she never washed herself, because she thought those people who did so were always taking cold, or laying the foundations of some dreadful disorder; her method was to besmear her face and neck all over with hog's lard, because that was soft and lubricating.'* (Pinks, 1865: 115)

This level of detail about Mrs Lewson tells a different kind of history, one that offers a rich portrait of one of the key Clerkenwell characters of her time. Pinks describes her rituals, her behaviours, and how she wore the dress of a bygone era. Ackroyd (2001: 470) was drawn to Pinks's description of Mrs Lewson, and reflects upon her particular choice of dress:

> *'There are many instances of old women for whom time has suddenly come to a halt, and who characteristically wear white as some emblem of death or virginity. It may be that, for those whose lives have been damaged by the turbulence and inhumanity of the city, it is the only way of withstanding chance, change and fatality.'*

Thus I chose to make reference to Mrs Lewson in *Skirting* to provide a useful example of a refusal to engage with many notions of social change and progress. In order to consider continuity and resistance – the themes I had become interested in exploring – I wanted to look at Mrs Lewson in the context of more recent characters in Clerkenwell. From the research being undertaken by VivaCity2020 I expressed a specific interest in the interviews conducted by the team led by Dr Mags Adams (see Chapters 4 and 5), which focus on residents' sensorial experiences. The interview transcripts proved to be very informative in establishing characters and themes to develop in both *Skirting* and *Flight*; however, in *Cheek by Jowl* it is the interviews that provide the structure of the video work. In this three-screen video work, the edited audio interviews present perceptions of the area by meshing together elements of stories and experiences of contemporary Clerkenwell residents. As with all the work in the series, some of the characters we hear in *Cheek by Jowl* are stuck physically or psychologically, and many express a sense of stress and anxiety at various changes to their environment. The current changes in and around Clerkenwell are a concern for many of the

Copyright Helen Bendon

Figure 13.2 *Cheek by Jowl* installation view, Urbis Manchester, 2007

current elderly population. They express sadness as to their social losses: how children can no longer play safely out in the streets; the fear of the impact of crime on their daily lives; and a fear of being left behind or not being able to stay here.

These reflections are taken from a sequence in *Cheek by Jowl* that clusters together residents' thoughts on pollution:

'It varies, some days there's almost like um a leady sort of acid, almost like a, an acrid smell that's there, especially on days like today where the sky's low and things sort of [cuts to a different voice] 'We used to have a pink carpet upstairs, it/ and well it does, because I notice it/ the whole edge of it was going black through the/ you know an oily dust, it's not just dust, it's sort of sticky.'[1]

By clustering together these reflections, I foreground the residents' sensorial experience of a kind of infiltration into their worlds. In *Cheek by Jowl* these thoughts are cut together with the wider fears of infiltration of the 'other' – be it unfamiliar languages and faces, or just a sense of change that they are not part of. For example, one resident asks of himself: 'Do I mind them being here? I think I do, if I'm honest,' and goes on to add 'I'd like to know who you are and where are you from, and if you're here for good.'[2] This fragmented structure of various voices plays with notions of belonging, fear and change. The role of editing is clearly divisive in this work, as comments and observations are pitched cheek by jowl, removing them from their original context, reworking the same source materials in an entirely new direction from the research team.[3] I felt it important to provoke these materials to bring to the fore something implicit in

the interviews, but perhaps something that was not part of the original agenda for collecting these materials. Through a re-listening and re-appropriation, we become complicit with the sense of difficulty, edge, or discomfort they express. This reworking of materials happened within a subjective creative context, taking the original materials to address a different set of research questions not explored elsewhere in the wider project.

The original interviews were conducted in residents' homes, which, it could be argued, provides a useful sense of opposition from which to reflect on their sensorial experiences of the environment beyond, and how they navigate between the two spaces. Therefore, when planning the visual materials for this work, I wanted to work with the boundaries (both physical and psychological) between public and private. In contrast to the voices, which all come from within the home, the visuals – a series of shots of front-facing windows – are from the outside looking in. The process of seeking permission and then filming into the residents' windows began to offer some insight into the importance of the window as a border between the private self and the public beyond. Issues of safety, privacy, personal space, freedoms and stillness are explored on this cusp. The sense of the private and public existing either side of a shaky pane of glass provided the tension investigated in this work.

Using multi-screen presentation allowed me to further exploit this sense of fragmentation of what is intended, implied or revealed (see Figure 13.2). What is said or implied is not always comfortable listening, but it is there. In questioning an unfalteringly positive notion of progress, something else is revealed in these voices – an otherwise unspoken racial tension, a difficulty, ambiguity, in their inability, lack of opportunity, or resistance to engage with change.

Artistic practices / community voices

Cheek by Jowl highlights some of the more difficult issues of how older residents do not feel engaged in the progress 'happening' around them, and how they fear change in the many forms in which they perceive it manifests. This state of 'staying the same' exists in all of the video works in different ways: *Flight* looks specifically at one character who seems to want to change and move but, for reasons never made explicit, is unable to; *Skirting* contains progress and resistance, movement and stillness in both content and structure.

The themes of continuity and resistance on the city fringe boundary are explored through the topography of the space itself – specifically, how the physical environment determines the activities within it. This sense of legacy imprinted in the physical environment is explored through working with intimate narratives in these video works, but it is not my intention to deny change, for indeed there is change, but it is *how* change engages the people that is interesting here.

The decline of manufacturing industries in many UK city fringe areas in the 1970s and 1980s (including Clerkenwell and neighbouring Shoreditch) opened up spaces for artists and designers to use, but this had a knock-on effect. Following the mavericks, the artisans, and the radicals come the property developers. Studios are no longer cheap and cheerful, but plush and expensive, so the artisans get managed or ousted as the boundaries shift and property prices rise. I interviewed Mike Franks, a local resident and businessman who was instrumental in establishing the Clerkenwell workshops for designers and artisans in the 1970s, and is now fighting developers taking over all the now trendy, hugely expensive workspaces.

Infamous graffiti artist Banksy, whose instantly identifiable stencilled images decorate the underpasses, railway bridges and street corners of London's East End (and now beyond), has – much the pity – acquired 'cultural value'. So much so that a resident of London's East End wrote an email to Banksy requesting that he stop his graffiti work in his area as it was feared he was causing an increase in the house prices (Banksy, 2004). Sociologist Sharon Zukin (1995: 112) notes that this 'symbolic economy' is at work in London's east fringes: 'These areas have accumulated a higher status because of their association with avant-garde cultural activity.' Banksy graffiti, once an interventionist symbol of the people's disillusionment and dissatisfaction, now has cultural currency, as the activities of the fringe become predated by the trappings of the city. In this sense the complex relationship between city and fringe is at its most ugly, with the push and pull of activities across the boundaries. These changes represent some kind of progress – shifts in land use, resurgence of activity, economic development – but they are not models of change that are particularly inclusive of the residents, and in some ways focusing on resistance or inability to change presents an oppositional stance to this kind of progress. With the fringe comes the underbelly, the darkness, but sometimes this darkness is preferable to the predation of the city.

Focusing on resistance and continuity in the works is a way of representing marginal or understated experiences. Going back to the approach of historian Pinks in the *History of Clerkenwell*, he did not simply produce a record of data; rather, his history also seems to evoke a *sense* of the area through its characters and their behaviours. There is no denying that the characters of the area play(ed) a part in shaping it. In this regard, my approach to this project takes a strong cue from Pinks in that there is no hierarchy of voices in what I have produced; more a fragmented composite history of some of the voices less likely to be heard in wider discussions about urban sustainability and development.

While not all of the anecdotes and experiences that I collected make an explicit appearance in the final work, they thread through the development stage, informing my practice with a series of social positions and perspectives from the area. With this approach I was able to work through ideas that draw upon individual, private experience to examine the formation of identity within this challenging fringe environment. To evoke a wider resonance, these moments were abstracted from their singular experience into metaphorical reconfigurations in the final works.

While I have firmly positioned the project with the everyday experiences of the residents of Clerkenwell, I must make it clear that it was not my intention to produce an 'authentic' representation or literal translation of the residents' experience in Clerkenwell (a problematic proposition, and one outside of the remit of the commission). There is a tension of facts and fictions, as the production of the video works employs a range of research methodologies from social science to historical accounts, from interview transcriptions to tall tales. This plurality of methodologies manifested due to working within an interdisciplinary project. There is the excitement of encountering new fields of knowledge but also the danger of assuming (and/or misusing) other practices' agendas. Hal Foster's (1996) text, The artist as ethnographer?, foregrounds these very concerns, noting that artists working in socially engaged practice are given a 'pseudo-ethnographic role' – one that presumes an ethnographic authority but fails to question these practices. While Foster does not deny that innovative ways of working with communities can result from interdisciplinary projects, he raises many issues relating to the ethical, political and cultural 'dangers' in this field, with particular reference to anthropology's roots in colonial 'othering'. These problematics, while understood, can easily debilitate engagement in community-based and/or interdisciplinary projects for fear of getting it 'wrong'.

In order to continue the dialogue with the environment itself, the work I produced was both shot (where possible) and exhibited in Clerkenwell. The work showed at Hooper's Gallery, Clerkenwell Close, in June 2006 as part of the London Architecture Biennale and Architecture Week. The exhibition was accompanied by talks with the researchers and a panel discussion with the artists, the principal investigator of the VivaCity2020 project, Professor Rachel Cooper, and representatives from the research teams and the local planning office, in order to develop links across disciplines and areas of practice.

Despite these approaches, working on the project did raise new and sometimes difficult questions for my practice – particularly to do with 'using' other people's stories and experiences, and a desire to represent something that is otherwise not represented. This came particularly to the fore during points of dissemination. Consultation, participation and involvement of local communities were primary methodologies in the research and development stages; however, in exhibiting the art works, it was certainly not the elderly from the social housing tower blocks who came to the exhibition. Even if the lifts had been working, their absence from the exhibition space was of no surprise to me, but perhaps this is where the idea of public engagement is noted as important in process as well as in dissemination. The opportunity to share experiences and views during the process of making this work constituted meaningful public engagement in the project. Bringing this to the gallery space (and subsequent discussions and conferences) engages *different* audiences with some of the issues raised in the work.

In the process of developing this body of work, I cannot deny my own authorial voice in the consideration of aesthetics, form and the selection of stories, behaviours and activities to visually represent. I have worked with their stories to create something new, which reflects upon residents' experiences and, in turn, feeds these reflections into the wider project.

The language of moving image practice

Collecting, organising and editing these episodes for *Skirting*, I created a series of fragmented narrative events of Clerkenwell women, past and present. These women going about their activities are of the fringes: there is poverty, crime, prostitution, sadness, stillness. I began working exclusively with female characters for a number of reasons – partly as a conscious decision to focus on intimate histories often overlooked or marginalised. The interview transcripts from the wider project provided a useful insight into approaching this level of intimacy – in, for example, describing women's relationships to home, or how women choose to move around the area by night. Also important was the taciturn manner in which many of these female characters have responded to change.

My exploration of space is very much informed by cinematic concerns, as I am often exploring space through a lens of some kind or another. The complex discourse around space and time is therefore something that recurs as a consideration in the resolution of my work. This seemed particularly pertinent to approaching this project in relation to continuity and progression. In the development of this work I was posing questions: How can the thematic concerns be explored visually – what composition of shots and construction of sequences enable a visual dialogue on the city fringe, marginality and the fragmentation of our understanding of place? How does one formally 'treat' narratives within the

Figure 13.3 Movement and stillness in *Skirting*

Copyright Helen Bendon

work in terms of camera angles, shot composition, repetitions, linking separate episodes, etc? Connected through the characters, and the spaces themselves, I wanted to create a sense of movement and progression. I used recurring motifs and repetition of actions and gestures to create a visual exploration of continuity. The shooting methodology was to fragment some characters in the frame, to explicitly reference the stealth of fringe activities, and to focus on the narrative implication of their movements and gestures (passing objects, whispering, running). There is a furtive sense of activity that the viewer is never fully allowed to see. These characters are constantly in motion, and in post-production pace shifts and beating soundtrack were also exploited to layer in a sense of menacing progression.

This frenetic activity is periodically broken by stasis – sometimes a character defiant in stillness, sometimes stubborn in demeanour, sometimes frozen through featuring inanimate 'characters' such as statues – all shot with static camera, often lingering to evoke stillness and containment (see Figure 13.3).

Relating specifically to ideas of progress that emerged in my approach to the project, *Flight* also plays on cinematic conventions of narrative progression and our expectation of cause and effect. Moving image practice, by its durational nature, allows for an interesting commentary on progress and development. This idea of progress, be it a small shift for an individual or a wider issue for the community, is not made explicit in this work but instead focuses on a sense of entrapment and stasis. In contrast to the other works produced, the narrative in *Flight* is focused in one space. The character in this work considers – and nearly acts on – a desire to move, change, progress.

She is placed amongst inanimate objects, such as ornaments, all representing moments of suspended animation – a bird, horse and carriage, etc. – but also a moth on the window, which is also held by the attraction to the light (see Figure 13.4).

Figure 13.4 The character in *Flight* is suspended, mid-flight, by her surroundings

Copyright Helen Bendon

We see her frenetically packing her things into a case, her movements impassioned with an urgency and determination. However, her immediate surroundings define and hold her in a state of stasis. *Flight* draws attention to the significance of space, the relationship between space and narrative progression, and between physical and psychological space.

Cheek by Jowl fragments space through the editing of multiple stories and accounts, as each character speaks independently of one another across the three screens. This is reinforced by the fact that we never connect a voice with a face – just a front window – a selected representation to the outside world. Moving image as a research language allowed the VivaCity2020 materials to be developed in a particular direction – one that marries themes with forms in its resolution and dissemination.

Reflections on practice-led research

The previous section briefly described elements of my approach to making the work, and indeed engages in discourses close to my own discipline. The work itself is obviously an outcome from this period, but there are also articulations *around* the work: discussions, process, work-in-progress reviews play a big part in the development of a broad interdisciplinary project, which brings to the fore issues around research methodologies.

In a project already involving such a diversity of practitioners, researchers and professionals there was already an openness to a range of disciplines, and an embracing of the research methodologies and professional practice skills that I bring as an artist-film-maker. For example, my approach – to employ narrative strategies to disseminate the research – offered a more intimate (personal story driven) and perhaps more accessible approach to engaging audiences. Being part of an interdisciplinary project allowed this kind of 'specialist' approach.

Louis Althusser (1990) sceptically asks: 'What in fact does the slogan of interdisciplinarity mask?' (p. 98). identifying the term is not about practice, or collaborative labour, but is an intellectual interdisciplinarity – an *ideological* position (p. 84). Althusser warns of interdisciplinary work slipping into the 'common theoretical ideology that silently inhabits the consciousness of all the specialists' (p. 97). Perhaps we do view the idea of interdisciplinarity as an ideological position: it somehow connotes virtue by implicitly evoking a knowingness of the importance of multiple approaches to complex subjects. It also suggests a more inclusive, democratic methodology. But this understanding of the term is still vague, and does not afford a questioning of what differing practices can offer each other; nor does this vagueness employ the rigour demonstrated *within* established practices.

A single-discipline approach would obviously be restrictive in findings and application when attempting to address the complexity of urban sustainability: therefore it is essential that VivaCity2020 is interdisciplinary. The nature of such projects means that the outcomes of the research are many, and therefore there are inevitable complications in sharing research that might be expressed by different authors in different forms, different languages, and indeed with different (software) systems. These are the inherent problems of interdisciplinarity as a practice. Anticipating such problems in designing the project encouraged me to engage in the complexity of how an interdisciplinary project would actually be conducted as well as be perceived. At best, interdisciplinarity both offers an understanding of the contribution (and limitations) made by each discipline and also suggests that new questions can be posed 'in the space that they open' (Althusser, 1990: 100). It is in this space for new questions that I embarked on this commission to challenge and develop my own practice.

The many voices, practices and methodologies on the VivaCity2020 project go some way to avoiding the reductive commonality that Althusser (1990) and Foster (1996) identify. Approaching the project as an artist in the ways outlined in this chapter inevitably provoked interesting discussion on research practices. It was important to think about what creative work can offer to the dialogue: how does the artwork (and the research methodology of an artist) contribute to the wider research project and a dialogue between design, social science and art practice?

Through a dialogue with the researchers and their materials, the project was reviewed at various stages to present work in progress and also to question our (sometimes) differing approaches to subject matter and methodology as artists, designers and scientists. There are undoubtedly problems and challenges involved in an interdisciplinary project (with community groups and researchers from other disciplines), but being part of a wider project allowed discussion to emerge across disciplines, and provided a platform on which to critique the methods and outcomes of the project. While maintaining our own discipline identity, procedures and preoccupations, there was a sense of being able to expand possibilities through the proximity of other disciplines. Discussions around consultation of communities, interview processes and the relationship between the artwork and the wider research concerns were discussed in both academic and exhibition environments throughout the project's duration. Creative practice outcomes afforded me certain freedoms in approach to my methodologies, perhaps denied to some of the other researchers. For example, the people I had interviewed had recommended I read Pinks's history and Gissing's novels, set in the streets of Clerkenwell in the nineteenth century, to get a sense of the area. These contextual layers provided a focus (for the wider project) on something that is regarded as incredibly important in the area – a sense of identity, and a sense of history. I was able to articulate these, both in discussions and also thematically in visual/aural form.

Again, I had to consider my role in the wider project – what could my research in the medium of the moving image offer that could not be expressed in other forms? By the very nature of my project, I am not trying to offer an overarching narrative. As stated, there is a process of selection – of stories and of organisation of shots in the edit. For example, the interwoven narratives in *Skirting* deny a straightforward linearity. The final shot, which is one of the characters striding determinedly on into the dark cloak of a Clerkenwell alley, lacks formal resolution and instead suggests a continuum beyond the film's duration. These formal considerations echo the thematic concerns of portraying the city fringe, in that they are in themselves resistances to a prescribed notion of progress. Both the form and content of *Skirting* become metaphors for continuity and resistance. Similarly, the other works produced do not offer definitive resolution.

The video works as research outcomes do not represent a definitive set of findings, nor is that the point. The anecdotal, observational and character-based investigations were more appropriate here than in other strands of the project. This is perhaps where the differences in our reporting/dissemination across the project come to the fore, but it serves to draw attention to how the different research methodologies have questioned and enriched the wider research project. While the project was initially framed to engage the public with the research, the cross-disciplinary engagement *within* the project became hugely important. The collaboration between artist and a research group outside my normal frame of reference and discipline has offered a genuine opportunity for sharing knowledge and perspectives to understand about place. In investing in such an initiative, the research consortia freely entered into a dialogue with the artists (Jess and myself) and were open to see what kind of knowledge could be shared across different practices. This synergy proved to be a valuable one for both parties, and I believe encouraged a broader engagement with the communities of Clerkenwell.

The project resulted in three strands: the body of work itself; the dissemination through exhibition and presentation at various stages; and, importantly, the dialogue generated through the process of the relationship between artists, communities and researchers. The role of a commissioned artist, or artist in residence, is not without problems. It is not easy to define precisely what the process of such a collaboration will lead to, or to anticipate a process so fraught with potential ethical, social and creative problems (in terms of engaging with materials, communities and points of dissemination, etc.). The dialogue itself cannot not eradicate these issues, but clearly identifies the need for this kind of provocation in a continual questioning of methods and practices in such a project.[4]

As an artist, of course, it is important for me to have made interesting work that is both developmental to my existing practice and which provides a challenging viewing experience for audiences. My approach to and resolution of the project was to constantly refocus on the micro personal experiences rather than the wider issues of sustainable urban living, to maintain a sense of everyday experience and narrative embedded in these streets. However, the works relate to the concerns of the wider project thematically, in that they attempt to deny the unquestioning approach to history, and to progress through the engagement of smaller individual fragmented narratives.

The role of the moving image in research practice allows a particular kind of exploration of space, which brings a different approach to, and view of, Clerkenwell to the research consortia, and to a wider audience. The ideas of resistance and continuity complicate the notion of progress that is inherent in discourse around urban development and regeneration. By highlighting the continuity of difficult aspects of fringe existence, I drew attention in the work to those who do not want to or who cannot be part of the kind of progress on offer – for example, families who become dispersed because of the increased cost of housing; council residents who cannot afford the right to buy; the influx of industries now trading there whose services do not provide for the locals; the independent creatives who are priced out. These people are becoming increasingly marginalised in the process of change. It is not my role to criticise these examples of progress, but in making this work and engaging in the discourse around it perhaps I have raised some alternative perspectives to the thrust of developing the 24-hour city.

The final works intentionally do not map the other researchers' materials to another medium, nor do they provide a clear voice of the community. There were limitations as to the mechanisms of local public engagement beyond the production of this work, but in engaging with the residents past and present in the conception of the work I was able to explore a tension that might not be represented elsewhere in the project. Investigating the area in terms of a complex dynamic between physical and psychological space introduces something less tangible to the project, which relates to senses, the affect of an area, and the relationship that people form between themselves and the space they inhabit.

Acknowledgements

The artist would like to thank all those who contributed to the research and production of this work, including: Nick Thomas, Film Office (Islington), Paul Cramer and the butchers at Smithfield Market, Father Paul Baggott of The Church of the Holy Redeemer, Paul Gilbert of Finsbury & Clerkenwell Volunteers and the Holy Redeemer Lunch Club Guests, Stephen Thake, Maxwell Hutchinson, Mike Franks, the Vivacity2020 and AUNT-SUE research teams and Joanne Leach, Vivacity2020 Project Manager. This chapter developed from a paper presented at the Design and Liveability Conference, Washington State University, Spokane (5 October 2006).

References

Ackroyd, P. (2001) *London the biography*. London: Vintage.

Althusser, L. (1990) *Philosophy and the spontaneous ideology of the scientists and other essays*. London: Verso.

Banksy (2004) *Cut it out*. London: Paranoid Pictures.

Foster, H. (ed.) (1996) The artist as ethnographer? In *The return of the real: The avant-garde at the end of the century*, pp. 171–204. Cambridge, MA: MIT Press.

Gissing, G. (1889) *The netherworld*. New York: Oxford World Classics.

Perdikogianni, I. & Penn, A. (2006) *Measuring diversity: A multivariate analysis of land use and temporal patterning in Clerkenwell*. Retrieved 15 January 2006 from http://www.vivacity2020.org/publications/academic.

Pinks, W.P. (1865) *The history of Clerkenwell*. London: J.T. Pickburn.

Zukin, S. (1995) *The culture of cities*. Oxford: Blackwell.

Being There Exhibition information from London Architecture Biennale 2006. Retrieved 1 October 2006 from http://www.architectureweek.org.uk/event.asp?eventURN=2141.

Footnotes

1 Original source material: interviews with Clerkenwell resident conducted by Dr Mags Adams.

2 Original source material: interviews with Clerkenwell resident conducted by Dr Mags Adams.

3 It should be noted that original source material was not used in the video works, to protect the identity of the residents who participated.

4 The dialogue continues as the work continues to be shown in a variety of contexts from film festival, to gallery space, to conference presentation, disseminating both the work and the processes to further audiences.

CHAPTER 14
PRESENT IN PUBLIC SPACE

Jessica Thom

Figure 14.1 19,545 people (Lambda print 2006)

Copyright Jessica Thom

I am interested in the role that photography plays as a tool for collecting and presenting information about our surroundings. I use photography and drawing to make images that explore how spaces are seen and experienced. I combine multiple viewpoints to make portraits of places that aim to be accessible and engaging. The images that form the Present in Public Space project were made in response to research carried out by Vivacity2020 researchers in Clerkenwell and Manchester. The work of Vivacity2020 continues to inform my practice as an artist.

As each work package was very different, my instinct as an artist was to look for a unifying factor between

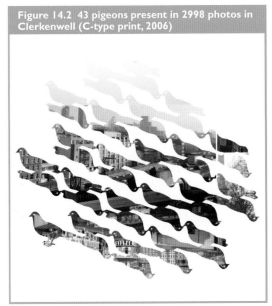

Figure 14.2 43 pigeons present in 2998 photos in Clerkenwell (C-type print, 2006)

Copyright Jessica Thom

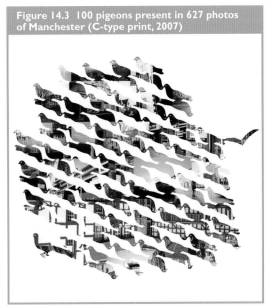

Figure 14.3 100 pigeons present in 627 photos of Manchester (C-type print, 2007)

Copyright Jessica Thom

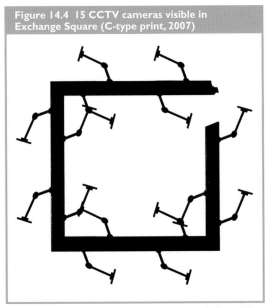

Figure 14.4 15 CCTV cameras visible in Exchange Square (C-type print, 2007)

Copyright Jessica Thom

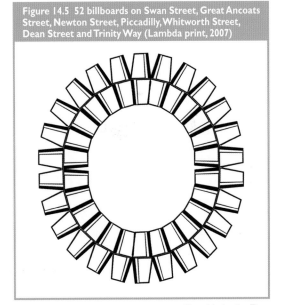

Figure 14.5 52 billboards on Swan Street, Great Ancoats Street, Newton Street, Piccadilly, Whitworth Street, Dean Street and Trinity Way (Lambda print, 2007)

Copyright Jessica Thom

them that I could use as a starting point for my creative exploration of their work. The Vivacity2020 research teams had taken many photographs as part of their research methodology, so it was these that I chose to focus on. I approached each work package and asked for images that they, or participants in their project, had taken in the fieldwork areas in Clerkenwell and Manchester. I hoped to compile these images, and the information contained within them, to reveal more about the fieldwork areas themselves as well as the preoccupations of the research teams.

Figure 14.6 107 trees on Swan Street, Great Ancoats Street, Newton Street, Piccadilly Street, Whitworth Street, Deansgate and Trinity Way (Lambda print, 2007)

Copyright Jessica Thom

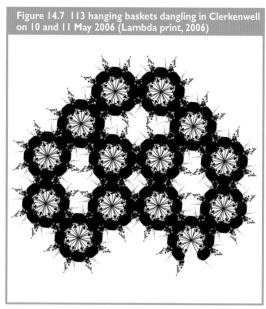

Figure 14.7 113 hanging baskets dangling in Clerkenwell on 10 and 11 May 2006 (Lambda print, 2006)

Copyright Jessica Thom

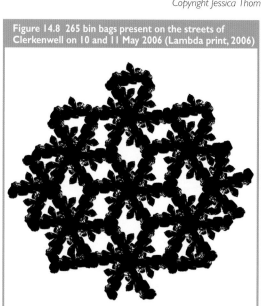

Figure 14.8 265 bin bags present on the streets of Clerkenwell on 10 and 11 May 2006 (Lambda print, 2006)

Copyright Jessica Thom

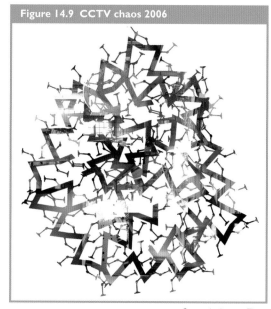

Figure 14.9 CCTV chaos 2006

Copyright Jessica Thom

I was given 3625 photographs altogether, of which 2998 were photos of Clerkenwell and 627 were photos of Manchester. Of these:

- 2319 (64%) of the photographs were taken by researchers

- 679 (19%) of the photographs were taken by Clerkenwell residents
- 627 (17%) of the photographs were taken by Manchester residents
- 275 (9%) of the Clerkenwell photographs were taken at night.

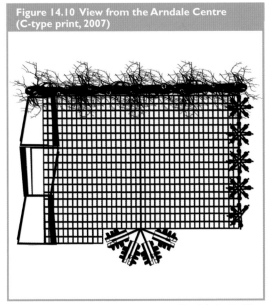

Figure 14.10 View from the Arndale Centre (C-type print, 2007)

Copyright Jessica Thom

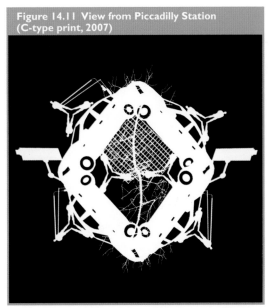

Figure 14.11 View from Piccadilly Station (C-type print, 2007)

Copyright Jessica Thom

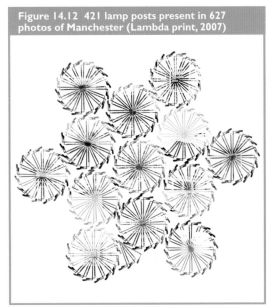

Figure 14.12 421 lamp posts present in 627 photos of Manchester (Lambda print, 2007)

Copyright Jessica Thom

I analysed the content of each photograph, looking at what and how often various objects appeared in them, from windows and advertising to feather boas and toilet rolls. I collated this information into a chart showing all the objects present in all the images, from the most common feature, which was windows, to the least common, which was a zebra.

I used the information from the chart to create new composite images that highlighted the most numerous, significant or memorable features of public space in Clerkenwell and Manchester. Each item on the chart was captured and depicted in the form of a symbol derived from the original photographic source. These symbols were then re-presented as a graphic image that combined the parts extracted from the photos alongside the numerical data derived from the fieldwork areas. The images presented numerical data as black or outlined symbols, and photographic data utilised the same symbols, but with parts of the original photographic image visible through it too.

The Present in Public Space series includes images that show the population of Clerkenwell and the number of traffic lights present in Clerkenwell, which I worked out by walking each street and counting

Figure 14.13 382 traffic lights (Lambda print, 2006)

Copyright Jessica Thom

the actual number present on the street. I used a similar method to collect information on the number of hanging baskets, bin bags, and trees in Clerkenwell, the number of CCTV cameras in Exchange Square, Manchester; and the number of advertising billboards and trees in Manchester.

Clerkenwell: final totals in size order (2998 photos)			
Windows	60787	Doors	2361
Railings	12691	People	1914
Advertising	6532	Lamp posts	1350
Vehicles	3644	Graffiti	695
Trees	3383	Signposts	483

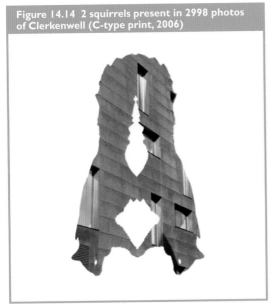

Figure 14.14 2 squirrels present in 2998 photos of Clerkenwell (C-type print, 2006)

Copyright Jessica Thom

Bin bags	458
For sale signs	340
Traffic bollards	329
Blocked-up windows	325
Burglar alarms	315
Traffic lights	240
Bikes	206
Flowers	184
CCTV	184
Benches	134
Grab rails	121
Tower blocks	115
Bus lanes	110
Tactile paving	96
Red traffic lights	95
Play equipment	91
Hanging baskets	90
Toilet rolls	68
Bus stops	66
Toilets	64
Pelican crossings	57
Buses	54

Sinks	47
Obstructed toilets	44
Pigeons	43
Recycling	43
People in fluorescent jackets	42
Soap	38
Taps	36
Telephone boxes	35
Mirrors	34
Clock faces	32
Red man at crossing	31
Sanitary bins	26
Art	23
Animal carcasses	22
Toilet brushes	20
Shopping trolleys	18
Cakes	17
Anti-war graffiti	16
Ice skates	15
Boats	14
Banksy stencils	13

Cuddly toys	13
Hand dryers	13
Emergency cords	13
Disabled symbols	13
Cattle troughs	13
Sandwiches	12
Finger over lens	12
Speed bumps	12
Cranes	12
Postboxes	12
Dogs	11
St Paul's Cathedral	11
Skips	8
Closed toilets	7
Sunsets	6
Tree stumps	6
Urinals	6
Changing beds	5
Blue plaques	5
Rubber gloves	4
Horses	4
Blocked-up doors	4
Angels	4
Trees growing out of gravestones	4
Wonky signposts	4
Green man at crossing point	4
Cats	4
Hooks	3
Congestion charge signs	3
Trains	3
Starbucks	2
Microphones	2
Squirrels	2
TVs	2
Marge Simpson	2

Stair chairs	2
Transparent toilet seats	2
Milk floats	2
Birds in flight	2
Flip-flops	2
Bullet holes	2
Tate Modern	2
London Eye	2
BT Tower	2
Big Ben	2
Cooker	2
Light nets	2
Bag in trees	2
Yellow police boards	2
Flower shrine	1
Topless man	1
Feather boa	1
Overhead projector	1
The Gherkin	1
Teapots	1
Bird's nest	1
Horse-drawn vehicle	1
Tripe seller	1
Guide and Brownie recruitment sign	1
Clamp	1
Wheelbarrow	1
Plane	1
Mermaid	1
Tandem bike	1
Folding bike	1
Zebra	1

VIVACITY2020: ARTISTS-IN-RESIDENCE

The artists working in the VivaCity2020 team responded uniquely to the situation presented to them. Helen responded to the residents – the users of Clerkenwell – as well as to its history, using verbal and written references. Jess took the visual research and re-analysed it from her own artist's visual perspective.

Both artists undertook a critical analysis of urban life in Clerkenwell and re-presented it with new insights. The value of the artists in such situations is not just in the finished artefact but in the process. The process of looking, 'the artist's gaze', the process of questioning and of making – this is a process everyone understands and therefore enjoys engaging with. This is invaluable to our understanding of the human condition in cities. Both the process and the product provided the researchers with a new perspective on how data/information could be used in a new and innovative way, thereby expanding our interdisciplinary horizons. This experience provides an example of how artists can be used to stimulate new perspectives when making decisions about our cities.

CONCLUSION

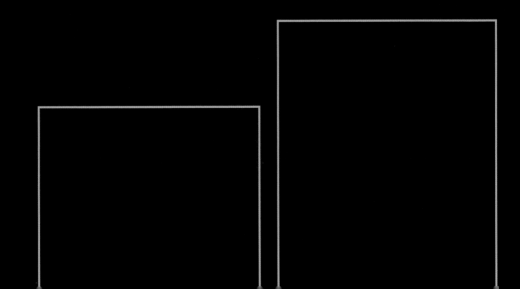

CHAPTER 15

THE ONGOING
SUSTAINABLE CITY
ENDEAVOUR

Rachel Cooper, Graeme Evans and Christopher Boyko

During the five years in which the research for this book has been undertaken, there has been a major shift in attitudes towards, awareness of and action on climate change, security, urbanisation, poverty, information technology and competing economies. Intimately intertwined with each of these and other global issues is sustainability. Yet, five years on, are we any more confident that we know more about the complex relationships between these issues and sustainability? And have we moved any closer to understanding how to design sustainable cities? The work undertaken on the VivaCity2020 project since 2003 has not, by any means, been comprehensive with regard to all aspects of sustainability; it was not designed to be. However, we have managed to undertake ground-breaking research through a transdisciplinary, multi-perspective lens, revealing both macro- and micro-scale issues as summarised at the end of each section. This final chapter cannot recapitulate the depth nor the breadth of all the findings found in each section. Nonetheless, it might be appropriate here to consider five overarching implications that have arisen from the research:

1: There is no such thing as a sustainable city – but we can create the capacity for sustainable improvement

It is clear, not only from the research on the VivaCity2020 project but also more generally, that achieving a sustainable city is an unobtainable Utopia. It is also clear that sustainability in urban planning and design is never addressed or considered consistently. A variety of decision-makers make decisions regarding the sustainability of urban development projects – or elements of urban development projects – but rarely are sustainability issues repeatedly discussed throughout the process. In addition, sustainability is rarely considered in a holistic manner when making decisions. Rather, decision-makers tend to address one or two sustainability issues in urban development projects – the most frequent being environmental issues – instead of assessing projects on a more thorough, multidimensional examination of sustainability (e.g., evaluating the social, economic, environmental, political and cultural dimensions). This is not to say that sustainability approaches must be equivalent in their spatial and temporal application.

Indeed, what the VivaCity2020 project has identified is that solutions are idiosyncratic, context-specific, and cannot be applied with a one-size-fits-all approach. Nonetheless, it is critical that as many dimensions of sustainability are considered and applied as possible throughout the urban design decision-making process. One way to ensure this is to develop a sustainability agenda early on in the process that is specific to a project, whether at a building, development or urban scale. The sustainability agenda should be revisited and modified by the key decision-making groups throughout the process, thus providing a 'living' resource from which to benchmark achievements, to negotiate and prioritise sustainable actions, and to inform socially responsible decisions.

Our work in IT suggests that virtual reality, GIS, space syntax and other modelling systems can facilitate the 'living' resource through the establishment of a legacy archive. The archive can provide a basis for the ongoing management and maintenance of the sustainable city by creating a vital virtual record of decisions, decision-makers, and the tools and resources used in decision-making. The original project's sustainability aims and objectives within the sustainability agenda also can be remembered over time, which is particularly beneficial when decision-makers are developing a comprehensive programme of building and urban maintenance and management. The maintenance and management programme ensures that sustainability continues to be regarded once an urban development project is constructed, and creates the capacity for ongoing sustainable improvements to our urban environments.

2: All cities are 24-hour cities – we need to consider density, diversity and intensity

It is clear that all places have a 24-hour rhythm. The difference between large cities and small towns and villages, however, is the level of intensity of 24-hour activity. Places that are denser and more economically, socially and culturally diverse are likely to have a greater impact on the environment and on inhabitants. We found on the VivaCity2020 project, for example, that many urban residents felt most concerned about doorstep issues such as rubbish, graffiti, antisocial behaviour and noise. Although not necessarily exclusive to large cities, these issues may be exacerbated by the relatively intense, 24-hour rhythm found in places such as London, Manchester and Sheffield.

Issues surrounding time and space, which feature prominently in the 24-hour rhythm of cities and impact on density, diversity and intensity, were explored particularly in Section 4 of this book. We found that the notion of time related to the temporal nature of consumption and production, as well as to their increasing spatial and symbolic conflation through the symbolic economy and the adaptation of

'space' (e.g., live–work, city branding and imaging). With space, we discovered that decision-makers and stakeholders often referred to both spatial separation (e.g., a major road dividing communities) and the combination of spatial 'uses' (e.g., office and residential) as persisting organically and organised. Nonetheless, for day-to-day existence, people felt that environmental management and spatial 'cohesion' were required to maintain liveability and avoid conflicts of use, both within and between groups, in dense, diverse, intensified areas.

For conflicts to be minimised, decision-makers must be more knowledgeable of the trends concerning the nature of density, diversity and intensity as they change over time. A critical dialogue is necessary both early and often when planning with the 24-hour rhythm of cities in mind. More guidance and experience are needed, for example, when planning for the dark, the evening and night-time economy and the abatement of noise and nuisance, and when trying to design out crime and reduce fear of crime. Thus knowing about current planning regulations and being savvy about how uses can be mixed (see the definition of mixed use recommended in Section 4) may help to reduce conflict and tension.

3: Hindsight and foresight – use them

Although our work focused on a five-year period from 2003 to 2008, it has been recognised that a historic perspective on the evolution and morphology of city life and spaces helps us to understand the present. The development of Clerkenwell, for instance, is clearly connected to its location near to the City of London. The way in which residents related to their neighbourhoods and communities was illustrated clearly through their understanding of the past, in terms both of associations with people and of the historic fabric of the urban environment. These associations were made increasingly salient through the representations of urban life in Clerkenwell created by our artists,

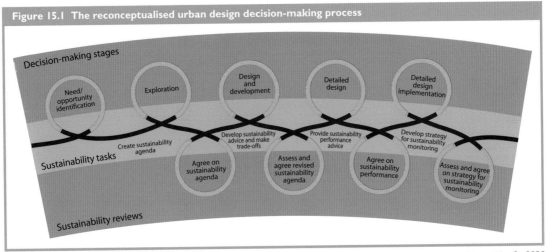

Figure 15.1 The reconceptualised urban design decision-making process

Decision-making stages

Need/opportunity identification — Exploration — Design and development — Detailed design — Detailed design implementation

Sustainability tasks

Create sustainability agenda — Agree on sustainability agenda — Develop sustainability advice and make trade-offs — Assess and agree revised sustainability agenda — Provide sustainability performance advice — Agree on sustainability performance — Develop strategy for sustainability monitoring — Assess and agree on strategy for sustainability monitoring

Sustainability reviews

Source: VivaCity2020

who were able to engage in a conversation with residents that was more intimate than the facts and figures gathered by the researchers.

Concomitantly, through a better understanding of the evolution and morphology of cities, we can begin to make predictions of future trajectories by looking at the cyclical and incremental nature of development and behaviour within the market, communities and households. Scientific and economic insights can now be represented through more comprehensive mechanisms, scenarios, modelling and so forth, as illustrated in Chapters 11 and 12. The use of these different tools and techniques – along with the legacy archive – can help us to develop an annotated narrative that will inform the process and give us ideas about what we need to do in the short- and long-term future to sustain our cities.

4: Everyone is a decision-maker – ensure their voices are heard and their stories are told

For more sustainable urban design decisions to occur, we need to do a better job of hearing and listening to the myriad voices that are affected by those decisions. In Section 2 of the book we revealed how residents provided rich insights into the quality of city life and the urban experience. Such knowledge is extremely valuable to decision-makers, particularly developers, designers and planners, who are responsible for creating and designing the places where these – and future – residents live.

In Section 6 we illustrated novel ways of facilitating engagement between professionals, scientists and the community through the medium of art. These types of mechanism are critical in the face of consultation weariness, and provide yet another way for voices to be heard and stories to be told. Finally, at the end of Section 1, we offered a way to categorise urban design decision-makers and stakeholders to ensure that more people's voices are heard throughout the lifetime of urban development projects (i.e., through the creation of a development team and a project sustainability group). We also revealed the underlying urban design decision-making process, which provides a platform to consider when and how to undertake consultation, and what tools and resources to use when consulting (the VivaCity2020 website, www.vivacity2020.org, provides an extensive array of such tools and techniques developed from the research project) (see Figure 15.1).

5: Policy response – make it flexible

Finally, it is clear that the multitude of challenges presented by the city is 'tricky' at best. Therefore we must ensure our governance and management structures are capable of detecting the challenges, and are flexible enough to respond. For instance, as discussed in Section 4, there is a clear challenge to reconsider now outdated land use classes, property investment vehicles and economic development strategies. Higher density and intensification, not just of housing and retail but also of public spaces, circulation (i.e., transport), informational flows and population growth is a reality. However, this reality suffers from being reduced to measures of dwelling densities, zoning, plot ratios and licensing controls. Regulatory development and change must keep pace with trends and be able to respond to enable flexible, sustainable growth and development (e.g., national policies must be flexible enough to support local approaches). Faster knowledge transfer between scientists and policy-makers is necessary to support such evidence-based policy.

Sheffield Hallam University Union Building, Sheffield

Box 15.1: UrbanBuzz

UrbanBuzz: Building Sustainable Communities was a £5 million, two-year programme to develop new ways of delivering genuinely sustainable forms of development and community in London and the wider south-east region. It was a joint venture between University College London and the University of East London, and ran through 2007 and 2008.

In spite of policy and best intentions, there is little confidence that today's developments will form thriving and vital sustainable communities. The problem is not a lack of policy, will or knowledge, but a lack of coordination. There seems to be a lack of the right knowledge in the right places to inform development. Both the urban supply network and the research base are fragmented along disciplinary and organisational lines, and this stands in the way of developing sustainable communities.

UrbanBuzz recognised that knowledge is transferred by people, working together to solve problems. This programme funded cooperation to help make sure it happened. It created a network of professionals and practitioners at every major link in the supply chain, and integrated these people – 'innovation fellows' – with leading-edge academics – 'business fellows'. They worked together to identify and work on live development projects. They brought together evidence-based and participative processes and new knowledge to develop sustainable communities. By working together to solve shared problems on projects, not only were academic disciplinary divisions bridged, but also organisational fragmentation in the urban supply network. Ultimately, successful networks and projects build belief that sustainable communities are possible. UrbanBuzz funded 28 projects to carry forward this agenda. Find out more about UrbanBuzz at http://www.urbanbuzz.org.

Box 15.2: Vivacity2020 internships

Internship 1: Sheffield

From November 2006 to May 2007 a senior researcher undertook an internship at Sheffield City Council, working with the urban design team within the planning and development division. For three or four days a week the researcher observed the urban design team and tried to map the process they used for making urban design decisions. From the observations, a number of recommendations were made to introduce sustainability into the strategic and daily decision-making by the urban design team:

- Hold a space syntax workshop for members of the urban design team and the planning division to understand how space syntax could be used to model pedestrian and vehicular flows, and whether space syntax could interface with other computer programs that are currently being used (e.g., the ArcView GIS).
- Further develop the checklist used in weekly urban design review meetings to incorporate additional sustainability criteria related to urban design.
- Hold a workshop or conduct a requirements-capture exercise within the planning and city development department to understand the local authority's familiarity with sustainability.
- Share VivaCity2020 information with decision-makers in the Council responsible for higher-level policy and masterplanning.
- Reconsider the structure of planning and development to enable a more multi-department approach to decision-making.
- Reconsider the structure of the urban design team to incorporate other departments (e.g., highways, environmental health), demonstrating the important role of urban design in overall planning.
- Add new kinds of people to the urban design team (e.g., urban historians, social scientists).
- Reconsider the communication systems between departments.
- Develop information technology to support project teams, rather than – or in addition to – department teams.

Box 15.2 (continued): Vivacity2020 internships

Internship 2: London

From December 2007 to April 2008 a senior researcher worked at Islington Borough Council with the planning policy team within the environment and regeneration division. For two or three days a week the researcher spent time understanding the context of planning policy in the Council, and identifying areas where evidence from the VivaCity2020 project could be used to support the planning policy team's core strategy issues and options (CSIO) document, which was being rewritten. The evidence was then reinterpreted into planning policy terms and incorporated into the CSIO document. Both during and at the end of the internship, the following recommendations were made:

- Propose a meeting between the planning policy team and a team of researchers from the University of Birmingham (working on the EPSRC SUE Birmingham Eastside project) to brainstorm about how best to categorise the core strategy issues.
- Create a web survey that examines communication between relevant teams within the environment and regeneration division.
- Act as a facilitator between a member of the policy team and another EPSRC project, SuScit, in an attempt to work together on a community consultation project in the Mildmay area of Islington.
- Hold an event (e.g., a CPD course) so that ESPRC-funded researchers have an opportunity to disseminate their relevant findings to the Council and other interested organisations.
- Create – and maintain – a legacy archive of contacts and details so that the policy team can obtain, and keep track of, information from various teams within environment and regeneration, but also within the Council as a whole. In so doing, the team could identify different possibilities for cross-cutting collaboration and demonstrate a more joined-up approach to planning.
- Use more GIS-based maps in the CSIO document to show spatial evidence that is already found within the Council's departments.

Moreover, the management structures set up within local authorities must respond more rapidly and holistically to the challenges of sustainability. Planning departments need to ensure greater collaboration and communication between internal departments managing such issues as waste, highways, transport and education. Planners must also be able to liaise proficiently with local and regional agencies (e.g., English Heritage, health trusts), local scientists and researchers, as these stakeholder groups can provide experience and knowledge to help make more informed design and planning decisions.

The final stage of the VivaCity2020 project involved developing a mechanism of direct knowledge transfer between the local authorities who participated in the work and other agencies. This was achieved in a number of ways. Two specifically are worth mentioning: the development of UrbanBuzz (see Box 15.1) and the use of internships in local authorities, undertaken by a senior researcher on the project (see Box 15.2).

Regarding the latter, this mechanism not only gave key decision-makers more specific access to the research data collected and the research team, but also enabled VivaCity2020 to gain insights into how knowledge was collected and used, and how decisions were made in practice. From these internships, we could make recommendations to local authority planners about how to approach sustainability through policy and practice, thus providing a faster, more flexible avenue for dialogue between the VivaCity2020 project and decision-makers and stakeholders.

The future

The work undertaken by the VivaCity2020 project and described in this book builds on a recognised body of knowledge on the design of sustainable cities. It is, as described in the Introduction, part of an ongoing body of work being undertaken in the UK using multidisciplinary teams. The work has resulted in the establishment of new tools and techniques to be used across research disciplines and in practice, as well as a new generation of urban sustainability researchers and practitioners. It has also resulted in (of course) new areas for research. We have only just begun to understand density, for instance, and how the different dimensions of density relate to one another and to wider issues, such as crime, cultural and economic diversity and intensity. The next step for us is to continue adding to our collective research knowledge base and to strive towards designing, creating and maintaining urban environments that are truly sustainable. This is an ongoing endeavour, however ...

APPENDIX I

VIVACITY2020 INDUSTRY PARTNERS AND COLLABORATORS

VivaCity2020 industry partners

Age Concern
Association of Town Centre Management (ATCM)
Brent Council
British Toilet Association (BTA)
Building Research Establishment (BRE)
Buro Happold CoSA
Centre for Accessible Environments (CAE)
Chapel Street Regeneration Strategy
CSC Construction Limited
EDAW
Environment Agency
Government Office for the North West (GONW)
Henry Boot PLC
Housing Corporation
Housing Federation North
Ian Finlay Architects
Ken Treadaway
Learian Designs Limited
London Borough of Camden
Manchester City Council
Mosscare Housing Limited
Novas-Ouvertures Group
Ordnance Survey
Peter Mapp and Associates
Royal Institution of Chartered Surveyors (RICS)
Royal National Institute for Deaf People (RNID)
Salford City Council
Sheffield City Council
Sheppard Robson
Space Syntax
Taylor Young
Westminster City Council

VivaCity2020 collaborators

Academy of Urbanism
Age Concern Sheffield
Arts Council
Asquith Brown Regeneration Agency Ltd (ABRA)
Building Design Partnership (BDP) Urbanism
Bourne Estate Tenants Association
Bradford University
British Council of Offices (BCo)
British Institute of Cleaning Science
British Urban Regeneration Association (BURA)
Building Design Partnership Ltd (BDP)
Cambridge University
Capita Property Consultancy
Central London Partnership
Centre for Cities (IPPR)
Centre for the Urban and Built Environment (CUBE)
Chamber Business Enterprises Ltd
Civic Trust
Commission for Architecture and the Built Environment (CABE)
Cranfield University
De Montfort University
Department of Communities and Local Government (DCLG)
Design Council
Edinburgh College of Art (ECA)
Edward Street and St George's Tenants' and Residents' Association
EKOS Consulting (UK) Ltd
English Heritage
Exeter University
Feilden Clegg Bradley Associates
Finsbury Estate Tenants and Residents Association
Future Inclusion Ltd
Glasgow Caledonian University
Goldsmiths University of London
Greater London Authority (GLA)
Greater Manchester Police (GMP)
Homes For Change Housing Co-operative

Homes for Islington
Hoopers Gallery
Igloo Regeneration Partnership
Imperial College London
Indigo Planning
Institute of Community Studies
Is There An Accessible Loo (ITAAL)?
Islington Council
Landmark Design for Public
Langdon House Tenants and Residents Association
Licensing Law Reform Project
Living Streets
London Borough of Brent
London Development Agency (LDA)
London South Bank University
Manchester Digital Development Agency (MDDA)
Manchester Disabled People's Access Group (MDPAG)
Manchester Joint Health Unit
Margery Street Community Centre
Michael Chambers Associates
MJ Gleeson Group
National Institute for Public Health and the Environment
New East Manchester Ltd
Partnership Solutions
Patronat Català Pro Europa
Pontiles Chambers
R. James Chapman Architect
Regeneration and Renewal
Regeneration Trust
Rigsby Venture Partners Ltd
Royal College of Art (RCA)
Royal Commission on Environmental Pollution
Scotland Europa
Sheffield City Council – Street Force
Sheffield First for Environment
Sheffield Homes Limited
Short and Associates, Chartered Architects
Southern Housing Federation
Spa Green TMO
Staffordshire Police

Staffordshire University
Stockholm University
Stockport Metropolitan Borough Council
Suscom
Tenants and Residents Association
Thames Gateway Development Corporation
Thames Gateway London Partnership
Thames Valley Housing Association
The Lighthouse
Triangle Tenants and Residents Association
Trinity Court Residents Association
Twynstra Gudde
University of Athens
University of Birmingham
University of Cambridge
University of Central England in Birmingham (UCE)
University of Dundee
University of Exeter
University of Greenwich
University of Leeds
University of Manchester
University of New South Wales
University of Quebec at Montreal (INRS)
University of Reading
University of Southampton
University of Strathclyde
University of Surrey
University of the West of England
University of Warwick
University of Westminster
University of Wolverhampton
Urban Splash
Urbis
Vienna University of Technology
W&G Sissons Ltd
WALK 21
Wates Group Limited
Weston Rise Estate Tenant Management Organisation (TMO)
WHAT_architecture

APPENDIX 2
EXPLAINING SPACE SYNTAX

Bill Hillier

Figure A.1 Space syntax complete representation of road network within the M25 (London)

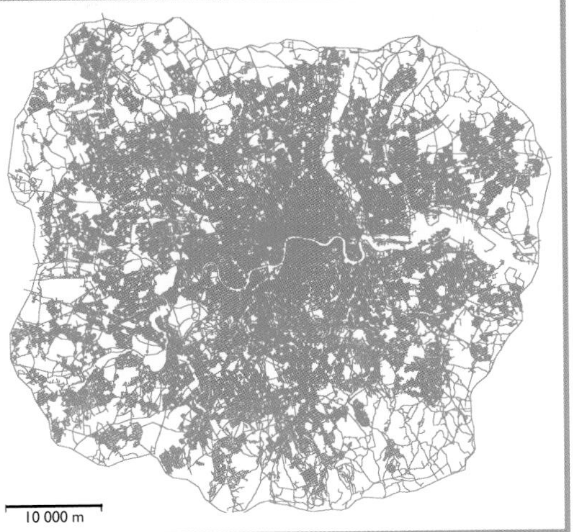

10 000 m

What is space syntax?

What is space syntax? From an urban point of view, it is four things:

- A family of techniques for analysing cities as the networks of space formed by the placing, grouping and orientation of buildings – street networks.
- A way of organising urban data structures in space across scales, from micro to macro, so as to relate spatial patterns to functional patterns at all scales, such as movement, land use, area differentiation, migration patterns and even social well-being and malaise, and crime.
- A set of theories, based on extensive empirical studies of cities, about how urban space networks relate in general to the social, economic and cognitive factors that shape and are affected by them.
- A set of theory-based techniques that can be used at all scales in evidence-based design and planning involving site-specific research. So we bring first-hand research into design and planning at the level of the project. More on this later.

The techniques have been applied to a large number of cities in different parts of the world, and to a large number of projects, and so a substantial database now exists of cities that have been studied at some level using space syntax.

How space syntax works

How does space syntax work? Historically most pre-syntax urban models take the urban area as the basic element (often administratively defined, as this is the way data on buildings, populations and activities are available), represent it as a point, and add a partial representation of the road network to carry flows between them. Movement flows are seen as resulting from the attraction between areas, inverse to the distance between them. These models are powerful and have important uses. But they do not work well at the level at which detailed urban design decisions are made. We need something more architecturally sensitive to the micro scale of urban design, preferably without losing sight of the macro scale.

So space syntax complements traditional planning models by working the other way round. It starts with a complete representation of the road network (Figure A.1) for the London region within the M25 – defining the basic element as the segment of a street between junctions – so a much smaller element. It then analyses the spatial relations

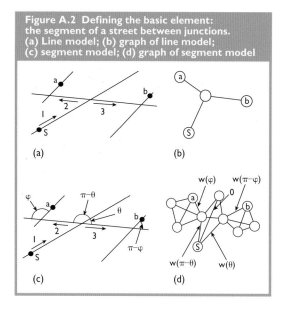

Figure A.2 Defining the basic element: the segment of a street between junctions. (a) Line model; (b) graph of line model; (c) segment model; (d) graph of segment model

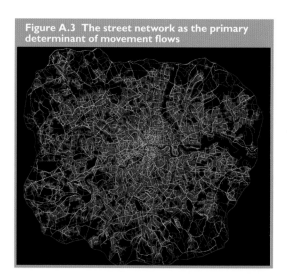

Figure A.3 The street network as the primary determinant of movement flows

between each segment and all the others. It then adds building, land use, density and activity information to the network, segment by segment. It does it this way round because its origins lie in architecture, rather than in planning. From the beginning, space syntax was about trying to find ways to answer architects' questions: Will it work if I do it this way? Is there a better way to do it? We had to work micro!

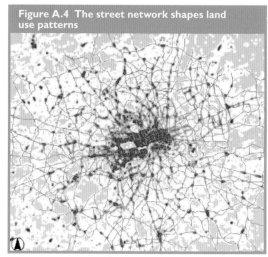

Figure A.4 The street network shapes land use patterns

The city-creating process

What are the advantages of this? In fact, by isolating and analysing the street network in the first instance we bring to light a very fundamental fact of cities: that the *structure* of the street network is in and of itself a – perhaps *the* – primary determinant of movement flows. Because the network structure shapes flows, it also shapes land use patterns, in that movement-seeking land uses seek locations that the grid has already made movement-rich, while other land uses, often including residence, migrate to less-movement-rich parts of the network. Economic values follow this process. With feedback and multiplier effects, this is the fundamental 'city-creating process' by which cities evolve from collections of buildings to living cities, with busy and quiet zones, often in close juxtaposition, and with differentiation of areas according to the detail of how they are embedded in the larger-scale grid.

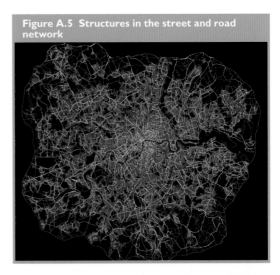

Figure A.5 Structures in the street and road network

Pervasive centrality

This is the process of self-organisation, by which cities acquire their generic form as foreground networks of linked centres at all scales set into a background network of primarily residential space. This is what we call pervasive centrality. Cities create local and global centrality in a much more intricate way than we have allowed, and it is this that makes them sustainable, because it means that, wherever you are, you are close to a small local centre and not far from a much bigger one. Figure A.6 shows the 168 largest centres in London within the M25, but there are ten times as many smaller centres. The intricate pattern of centres emerges from the structure of the network. So the space syntax theory of the city says that the pattern in Figure A.6 is emergent from the space network in Figure A.5. So what is the pattern in Figure A.5? What do the colours mean?

Movement potentials as structures

The patterns of colours are what we call structures in the street and road network. They are essentially measures of different kinds of movement potential of each street segment. Red means high movement potential, blue means low. These potentials matter because movement is the lifeblood of the city, and the means to the dense patterns of human contact that are the raison d'être of the city.

So how do we measure movement potential? Essentially in two ways, reflecting the fact that every human trip involves two things:

• Selecting a destination from an origin – deciding where to go – call it the to-movement element of the trip

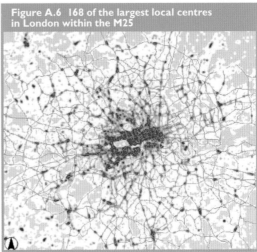

Figure A.6 168 of the largest local centres in London within the M25

• Selecting the spaces to pass through on the way to the destination – selecting the route to get there – call it the through-movement component of the trip

Selecting destinations is shaped by accessibility. We all make a large number of small trips and a small number of large trips, so destinations that are closer in general to more origins will have more potential as destinations. This is why people try to put shops in locations that are more accessible to more other locations.

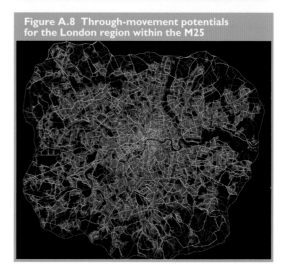

Figure A.7 To-movement potentials for the London region within the M25

The accessibility of all street segments to and from all others can be measured using standard mathematical techniques. When we make these measures and colour segments from red for high potential through to blue for low, we see structure emerge in the urban grid. In Figure A.7 we see the to-movement potentials for the London region within the M25. Through-movement potential can be calculated similarly using standard network measures, with the outcome shown in Figure A.8. By the way, if we analyse Tokyo we find very similar patterns.

People use least-angle-change routes

But there is a hidden problem. Both selecting accessible destinations and deciding on good routes depends on how people calculate spatial distances. There are debates in cognitive science about this. Do people calculate the routes that are actually shorter? Or do they favour less complex routes with fewer turns? Or do they try to minimise angular changes in direction? All have been suggested.

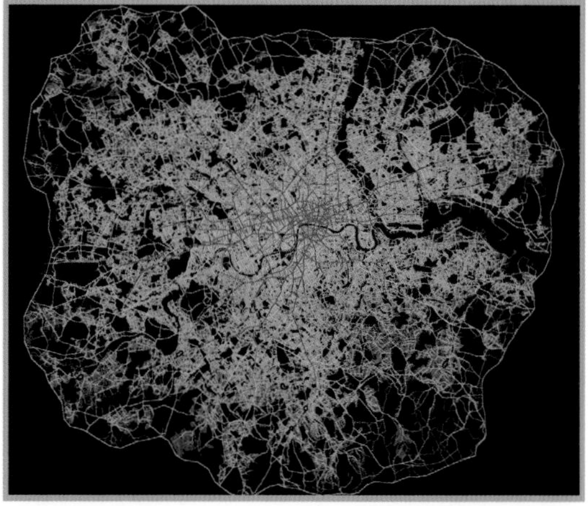

Figure A.8 Through-movement potentials for the London region within the M25

We found the answer by analysing large numbers of movement flow patterns in urban areas and comparing them with different ways of analysing the grid: shortest paths, fewest turns paths, least-angle paths, and so on. We find that insofar as people make spatial (as opposed to temporal) calculations in defining routes, they do not calculate distances directly but use a mental model of the geometry and connectivity of the urban grid and seek to minimise distance by minimising angular change on routes. In effect, when they think they are calculating distances, people are really using a geometric mental model of the network, trying to head for the destination as linearly as possible. Both the models on the previous page reflect the least-angle definition of distance. As I will show you, if we used real metric distance the results would be quite different and pretty well nonsense.

Restricted radius measures

One more factor needs to be taken into account: that we make different judgements about routes depending on the length of trips. If we are going from Kingsway to Hampstead, for example, we shall tend to use more global routes, whereas if we are

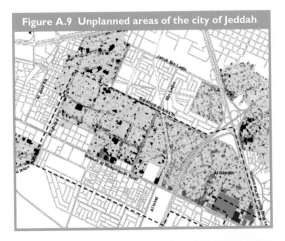

Figure A.9 Unplanned areas of the city of Jeddah

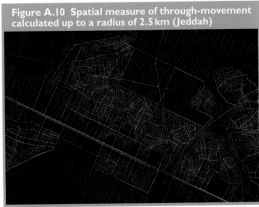

Figure A.10 Spatial measure of through-movement calculated up to a radius of 2.5 km (Jeddah)

First we find that in general the movement potential measures (in fact the least-angle version) agree with actual flows, with something between 60% and 80% accuracy. To predict actual flows, of course, we need to, and do, take other features into account. But the key thing is that the structure of potentials is so powerful that it is more or less the key to the structure–function relation in cities, as well as the key to designing outcomes that will actually happen.

Urban structure is geometric, not metric

We can show graphically, as well as statistically, that these measures – to- and through-movement potentials, with a least-angle definition of distance and calculated at different radii – identify meaningful structures in the urban grid. The following example is taken from a recent masterplanning study of Jeddah by Space Syntax Limited. In Figure A.9 we see one of the unplanned areas of the city of Jeddah with all the shops marked in red, clearly the result of some kind of organic process. In Figure A.10 we see our spatial measure of through-movement – and hence of passing trade potentials – calculated up to a radius of 2.5 km, so allowing only for trips up to this length. The agreement between the two patterns is not perfect, but it is remarkably good.

going to, say, Soho Square, we shall select more localised routes. We build this into our model by calculating our measures at different radii – that is, for trips up to a certain length.

Now with this matrix of measures of to- and through-movement potentials, using different definitions of distance and applying them at different radii, we have a very powerful tool for bringing to light the structure of cities and its relation to how they are functioning.

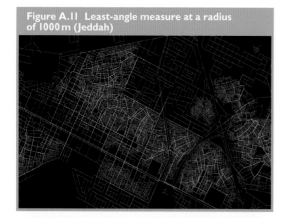

Figure A.11 Least-angle measure at a radius of 1000 m (Jeddah)

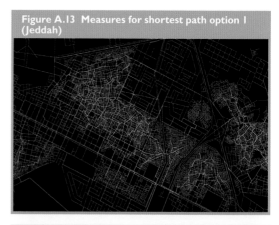

Figure A.13 Measures for shortest path option 1 (Jeddah)

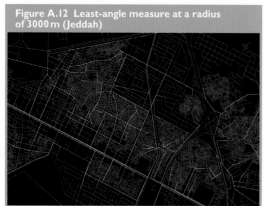

Figure A.12 Least-angle measure at a radius of 3000 m (Jeddah)

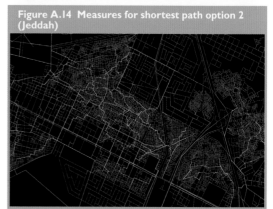

Figure A.14 Measures for shortest path option 2 (Jeddah)

But we can do better. In Figure A.11 we see the least-angle measure at a radius of 1000 m, and in Figure A.12 at 3000 m. The focus shifts from the smaller-scale northern centres to the larger-scale southern centre, closer to the Mecca Road. When the measures are repeated for shortest path distance, in Figures A.13 and A.14, the result is a maze of complex paths, which do not reflect the functional pattern at all. The orthodox preference for shortest paths models would conceal such effects.

Metric analysis at best finds the taxi driver's routes

In fact, if we show the unrestricted radius pattern for Jeddah for least-angle through-movement (Figure A.15) and metric, or shortest path through-movement (Figure A.16) with identical colour spectrum adjustment for the local range, we find

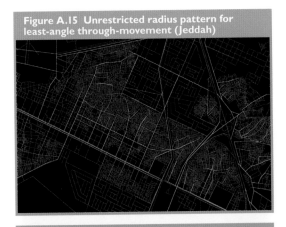

Figure A.15 Unrestricted radius pattern for least-angle through-movement (Jeddah)

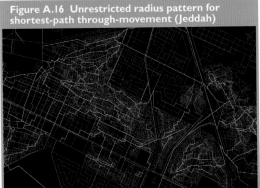

Figure A.16 Unrestricted radius pattern for shortest-path through-movement (Jeddah)

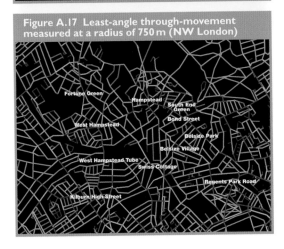

Figure A.17 Least-angle through-movement measured at a radius of 750 m (NW London)

that while the angular measure still identifies the main functional structure, the metric measure identifies a bizarre network of highly complex routes with no references to the emergent functional structure. At best it finds the taxi drivers' routes, but in this case even this is not realistic. The structure–function relation in cities is geometric, not metric.

But let us look closer to home and try to throw some light on London's spatial patterning. Looking down on part of north-west London, what you cannot see is its distribution of 'urban villages'. But they can be seen in the analysis in Figure A.17 of the street network, using the least-angle through-movement measure at a radius of 750 m. This makes singularly clear the intricate way in which the evolution of London has created a network of – in this case small-scale – centres, shown by the red and orange segments, set into a background of residential space, shown in green and blue segments. Remember this is purely a mathematical analysis of the street network.

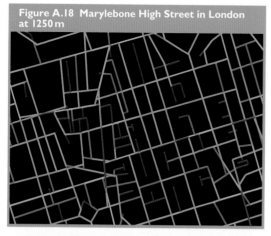

Figure A.18 Marylebone High Street in London at 1250 m

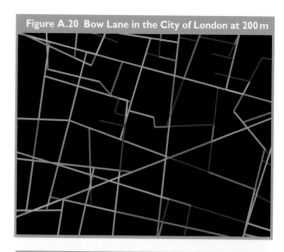

Figure A.20 Bow Lane in the City of London at 200 m

Figure A.19 Lamb's Conduit Street at 250 m

Figure A.21 Leadenhall Market area in the City of London at 250 m

The following figures show how Marylebone High Street in London appears at 1250 m (Figure A.18), Lamb's Conduit Street at 250 m (Figure A.19), Bow Lane in the City of London at 200 m (Figure A.20), and the Leadenhall Market area in the City of London at 250 m (Figure A.21).

A testable theory and method

So we have a testable theory of how urban space is organised and how it works. It brings to light structures of various kinds in the urban grid. These structures are powerfully related to functional patterns. What is more, we understand why. The underlying theory accounts for it. So we have a method that is theory based, testable and transparent.

What can we do with it? Well, first we can use it as a frame for all kinds of urban data by simply adding data to the model segment by segment: movement flows, land uses, densities, demographic information, land and rental values and so on.

We then have a tool for asking spatial questions of the city, of the form: is there a spatial dimension to this or that urban problem — to social malaise, to migration patterns, crime distributions, to the success of areas? All these are areas that we have investigated using space syntax.

The movement–place relation

But we also learn principles about the form and functioning of cities that are critical to design and planning. The most critical are:

- the grid–movement relation is the key to self-organisation
- measures of movement potentials at different radii identify key local and global structures in the network
- the most important of which is the 'dual network' theory of pervasive centrality.

The most important lesson for design and planning from all this is that movement creates place. For decades, professional specialisations have led us to think of movement as between places, and so separate from place-making. Here we have shown that movement is intrinsic to place, and the life of places is deeply bound up with how the internal structure of a place is related to its spatial context. This is where the change in design thinking through strategic urban design has to come. Place-making starts with understanding movement potentials, local and global, and the relation between the two.

How then can the methods – always embedded in the accompanying theory – be applied to real design and planning projects?

We first build a model of the urban context of a proposed development – often these days a whole-city model or even a regional model (we have quite a large stock of cities by now!).

We then test the model against existing movement and land use patterns, often gathering primary data for the purpose. Given the tested model, we can then work with the designers in sketch design experimentation. What happens if we do this, or that? We literally draw the spatial structure of the proposal into the model and re-run the model. This process, by the way, almost always gives rise to new ideas that come from the syntactic analysis, and which were not in the frame at the start of the project.

We call this process of bringing new kinds of directly observed data into the model 'site-specific research'. It means that design is always informed by a real understanding of what is currently happening on or in the vicinity of the site. This is another innovation in evidence-based design that we think will be seen as increasingly important.

This is what was done on such highly successful spatial re-engineering projects as Trafalgar Square and Nottingham's Market Square. In both cases the design changes came from the space syntax analysis, which was able to show exactly what changes would make the huge difference that actually came about in the two squares.

But on the basis of its ability to synthesise complex patterns of urban data on the basis of a functionally intelligent analysis of spatial networks, and to work simultaneously across all urban scales, space syntax is increasingly being used as a masterplanning tool, not only at the scale of the urban area and the larger context, as at the Elephant and Castle, but also at the scale of the city and its region, for example as lead partner in the masterplanning of Jeddah in Saudi Arabia. This study, which can be accessed through www.spacesyntax.com, is, we believe, a new kind of masterplanning, giving a new, testable meaning to evidence-based and theoretically informed design and planning.

Further Reading

Hillier, B. (1996) *Space is the machine*. Cambridge: Cambridge University Press (paperback 1998; e-edition 2007; Chinese translation 2008).

Hillier, B. (2002a) A theory of the city as object: how the social construction of urban space is mediated by spatial laws. *Urban Design International*, **7**, 153–179.

Hillier, B. (2002b) Society seen through the prism of space. *Urban Design International*, **7**, 181–203.

Hillier, B. (2006) The golden age for cities? How we design cities is how we understand them. *Urban Design*, (100), 16–19.

Hillier, B. (2007) Metric and topo-geometric properties of urban street networks: some convergencies, divergencies and new results. Keynote paper for the Sixth Space Syntax Symposium, Istanbul.

Hillier, B. (2008a) The new science of space and the art of place. In T. Haas (ed.), *New urbanism and beyond*, pp. 30-39. New York: Rizzoli.

Hillier, B. (2008b) Space and spatiality: what the built environment needs from social theory. *Building Research and Information*, **36** (3), 216–230 (special issue on the importance of theory).

Hillier, B. & Hanson, J. (1984) *The social logic of space*. Cambridge: Cambridge University Press (paperback 1989).

Hillier, B. & Iida, S. (2005) Network effects and psychological effects: a theory of urban movement. In A.G. Cohn & D.M. Mark (eds), *Spatial information theory*, Lecture Notes in Computer Science 3603, pp. 473–490. Berlin: Springer Verlag.

Hillier, B. & Vaughan, L. (2007) The city as one thing. *Progress in Planning*, **67** (3), 205–230 (special issue on space syntax research on space as an aspect of social segregation).

Turner, A., Hillier, B. & Penn, A. (2005) An algorithmic definition of the axial map. *Environment & Planning B*, **32** (3), 425–444.

INDEX